The Legacy of
Genghis Khan

Michigan Slavic Publications is a nonprofit organization associated with the Department of Slavic Languages and Literatures of the University of Michigan. Its goal is to publish titles which may be of marginal interest from the commercial point of view but which substantially enrich the field of Slavic and East European studies. The present volume, number 33 in the series *Michigan Slavic Materials*, is the second selection of Trubetzkoy's works in this series, the first being *Three Philological Studies*, 1963, long out of print. N. S. Trubetzkoy's essays on culture, ethnology and politics—each appearing for the first time in English translation—shed light on themes that have preoccupied Russian intellectuals for centuries. On the hundredth anniversary of Trubetzkoy's birth—coinciding with a new era of rapid change in Russia—the reader is sure to find these essays both challenging and controversial.

Michigan Slavic Publications

Michigan Slavic Materials, No. 33

N. S. Trubetzkoy, Vienna 1930s

Nikolai Sergeevich Trubetzkoy

THE LEGACY OF GENGHIS KHAN

and
Other Essays on Russia's Identity

edited, and with a postscript, by
Anatoly Liberman

preface by
Viacheslav V. Ivanov

Michigan Slavic Publications
Ann Arbor 1991

Library of Congress Cataloguing-in-Publication Data

Trubetskoi, Nikolai Sergeevich, kniaz', 1890-1938.
The Legacy of Genghis Khan and Other Essays on Russia's Identity /
Nikolai Sergeevich Trubetzkoy ; edited, and with a postscript, by
Anatoly Liberman ; preface by Viacheslav V. Ivanov.
      p.   cm. – (Michigan Slavic Materials ; no. 33)
      Includes bibliographical references and index.
      ISBN 0-930042-70-0
      1. Soviet Union—Ethnic relations. 2. Nationalism—Soviet
Union. 3. Minorities—Soviet Union. 4. Soviet Union—Politics and
government—1985- 5. East and West. 6. Eurasianism. I. Title. II.
Series.
PG13.M46 no. 33
[DK33]
491.8 s—dc20
[305.8'00947]   91-27783
                                                                CIP

Translated by Kenneth Brostrom and Anatoly Liberman; see
individual credits at the beginning of each article.

Cover design and typography by Ross Teasley.
Cover based on graphics made by Pavel Tchelitchew (1898-1957) for
the Eurasian collection *Iskhod k Vostoku*, Sofia 1921.

Michigan Slavic Publications
Department of Slavic Languages and Literatures
University of Michigan
Ann Arbor, MI 48109-1275, USA
phone (313) 763-4496
fax (313) 764-3521

Note on Transliteration

Russian personal and place names are transliterated throughout in accordance with the modified Library of Congress system employed by *Slavic Review*. Exceptions are made for Russians whose names have become fixed in a different transliteration (e.g., Gogol, Mirsky, Trotsky, Vernadsky). The surname Trubetzkoy is treated variously: N. S. Trubetzkoy is always transliterated thus, while other members of the family appear in a transliteration based on the history of their publication (or lack thereof) in languages other than Russian. This is not a completely satisfactory solution, but it seemed the simplest.

The few Old Church Slavonic and Russian linguistic items that occur in the body of the text are transliterated according to the system long used by Slavic linguists in the U.S. and specified by the *Slavic and East European Journal*.

ACKNOWLEDGMENTS

The editorial board is particularly grateful to Ladislav Matejka, who initiated this project in his former capacity as managing editor of Michigan Slavic Publications, and to Anatoly Liberman for his inspiration and expert hand throughout the process of preparing these articles for publication, as well as for his highly insightful postscript. Our gratitude goes, in addition, to Kenneth Brostrom for his dedication and skill as primary translator, and to Susan Larson and Timothy Sergay, who participated in the translating during the initial stages of this project. Many thanks are due as well to Ann Podolski, who labored cheerfully and efficiently on the word processing of a very messy manuscript. Finally, it is our pleasant duty to acknowledge a generous publication grant from the Wheatland Foundation. Ultimate responsibility for any defiencies in the final shape of this volume, however, rests with the Editorial Board of Michigan Slavic Publications.

For the Editorial Board
Benjamin Stolz and Jindřich Toman

CONTENTS

Preface

Prince Nikolai Sergeevich Trubetzkoy belonged to a generation of Russian scholars, thinkers, and artists that was destined to make remarkable discoveries and to pass through much suffering. Since Trubetzkoy's biography is discussed in detail in the Postscript by Anatoly Liberman, I will limit myself to a few brief observations.

Trubetzkoy began his scholarly activities at an amazingly early age. His close friend and collaborator Roman Jakobson told me about an unrealized meeting between Trubetzkoy and Bogoraz-Tan, the well-known Petersburg expert in Paleo-Siberian languages. Bogoraz knew Trubetzkoy through an exchange of scholarly letters. On a visit to Moscow, Bogoraz decided to seek out his correspondent, and set off for the home of the Trubetzkoys. After ringing the bell, he asked for Prince Nikolai Sergeevich. In answer to the call "Kolen'ka," a little boy in short trousers came running to the door. Bogoraz (a member of the People's Will who had been exiled to Siberia and there had studied the languages and customs of the local inhabitants) decided that this aristocratic family had played a cruel joke on him; he became incensed and left, and so did not speak with Trubetzkoy, who had written him such mature scholarly letters.

This altogether plausible anecdote could be expanded upon by relating the incredible range of the speculations contained in the articles published by Trubetzkoy during his youth. Just one of his short notes, "Caucasian Parallels to the Phrygian Myth about Birth from Stone (= Earth)," published when he was eighteen years old (his very first published works appeared when this young scholar was only fifteen!), would suffice to convince one of the brilliance of his scholarly intuition. The conjectures contained in this article were confirmed by the discovery of ancient eastern texts, which were found much later (for greater detail, see my commentary on the republished version of this article in Trubetzkoy's *Selected Works on Philology* [*Izbrannye trudy po filologii*, Moscow: Progress, 1987]. Trubetzkoy was already in a hurry during his adolescence, as if he anticipated his early death.

Trubetzkoy's first scholarly efforts concern the fields of ethnology (anthropology in the broad sense of the term) and folklore. From the age of thirteen he regularly attended the meetings of the Ethnographic Section of the Society of Science, Anthropology, and Ethnography at Moscow University. When Trubetzkoy was elected an honorary member of the Finno-Ugric Society at the end of his short life, he recalled that "when I was a gymnasium student in the fifth class, I was already fascinated by the *Kalevala* and Finno-Ugric ethnography" (*LN*, p. 455). He spoke of these pursuits as "his first scholarly love."

The study of prosody and music was also among Trubetzkoy's early interests. He studied the folk music and songs of both the Finno-Ugric peoples and the Russians. He was not yet seventeen years old when he began to compare the vocabularies of Kamchadal and other "Arctic" (Paleo-Siberian) languages with the lexicons of the Samoyed languages. Later, as a university student, Trubetzkoy studied the languages of the Northern Caucasus; one of his major linguistic achievements was the compilation of a comparative historical grammar of these languages.

From what has been said, it is apparent that Trubetzkoy was occupied with a wide range of anthropological problems and that while still very young he dealt with them on the basis of materials drawn from the languages and cultures of various Eurasian peoples. As time passed, the full range of anthropological-humanistic studies continued to occupy him; but in order to utilize in his work techniques comparable to those of the exact sciences, he decided to master classical comparative historical linguistics. He considered it the only humanistic discipline in possession of a scientific method, in contrast to other branches of the humanities that had not advanced beyond alchemy.

Trubetzkoy mastered the rigors of Neogrammarian comparative historical linguistics, which was current at the time. He worked first in Moscow, in a recently established program in comparative linguistics reflecting the exacting standards of F. F. Fortunatov and taught by Professor Viktor Porzhezinskii; there was only one other student, Mikhail Nikolaevich Peterson (who—after overcoming unbelievable difficulties—taught me and my comrades comparative linguistics at Moscow University at the end of the forties, when it was forbidden). Trubetzkoy then studied at Leipzig, where he attended lectures with Leonard Bloomfield, who later founded American descriptive linguistics, and with Lucien Tesnière, one of the originators of modern structural grammar. Trubetzkoy very quickly abandoned the principles of the Neogrammarian scholarship he had mastered. In a discussion of a work published in 1915 in the area of comparative historical phonetics by the great Neogrammarian Shakhmatov, young Trubetzkoy subjected the methods of the linguists of the preceding generation to devastating criticism. From this time forward, his efforts were directed toward the elaboration of more exact methods, at first in historical and later in descriptive linguistics.

One of Trubetzkoy's characteristics as a scholar was his persistent striving toward the creation of whole new areas of knowledge. During the *Sturm und Drang* period of the Prague Linguistic Circle, of which Trubetzkoy was to become one of the preeminent members after the middle twenties (he had settled in Vienna but traveled to Prague for meetings with Roman Jakobson and other members of the Circle), he established and developed a series of areas in linguistics that were either nonexistent or altogether different in nature before his appearance on the scene. Besides phonology, whose development during the Prague period he summed up in his magisterial book *Grundzüge der Phonologie*, one can mention morphophonemics, the *Sprachbund* theory, which on its most inclusive level dealt not only with the languages but with the cultures of diverse ethnic groups linked to one another geographically—a theory illuminated by articles included in this book—and the history of literary languages, which is also discussed in the present volume. Trubetzkoy left nothing that he came to understand unchanged.

I will attempt to demonstrate this using the example of comparative historical Indo-European linguistics, the discipline that Trubetzkoy mastered in his youth in order to acquire methodological rigor. He subjected the fundamental principles of this discipline to a radical reexamination in a paper which he read at the end of 1936 at a session of the Prague Linguistic Circle. His paper "Thoughts on the Indo-European Problem" emphasized the purely linguistic nature of the problem. Trubetzkoy's utilization of the existing body of knowledge about the typology not only of phonological but of grammatical systems allowed him to specify the place of Indo-European among the other Eurasian linguistic types. The subsequent development of linguistics and associated disciplines has shown to what a significant degree Trubetzkoy was here once again ahead of his time. The alliances between the Indo-European languages and other contiguous languages, which are examined on the most inclusive level in Trubetzkoy's paper, remain to this day the center of attention for scholars who study them both on the level of the typological connections among languages and from the perspective of their historical kinship (more problematical for Trubetzkoy). For Trubetzkoy (and it is here that the principal distinction between him and earlier comparative linguists can be seen), the important thing was not establishing the kinship between languages but clarifying how contiguous languages partially assimilate to one another. While proceeding in this direction he also tried to solve the riddle of Indo-European unity, anticipating in this effort much that would be said subsequently on this question by linguists such as Vittore Pisani.

A geographical (that is, an essentially spatial) approach—behind which one can glimpse a spatial-temporal approach close in the final analysis to that of the exact sciences—initially played an essential role in the formation of Trubetzkoy's Eurasian views, as it did in the views of his allies in the Eurasian movement. He based his arguments first of all on linguistic and cultural alliances established through this approach over the entire territory of the Eurasian continent. A basic position in all his linguistic and culturological research was his rejection of national "egocentricity." With regard to a trilogy first conceived in 1909-1910, parts of which were published beginning in 1920 (some of these parts are included in the present volume), Trubetzkoy said: "The first part was to have the title 'On Egocentricity' and was dedicated to the memory of Copernicus; the second part was called 'On True and False Nationalism,' with a dedication to Socrates; finally, the third part, entitled 'The Russian Element,' was to be dedicated to the memory of Emelian Pugachëv" (*LN,* p. 12). The essential purpose of the first part (appearing ten years after the formulation of this basic conception with the "more striking" title *Europe and Mankind* [Evropa i chelovechestvo] and without the dedication to Copernicus, which the more mature author considered pretentious) was, in Trubetzkoy's words, to compel readers "to understand that neither 'I' nor anyone else is the salt of the earth, that all peoples and cultures are equal in value, that there are no 'greater' and 'lesser'" (*LN,* p. 13).

Insofar as Trubetzkoy insisted on the necessity of a special path for Russia (understood as a part of Eurasia) that was distinct from the "Romano-Germanic" (i.e., the Western) path, his idea can be associated with the idea of a new generation of Slavophiles. In the never-ending intellectual struggle between the adherents of an orientation toward the West and those who urge looking toward the East, Trubetzkoy unquestionably is in the camp of the latter. It seemed to him that Russia could find her own true path only after she had been reunited with the Eurasian cultural tradition from which she had been torn away in recent centuries, especially after the reforms of Emperor Peter the Great.

In practice, the point of view which the young Trubetzkoy compared with the Copernican also boiled down to a search for cultural principles distinct from the Romano-Germanic (West European). It is obvious that one could ask why the union between the Eurasian, Genghis-Khanian element and the Orthodox element (Byzantine in origin), which Trubetzkoy uncovered—with considerable evidence—in Russia's history, was more organic than the subsequent merger of these same elements with the Western European. But we leave it to the readers themselves to ponder the many questions that Trubetzkoy's perceptiveness opened up for us.

There is much in his ideas that is paradoxically contra-dictory. It was the undemocratic nature of the consequences of the Pugachëv rebellion that attracted Prince Trubetzkoy. This is why he reacted to the "ideocracy," whose creation he was witnessing in his native land, with much greater interest than others among his contemporaries who shared with him the hardships of emigration. But if we look closely at the intellectual landscape of Europe at the beginning of the thirties, we discover that Trubetzkoy's social ideals were not so different from the aspirations of many of the foremost minds of that time. No matter how different Ezra Pound was, let us say, from George Bernard Shaw or Thomas Mann, all of them (and many others) marked out a path that for a time brought them into the orbit of authoritarian thinking. The failures of the democracies of that time are all too obvious, and some of the judgments rendered upon them (and evident in Trubetzkoy's work as well) are true to the point of being banal. But from this it certainly does not follow that it was necessary to proceed as far along the path toward the development of ideocracy as Trubetzkoy proposed.

Rather than quarreling with these ideas that clash so dissonantly with the current arguments of the intelligentsia against totalitarianism, it is possible to agree with Trubetzkoy's ideas about personalism as the basis for the emergence of human individuality in every society. Many of his ideas that relate to new areas of scholarship (in particular, those relating to personality) are original and up-to-date. Everyone who thinks about the next century of humanistic studies needs to become acquainted with Trubetzkoy.

Viacheslav V. Ivanov

Летит, летит степная кобылица
И мнёт ковыль . . .

The mare of the steppe flies on and on,
and tramples the feather-grass . . .

—Alexander Blok
"On Kulikovo Field," 1908

N. S. Trubetzkoy
Essays

1 Europe and Mankind*

I bring the present work to public attention not without some apprehension. The ideas expressed in it took shape in my mind more than ten years ago. Since then I have often discussed them with various people, wishing either to verify my own opinions or to convince others. Many of these discussions and debates were quite useful to me, because they forced me to rethink my ideas and arguments in greater detail and to give them added depth. But my basic positions have remained unchanged.

Quite clearly, I could not limit myself to chance discussions, and to test the correctness of my theses I had to submit them to a much broader audience, that is, to publish them. I did not do so, because—especially in the beginning—I came away from numerous conversations with the impression that most of my listeners simply did not understand me. And they failed to understand me not because I expressed myself awkwardly, but because, for most educated Europeans, ideas like mine are almost viscerally unacceptable; they contradict certain immovable psychological principles that underlie European thought. They considered me a lover of paradoxes and viewed my arguments as trickery. In such circumstances discussion lost all meaning and purpose for me: discussion can be productive only when each side understands the other and when both speak the same language. Since I was meeting with almost total lack of understanding, I did not consider it the appropriate time to publish my ideas, and I waited for a more propitious

*Originally as *Evropa i chelovechestvo,* Sofia: Rossiisko-Bolgarskoe knigoizdatel'stvo, 1920. Translated by Kenneth Brostrom.

moment. And if I now make bold to appear in print, it is because I have been encountering with increasing frequency understanding and even sympathy for my basic positions. Many people have arrived at the same conclusions as I. Obviously a shift has occurred in the thinking of a substantial number of educated people.

The Great War and especially the subsequent "peace" (which even now must be written in quotation marks) shook our faith in "civilized mankind" and opened the eyes of many people. We Russians find ourselves in a special situation: we were witnesses to the sudden collapse of what we used to call "Russian culture." Many of us were struck by the speed and ease with which this occurred, and many began to ponder the reasons for these events. Perhaps the present study will help some of my compatriots examine their own thoughts on this matter. Some of my positions could be illustrated with a large number of examples drawn from Russian history and Russian life. Although this would perhaps make my account more engaging and lively, the clarity of the general plan would suffer from such digressions. I might add that, in proposing these relatively new ideas, I have placed especially high value on the clarity and consistency of their presentation. Moreover, my ideas pertain not only to Russians but to peoples whose origins are in neither the Romance nor the Germanic groups, but who have in some way adopted European culture. If I publish my book in Russian, it is only because "home is where the heart is" and because I attach very great importance to the acceptance and assimilation of my ideas by my fellow countrymen.

In bringing these ideas to the attention of the reader, I would like to pose a question each person *must* answer for himself or herself. There are only two alternatives: Either my ideas are *false*, and they must then be refuted logically, or they are *true*, and they must lead to practical conclusions.

Agreement with these positions obliges everyone to further work. If they merit acceptance, they must be developed further and applied to concrete reality, and numerous practical questions must be reviewed from this new perspective. Many people are currently preoccupied with the "revaluation of values." My ideas, for those who will accept them, will serve as one indicator of the direction in which this revaluation should proceed. Certainly the theoretical and practical work which will follow acceptance of my theses must be a collaborative effort. One individual can advance an idea or raise a banner, but many minds are needed to develop an idea into a system and to put it into practice. I call upon all those who share my convictions to join in this effort. Thanks to several chance encounters, I am convinced that such people exist. They need only to agree to a joint effort; and if my book happens to serve as an inducement or a means to such collaboration, I will consider my goal achieved.

On the other hand, certain moral obligations also fall upon those who reject my positions as false. For if my ideas indeed are false, they are then *harmful*, and an effort should be made to disprove them. And since (I dare to hope) they have been proved logically, they should be disproved no less logically. This must be done to preserve from error those who have come to believe in these ideas. The author himself will abandon without regret the unpleasant, disturbing ideas that have been plaguing him for more than ten years if someone can demonstrate to him logically that they are incorrect.

All those who in one way or another wish to react to my brochure are requested to forward offprints, clippings, or simply letters to the following address: N.S. Trubetzkoy, docent, Faculty of History and Philology, University of Sofia, Sofia, Bulgaria.

Chapter I

The positions that any European can take on the national question are rather numerous, but all of them fall between two extremes: chauvinism and cosmopolitanism. Every form of nationalism is a synthesis of chauvinism and cosmopolitanism, an attempt to reconcile these concepts. The European views chauvinism and cosmopolitanism as opposites. Yet this formulation is wrong. If we examine chauvinism and cosmopolitanism more closely, we will see that there is no fundamental difference between them, that they are two stages, two aspects of the same phenomenon.

The chauvinist proceeds from the *a priori* conviction that his nation is the best in the world. The culture created by his nation is better and more refined than all other cultures. His nation alone has the right to dominate and rule over other nations, who are supposed to subordinate themselves to it, adopt its beliefs, language, and culture, and merge with it. Everything that stands in the way of his great nation's ultimate triumph must be forcefully swept aside. This is how the chauvinist thinks, and, accordingly, how he acts.

The cosmopolitan rejects national distinctions. If such distinctions exist, they should be eradicated. Civilized mankind should be a single entity and have one culture. Uncivilized nations should accept and adopt this culture, join the family of civilized nations, and proceed with them along the path of world progress. Civilization is a higher good for which national traits should be sacrificed.

Formulated in this way, chauvinism and cosmopolitanism certainly appear to be distinctly different: In the former, supremacy is claimed for the culture of a particular ethnographic-anthropological group, and in the latter, for the culture of supraethnographic humanity. But what meaning do European cosmopolitans attach to the terms "civilization" and "civilized mankind"? By "civilization" they mean the culture created jointly by the Romano-Germanic nations of Europe, as well as by the nations that have adopted European culture. By "civilized nations" they again mean precisely these same nations.

The culture that ought to dominate the world (according to the cosmopolitan) after all other cultures have been eliminated turns out to be the culture of the very same ethnographic-anthropological group whose supremacy is the lodestar of the chauvinist's dreams. There is no fundamental difference here. The national, ethnographic-anthropological, and linguistic unity of each European nation is a relative matter. Every one of them is an aggregate of small, diverse ethnic groups, each with its own dialectal, cultural, and anthropological traits but linked by the bonds of kinship and common history—the source of a common stock of cultural assets. The chauvinist who proclaims his nation to be the crown of creation and the sole repository of everything perfect is the champion of a whole group of ethnic units. In addition, the chauvinist wants other nations to merge with his own, to lose their individuality. The chauvinist treats members of nations that have done this (i.e., have lost their national individuality and assimilated the language, beliefs, and culture of his nation) as his own; he will praise their contributions to his culture, but only if they have assimilated the spirit so dear to him and have been completely successful in abandoning their former national psychology. Chauvinists always approach with some suspicion those foreigners who have merged with the dominant nation, especially if their assimilation occurred in the recent past. In principle, however, no chauvinist will reject them. Incidentally, the names and anthropological attributes of many European chauvinists indicate quite clearly that these people do not belong to the nation whose supremacy they are proclaiming with such fervor.

If we now consider the European cosmopolitan, we will see that he is not essentially different from the chauvinist. The "civilization," the culture which he considers the best and to which, in his view, all other cultures should give way, also represents a stock of cultural assets common to several nations linked together by the bonds of kinship and common history.

Whereas the chauvinist disregards the individual characteristics of ethnic groups within his nation, the cosmopolitan ignores particular characteristics of the cultures of individual Romano-Germanic nations and takes into account only the traits that comprise the common cultural stock. He also acknowledges the cultural value inherent in the activities of non-Romano-Germanic people who have fully accepted Romano-Germanic civilization—that is, people who have renounced everything contrary to the spirit of this civilization and exchanged their national dress for Romano-Germanic garb. This is precisely like the chauvinist, who considers foreigners and outsiders "his own" if they have been completely assimilated by the ruling nation! Even the hostility that cosmopolitans feel toward chauvinists and toward everything that glorifies the cultures of individual Romano-Germanic nations has a parallel in the chauvinist's world view. Chauvinists always respond with hostility to attempts by individual parts of their nation to achieve separation. They try to wipe out any local characteristics that can destroy the unity of their nation.

Thus the parallel between chauvinists and cosmopolitans is all-inclusive. The same attitude toward the culture of the ethnographic-anthropological group to which a person belongs marks both. The chauvinist is simply concerned with a narrower ethnic group than the cosmopolitan; but even the chauvinist's group is not entirely homogeneous, while the cosmopolitan is ultimately concerned with a specific ethnic group. The difference is quantitative, not qualitative.

In evaluating European cosmopolitanism one must always remember that terms such as "humanity," "universal human civilization," and so forth, are extremely imprecise and that they mask very definite ethnographic concepts. European culture is not the culture of all humanity; it is a product of the history of a specific ethnic group. The Germanic and Celtic tribes were exposed in varying degrees to the influence of Roman culture, and they intermingled extensively; from elements of their own national culture and Roman culture they created a common pattern of daily living. As a result of shared ethnographic and geographic conditions, they lived according to this common pattern for a long time; thanks to regular contacts with one another, the common elements in their *mores* and history were so strong that a sense of Romano-Germanic unity was always subconsciously alive among them. Eventually, as with so many other peoples, they developed an interest in the origins of their culture. Their encounter with the monuments of Roman and Greek culture brought to the surface the concept of a supranational, "world" civilization—an idea characteristic of the Greco-Roman world and based on ethnographic and geographic considerations. In Rome, the "entire world" meant only *orbis terrarum*, that is, the peoples inhabiting the Mediterranean basin and areas close to it; through regular contacts with one another they developed a number of common cultural assets and finally merged, owing to the leveling influence of Greek and Roman colonization and to Roman military supremacy. In any case, the cosmopolitan ideas of antiquity became the basis for education in Europe. In the fertile soil provided by the subconscious sense of Romano-Germanic unity, these ideas gave rise to the theoretical foundations of so-called European cosmopolitanism, which it would be more correct to call quite bluntly *pan-Romano-Germanic chauvinism.*

This is the real historical basis of European cosmopolitan theories. But the psychological basis of cosmopolitanism is the same as that of chauvinism. It is a variant of a subconscious bias, a particular psychology, that is best called *egocentricity.* A person with a clearly defined egocentric psychology subconsciously considers himself to be the center of the universe, the crown of creation, the best, the most perfect of all beings. Confronted by two other human beings, the one closer to him, more like him, is the better, while the one less like him is worse. Consequently, this person considers every natural group of human beings to which he belongs the most perfect: his family, estate, nation, tribe, and race are better than all other analogous groups. Similarly, his species, the human race, is more perfect than all other mammals, and mammals are more perfect than other vertebrates, while animals are more perfect than plants, and the organic world more perfect than the inorganic. To some degree everyone is captive to this psychology. Even science has not freed itself from it completely, and every victory it achieves in liberating itself from egocentric biases is accomplished with very great difficulty.

The psychology of egocentricity permeates the world view of many people. Rarely does anyone succeed in freeing himself from it entirely, but its most extreme manifestations are readily noticeable, their absurdity is obvious, and they therefore tend to elicit condemnation, protest, or derision. A person convinced that he is better and more intelligent than others and that everything about him is as good as can be will be held up to ridicule; and if he is also aggressive, he will receive well-deserved knocks on the noggin. Families naively believing that all their members are brilliant, wise, and beautiful become the object of ridicule, and their acquaintances tell amusing stories about them. Such extreme manifestations of egocentricity are rare and are usually met with active resistance, but the situation is quite different when egocentricity is spread over a broader group. Although resistance usually occurs here as well, the egocentricity is more difficult to arrest. The matter usually ends in a struggle between two egocentric groups, and the victorious group remains with its convictions. This happens, for example, in class and social struggles.

The bourgeoisie, when it overthrows the aristocracy, is as convinced of its superiority over all other estates as is the overthrown aristocracy. In its struggle with the bourgeoisie, the proletariat also considers itself the "salt of the earth," the best of all social classes. Here the egocentricity is clear, and individuals with a broader outlook usually know how to rise above it. But it is more difficult to free oneself from such biases when ethnic groups are involved. In this case people differ greatly in their ability to recognize the true nature of egocentric bias. Many Prussian Pan-Germans condemn their countrymen who elevate the Prussians above all other Germans, and they consider their jingoism ludicrous and narrow-minded. However, the proposition that the German tribe as a whole represents the flower, the *non plus ultra* of mankind, creates no doubts in their minds, and Romano-Germanic chauvinism (i.e., cosmopolitanism) is beyond their reach. The Prussian cosmopolitan is equally indignant with his Pan-German compatriot, branding him a narrow-minded chauvinist and never noticing that he is himself a chauvinist, albeit Romano-Germanic and not German. Thus everything here is a matter of degree: One is more sensitive to the egocentric basis of chauvinism, the other less so. In any case, the sensitivity of Europeans to this issue is unquestionably limited; rarely does anyone rise above cosmopolitanism (i.e., Romano-Germanic chauvinism), and I do not know of any Europeans who consider the cultures of so-called savages equal to their own. Apparently such Europeans do not exist.

It is now quite clear how a thoughtful Romano-German ought to regard both chauvinism and cosmopolitanism. He should recognize that an egocentric psychology underlies both. He should admit that this psychology is an illogical frame of reference, and that it therefore cannot serve as the basis for any theory. Moreover, it should not be difficult for him to understand that egocentricity is by its very nature anticultural and antisocial and that it hinders community life in the broad sense of the term (i.e., free contacts among all people). It should be obvious to everyone that egocentricity of any sort can be vindicated only by force, that it always falls to the lot of the victor alone. This is why Europeans do not move beyond Pan-Romano-Germanic chauvinism; any single nation can be conquered by force, but collectively the Romano-Germans are so strong that no one can prevail against them.

However, as soon as all of this penetrates the consciousness of our hypothetical Romano-German, who is both perceptive and thoughtful, a conflict will immediately arise in his soul. His spiritual culture and world view rest on the conviction that a

subconscious spiritual life and its attendant biases should yield
to the demands of reason and logic, and that every theory must
be built upon logical, scientific foundations. His consciousness
of what is right presupposes rejection of principles that hinder
free contacts among people. His ethics are opposed to the
resolution of problems by brute force. And suddenly it turns
out that the foundation of cosmopolitanism is egocentricity!
Cosmopolitanism, the crowning glory of Romano-Germanic
civilization, rests upon foundations that contradict the most
deeply held beliefs of this same civilization! The very root of
cosmopolitanism—this religion for all humanity!—turns out to be
the anticultural principle of egocentricity. This impasse is tragic,
and there is only one way out of it. A thoughtful Romano-
German should renounce chauvinism and cosmopolitanism
forever, and with them all views that occupy the middle ground
between these two extremes.

But what attitude toward European chauvinism and
cosmopolitanism is appropriate for non-Romano-Germans—that
is, for representatives of the ethnic groups which took no part in
the creation of so-called European civilization? Egocentricity
deserves condemnation not only within the context of European
Romano-Germanic culture, but in any culture, for it is an
antisocial frame of reference that destroys every form of
cultural communication between human beings. If certain non-
Romano-Germanic chauvinists preach that their nation is a
chosen people to whom all other nations should bow down,
then they must be resisted by their fellow countrymen. But what
if there are individuals in such a nation who advocate the
supremacy not of their own, but of some other people, and they
urge their compatriots to merge with this "nation for all
mankind"? Such an appeal would not be egocentric, but quite
the opposite, and one could not condemn it as one does
chauvinism. But is the essence of a doctrine not more important
than the person of its advocate? If the supremacy of nation A
over nation B were advocated by a member of nation A, this
would be chauvinism, a manifestation of egocentric psychology;

and such an appeal would have to be rejected, and quite legitimately, by both A and B. But does the matter change fundamentally as soon as the voice of a representative of nation A is joined by the voice of a representative of nation B? Of course not. Chauvinism remains chauvinism. The protagonist in this hypothetical scenario is the representative of nation A. The will to enslave (the true meaning of all chauvinistic theories) finds its voice in him. While the voice of the representative of nation B may be louder, it is of lesser significance. Representative B has merely come to believe the argument of representative A, or he is convinced of the strength of nation A, or has allowed himself to be carried away, or perhaps he was simply bribed. Representative A fights for himself; representative B for someone else. It is A who speaks through B, and we can always consider the preachments of the latter to be camouflaged chauvinism.

On the whole, this line of reasoning is rather purposeless; such matters are not deserving of prolonged, logical argumentation. Everyone knows how he would respond to a fellow countryman if he began urging his people to renounce their faith, language, and culture, and to pursue assimilation by a neighboring nation (let us call it nation X). Everyone would consider such an individual to be a madman, or a dupe of nation X who had lost his own national pride, or a paid emissary of nation X sent to conduct propaganda. In any case, everyone would spot a chauvinist from nation X standing behind such a person, controlling his words at the conscious or subconscious level. Our attitude toward such proselytizing would not be determined by the fact that it comes from a compatriot, since we would certainly recognize that its origins were located in the nation whose supremacy was being advocated. There can be no doubt that our attitude to such proselytizing would be extremely negative. No normal nation, particularly no nation organized into a state, can voluntarily allow the destruction of its national individuality in the name of assimilation, even if by a more advanced nation. Any nation that respects itself would respond to the chauvinistic provocations of foreigners like Leonidas of Sparta: "Try to take us," it would say, and rise up in arms to defend its independence, even if defeat were inevitable.

All of this seems obvious, and yet people very often do not act in the way we have suggested. European cosmopolitanism, which, as we have noted, is nothing more than pan-Romano-Germanic chauvinism, has spread among non-Romano-Germanic peoples with great speed and ease. There are already many such cosmopolitans among the Slavs, Arabs, Turks, Indians, Chinese, and Japanese. Large numbers of them are even more orthodox than their European counterparts in their renunciation of national characteristics, in their contempt for every non-Romano-Germanic culture, and so forth. How are we to explain this contradiction? Why does pan-Romano-Germanic chauvinism enjoy such unchallenged success among the Slavs, while a mere hint of Germanophile propaganda puts them immediately on their guard? Why do Russian intellectuals reject with indignation the notion that they might serve as tools of German Junker nationalists, and yet not feel repelled by the idea of subordination to pan-Romano-Germanic chauvinists? The hypnotic power of words has concealed the answer.

The Romano-Germans have always been so naively convinced that they alone are human beings that they have called themselves "humanity," their culture "universal human culture," and their chauvinism "cosmopolitanism." Their terminology has allowed them to conceal the real ethnographic content of these concepts, which have thus become palatable to other ethnic groups. When selling to foreign peoples the products of their material culture which can indeed lay claim to universality (armaments and mechanical means of conveyance), the Romano-Germans pawn off their "universal" ideas, presenting them in a form that conceals their ethnographic nature.

The dissemination of so-called European cosmopolitanism among non-Romano-Germanic nations is the result of a simple misunderstanding. Those who have been taken in by the propaganda of Romano-Germanic chauvinists have been misled by the terms "humanity," "universally human," "civilization," "world progress," and so forth. These terms have been understood literally, while they actually conceal very specific and very narrow ethnographic concepts. The "intellectuals" in non-Romano-Germanic nations who have been duped by the Romano-Germans should realize their error. They should realize that the culture offered to them as universal human civilization is in fact the culture of the Romano-Germanic peoples. Recognition of this truth should change their attitude toward the culture of their own nation and force them to ask whether it is wise to try, in the name of "universally human" ideals (actually, Romano-Germanic—that is, foreign), to impose a foreign culture on their nation, at the same time eradicating the features of their own national uniqueness. They can answer this question only after a mature and rational examination of Romano-Germanic claims to the title "civilized mankind." They can decide whether to accept or reject Romano-Germanic culture only after answering a number of questions: (1) Can one prove objectively that the culture of the Romano-Germans is more advanced than any other culture which now exists or has existed on earth? (2) Is the complete assimilation of a culture created by another people possible without an anthropological merger of both peoples? (3) Is the assimilation of European culture (insofar as such assimilation is possible) a good or a bad thing?

These questions must be posed and answered in one way or another by everyone who understands the essence of European cosmopolitanism to be pan-Romano-Germanic chauvinism. And universal Europeanization can be accepted as necessary and desirable only if the answers to all these questions are affirmative. A negative answer means that Europeanization should be rejected, and two new questions should be posed: (4) Is universal Europeanization inevitable? (5) How should we combat its negative consequences?

In the following pages I will attempt to answer these questions. However, to ensure the correctness and, more importantly, the usefulness of the answers, we invite our readers to reject for the time being their egocentric biases, the idols of "universal human civilization," and, more generally, the mode of thought characteristic of Romano-Germanic scholarship. This renunciation is not a simple task, because the biases in question are deeply rooted in the consciousness of every person with a European education. However, this is the only way to achieve objectivity.

Chapter II

We have already noted that acceptance of Romano-Germanic culture as the most perfect of all historical cultures is rooted in the psychology of egocentricity. In Europe the notion of the absolute superiority of European civilization is viewed as a fundamental principle which has been established more or less scientifically. But the scientific nature of the proof is illusory, since the understanding of evolution present in European ethnology, anthropology, and the history of culture is itself permeated with egocentricity. Concepts such as the "evolutionary scale" and "stages of development" are all thoroughly egocentric. At their foundation is the idea that the development of the human species has proceeded and still proceeds along the path of so-called world progress, which is conceived to be a straight line. Mankind has moved along this straight line, but certain nations stopped at various points and have remained there, "running in place," while other nations managed to advance somewhat farther before they, too, stopped and began "running in place," and so on. Consequently, an overview of mankind as it exists today enables us to observe the entire evolutionary process, because at every step there stands some nation that got stuck and is "running in place." Thus, mankind represents something like a film of evolution that has been unwound and spliced; and the cultures of various nations are distinguished from one another as separate phases, as consecutive steps along the common path of world progress.

Even if we acknowledge that this conception of the relationship between reality and evolution is correct, we still will not be able to reconstruct the evolutionary process. To ascertain which evolutionary phase is represented by any given culture, we need to know where both ends of the straight line of world progress are located. Only then would it be possible to measure the distance separating a given culture from both ends of the scale and to determine its place in the evolutionary scheme. But we cannot locate those beginning and end points without first reconstructing the evolutionary scheme. The result is a vicious circle: to reconstruct the evolutionary scheme, we must know its beginning and end points, and to ascertain its beginning and end points, we must reconstruct the evolutionary scheme. The only way out of it is to discover in some suprascientific, irrational way that some particular culture is the beginning or end point of evolution. This cannot be done scientifically and objectively; this concept of evolution identifies nothing in individual cultures that would indicate their distance from the beginning or end points of evolution. Objectively, we can identify in particular cultures only those characteristics that are, to a greater or lesser degree, similar. On the basis of these characteristics we can group the cultures of the world, so that those exhibiting the greatest degree of similarity are close together, while those less similar are separated from one another. That is all we can do on an objective basis. But even if we succeeded in doing this and constructed a continuous chain, we still would not be in a position to determine the beginning and end points of the chain with complete objectivity.

Let us illustrate our meaning with an example. Imagine seven squares, each of them painted with one of the colors of the rainbow; they are arranged in a straight line in the following order, from left to right: green, blue, indigo, violet, red, orange, and yellow. Now let us mix them up and ask someone who did not see their original order to arrange them again in a straight line, so that each secondary color is located between two primary colors. It is clear that the individual we have selected can arrange the squares in the original order only by chance, the probability of doing so being 1 out of 14. An investigator who is given the task of arranging in evolutionary order the peoples and cultures extant today is in precisely the same situation. Even if he places every culture between the two that are most like it, he still will not know which end to start from, just as it would be impossible to guess in our experiment that one should begin with the green square, and that the blue one should be to the left, not to the right of it. The only difference is that there are many more than seven cultures to be grouped, so the number of possible solutions will be much larger than fourteen; since only one of them will be correct, the chances of solving this problem are incomparably smaller than in our experiment with the colored squares. Therefore, if the pervasive understanding of evolution in European scholarship is true, the pattern of mankind's evolution still cannot be reconstructed. But Europeans maintain that they have in fact reconstructed the general line of this evolution. How is this to be explained? Has a miracle occurred? Have European scholars had access to a supernatural revelation from some mysterious source, enabling them to locate the beginning and end points of evolution?

If we look closely at the results of the work of European scholars and at the scheme of human evolution they have constructed, we find behind the mask of supernatural revelation the same, altogether familiar egocentricity. It, and only it, signaled for Romano-Germanic scholars—ethnologists and historians of culture—the location of the beginning and end points of human development. Rather than remaining objective and admitting that the hopelessness of their position can only be ascribed to an understanding of evolution which is in need of correction, Europeans have simply accepted the idea that they and their culture represent the apotheosis of human evolution; and in the naive belief that they had found one end of the postulated evolutionary path, they quickly reconstructed the entire journey. The possibility that recognition of Romano-Germanic culture as the apotheosis of human evolution is merely a convention and a monstrous *petitio principii* is an idea that has occurred to no European thinker. Their egocentricity has proven so strong that no one has challenged this view, and it has been accepted without reservation, as something obviously true.

This is how the "scale of human evolution" came into being. The Romano-Germans and the nations that have adopted their culture are located at its top; the "highly cultured nations of antiquity" (i.e., nations whose cultures are closely aligned with and similar to European culture) stand on the next rung down. Next come the cultured peoples of Asia; literacy, state organization, and several other traits of their cultures make them to some degree like the Romano-Germans. The same holds for the "ancient cultures of America" (Mexico, Peru); however, these cultures resemble Romano-Germanic culture to a lesser degree, and they are accordingly located somewhat lower on the evolutionary scale. Nevertheless, all these peoples have so many features in their cultures that are superficially similar to the Romano-Germans that they are deemed worthy of the label "cultured." Below them stand the "culturally underdeveloped nations," while "the uncultured" and "savages" are placed at the very bottom. The last are the representatives of the human race who least resemble the contemporary Romano-Germans.

From this perspective, the Romano-Germans and their culture do indeed represent the summit of human achievement. Of course, Romano-Germanic historians of culture modestly add that "mankind" may in time progress still farther; the inhabitants of Mars may be more advanced than we are in a cultural sense, but on earth we Europeans are presently more advanced, more perfect than anyone else.

This scheme lacks the force of objective, convincing proof. The Romano-Germans do not consider themselves the "crown of creation" because science has proved the existence of the scale of evolution; to the contrary, European scholars place the Romano-Germans at its top solely because they proceed from an *a priori* belief in their own perfection. Egocentricity is the decisive factor here. Objectively speaking, this scale represents the classification of peoples and cultures using the degree to which they resemble contemporary Romano-Germans as the only measure. The evaluative element that creates from this classification a scale measuring degrees of perfection is not objective; it is the product of subjective egocentricity. Thus, the classification of peoples and cultures that is accepted in European scholarship is incapable of demonstrating objectively the superiority of Romano-Germanic civilization to the cultures of other peoples. We would do well to remember the saying, "A turkey's not a peacock, however he struts." If we examine the proofs that are adduced in favor of the great perfection of Romano-Germanic civilization, which stands at the top of the "evolutionary sacle" by comparison with the culture of "savages" who supposedly "stand at the lowest stage of development," we note with surprise that all these proofs are founded either on a *petitio principii* of egocentric prejudices or on an optical illusion caused by that very egocentric psychology. Objective scientific proofs are completely lacking.

The simplest and most widespread proof of the alleged perfection of Romano-Germanic civilization is the fact that Europeans always conquer "savages"; when "savages" engage in battle with Europeans, the struggle always ends in victory for the "whites" and defeat for the "savages." The crudeness and naivete of this "proof" should be apparent to every fair-minded person. This argument shows clearly how much the worship of brute force—a fundamental characteristic of the tribes that created European civilization—is still alive in the consciousness of every descendant of the Gauls and Teutons. The Gallic "Vae victus!" [Woe to the conquered!] and Teutonic vandalism, both of which acquired system and weight from the traditions of the Roman soldiery, emerge here in all their glory, although concealed behind the mask of objective scholarship. And yet this argument can be encountered in the works of the most enlightened European "humanists." It is pointless to analyze its logical incoherence. Although European historians attempt to array it in the mantle of science by means of theoretical allusions to "survival of the fittest" and "natural selection," they cannot elaborate this historical point of view consistently. They are constantly forced to admit that victory has often fallen to the lot of "less cultured peoples." History provides numerous instances of the conquest of settled peoples by nomads (although nomads, who are very distinct in their mode of life from contemporary Romano-Germans, are always placed lower than settled peoples on the evolutionary scale). All the "great cultures of antiquity" recognized by European scholarship were destroyed by "barbarians." The point is often made that these cultures had already reached a state of decay and degeneration by the time they fell, but in many cases this thesis is difficult to prove. Since European scholarship cannot accept the proposition that the victorious nation is always more advanced culturally than the vanquished, no definitive conclusions can be drawn from the simple fact of the Europeans' victory over "savages."

Another argument, no less widespread but even less well founded, is that "savages" are incapable of grasping certain ideas of European origin and should therefore be viewed as "lower races." The psychology of egocentricity is particularly vivid in this notion. Europeans are quite oblivious to the fact that if "savages" are incapable of understanding some of the ideas of European civilization, the cultures of these "savages" are equally inaccessible to them. There is a well-known story about a Papuan who was taken to England and given a university education, but who began to pine for his homeland and fled to it, abandoning his European clothing; he began to live again like the "savage" he had been before his trip to England, so that not a trace of European culture remained in him. Forgotten are the numerous anecdotes about Europeans who, having decided to "simplify their lives," settled among "savages"; they discovered rather quickly that this new milieu was intolerable, and they abandoned it for life as it is lived in Europe. It is common to assert that European civilization is so difficult for "savages" to understand that many who have attempted to "become civilized" have lost their minds or become alcoholics. However, in those instances—rare, to be sure—when well-intentioned European "eccentrics" have attempted to assimilate the culture of some "savage" tribe (i.e., to accept not only the external, material life style of the tribe but also its religion and beliefs), the same fate has usually befallen them. It is sufficient to recall Gauguin, the talented French painter, who tried to become a Tahitian and who discovered that the price of this undertaking was madness, and later alcoholism, and who died ignominiously in a drunken brawl. Obviously, the point is not that "savages" are lower in development than Europeans, but that their culture is not developing in the same direction; Europeans and "savages" differ fundamentally from one another in the basic patterns of their everyday lives and in the psychology produced by these patterns. Since the psychology and culture of "savages" have almost nothing in common with the psychology and culture of Europeans, complete assimilation of these alien spiritual and material patterns is impossible for both sides. Because this impossibility is mutual—it is as difficult for a European to become a "savage" as it is for a "savage" to become a European—one cannot reach any conclusions here about who is higher and who is lower in development.

The considerations examined above regarding the superiority of Europeans over "savages" are occasionally encountered in scholarly works, but their proper place is in the naive, superficial opinions of ordinary people. The arguments characteristic of scholarly literature appear much more sophisticated, but closer inspection shows them to be based on egocentric biases as well. For example, one often encounters the argument that "savages" are very much like children. This assumption is not surprising, because "savages" do create in observers the impression of being grown-up children. So the logical conclusion is that they are "suffering from arrested development" and that they stand lower on the evolutionary scale than Europeans, who are genuinely adult. In this European scholars once again exhibit a lack of objectivity. They completely ignore the fact that the impression of "grown-up children" is *mutual*, which is to say that the savages also view Europeans as grown-up children.

From a psychological point of view, this fact is very interesting, and its significance can only be explained by examining what Europeans mean by the term *savage*. We have already observed that European scholarship uses this word to refer to people who are psychologically and culturally most distant from contemporary Romano-Germans, and it is in this fact that we must seek the explanation for the above-mentioned puzzle. The following conditions should be borne in mind: (1) the psychology of every human being consists of inherited and acquired traits; (2) among inherited psychological traits one must distinguish those which are individual, familial, tribal, and racial, as well as those attributable to the human species, to all mammals, and to all animals; (3) acquired traits depend on the environment in which an individual exists—on his familial traditions and those of his social group or class and on the culture of his people; (4) in infancy the psyche consists entirely of inherited traits, but with time these traits are supplemented in increasingly greater measure by acquired traits, so that some inherited traits are suppressed or disappear altogether; (5) we can understand and interpret in another human being only those psychological traits that he has in common with us.

It follows that when an encounter occurs between two individuals from the same environment who have been educated in the same cultural traditions, they understand one another's psyche almost completely, because they have in common virtually every trait, except those that are individual and innate. But when such an encounter occurs between two individuals who belong to two distinct and completely dissimilar cultures, they will notice and understand only a few inherited traits in the psychology of the other, but acquired ones will not be understood and perhaps not even noticed, for here they have nothing in common. The more the culture of the observer differs from that of the observed, the fewer acquired psychological traits the former will notice in the latter and the more the psychology of the observed will seem to the observer to consist solely of inherited traits. And a psychology in which inherited traits predominate over acquired ones always appears very simple. The psyche of any human being can be represented by a fraction in which the numerator is the sum total of inherited traits accessible to our perception and the denominator the sum total of acquired features. The larger the fraction (i.e., the smaller the denominator is in relation to the numerator), the more elementary the psyche will appear. Conditions (3) and (5) above make it clear that the more the culture and social environments of the observed and the observer differ, the larger the fraction will be.

Since "savages" are those peoples who differ most in their culture and everyday life from contemporary Europeans, it is clear why their psychology must inevitably seem elementary to Europeans. And from everything that has been said it is also clear that this impression must be mutual. The notion that "savages" are grown-up children is based on this optical illusion. We notice only inherited traits in the psychology of "savages," because we have only these in common with them (condition 5). Their acquired traits are alien and incomprehensible to us, since they are based on cultural traditions completely different from ours (condition 3). The psychology in which inherited traits predominate and acquired traits are virtually absent is the psychology of the child (condition 4). Therefore, the "savage" seems to us to be a child.

One other consideration is of importance here. If we compare two children—a young "savage" and a young European—we will notice that they are much closer to one another psychologically than their fathers. They do not yet possess the acquired traits that will appear later; but they share many of the elements entering into the psychologies of the human species, mammals, and animals, while the psychological distinctions introduced by race, tribe, family, and individual personality are not yet very great. Over time a certain portion of this common stock of inherited traits will be effaced or altered by acquired traits, and the other part will remain unchanged. But these two parts will differ from one another in their composition. The "savage" will lose A and retain B and C; the European will lose B and retain A and C. To this the "savage" will add acquired traits D, while the European will add acquired traits E.

When an adult European meets an adult "savage" and begins to observe him, he will find elements B, C, and D in the psychology of the "savage." Of these, element D will prove to be alien and incomprehensible to him, since this element is acquired; it is conditioned by the culture of the "savage," a culture having nothing in common with European culture. Element C will be common to the adult "savage" and the adult European, and thus fully comprehensible to the latter. Element B is not present in the psychology of the adult European, but he knows that he possessed it in infancy and that it exists in the psychology of the children of his people. Consequently, the psychology of the "savage" will inevitably strike the European as a mixture of elementary psychological traits found in adults with traits characteristic of a child. The psychology of the European will strike the "savage" in the same way and for the same reasons.

This optical illusion is also the source of another phenomenon—the similarities that Europeans have found between the psychologies of "savages" and animals. We have already noted that a young "savage" differs very little in his psychology from a young European. If we now add a young animal to these two young children, we will be forced to recognize that the three have something in common, namely, psychological traits characteristic of all mammals and of all animals. These traits may not be numerous, but they exist; we will designate them as x, y, and z. Over time the young European will lose x, and the "savage" will lose y; the animal will retain x, y, and z. But the traits of animal psychology retained by the three subjects will not be preserved in their original form: the psychological characteristics of adult animals always differ to some degree from the characteristics of the young animals from which they developed. Consequently, traits x, y, and z will become x', y', and z' in an adult animal. In a European, traits y

and z will become y' and z'; and traits x and z will become x' and z' in an adult "savage."

When an adult European observes an adult "savage" he notices, among other things, trait x'. How does he interpret it? This trait does not exist in his own psychology, and it has a different form (namely, x) in the psychology of the children of his people. However, the European can observe x' directly in the psychology of adult animals. It is therefore quite natural for him to define x' as characteristic of animals, and because of its presence in the psychology of the "savage," to consider the latter a person akin to animals in his development. This also applies to the "savage" who sees in the European trait y', which is alien to his own psychology but known to him from animals; he will interpret it exactly as the European interprets trait x' in the psychology of the "savage."

All of the above helps us to understand the first impression that people from radically different cultures make upon each other. Each will see and understand in the other only those traits which they have in common (i.e., inherited psychological traits), and will inevitably consider the psychology of the observed person to be elementary and childlike. Perceiving in the person observed traits that are familiar to himself from his own childhood but subsequently lost, the observer will consider the subject a man whose development is arrested, a man who, although adult, is endowed with traits of a child's psychology. Further, certain traits of the observed subject will strike the observer as close to the psychology of animals. As far as nonelementary traits (i.e., acquired traits linked to a culture alien to the observer) are concerned, they will remain completely incomprehensible and will strike the observer as oddities or eccentricities. This combination of childishness and eccentricity turns any person from a profoundly alien culture into a freak. And this impression will be mutual. When representatives of two maximally different cultures meet, each will seem to the other funny and freakish — in a word, "savage."

We know that the European experiences precisely such feelings at the sight of a "savage", but we also know that "savages" at the sight of a European are either frightened or react to every one of his displays with explosions of Homeric laughter. So the notion that the psychology of the "savage" is similar to that of children and animals is based on an optical illusion. This illusion preserves its force not only with reference to savages, that is, peoples who differ maximally from the contemporary Romano-Germans but also to all peoples of non-Romano-Germanic culture. The difference will be only a matter of degree. In observing a representative of a culture "not our own" we will understand among his acquired psychological traits only those which we also have, that is, which are connected with elements of culture common to each of us. Acquired traits based on sides of his culture which have no equivalent in our own, will remain incomprehensible for us. As concerns elements of the innate psyche, they will almost all turn out to be understandable for us, though some of them will seem like childish traits. Thanks to the fact that we will understand the innate psyche of that observed nation almost completely, and the acquired psyche only to the extent that the culture of that people is similar to ours, the correlation of the innate and acquired sides of his psyche will always seem incorrect to us, with the preponderance on the side of the innate; and the more the culture of a given people differs from ours, the greater that preponderance will be. It is natural, therefore, that the psychology of a people with a culture that is unlike our own will always seem more primitive.

Such an evaluation of another human being's psychology is observable not only between two nations but between social groups within the same nation if social differences are very great and if the upper classes have adopted a foreign culture. Many Russian intellectuals, physicians, officers, and nurses, when dealing with the common people, say that they are like grown-up children. On the other hand, judging by their folk tales, the common people perceive certain eccentric, naive, childlike psychological traits in the upper classes.

Although the European conceptualization of the psychology of the savage is based on an optical illusion, it is still the predominant element in the pseudoscholarly formulations of European ethnologists, anthropologists, and historians of culture. The most important methodological consequence of this conceptualization is that it has allowed scholars in these fields to lump together the most diverse peoples under the headings "savage," "culturally underdeveloped," and "primitive." We have already noted that these terms are used to refer to peoples whose cultures differ radically from contemporary Romano-Germanic culture. This subjective and therefore negative feature is the only one these peoples have in common. Since it is the source of the optical illusion that gave rise to the undifferentiated assessment of the psychology of such peoples by Europeans, it has caused the latter to accept their own assessment as an objective and empirically verifiable feature, and they have categorized all peoples who are equally distant culturally from contemporary Romano-Germans as "primitive." European scholars can ignore the fact that peoples who are very different from one another culturally (e.g., the Eskimos and the Kaffirs) fall into the same category because the specific differences between various "primitive peoples" (as long as their cultures are equally distant from Romano-Germanic culture) are all equally alien and incomprehensible to Europeans. They are therefore dismissed as traits of little significance. European scholarship deals confidently with this multitudinous group and with the concept of "primitive peoples" (based on a subjective and indeterminate characteristic) as if it had an altogether real and homogeneous entity at its disposal. Such is the impact of egocentricity on European evolutionary science.

There is another argument in favor of the superiority of Romano-Germanic civilization over every other culture; it is based upon the very same optical illusion and, consequently, on the habit of evaluating other peoples by the degree to which they resemble contemporary Romano-Germans. This argument, which can be called "historical," is looked upon in Europe as the most weighty of all, and historians of culture refer to it especially often. It asserts that the ancestors of contemporary Europeans were also "savages" at one time and that contemporary "savages" are at a stage of development which Europeans left behind long ago. This argument is supported by archeological discoveries and by the testimony of ancient historians allegedly showing that the *mores* of the distant ancestors of the contemporary Romano-Germanic peoples exhibited all the typical features of contemporary "savages."

The flimsiness of this argument becomes obvious as soon as we recall the artificiality of the concept of "savage" or "primitive" peoples, a concept that joins the most diverse of the world's peoples together on the basis of a single characteristic, namely, the extreme cultural differences that separate them from contemporary Romano-Germans. Like every culture, European culture has changed and reached its present-day state only gradually, after a long evolution. In every epoch, the culture of the Europeans was somewhat different, and it is only natural that it would be closer to its present state in epochs closer to our own time than it was in more remote epochs. In the remotest epochs of the past, the culture of the Europeans differed most of all from contemporary "civilization"; at that time the culture of the ancestors of Europeans was *maximally* differentiated from contemporary European culture. But all cultures maximally differentiated from contemporary European civilization are lumped together by European scholars as "primitive"! It is therefore quite natural that the culture of the distant ancestors of contemporary Romano-Germans should fall into the same category. But once again, no empirically verifiable conclusions can be drawn from this fact. Given the indeterminacy of the concept of primitive culture, the fact that the epithet "primitive" is applied by European scholars to the culture of the most ancient ancestors of the Romano-Germans and to the culture of the present-day Eskimos and Kaffirs does not prove that these cultures are *identical;* it only proves that they are equal in their differentiation from contemporary European civilization.

Here I would like to touch upon another detail of European theories about "savages," a detail that is closely connected with the "historical argument." When Europeans succeed (rather rarely, to be sure) in penetrating the history of some contemporary "savage" tribe, it always turns out that the culture of this tribe has never changed at all over time or that it has "gone backward." In the latter case, present-day "savages" are said to embody the results of this regression—the gradual brutalization of a people that once stood at a "higher level of development." Such conclusions are once again based on the same optical illusion and on egocentric prejudices.

This view of the history of "savages" can best be illustrated graphically. Let us imagine a circle whose center (point A) is the locus of contemporary European culture. The radius of this circle represents the maximum cultural differentiation from contemporary Romano-Germans. Consequently, the culture of any contemporary "savage" tribe can be represented by some point B on the circumference of the circle. But the culture of this tribe is located at point B only at the present moment. In the past this culture had a different form, which can be designated by some point C not coincident with point B. Where should this point be located? There are three possibilities.

First, C can be located at some other point on the circumference of the same circle (Figure 1). According to our proposition, AC will then be equal to AB. In other words, it will turn out that the culture of our "savage" tribe was maximally differentiated from con-temporary European culture in this earlier historical epoch. And since European scholarship lumps together as "primitive" all cultures maximally differentiated from European civiliza-tion, the European scholar will

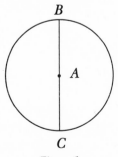

Figure 1

recognize not signs of progress but only immobility and stagnation, no matter how large the arc CB that represents the distance traversed by the culture of this "savage" tribe from that past epoch to the present.

In the second case, C can be located within the circle. Here AC will be less than AB; in other words, the culture of the "savage" tribe has moved in a direction away from the point representing the contemporary culture of Europeans. The European scholar, who considers his culture the peak of earthly perfection, can interpret this movement only as regression, decline, or as a descent into barbarism.

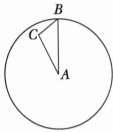

Figure 2

Finally, in the third case, C can be located outside the circle. Here AC is greater than the radius AB (i.e., greater than the maximum distance from the culture of contemporary Romano-Germans). But quantities greater than the maximum are beyond the reach of the human mind and our powers of perception. The horizon of the European standing at point A is limited by the circumference of the circle, and he sees nothing that lies beyond it. Therefore, the European must project point C

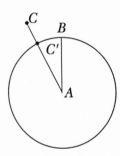

Figure 3

onto the circumference of the circle (C'), and this third case will be reduced to the first and to its conclusion: immobility or stagnation.

The European evaluates the histories of peoples whose cultures differ in varying degrees from the contemporary Romano-Germanic just as he does the history of "savages." Strictly speaking, the European observes real "progress" only in the history of Romano-Germanic culture itself; in that history there occurs quite naturally a continual, gradual movement toward the present state of the culture, which is arbitrarily declared the peak of perfection. As far as the history of any non-Romano-Germanic people is concerned, unless it ends with the importation of European culture, all its later stages (those closest to the present) are inevitably viewed by European scholars as steps in a period of stagnation or decline. These scholars note with satisfaction that such a people "has set out on the path of universal human progress" only when it has its rejected their national culture and succumbed to blind imitation of the Europeans.

Thus the "historical argument"—the most cogent and persuasive in the eyes of Europeans—turns out to be as inconclusive as all the other arguments in favor of the superiority of the Romano-Germans over "savages." To many it may seem that I am indulging in sophistry and juggling with general principles. They will say that despite all the logic of my arguments, the superiority of the European over the "savage" remains an indisputable, objective, and self-evident truth, which cannot be proved precisely for that reason. Axioms are accepted without proof, like the facts of our immediate perceptions (e.g., the fact that the paper on which I am writing is white). However, self-evident things require no proof only if they are objective. It may be obvious to me subjectively that I am in all respects better and more intelligent than my acquaintance N; but since this fact is not self-evident to N himself nor to many of our mutual friends, I cannot consider it objective. The question of the superiority of Europeans over "savages" is the same sort of thing. Let us not forget that those who want to provide the answer to this question are Europeans themselves—the Romano-Germans—or people who do not belong to their race but who are hypnotized by their prestige and have fallen completely under their influence. Even if the superiority of the Romano-Germans is self-evident to these judges, this is a subjective and not an objective judgment, and it requires objective proof. But such proofs do not exist; the foregoing discussion has demonstrated this quite clearly.

We are told to compare the intellectual baggage of a cultured European with that of any Bushman, Botocudo, or Veddah: Is the superiority of the first over the others not obvious? It is my contention that the obviousness of this conclusion is subjective and that it vanishes as soon as we take the trouble to investigate the matter carefully and without bias. The "savage," if he is a good hunter possessing all the qualities that his tribe values (and only such a "savage" can be compared with a cultured European), has a mind that contains an enormous and diverse store of concepts and information. He has learned to perfection the life of the nature that surrounds him, he knows all the habits of the animals and subtleties of their behavior that escape the experienced eye of the most observant European naturalist. His knowledge is hardly disordered or chaotic; rather, it is systematized—true, not according to the rubrics by which a European scholar would organize it, but according to others that suit the practical objectives of the hunter's life. In addition to this practical knowledge derived from experience, the "savage" knows the mythology of his tribe (often quite complex), its moral code, the rules and prescriptions of etiquette (sometimes also quite complex), and finally, some and perhaps many works from the oral literature of his people. In short, the mind of the "savage" is "full," despite the fact that the materials filling it are utterly different from those filling the head of the European. Consequently, the intellectual baggage of the "savage" and the European must be viewed as neither comparable nor commensurable; the question of the superiority of one over the other cannot be resolved.

European culture is also said to be more complex than that of the "savage." But this relation between the two cultures can hardly be said to hold true for all of their component parts. Cultured Europeans take pride in the elegance of their manners, in their refined politeness. But the rules of etiquette and the conventions of social life among "savages" are often more complex and elaborate than among Europeans, not to mention the fact that all members of a "savage" tribe are subject to this code of decorum, whereas among Europeans refinement and decorum are associated only with the upper classes. In their preoccupation with external appearance, "savages" often go much farther than Europeans: note the intricate tatooing of Australians and Polynesians and the extremely complicated hairdos of African women. Even if tatooing and hairdos could be dismissed as purposeless eccentricities, there are some unquestionably useful institutions in the cultures of certain "savages" that are more complex than their European counterparts. A good example is the way in which sexual relations, the family, and marriage are handled. How crudely this question is resolved in Romano-Germanic civilization, where monogamous families, officially protected by law, co-exist with unbridled sexual freedom, which society and state theoretically condemn but in practice permit! Compare this with the elaborate institution of group marriage among the Australians, where sexual relations occur within very rigid boundaries; and yet, in the absence of individual marriage, measures are taken to avoid incest and to ensure the well-being of children.

Generally speaking, a greater or lesser degree of complexity says nothing about the level of perfection reached by a culture. Evolution just as often moves in the direction of simplification as in the direction of greater complexity, so the degree of complexity cannot serve as a measure of progress. Europeans understand this very well, and they use this yardstick only when it facilitates self-glorification. When a "savage" culture proves to be more complex in some respect than European culture, Europeans, far from considering greater complexity a sign of progress, ascribe it to "primitiveness." This is how European scholarship interprets the aforementioned examples—the elaborate etiquette of "savages," their preoccupation with body decoration, even the ingenious Australian system of group marriage—all of this turns out to be a manifestation of a low cultural level. In so doing, Europeans disregard even their precious "historical argument," because there never was a moment in the prehistory of the Gauls and the Teutons (and the Romans) when any of these allegedly primitive "savage" traits actually occurred. The ancestors of the Romano-Germans knew nothing about elaborate body decoration, tatooing, or fantastically complex hairdos, they cared even less about "good manners" and politeness than our contemporary Germans and Americans, and their families were structured for centuries according to an unchanging pattern.

Europeans disregard the historical argument in numerous instances where its logical application would not support European civilization. Much in contemporary European culture that is taken for the very latest thing, the summit of newly achieved progress, also occurs among "savages," but there it is looked upon as a sign of extreme primitiveness. Futurist paintings by Europeans are treated as of the highest refinement in aesthetic taste; but very similar works by "savages" are seen as naive experiments, signs of the first stirrings of a primitive art. Socialism, communism, anarchism—all are the "shining ideals of a future, higher progress," but only when they are preached by a contemporary European; when these same "ideals" are realized in the life of "savages," they are immediately interpreted as manifestations of primitive brutishness.

There are and can be no objective proofs of the superiority of Europeans over "savages," because in comparing various cultures to one another, Europeans know only one criterion: What resembles us is better and more perfect than anything that does not resemble us. But if Europeans are not more advanced than "savages," then the evolutionary scale or ladder discussed above collapses. If its top rung is no higher than its base, then it is obviously no higher than the other rungs between the top and the bottom. Rather than a ladder we obtain a horizontal plane; rather than the principle of arranging peoples and cultures according to degrees of perfection, we obtain a new principle of the equal worth and qualitative incommensurability of the cultures and peoples on this earth. The element of evaluation should be banished once and for all from ethnology, the history of culture, and from all the evolutionary sciences, because evaluation is inevitably based on egocentricity. No one is higher, and no one is lower. Some are similar, and others are not. To declare that those who are like us are higher and those unlike us lower is arbitrary, unscholarly, and in the final analysis, simply ignorant. When the European evolutionary sciences, in particular ethnology, anthropology, and cultural history, have overcome this deeply rooted egocentric prejudice and freed themselves from its consequences in their methods and conclusions, only then will they become scientific disciplines. To date they are at best a means to deceive people and to justify in the eyes of Romano-Germans and their henchmen the imperialistic, colonial policies and the vandal-like cultural "mission" of the Great Powers, Europe, and America.

Thus, the first of the questions posed above, "Is it possible to prove objectively that the culture of the contemporary Romano-Germans is more advanced than all other cultures that exist or have existed on earth?" must be answered in the negative.

Chapter III

We will now attempt to answer the following question: Is it possible for any nation to assimilate *in toto* a culture created by another nation? By complete assimilation we mean the following: the culture of the foreign nation is absorbed to such a degree that it becomes the "native" culture of the borrowing nation, continuing there its development exactly as "at home," so that the creator of the culture and its borrower merge into a single cultural entity.

To answer such a question, one must know the laws governing the life and development of cultures. The existing European scholarship in this area knows virtually nothing about these laws, since, owing to the egocentric prejudices discussed above, sociology pursues the same false course as all the other evolutionary sciences in Europe. It has failed to generate either objective scholarly methods or reliable conclusions, and remains at the level of alchemy. Certain tenable perspectives on the method that ought to be used in sociology and on the mechanics, or dynamics, of social phenomena sometimes turn up in the works of European sociologists; but they never maintain their methodological principles consistently to the end of their argument and invariably lapse into egocentric generalizations about the development of "mankind." This passion for hasty generalizations (always incorrect owing to the falsity of the concepts "mankind," "progress," "primitiveness," etc.) is characteristic of all sociologists, making it especially difficult to put their conclusions to use.

One of the most outstanding European sociologists of the last century (unfortunately, little known and misunderstood in Europe) was the French scholar Gabriel Tarde; in his general views on the nature of social processes and the methods of sociology, he seems to have come closer to the truth than anyone else. But the passion for generalizations and a desire to describe the entire evolution of "mankind" immediately after defining the elements of social life ruined the work of this astute scholar. Moreover, he was imbued like all Europeans with egocentric prejudice, and he could not accept the idea of the equal value and qualitative incommensurability of peoples and cultures; he could not think of "mankind" other than as an indivisible whole, with separate parts arranged on an evolutionary scale; nor could he abandon concepts like "universally human" and "world progress." Consequently, although I agree in large part with a significant number of points in Tarde's sociological ideas, I must correct them in several very significant ways. However, it is from the perspective provided by his sociological system that I will approach the question posed above.

The life and development of every culture consists of the uninterrupted emergence of new cultural assets. By cultural asset I mean every purposeful creation by a human being that becomes the common property of his compatriots. This could be a legal standard, a work of art, an institution, a technical device, or a scientific or philosophical thesis, so long as it meets specific physical or spiritual needs or is accepted by all or some representatives of a given people for the satisfaction of such needs. The emergence of every new cultural asset can be called an invention (Tarde's term). Every invention is a combination of two or more existing cultural assets or of their various components. However, a new invention cannot be completely broken down into its components, and it always contains an additional element: the method of combination itself and the imprint of its creator's personality. Once it has appeared, an invention passes to other people through imitation (also Tarde's term). This term must be understood in its broadest sense, from reproduction of the cultural asset or reproduction of the means of satisfying a particular need with its help to "sympathetic imitation" (i.e., subordination to a newly created norm, acceptance of a given idea as true, or profound regard for the merits of a particular work). During the process of imitation, a new invention may clash and enter into conflict with another one or with an older cultural asset; a struggle for supremacy ensues between them (*duel logique*, according to Tarde), and one value replaces the other.

A particular invention becomes a fact of social life, an element of culture, only after it has overcome all obstacles and spread through imitation to the entire community. The culture of any nation at any moment always represents the sum total of the inventions that have been accepted by the present and earlier generations. The life and development of culture can thus be reduced to two elementary processes— invention and dissemination (Tarde's *invention* and *propagation*)—together with the almost inescapable (but not inevitable) factor, struggle for acceptance (*duel logique*). It is not difficult to see that these two fundamental processes have much in common: insofar as any invention is inspired by earlier inventions, or better, by existing cultural assets, it can be viewed as a combined imitation, or, in Tarde's expression, as the clash in an individual consciousness of two or several imitative waves (*ondes imitatives*). The difference consists only in the fact that during the process of invention there is no struggle between conflicting values (*duel logique*) in the narrow sense of the word; no value replaces any other, for they are synthesized and merged into a single whole, whereas during the process of dissemination the clash of values does not create a new value but only eliminates one of those in conflict.

Both invention and dissemination can be considered two aspects of the process of imitation. The special feature of Tarde's thought is that he recognizes as the fundamental principle of social life only the basic psychological process of imitation, which always occurs in the brain of an individual but establishes at the same time links with other people; it refers therefore not only to individual, but to an interpersonal psychology (Tarde's *interpsychologie*).

Now I will attempt to formulate the conditions necessary for the continual emergence of inventions (i.e., for the development of culture). Before all else, this development requires the existence of a complete stock of cultural assets in the consciousness of a given community—that is, previously created assets that have passed through the stage of struggle. As was stated above, every new invention comprises elements of existing cultural assets, according to the principle *ex nihilo nihil fit*. While every new invention is directed toward the satisfaction of a particular need, it evokes at the same time new needs or alters old ones, resulting in a search for new ways to satisfy them. All of this makes a close connection between new inventions and the existing stock of cultural assets absolutely indispensable.

To develop successfully, this common stock of cultural assets—the inventory of the culture—must be passed on by tradition: it is through imitation of the older generation that every new generation must assimilate the culture in which the older generation grew to adulthood after acquiring it from their own predecessors. The culture received through tradition is for every generation the point of departure for ongoing invention; this is an essential condition for the continuous, organic development of a culture. Finally, heredity plays a most important role in the development of culture (a factor underestimated by Tarde). Heredity supplements tradition, and it is with its help that the tastes, predispositions, and temperaments of those who created the cultural assets in the past are transmitted from generation to generation; it also facilitates the organic development of the culture.

The same conditions that are needed for the emergence of inventions are indispensable for their *dissemination (propagation des inventions)*—the other fundamental process in the development of culture. The presence of a common stock of cultural assets is necessary because it determines the need that is to be satisfied by an invention; and the invention can take root only if the need that brought it into existence is identically present in both the inventor and in society. Further, the successful dissemination of any invention is guaranteed for the most part by the readiness of society to accept it; and this readiness assumes that the elements comprised by the invention already exist in the consciousness of society. We know that the elements of every new invention are drawn from the common stock of assets; consequently, this common stock, identical for inventors and imitators, is a necessary condition for an invention's dissemination. But the presence of a common stock of cultural assets is not, in itself, sufficient for this to happen. It is important that all these values and their constituent elements be arranged in the consciousness of the inventor and of society in approximately the same way, so that their interrelationships in both cases are identical. This is possible only within the context of a single tradition. Finally, for an invention to be accepted by all or by the majority of people, it is necessary that the tastes, predispositions, and temperament of its creator not contradict the psychological *gestalt* of society; and for this a common heredity is required.

After these preliminary remarks on general sociology, we can turn to the question that interests us: Can any people assimilate a foreign culture completely? Let us imagine two nations—nations A and B—each with its own culture (a nation is inconceivable without a culture in the definition we have given to the term), and these two cultures are different. Now let us assume that nation A borrows the culture of nation B. Can this culture develop subsequently in the same direction, with the same spirit, and at the same tempo on the soil of nation A as it will on the soil of nation B? For this to happen, we know that after the borrowing it would be necessary for nation A to receive a stock of cultural assets, a tradition, and a heredity identical to those of nation B. Of course, none of these is possible. Even if nation A assimilates the entire inventory of nation B's culture, the common stocks of cultural assets will be different for both nations; especially at first, nation A will add to the borrowed stock of nation B the inventory of its previous culture, which nation B does not possess. Even if great pains are taken to eradicate the remainders of the previous national culture, it will live on after the borrowing, if only in the national memory of A. As a result, the tradition of nation A will turn out to be quite different from that of nation B. Finally, heredity cannot be borrowed without an anthropological merger of nations A and B; but even if such a merger were to occur, the heredity produced by crossbreeding A and B will be different from that of B alone. Thus, immediately after the borrowing the conditions affecting the life of nation B's culture on the soil of nation A will diverge radically from the conditions affecting its life on its native soil.

The first steps taken by a culture after it has been transferred to a foreign soil are decisive for its future development. The most critical factor here is the absence of an organic tradition. Numerous elements of nation B's culture are learned and assimilated by small children in nation B; these elements will be assimilated by adults in nation A. The natural source of tradition in nation B is the family; initially, the family in nation A cannot transmit the new culture in its pure form to the younger generation, and it must be instilled through school or through organizations that are here quite artificial—the army, factories, workshops, and so on. While they are receiving the traditions of the new, borrowed culture from such sources, the younger generation also retains the traditions of their former national culture, which are passed on by the family and reinforced by its authority for a long time. They quite naturally combine both traditions and create a mixture of concepts drawn from the two distinct cultures. This mixture is created in every individual consciousness, although imitation of others also plays a role. In general, everyone produces his or her own mixture, and all of them are to some degree different, depending on the variable conditions of individual life experiences; for people with similar biographies, the differences are naturally not very great.

Be that as it may, when the younger generation ceases to be the receiver of culture and becomes its transmitter, it will give the next generation not the unadulterated tradition of nation B's culture, but a tradition that mixes the cultures of A and B. The next generation, which receives the culture of nation B in a more or less unadulterated form from school and similar sources, will receive the mixture of A and B from the family and from free contacts with their elders; they will produce a new mixture from these elements and pass on its traditions to the next generation, and so on. The culture of nation A will always remain a mixture of cultures A and B; and at any moment the element of culture A will always be somewhat stronger in the older generation than in the younger, and the family will be closer to A than other institutions. In time some elements of culture A will penetrate the tradition acquired by the younger generation at school as well, so it will also acquire the character of a mixture. Ultimately the entire culture of nation A will become an amalgam of two cultures, while the culture of nation B will remain homogeneous. It follows that complete identity in a cultural sense between nations A and B will not occur.

Since every invention comprises elements of existing cultural assets, the sum total of possible inventions at any given moment depends on the total number of cultural assets available to a given people. And since there can never be complete identity between nations A and B with respect to their stocks of cultural assets, it follows that the total number of possible inventions in both cultures can never be identical. In other words, the culture of nation B (the creator) and the culture of nation A (the borrower) will continue to develop, but in different directions. To this we must add the differences in tastes, predispositions, and temperaments conditioned by differing heredities. Finally, all of this is often complicated by differing geographic conditions (consider the question of costume) and anthropological types.

Thus we must admit that it is impossible for one nation to assimilate the culture of another nation completely.

History provides no refutations of this conclusion. Wherever complete assimilation of a foreign culture is alleged, closer scrutiny reveals that this assimilation is merely apparent, or that it became possible because of an anthropological merger of the nation that created the culture with the nation that borrowed it.

Hellenism and Romanization are often cited as historical examples of the assimilation of the culture of one nation by another. However, these examples are not very convincing. We know that a mixture of ancient Greek culture with indigenous cultures occurred in Hellenized countries. Elements of Greek culture and the Greek language served as the cement that connected these mixed cultures together. We also know that some elements of foreign cultures penetrated Greece, so that the Greeks themselves acquired a mixed culture. There was no "nation B" here that created the culture or "nation A" that borrowed it; there were nations A, B, C, and so on, which borrowed individual elements from one another's cultures after they entered into many-sided spirited cultural relations.

Two aspects of Romanization need to be distinguished. The Romanization of the Italian peninsula cannot be viewed as an example of cultural assimilation, because Roman culture during the republican epoch differed very little from the culture of the other urban communities of Italy. A single culture with minor local variations prevailed throughout the entire peninsula, and Romanization consisted essentially in the victory of Latin over the other dialects of Italy, most of which were closely related to the dialect of Rome in any case. The Romanization of the more distant provinces of the Empire (Gaul, Spain, Britain, etc.) was of a different nature, because each people had its own culture. Here a number of circumstances must be taken into account. Romanization occurred very gradually in these areas. At first the Romans built roads and established military settlements that were used only by the Italian soldiery, and only later by recruits from the local population. In time the institutions of Roman government and Roman law were introduced. In the area of religion, only the cult of the emperor was obligatory; other Roman cults were not deliberately introduced but were brought into the provinces by Roman soldiers, where they coexisted peacefully with native cults. In the area of material culture— clothing, shelter, and tool production—the provincial "barbarians" maintained their cultural uniqueness for a very long time, and they were acculturated only gradually, owing to their active commercial relations with other provinces and with Rome. Consequently, the culture of the Romanized provinces was always mixed. What is more, the Roman culture forced upon these regions in one way or another during the Empire was in fact a motley mixture of elements drawn from the diverse cultures of the Greco-Roman world. The result represented not assimilation by various tribes of the culture created by one people, but eclecticism, a synthesis of several cultures. That local cultures continued to exist and develop among the folk masses became evident at the end of Roman rule, when they reemerged, liberated from the leveling influence of the capital, and gave birth to the cultures of the peoples of the Middle Ages.

These examples show that it is wrong to identify the merger of cultures with the assimilation of a foreign culture. As a general rule, only a mixture of cultures is possible in the absence of an anthropological merger. Conversely, assimilation is possible only with an anthropological merger. This can be seen, for example, in the assimilation of the culture of China by the Manchu, the culture of Egypt by the Hyksos people, the culture of the Slavs by the Varangians and the Turko-Bulgarians, and so on. The assimilation of the culture of the Germans by the Prussians, Polabians, and Lusatians (not yet complete in the last case) are analogous cases.

Hence, the second of the questions posed above, "Is it possible for an entire nation to assimilate *in toto* a culture created by another nation without their anthropological merger?" must also be answered in the negative.

Chapter IV

The third question reads as follows: Is the assimilation of European culture good or bad (insofar as such assimilation is possible)? This question must be formulated more precisely, taking into account the results of the previous queries. We already know that Romano-Germanic culture is objectively neither higher nor more advanced than any other culture and that complete cultural assimilation is possible only in conditions created by an anthropological merger. It would seem to follow that our question is relevant only to nations that have merged with the Romano-Germans. However, in regard to such nations this question proves to be meaningless, for as soon as the anthropological merger is complete, the nation in question is no longer completely non-Romano-Germanic. From its perspective Romano-Germanic culture and the culture of the people who merged with the Romano-Germans are both native cultures, and it must choose between them.

Romano-Germanic culture is in no way better than any other culture, but neither is it essentially worse. So for the nation involved it generally makes no difference whether it adopts this culture or not. Of course, even if it does so, it will still differ from pure Romano-Germans in a heredity that does not fully correspond to its culture, just as a choice in favor of the other culture will produce an analogous result, because Romano-Germanic blood flows in its veins. Therefore the question whether Europeanization is desirable for nations that have merged anthropologically with the Romano-Germans is meaningless. As for nations that have not merged anthropologically with the Romano-Germans, it is clear from the foregoing that they cannot be completely Europeanized (i.e., they cannot assimilate Romano-Germanic culture completely). However, we also know that, despite this impossibility, many nations exert immense efforts in pursuit of such assimilation. It is for them that our question has meaning. We must explore the consequences of such efforts and determine whether these consequences are beneficial and desirable from the perspective of the nation in question.

In demonstrating that a given nation cannot assimilate the culture of another nation completely, I sketched out in general terms the development of culture in a hypothetical nation A that has borrowed the culture of some nation B. We now must substitute the Romano-Germans for nation B and a Europeanized, non-Romano-German nation for A, and describe the results more concretely. The most important of these are produced by the characteristic of the Romano-Germans and their culture which I have defined as egocentricity. The Romano-German views himself and everything like himself as higher, and everything different from himself as lower. In the domain of culture he cherishes only that which does or could constitute an element in his own contemporary culture; everything else is without value in his eyes or is evaluated according to the degree it resembles analogous elements in his culture. Europeanized nations or those striving to be Europeanized are infected with this Romano-Germanic psychological trait, but because they are unaware of its egocentric basis, they do not actually think and behave like Europeans. On the contrary, they evaluate everything, including themselves and their own culture, from the Romano-Germanic viewpoint. This is what characterizes instances of Europeanization viewed as specific examples of nation A borrowing the culture of nation B.

The culture of nation A will always represent a mixture of elements from its old national culture (which we will designate α) and elements borrowed from nation B (which we will designate β), while the culture of nation B will consist exclusively of homogeneous elements (β). It follows that culture A (of a Europeanized, non-Romano-Germanic nation) contains more cultural assets than culture B (of a Romano-Germanic nation). Since the sum total of cultural assets determines the number of possible inventions, this number in a Europeanized nation is greater than in a Romano-Germanic nation. At first glance this would appear to be a profitable state of affairs for a Europeanized nation, but this is not the case. The fact of the matter is that the number of *potential* inventions is never equal to the number of inventions actually realized. Most inventions perish in mutual conflict or in clashes with the older cultural assets they oppose; and the greater the number of potential inventions, the longer and more bitter will be the struggle for recognition (Tarde's *duel logique*). It turns out that the cultural work of a Europeanized nation is carried out in conditions far less favorable than those found in a native Romano-Germanic nation. The former must grope about in various directions, spending its energies on efforts to coordinate elements from two diverse cultures, efforts that for the most part lead to nothing; it must seek out homologous elements in the store of assets from two cultures, while a native Romano-Germanic nation moves along a well-worn path, looking neither to the right nor left and concentrating its efforts on the coordination of elements from a single culture—homogeneous elements bearing the familiar stamp of its own national character.

A specific instance of Europeanization—as opposed to cultural borrowing in general—also involves the logical consequences noted above. Since the culture of a Europeanized nation consists of assets α (purely national) and β (borrowed from the Romano-Germans) and since every invention consists of elements drawn from existing cultural assets, the inventions created by a Europeanized nation will theoretically belong to one of three types: $\alpha + \alpha$, $\alpha + \beta$, or $\beta + \beta$. From the point of view of the Romano-German, inventions of the type $\alpha + \alpha$, which do not contain any elements drawn from Romano-Germanic culture, are utterly valueless. Many inventions of the type $\alpha + \beta$ will certainly strike the Romano-German as distortions of European culture, because they contain, together with β, an element α, which drives a wedge between them and contemporary Romano-Germanic culture. The Romano-German will accept without question only those inventions of the type $\beta + \beta$ that reflect the tastes, predispositions, and temperaments characteristic of Romano-Germanic heredity. Since the heredity of a Europeanized nation is different, it is clear that many works of the type $\alpha + \beta$ will not meet this requirement and will be rejected by the Romano-Germans. Not only is the cultural work of a Europeanized nation, in comparison with a Romano-Germanic nation, extremely difficult and hemmed in by obstacles, but it is a thankless undertaking. From the perspective of the native European, a good half of it is unproductive and purposeless. And since a Europeanized nation borrows its evaluations of culture from the Romano-Germans, it must reject the inventions that cannot gain recognition in Europe. Clearly its work becomes in large measure the labor of Sisyphus.

The consequences that ensue from all of this are not difficult to understand. During any given period of time a Europeanized nation will produce only a very small number of cultural assets acceptable to other nations of European culture, while native Romano-Germans will produce many. Because all of them will be added to the common stock of Romano-Germanic culture, becoming thereby indisputably authoritative, the Europeanized nation will also have to accept them. This nation will always receive more than it can give away; its cultural imports will always exceed its cultural exports, a situation that automatically places it in a dependent position vis-à-vis native Romano-Germanic nations.

One must add that the preponderance of imports over exports and the differences between the psychological inheritance of a Romano-Germanic nation and that of a Europeanized nation confront the latter with great obstacles to the assimilation and dissemination of new inventions. In general, the Romano-Germans absorb only inventions that bear the stamp of all-Romano-Germanic psychology, which is transmitted through heredity and tradition; everything that contradicts this psychology can be branded as "barbarous" and discarded. A Europeanized nation is in a different position; it must be guided not by its own, but by a foreign, Romano-

Germanic psychology, and it must accept without protest everything that genuine Romano-Germans create and consider valuable, even if it conflicts with its national psychology and is poorly understood. This obviously complicates the assimilation and dissemination of imported inventions (and, as we know, the imported inventions are always more numerous than the indigenous in a Europeanized nation). It goes without saying that the constant difficulties encountered during assimilation of these imported inventions must have a harmful impact on the prudent expenditure of a Europeanized people's national energies; even without this they must waste a great deal of effort on the unproductive coordination of two diverse cultures (inventions of the type $\alpha + \beta$) and on development of the remnants of their own national culture (inventions of the type $\alpha + \alpha$).

The disadvantages that confront a Europeanized nation in the course of its cultural work are not exhausted by these impediments. A most grievous consequence of Europeanization is the destruction of national unity, the dismemberment of a people's national body. We have already seen that during the course of borrowing from a foreign culture, each generation works out its own mixture, its own canonized synthesis of the elements of the national and the foreign culture. Thus every generation in a nation that has borrowed a foreign culture has its own particular culture, and the distinctions between "fathers and sons" will always be sharper than in a nation whose culture is homogeneous. What is more, it very rarely happens that an entire nation succumbs to Europeanization at one stroke, all its parts having imbibed precisely the same amount of Romano-Germanic culture. This can happen only when a nation is very small and weakly differentiated.

For the most part, Europeanization occurs from the top down—that is, it first embraces the upper classes (the aristocracy, the urban population, certain professions) and then spreads gradually to the other parts of the nation. This process is rather slow, and many generations succeed one another while

it is underway. I have noted that the efforts of several
generations are required for the assimilation of a foreign
culture. Every generation works out a synthesis for itself, and
the borrowed elements in it predominate over elements from
the old national culture only to the extent that previous
generations have been successful in bringing the two cultures
together. At any given moment, the parts of the nation that first
underwent Europeanization display a cultural silhouette closer
to that of the Romano-Germans than other parts. It follows that
the different parts of a Europeanized nation (classes, estates,
professions) represent various stages in the assimilation of
Romano-Germanic culture (i.e., combinations of the elements
of the native and the foreign culture that vary both in kind and
proportions). These various groups are not parts of a single
national whole but isolated cultural units, separate peoples, as it
were, each with its own culture, traditions, habits, ideas, and
language. Social, material, and professional differences are
much greater in Europeanized nations than in Romano-
Germanic nations precisely because ethnographic and cultural
distinctions have been added to them.

The adverse consequences of this situation are everywhere to
be seen in the life of a Europeanized nation. The dismemberment of the national body tends to intensify class struggle, it
complicates movement from one social class to another, it
further impedes the dissemination of new habits and inventions,
and it hinders cooperation among the various parts of the
nation in cultural work. Such conditions inevitably weaken a
Europeanized people and place them in an extremely
disadvantageous position vis-à-vis native Romano-Germans.
Their social life and cultural development are beset with
difficulties unknown to the Romano-Germans; as a result, they
become unproductive, they create little, and they do it slowly
and with great difficulty. They display the same sluggishness in
the assimilation and dissemination of inventions. Such a nation
can always be considered backward from a European point of
view. Since its culture constitutes a mixture of Romano-

Germanic and indigenous elements and always differs from contemporary Romano-Germanic culture, genuine Europeans will naturally consider this people to be lower than themselves.

A Europeanized nation is forced to look upon itself in the very same way. It has adopted together with European culture the European scale for cultural evaluation, and it cannot help noticing that its cultural productivity is meager, that its cultural exports are developing hardly at all, that new ways of thinking spread very slowly and with difficulty, and that most of its people are scarcely touched by Romano-Germanic culture, which it considers "higher." In comparing itself with native Romano-Germans, a Europeanized nation comes to view them as superior; and this perception together with the now habitual complaints about its own inertia and backwardness gradually lead to a loss of self-respect. This nation also learns to evaluate its own history from the standpoint of the native European; everything that contradicts European culture is perceived as evil and as a sign of backwardness, whereas the decisive turn toward Europe is considered the high point in its past. Everything later borrowed from Europe is viewed as progress, and every deviation from European norms as reaction. Gradually this nation begins to despise everything that is characteristically its own and national. If we also take into account the dismemberment of the national body, the weakening of social links among its parts owing to the absence of a single culture and of a common cultural language, we can understand why patriotism is always very weakly developed in a Europeanized nation. Patriotism and national pride are only occasionally encountered, while national self-assertion boils down for the most part to the ambitions of the rulers and the leading political circles.

Absence of belief in oneself is a very great liability in the struggle for existence. In private life one constantly observes how shy people who are lacking in self-esteem and accustomed to self-abasement often exhibit indecisiveness and insufficient steadfastness of purpose, how they allow others to "walk all over them," and how they finally fall under the sway of people who are more resolute and self-assured (although often much less talented). Likewise, nations that lack patriotism, that have an undeveloped sense of national pride, always yield to nations that are strongly patriotic and self-confident. This is why Europeanized nations are usually in a dependent, subordinate position vis-à-vis the real Romano-Germanic nations.

All of these negative consequences are contingent upon the fact of Europeanization—the degree of Europeanization is not significant here. We know that the elements of the old indigenous culture retreat farther into the background with each generation, so that in time a nation striving for Europeanization should finally become completely Europeanized (i.e., receive from the older generation a culture comprising elements exclusively of Romano-Germanic origin).

This is an extremely slow process, the more so because it affects the various social strata of a Europeanized nation very unevenly. But even when the process comes to an end, a Europeanized people will retain the permanent, inherited predispositions of its national psychology; these non-Romano-Germanic predispositions will interfere with productive creative work and hinder the successful and rapid assimilation of the new cultural assets created by native Romano-Germans. So even after attaining the final degree of Europeanization, this nation—already hampered in its development by the gradual cultural leveling of all its constituent parts (a long and difficult process) and by the eradication of its national culture—still will not be on an equal footing with the Romano-Germans and will continue to "fall behind." The fact that this nation is obliged to participate in cultural contacts and cultural exchange with the Romano-Germans from the very beginning of its Europeanization makes this "backwardness" absolutely inevitable.

But one should not be reconciled to this inevitability. Any nation that does not reject its "backwardness" quickly falls prey to some neighboring or distant Romano-Germanic nation, which then deprives this "backward member of the family of civilized nations" of its economic, and later its political independence; it begins to exploit its prey shamelessly, bleeds it white, and transforms it into "ethnographic material." But the nation that wishes to struggle against the law of eternal backwardness confronts an equally unhappy fate. To guard itself against threats from abroad, a "backward," Europeanized nation must maintain parity with the Romano-Germanic nations, at least in its military and industrial technology. But since, for reasons noted above, a Europeanized nation is unable to innovate as rapidly in this area as native Romano-Germans, it must generally restrict itself to borrowing and imitating foreign inventions. Its backwardness continues to exist even in the area of technology. But in this case, despite certain chronic delays, the technical level is more or less uniform, and the difference from the Romano-Germans consists rather in the lower intensity of industrial activity.

The necessity of overtaking the Romano-Germans is felt less strongly and persistently in other areas. Nevertheless, the distance from the Romano-Germanic level, the "backwardness" in these areas, makes itself felt very acutely. And the worst aspect of these feelings is precisely their sporadic quality: the elimination of the consequences of these sporadic feelings of backwardness is possible only through equally sporadic historical leaps. Europeanized nations, finding it impossible to keep pace with the Romano-Germans and so gradually falling behind, try to catch up from time to time by attempting long leaps. Such leaps disrupt the entire course of historical development. A nation must cover very quickly a distance that the Romano-Germans covered gradually and over a much longer period of time. It must skip several historical rungs and create overnight, *ex abrupto*, what arose in Romano-Germanic nations as the result of a "series of historical changes." The consequences of such "leaping" evolution are genuinely terrible. Every leap is inevitably followed by a period of apparent (from the European standpoint) stagnation, when it is necessary to bring order to the culture, to coordinate the results achieved by a leap in a particular area with the other elements of the culture. During this period of "stagnation," the nation again falls even farther behind. The histories of Europeanized nations are always characterized by brief periods of rapid "progress" alternating with more or less protracted periods of "stagnation." In destroying the wholeness and the unbroken incrementalism of the historical process, such historical leaps also disrupt tradition, which is already fragile in a Europeanized nation.

Let us emphasize: Unbroken tradition is a prerequisite for normal evolution. Leaps and jumps create a temporary illusion that the "common European level of civilization" has been achieved, but they cannot advance a nation in the true sense of the word. Leaping evolution wastes national energies, which are already overburdened owing to the very existence of Europeanization. Just as a person who, in trying to keep pace with a speedier companion, will become exhausted and collapse after resorting to long jumps to catch up, so a Europeanized nation will perish after choosing such an evolutionary path and squandering there its national energies. And all of this will happen while faith in oneself is lost, and without the sustaining sense of national unity which was destroyed long before by the fact of Europeanization.

Thus, the consequences of Europeanization are so deleterious and appalling that it must be considered an evil, not a blessing. I have deliberately left out of my discussion several negative aspects of Europeanization that are recognized regretfully by the Europeans themselves—vices and habits that damage the health, diseases introduced by European "culture bearers," militarism, and the drab and restless life of an industrialized society. These "companions of civilization," which soft-hearted European philanthropists and aesthetes lament, are not peculiar to Romano-Germanic culture. Every culture has vices and destructive customs that are often borrowed by other peoples, but altogether apart from assimilation of the entire culture. Many of these customs were borrowed by the Europeans themselves from tribes they consider lower and "underdeveloped"; the smoking of tobacco, for example, was copied by Europeans from the North American "savages." As far as militarism and capitalism are concerned, the Europeans always promise to correct these failings, choosing to view them as transitory historical episodes. All of these negative aspects of European civilization are debatable, which is why I have not discussed them. I have discussed only phenomena that are immediate consequences of the very nature of Europeanization and that affect the very nature of social life and culture in a Europeanized nation.

In summary, it has been necessary to answer all three questions posed above in the negative.

Chapter V

But if European civilization is in no way higher than any other, if complete assimilation of a foreign culture is impossible, and if efforts to achieve complete Europeanization promise all non-Romano-Germanic nations a miserable and tragic future, then it is obvious that these nations must combat Europeanization with all their strength. It is here that we must confront a terrible question: What if this struggle is impossible and Europeanization of the world is an inescapable, universal law?

There is much to suggest that this may indeed be the case. Whenever Europeans encounter a non-Romano-Germanic nation, they bring to it their goods and their guns. If the nation shows no resistance, the Europeans conquer it, make it a colony, and Europeanize it by force. If the nation considers resisting, then it must acquire guns and the latest European technology. To do this, it is necessary to have factories and plants and to master the European applied sciences. But factories are inconceivable without the European socio-political order, and the applied sciences are unthinkable without the pure sciences. Consequently, in order to resist Europeans, a nation must assimilate contemporary Romano-Germanic civilization in its entirety and succumb to Europeanization voluntarily. To resist or not to resist—in both instances, Europeanization appears unavoidable.

The foregoing can create the impression that Europeanization is an inevitable consequence of European military technology and industrial production. But military technology is a consequence of militarism, and industrial production a consequence of capitalism, neither of which is eternal. Both arose historically, and, according to the predictions of European socialists, they will soon perish, making way for a new socialist order. It turns out that opponents of universal Europeanization must hope for the establishment of a socialist order in the countries of Europe. But this is simply a paradox. Socialists, more than any other Europeans, depend on the International and on militant cosmopolitanism, the true nature of which I exposed at the outset of my argument. This is no accident. Socialism is possible only in the context of universal Europeanization (i.e., the leveling of all national cultures on earth and their subordination to a uniform culture and a common way of life). If a socialist order were to be established in Europe, the first order of business for the European socialist states would be to impose this system everywhere by fire and sword and then to exercise great vigilance to prevent apostasy; otherwise any small corner of the world that remained untouched by socialism would turn into a new breeding ground for capitalism. To protect the socialist order, Europeans would have to maintain their military technology at previous levels while remaining armed to the teeth. And since the militarization of one part of "mankind" is always a threat to the independence of its other parts (which, despite protestations to the contrary, will feel uncomfortable living next to heavily armed people), a state of armed coexistence will gradually become everyone's lot.

Inasmuch as the Romano-Germanic nations have long since grown accustomed to using imported products in their material culture and to satisfy basic needs, international, and especially colonial trade will continue under socialism, and with a nature shaped by the characteristics of a socialist economy. First and foremost, the Romano-Germanic countries will continue as before to export industrial goods. Thus, the two stimuli behind Europeanization—military technology and industrial production—will not disappear under socialism, while new stimuli will be added to them owing to the requirement that a uniform socialist order exist everywhere—an inevitable requirement, since socialist states can trade only with one another.

As for the adverse consequences of Europeanization discussed above, they will remain intact under socialism. These consequences will even be intensified under socialism because the social and political uniformity required of all nations will force Europeanized peoples to devote even greater energies to the imitation of native Europeans. Only one of these adverse consequences, namely, the cultural dismemberment of the national body of each Europeanized nation, will supposedly disappear under socialism because of the absence of classes and estates in a socialist society. However, classes and estates disappear only in theory; in reality the division of labor will lead to stratification according to professions, and this stratification will always be more pronounced among Europeanized peoples than among native Romano-Germans for reasons noted above. What is more, the necessity of maintaining a common level of "civilization" under socialism will force the Romano-Germans to whip up and spur on "backward" nations. And since "national prejudices" will have yielded to triumphant cosmopolitanism by that time, it is obvious that representatives of the native Romano-Germanic nations or of nations that have assimilated Romano-Germanic culture most fully will assume leading roles in all the Europeanized socialist states, specifically as instructors and, to some extent, rulers. Ultimately, the Romano-Germans will preserve the privileged position of aristocrats in "the family of socialist nations," while the "backward nations" will gradually become their slaves.

Thus the nature of the socio-political system in the Romano-Germanic states has no bearing whatever on the inevitability of Europeanization and its negative consequences. Whether the Romano-Germanic states are capitalist or socialist, this inevitability will remain. It does not depend on militarism or on capitalism but on the insatiable greed that characterizes those international predators, the Romano-Germans, and on the egocentricity that saturates their notorious "civilization."

Chapter VI

How is the inevitability of universal Europeanization to be resisted? At first glance it appears that the only possibility is a general uprising against the Romano-Germans. If mankind—not the "mankind" the Romano-Germans like to discuss, but genuine mankind, the majority of which consists of Slavs, Chinese, Indians, Arabs, Negroes, and other peoples, all of whom, regardless of color, are groaning under the heavy Romano-Germanic yoke and squandering their national energies on the production of raw materials for European factories—if this mankind could unite in a common struggle against the oppressors, it would probably succeed sooner or later in overthrowing the hateful yoke and sweeping these predators and their culture from the face of the earth. But how could such an uprising be organized? Is this not an unattainable dream? The more we examine such a plan, the clearer it becomes that it is impossible and that the struggle is hopeless if this is the only method of resisting universal Europeanization.

However, the situation is not so hopeless. As I have stated, one of the principal conditions for the inevitability of Europeanization is the egocentricity that permeates Romano-Germanic culture. One cannot expect that they will correct this fatal flaw themselves, but Europeanized non-Romano-Germanic peoples can purge European culture of egocentricity entirely during the process of assimilation. If they succeed in this attempt, the borrowing of individual elements of Romano-Germanic culture will no longer have the detrimental effects discussed above and will actually enrich their national culture. If, in their encounter with European culture, these peoples remain free of the prejudices that make them see all its elements as absolutely perfect, they will have no reason to borrow this culture in its entirety or to attempt to destroy their own culture for its sake, or to regard themselves as backward, retarded members of the human race. Looking upon Romano-Germanic culture as merely one among many, they can borrow only those elements that suit them and make sense; subsequently they can modify these elements in accordance with their national tastes and needs, and ignore entirely the Romano-Germans' way of evaluating these modifications from their egocentric perspective.

There can be no doubt that such a situation is possible. No examples from the past contradict it. True, history teaches us that no Europeanized nation has been able to maintain this sober attitude toward Romano-Germanic culture. Many nations originally planned to borrow only the most essential things from it, but over time they gradually succumbed to the hypnotism of Romano-Germanic egocentricity and forgot their original intentions; they began to borrow indiscriminately, perceiving their ideal in the complete assimilation of European civilization. Initially Peter the Great wanted to learn military and naval technology from the "Germans," but he got carried away by the process of borrowing and adopted many things that had no direct bearing on his fundamental goal. Nevertheless, he always realized that sooner or later Russia would acquire everything she needed from Europe and that she should then turn her back and develop her culture freely without trying to emulate the West. But he died and left no successors prepared to continue his policy.

The entirety of Russia's eighteenth century was devoted to the trivial, demeaning aping of Europe. By the end of the century the minds of the upper strata of Russian society were already saturated with Romano-Germanic prejudices and biases; the nineteenth and the beginning of the twentieth centuries were devoted to efforts to Europeanize all aspects of Russian life, and Russia took on the characteristics of the "leaping evolution" discussed earlier. The same process is about to happen before our very eyes in Japan, which first wanted to borrow only military and naval technology from the Romano-Germans but gradually went much farther in its imitative efforts, so that now a significant part of "educated" society there has assimilated Romano-Germanic ways of thinking. To date Europeanization in Japan has been tempered by a healthy sense of national pride and respect for national traditions, but no one knows how long the Japanese will remain this way.

Even if my solution to the problem of Europeanization has no historical precedents, it does not follow that a solution is itself impossible. The entire matter boils down to the fact that the true nature of European cosmopolitanism and of other European theories rooted in egocentric prejudice has not been understood. The intelligentsia of Europeanized nations (i.e., those people who are most open to the spiritual culture of the Romano-Germans) trustingly followed Romano-Germanic ideologists, never feeling the jagged reefs beneath their feet, because they have been unaware of the triviality of the psychology of egocentricity and thus unable to combat this aspect of the European influence. Everything will change dramatically as soon as the intelligentsia comes to grips with the truth and approaches European civilization objectively and critically.

The center of gravity must be shifted to the *psychology* of the intelligentsia in Europeanized nations, because this psychology requires a radical transformation. This intelligentsia must tear away the blindfold placed upon its eyes by the Romano-Germans and free itself from the specter of Romano-Germanic ideology. It must understand clearly, once and for all:

—that is has always been deceived;

—that European culture is not an absolute, it is not a universal human culture, but merely the creation of one limited, distinct ethnic or ethnographic group of nations sharing a common history;

—that European culture is obligatory only for the group of nations that created it;

—that it is not more perfect or "higher" than a culture created by some other ethnographic group, for there are no "higher" or "lower" cultures, only cultures and peoples that resemble one another to a greater or lesser degree;

—that the assimilation of Romano-Germanic culture by a people that has not participated in its creation is therefore not an unconditional blessing or a moral imperative;

—that complete, organic assimilation of Romano-Germanic culture (or of any foreign culture), that is, an assimilation which allows the borrower to create in the spirit of, and in lockstep with, those who actually created it, is possible only after an anthropological merger with the Romano-Germans, or better, after an anthropological ingestion of that nation by the Romano-Germans;

—that without such an anthropological merger only a surrogate of complete assimilation is possible, when only the "static" but not the "dynamic" part of the culture is assimilated (i.e., a nation that has assimilated the contemporary state of European culture turns out to be incapable of developing it further; and each new change in the elements of this culture must again be borrowed from the Romano-Germans);

—that under such circumstances this nation must give up independent cultural creation completely, live in the reflected light of Europe, and turn into an ape that imitates the Romano-Germans tirelessly;

—that, consequently, such a nation will always "lag behind" the Romano-Germans (i.e., assimilate and reproduce various stages in the cultural development of Europe, but always after a certain delay—and in relation to native Europeans, from a disadvantageous, subordinate position, from a state of material and spiritual dependence on them;

that Europeanization is an *unquestionable evil* for every non-Romano-Germanic nation;

that this evil can and must be fought as forcefully as possible.

All of this must be understood not superficially but viscerally; it must be felt, experienced, endured. The truth must stand in all its nakedness, without adornments or traces of the enormous deception in which it is still enveloped. Compromises must be ruled out: If it's to be war, then let it be war.

All of this presupposes a revolution in the psychology of the intelligentsia of non-Romano-Germanic nations. The essence of this revolution will be an understanding of the relativity of what has long seemed absolute: the benefits of European "civilization." The rejection of this old view must be unhesitating and complete. To carry out such a program is extremely difficult, *but there is no other way.*

A revolution in the consciousness of the intelligentsia of non-Romano-Germanic peoples will bring the activity of universal Europeanization to an inevitable end. After all, to the present day this very intelligentsia has been the champion of Europeanization; in its belief in cosmopolitanism and the "benefits of civilization," and in its regrets about the "stagnation" and "backwardness" of its own nation, it has labored to acquaint its compatriots with European culture, at the same time forcefully destroying the age-old foundations of its own unique traditions. In fact, the intelligentsia of the Europeanized countries has gone even farther in this direction by pushing not only its own people toward European culture but also neighboring countries. Consequently, the members of the intelligentsia have served as the Romano-Germans' principal agents. If they now realize that Europeanization is an unmitigated evil, and cosmopolitanism a brazen lie, they will no longer assist the Romano-Germans, and the triumphant march of "civilization" will cease. Without the support of Europeanized peoples, the Romano-Germans will not be able to continue the spiritual enslavement of the whole world. Quite simply, upon realizing its mistake, the intelligentsia of Europeanized nations will not only stop helping the Romano-Germans, but it will try to thwart them, at the same time opening the eyes of other peoples to the true nature of the "benefits of civilization."

In this great and difficult work to liberate the world from spiritual slavery and from the hypnosis of the "benefits of civilization," the intelligentsia of all the non-Romano-Germanic nations that have set out on the path to Europeanization or are planning to do so must act together in a spirit of full

cooperation and agreement. They must never lose sight of the
true problem and not be distracted by nationalism or by partial,
local solutions such as Pan-Slavism and other "pan-isms." One
must always remember that setting up an opposition between
the Slavs and the Teutons or the Turanians and the Aryans will
not solve the problem. There is only one true opposition: the
Romano-Germans and all the other peoples of the world—
Europe and Mankind.

2 On True and
False Nationalism*

An individual can maintain any of a variety of possible attitudes toward his national culture. The attitude of the Romano-Germans is shaped by a specific psychology which can be called egocentric. "A person with a clearly defined egocentric psychology subconsciously considers himself to be the center of the universe, the crown of creation, the best, the most perfect of all beings. Confronted by two other human beings, the one closer to him, more like him, is the better, while the one less like him is worse. Consequently, this person considers every natural group of human beings to which he belongs the most perfect: his family, estate, nation, tribe, and race are better than all other analogous groups."[1]

This psychology is characteristic of the Romano-Germans, and it shapes their evaluations of all other cultures. Consequently only two general attitudes toward culture are possible for them: either the culture to which the evaluator (a German, a Frenchman, etc.) belongs is the highest and most advanced in the world, or this distinction is attributed not to one national cultural variant but to the sum total of the closely related cultures created by the collective efforts of all the Romano-Germanic peoples. The first type is known in Europe as narrow chauvinism (German chauvinism, French chauvinism, etc.), while the latter is best described as "Pan-Romano-Germanic chauvinism." However, "the Romano-Germans have always been

*Originally as "Ob istinnom i lozhnom natsionalizme," *Iskhod k Vostoku,* Sofia 1921, pp. 71-85. Translated by Kenneth Brostrom.
[1]See my *Europe and Mankind* [p.7 in this volume].

so naively convinced that they alone are human beings that they have called themselves 'humanity,' their culture 'universal human culture,' and their chauvinism 'cosmopolitanism.'[2]

Non-Romano-Germanic nations that have assimilated European culture usually assimilate with it the Romano-Germanic assessment of that culture; they are taken in by fraudulent terms such as "universal human civilization" and "cosmopolitanism," which conceal the narrow ethnographic content of these ideas. As a result, these nations do not base their assessment of cultures on egocentricity but on a kind of "excentricity," or more precisely, on "Eurocentricity." We have spoken elsewhere about the inevitable, disastrous consequences of Eurocentricity for Europeanized, non-Romano-Germanic nations.[3] The intelligentsias of such nations can escape these consequences only by accomplishing a fundamental reversal in their thinking and in their methods of appraising cultures, this after they have realized clearly that European civilization is not a "universal human culture" but merely the culture of a particular ethnographic group, the Romano-Germans; for them alone is this culture mandatory. Such a reversal should fundamentally alter the attitudes of Europeanized, non-Romano-Germanic peoples toward all the problems of culture, and their anachronistic, Eurocentric judgments will be replaced by others based upon a completely different set of premises.

The first duty of every non-Romano-Germanic nation is to overcome every trace of egocentricity in itself; the second is to protect itself against the deception of "universal human civilization" and against all efforts to become "genuinely European" at any cost. These duties can be expressed by two aphorisms: "Know thyself" and "Be thyself."

The struggle against one's own egocentricity is possible only when there is true self-awareness. True self-awareness will show a person or his place in the world; it will teach him that he is not the center of the universe or of the earth. But this same self-

---

[2]Ibid. [p. 4-7 in the present edition].
[3]See Chap. 5 of *Europe and Mankind*.

awareness will also lead him to an understanding of the nature of people (and of nations) in general—that not only a subject who seeks self-awareness but all those who resemble him are neither the center nor the apotheosis of anything at all. From an understanding of their own natures, individuals (and nations) come, through growing self-awareness, to a full awareness of the equal value of all persons and nations. A logical consequence of these new understandings is an affirmation of one's own uniqueness, the determination to be oneself: and not merely the determination, but the ability, for the man who does not know himself cannot be himself.

An individual can remain unique, never falling into internal contradictions and never deceiving himself and others only after he has come to understand his own nature clearly and completely. And it is in the achievement of this harmonious personal wholeness, based upon a clear and full understanding of one's own nature, that the greatest earthly happiness is attained. Here, too, is to be found the essence of moral behavior, for when true self-awareness is achieved, the voice of conscience is heard most clearly; a person who lives so as to remain honest with himself and avoid internal contradictions will certainly be moral, and he will discover the greatest spiritual beauty accessible to any human being. For self-deception and inner contradictions, which are inevitable without genuine self-awareness, always make a man spiritually ugly. Moreover, the highest wisdom, both practical and theoretical, is to be found in self-awareness, for all other knowledge is vain and illusory. Finally, it is only after people (and nations) have attained a uniqueness based on self-awareness that they can be certain they are realizing their purpose on earth, that they are becoming what they were created to be. Self-awareness is the single, highest goal in this life for any human being. It is a goal—but it is also a means.

This idea is not new; on the contrary, it is very old. Socrates expressed it twenty-three centuries ago, but did not invent his γνῶθι σαυτόν: he read it in an inscription on the temple at

Delphi. However, he was the first to formulate this idea clearly, the first to understand that self-awareness is both an ethical and a logical problem, that it is just as much a matter of right living as it is of right thinking. This vitally important dictum, "Know thyself," identifies a problem that is superficially the same but essentially different for every person, owing to its merger of the relative and subjective with the absolute and universal; it is a principle that is equally applicable to everyone, without regard to nationality or historical period, because it is unlimited by time and circumstance. This principle remains valid today for nations as well as individuals. It would be easy to demonstrate that not one of the world's religions rejects or ignores Socrates' dictum; several have affirmed it and elaborated upon it. One could also show that the majority of a-religious ideas are quite compatible with this principle.[4] However, further discussion of these matters would lead us too far afield.

The results of self-awareness can be diverse because they depend not only on the self-knowing individual but on the

[4]The dictum "Know thyself" is based upon a certain philosophical optimism, upon the belief that human nature (and all creation) is essentially good, reasonable, and beautiful, and that everything bad in life (evil, ugliness, senselessness, suffering) is a result of a deviation from nature, the fruit of man's inadequate understanding of his true essence. Consequently, Socrates' dictum is completely unacceptable only to proponents of extreme philosophical pessimism. For example, a consistent Buddhist who views everything that exists as evil, senseless, ugly, and inseparable from suffering must reject Socrates' principle. The only way out for such a Buddhist is suicide, not physical suicide (pointless, owing to the doctrine of the transmigration of souls) but spiritual—the destruction of his spiritual individuality, that is, in Buddhist terminology, "nirvana" or "the total conquest of birth and death." However, most Buddhists are not so consistent and limit themselves to a theoretical acceptance of certain fundamental principles enunciated by Buddha. In practice they are adherents of a morally indifferent polytheism, and as such, they can accept Socrates' dictum up to a certain point.

extent and the form of the knowledge itself. The labors of a Christian ascetic, which are directed toward overcoming temptation and becoming what God created man to be, are essentially a kind of self-awareness achieved through Heavenly guidance and constant prayer. It brings the ascetic not only to a high degree of moral perfection but to mystical insights into the meaning of creation and existence. The self-awareness of Socrates, which was devoid of specific metaphysical content, led to psychological harmony, wise conduct, and even to certain insights into worldly affairs—all of this coupled with complete metaphysical ignorance. In some individuals self-awareness happens under the predominant influence of logical reflection, while in others, irrational intuition plays a decisive role. The forms of self-awareness are variable in the extreme. The important thing is that a clear, more or less complete vision of oneself is achieved, an unambiguous understanding of one's own nature and of the proportional weights of all its elements and manifestations in their mutual interrelations.

All of this applies not only to individual but to collective self-awareness. If one views a people simply as a psychological entity, a collective individuality, one must admit that some form of self-awareness is both possible and necessary to it. Self-awareness has a logical connection with the concept of individuality: Where there is individuality, there can and should be self-awareness. And if, in the life of the individual, self-awareness is the all-encompassing goal that incorporates all the happiness accessible to him, all the goodness, spiritual beauty, and wisdom attainable by him, then it is the same universal principle for the collective individuality of a nation as well. The special feature of this collective individuality is that a nation lives for centuries and changes constantly during that time, so the fruits of national self-awareness in one epoch will not be valid in the next. However, they will always establish a point of departure for every new effort to achieve self-awareness.

"Know thyself" and "Be thyself" are two aspects of the same affirmation. True self-awareness is expressed externally in the unique, harmonious life and activity of the individual. The analogue for a nation is its unique national culture. A nation has come to know itself if its spiritual nature and individual character find their fullest, most brilliant expression in its national culture, and if this culture is thoroughly harmonious (that is, its components do not contradict one another). The creation of such a culture is the true goal of every nation, just as the goal of each of its members is to achieve a life style that embodies his or her unique spiritual essence fully, brilliantly, and harmoniously. These two tasks—the national and the individual—are intimately related; they complement and condition one another.

In pursuing self-awareness, every individual comes to know himself as a member of a nation. The emotional life of the individual always contains elements of the national psyche, just as his spiritual makeup necessarily contains traits of the national character that combine in various ways, both with one another and with other traits whose origins are located in himself as an individual and in his family and social class. Self-awareness allows these national traits, in their merger with an individual nature, to be affirmed and enhanced. When an individual begins to "be himself" through self-awareness, he inevitably moves toward becoming an outstanding representative of his people. His life, being a full and harmonious expression of his consciously understood, unique individuality, inevitably embodies national traits. If this individual is engaged in work that is culturally creative, his efforts will bear the stamp of his personality and will thus reflect the national character; in any case, they will not contradict this character. But even if an individual does not participate actively in culturally creative undertakings and merely assimilates their products passively or participates as a menial in some area of his nation's cultural life, even in this case the fact that his life and activities embody certain traits of the national character (primarily tastes and predispositions) will serve to heighten and intensify the national qualities of his people's everyday life. It is everyday life that inspires the creator of cultural assets, that supplies him with both tasks and material for his creations. Thus it is that individual self-awareness facilitates the uniqueness of a national culture, a uniqueness which is the correlate of national self-awareness.

Conversely, a unique national culture is helpful in the acquisition of individual self-awareness. It facilitates complete understanding of those traits in an individual's psychology which are manifestations of the common national character. All such traits are prominent, vivid elements in a genuine national culture, and this enables each individual to find them easily in himself, to come to know them (through culture) in their true lineaments, and to evaluate them properly in the perspective of common daily life. A harmonious and unique national culture enables every member of the national whole to be himself, and to remain so, while being at the same time in constant contact with his compatriots. In such circumstances an individual can participate in the cultural life of his nation with complete sincerity and without pretending to others or to himself that he is something he has never been and never will be.

It is now apparent that a strong inner connection and constant interaction exist between individual and national self-awareness. The greater the number of people in a nation who "know themselves" and are "being themselves," the more successful efforts will be to achieve national self-awareness and to create a unique national culture, which will guarantee in turn that profound individual self-awareness can be achieved. The felicitous evolution of national culture is possible only when this interaction between individual and national self-awareness exists. Otherwise the national culture may cease to develop at a certain point, while the national character, which is composed of the characters of individuals, will still change. If this happens, the concept of a unique national culture will lose its meaning. The culture will no longer evoke a lively response in its bearers; it will cease to be the embodiment of the national spirit, and will become a kind of traditional hypocrisy that encumbers rather than expediting individual self-awareness and uniqueness.

If the highest earthly ideal for a human being is perfect self-awareness, then it follows that the only authentic culture is one that facilitates such self-awareness. In order to do this, a culture must embody those elements common to the psychology of all or most of the individual members of the culture (that is, it is an aggregate of the elements of the national psychology). Moreover, the culture must manifest these elements vividly and prominently, because the more vivid they are, the easier it is for each person to attain *through the culture* a full knowledge of them in himself. In other words, the only authentic culture is a completely unique national culture, because it alone can fulfill the ethical, aesthetic, and even utilitarian requirements incumbent upon every culture. If a person can be acknowledged as truly wise, virtuous, beautiful and happy only after he has "come to know himself" and "be himself," then the same applies to an entire nation. But here it means "to possess a unique national culture." If one requires that a culture provide "maximum happiness for the greatest number of people," this changes nothing. True happiness is to be found not in comfort and not in the satisfaction of personal needs, but in an equilibrium, a harmony among all the elements of spiritual life (including those "needs"). No culture can give individual human beings this happiness: happiness lies within, and self-awareness is the only path to it. A culture can help an individual become happy because it facilitates self-awareness. But it can do this only if it is completely, manifestly unique.

Thus the cultures of all nations should be different. Each nation should manifest all its originality in its culture, and in such a way that its elements, which are imbued with the same national coloration, are in harmonious relation. The greater the differences between the national psychologies of particular nations, the greater will be the differences between their national cultures. Nations similar to one another in their characters will have similar cultures. But a universal human culture, identical for all nations, is impossible. Given the great diversity among national characters and psychological types, such a "universal culture" would lead either to satisfaction of purely material needs at the expense of the needs of the spirit or to the imposition on all nations of forms of life reflecting the national character of a single ethnographic type. In either case, this "universal" culture would not meet the requirements incumbent upon every genuine culture: it would bring true happiness to no one.

Therefore, efforts to achieve a universal human culture must be repudiated, and conversely, the efforts of any nation to create its own distinctive culture are fully justified, while cultural cosmopolitanism and internationalism merit unequivocal condemnation. However, not every type of nationalism is logically or morally justified. There are various kinds of nationalism, some false and some true, and the only indispensable, objective guide for a nation's conduct is a true nationalism. The only kind of nationalism which can be acknowledged as true, as morally and logically justified, is a nationalism that has its origins in a unique national culture or is directed toward such a culture. The actions of a true nationalist must be guided by the idea of this culture. He will defend it and struggle for it. He must support everything that facilitates a unique national culture and reject everything that interferes with it.

However, if we apply this measure to the existing forms of nationalism, we will soon be convinced that the majority of them are false. Most frequently encountered are nationalists who do not consider the uniqueness of their nation's culture to be important. All their efforts are directed toward achieving national independence regardless of the cost; they want their nation to be recognized by the "great" powers as a full and equal member in the "family of nation-states," and to be like these "great" nations in all things. This type of nationalist is found especially often in "small," non-Romano-Germanic nations, where he appears in particularly outlandish, almost grotesque forms. Self-awareness plays no role whatever in such nationalism, because its proponents have absolutely no desire to "be themselves"; to the contrary, they want to be like others, like the "big" people, like the "masters"—even when they are often neither big nor masterful themselves.

When historical conditions cause a nation to become subject to the power or economic supremacy of another nation altogether alien to it in spirit and it cannot create a unique national culture without liberating itself from this domination, efforts to achieve national independence are fully justified on moral and logical grounds. However, these efforts are appropriate only when they are undertaken in the name of a unique national culture; national independence as an end in itself is senseless. And nationalists of the type under discussion regard national independence and great-power status as ends in themselves. What is more, they are willing to sacrifice their own national culture to these ends. To make their people exactly like "real Europeans," they strive to impose not only alien Romano-Germanic forms of government, law, and economic life on their people but their ideas, art, and the bric-a-brac of European daily life as well. Europeanization—that is, the effort to reproduce general Romano-Germanic patterns in every area of life—results ultimately in complete loss of every trace of national uniqueness; soon the infamous "native language" is the only unique thing remaining in a nation led by such nationalists. And after this language has become "official" and begins to adapt to foreign concepts and patterns in everyday life, it will become distorted by the incorporation of an enormous number of clumsy neologisms and Romano-Germanic words and phrases. Frequently, the official language becomes incomprehensible to ordinary people in "small" states that have opted for this brand of nationalism, especially those who have not yet succeeded in becoming denationalized and depersonalized to the level of "democracy in general."

It is obvious that a nationalism which strives not for national uniqueness and national self-realization but for a close resemblance to the "Great Powers" can never be considered true. It is based not on self-awareness but on petty conceit, which is the opposite of self-awareness. The term "national self-determination," which proponents of this type of nationalism like to use, especially when they belong to one of the "small nations," can lead only to confusion. Actually there is nothing "national" and no "self-determination" whatever in this set of attitudes, and this is why national liberation movements often incorporate socialism, which always contains elements of cosmopolitanism and internationalism.

Another form of false nationalism is present in militant chauvinism, which is essentially an effort to disseminate the language and culture of one's own nation among the greatest possible number of foreigners after first destroying in them the last traces of their own national uniqueness. The falsity of such nationalism is obvious without detailed argument. The uniqueness of a particular national culture acquires value only from the degree to which it harmonizes with the psychology of its creators and bearers. When this culture is transplanted to a nation with a different psychology, all the meaning of its uniqueness disappears and the value of the culture itself changes. The fundamental error of militant chauvinism lies in its lack of attention to the relationship between every culture and its individual ethnic representatives. Such chauvinism is rooted in arrogance and denial of the equal worth of all peoples and cultures—in a word, in egocentric self-exaltation—and it is inconceivable in conjunction with genuine national self-awareness. Thus it also stands in opposition to true nationalism.

A special form of false nationalism is to be found in the cultural conservatism that artificially identifies national uniqueness with certain cultural assets or patterns of living created in the past and rejects the possibility of change in them, even when they no longer embody the national psyche in a satisfactory way. Here, as with militant chauvinism, the living bond between culture and the psyche of its bearers is ignored, and absolute value is attached to culture independent of its relation to the people: "The culture is not for the people, but the people for the culture." Once again this destroys the moral and logical meaning of uniqueness as the correlate of the continuous process of attaining national self-awareness.

It is apparent that the aforementioned types of false nationalism have practical consequences that are catastrophic for the national culture. The first leads to a loss of national identity, to the denationalization of the culture; the second to a loss of racial purity by the bearers of the culture; the third to stagnation, the precursor of death.

Obviously, the different forms of false nationalism can combine to produce mixed types. But they all share one common feature: their foundations cannot rest upon national self-awareness in our sense of the word. However, even those variants of nationalism which seem to derive from national self-awareness and strive for a national culture are not always true. The problem is that self-awareness is often understood too narrowly and achieved incorrectly. True self-awareness is frequently obstructed by some label which, for whatever reason, a nation has attached to itself and will not relinquish. For example, the cultural orientation of the Romanians is strongly conditioned by the fact that they consider themselves a nation with a Romance language and culture, this because a small detachment of Roman soldiers constituted long ago one of the elements from which Romanian nationality developed. Similarly, contemporary Greek nationalism (a mixed type of false nationalism) redoubles its own falsity through the one-sided view Greeks have of their own origins: although they are in fact a mixture of several ethnic groups that share a lengthy cultural evolution with other "Balkan" peoples, they consider themselves descendants of the ancient Greeks alone. Such aberrations result from the fact that self-awareness has not been achieved organically, it is not the source of this particular nationalism but merely an attempt to provide it with a historical justification for its jingoistic, chauvinistic tendencies.

The process of examining the various types of false nationalism underscores by contrast what true nationalism should be. As a product of national self-awareness, it affirms the necessity of a unique national culture; it establishes this culture as its supreme task, and it appraises every aspect of domestic and foreign policy and every stage of the nation's history from the perspective of this task. Self-awareness gives true nationalism the kind of self-sufficiency that prevents it from imposing its culture on other peoples by force and from imitating slavishly others which are alien in spirit and enjoy, for whatever reason, special prestige within a particular anthropo-geographic area. The true nationalist displays no nationalistic arrogance or ambition in his attitudes toward other peoples. Because his world view rests upon self-awareness, he will be by nature peace-loving and tolerant of all foreign expressions of uniqueness. He will also be opposed to the artificiality of national isolation. Because he fully understands the unique psyche of his own people, he will be especially sensitive to characteristics in other peoples that are similar to those in himself. And if another people has succeeded in giving one of these characteristics felicitous expression in some cultural asset, the true nationalist will not hesitate to imitate this work after adapting it to harmonize with his own unique culture's inventory of cultural assets. Two peoples of similar national character who are in contact with one another and under the leadership of true nationalists will always have very similar cultures, owing to the free exchange of cultural assets that are acceptable to both sides. This cultural unity is fundamentally different from the artificial unity resulting from one's nation's efforts to subjugate a neighbor.

If we examine in light of these considerations the kinds of Russian nationalism existing in the past, we will be forced to admit that true nationalism is nowhere to be found in post-Petrine Russia. The majority of educated Russians have not wanted to "be themselves"; they have dreamed of becoming "real Europeans." And because Russia could not become a genuine European state, despite all her longing, many of us came to despise our "backward motherland." Consequently, until very recently most Russian intellectuals have shunned any kind of nationalism. Others have called themselves nationalists, but they have understood nationalism as the drive to become a great power, to acquire military and economic might, to achieve a brilliant international position for Russia. To achieve these goals, they considered it necessary for Russian culture to approximate as closely as possible the Western European model. The demands of certain Russian "nationalists" for "Russification" have reflected the same slavish attitude toward the West. This has meant the encouragement of a shift to Orthodoxy, the compulsory introduction of the Russian language, and the replacement of foreign with more or less awkward Russian place names. And these things were done only because "this is the way the Germans act—and the Germans are a cultured people."

At times this urge to be a nationalist because the Germans are nationalists found more elaborate expressions. Since the Germans base their nationalistic lordliness upon their contributions to the creation of culture, our nationalists have also tried to identify some sort of unique, twentieth-century Russian culture, exaggerating to near cosmic proportions the significance of any work by a Russian or even by some non-Russian subject if it deviated ever so slightly from the Western European pattern, declaring it to be "a valuable contribution by Russian genius to the treasure house of world civilization." An even better parallel: As a counterpart of Pan-Germanism, Pan-Slavism was created, and the mission of unifying all the Slavic nations that were "treading the path of world progress" (that is, were exchanging their uniqueness for the Romano-Germanic model) was accepted by Russia as her own, so that Slavdom might assume its "proper" or even the leading place in the "family of civilized nations." During the period immediately preceding the Russian Revolution, this tendency in westernizing

Slavophilism became fashionable even in circles that had formerly considered the word "nationalism" indecent.

However, Slavophilism in the more distant past can hardly be considered a pure form of true nationalism. It is quite easy to spot in it the three forms of false nationalism discussed above, with the third type dominant initially, and later the first and second. There has always been a tendency to construct Russian nationalism according to the Romano-Germanic model. Thanks to these qualities, Slavophilism was bound to degenerate, despite the fact that a feeling for uniqueness together with the principle of national self-awareness were its points of departure. These matters were not understood clearly or formulated adequately.

Only isolated individuals have been concerned with true nationalism, which is based entirely upon self-awareness and demands in its name a restructuring of Russian culture guided by the spirit of uniqueness. True nationalism has never existed as a socio-historical tendency. It must be created in the future. And this will require that reversal in the consciousness of the Russian intelligentsia which we discussed at the outset of this article.

3 The Upper and Lower Stories of Russian Culture*
(The Ethnic Basis of Russian Culture)

Every differentiated culture inevitably contains two components that can be figuratively termed the "upper" and "lower stories" of the edifice of that culture. By "lower story" we mean the stock of cultural assets that meets the needs of the so-called folk masses. When such assets originate in the midst of the common people themselves, they are rather elementary and lack the imprint of individual creativity. And when cultural assets migrate from the upper to the lower story, they necessarily become somewhat depersonalized and simplified as they are adapted to a context created by assets exclusively of "lower" origin.

The upper story of the cultural edifice is different in nature. The cultural assets of a nation's broad masses cannot meet the needs of all its members; many who are dissatisfied with the form of some generally accepted asset will attempt to improve it by adapting to their personal tastes. Altered in this way, an asset may become inaccessible to the masses but appeal to the tastes of those who in one way or another occupy positions of authority in the society. In this case the asset will enter the stock of assets belonging to the upper story of the culture. It follows that the assets found in this "upper stock" are created either by or for the society's ruling elite; they are responses to more refined needs and more demanding tastes. Consequently, such

*Originally as "Verkhi i nizy russkoi kul'tury. Etnicheskaia osnova russkoi kul'tury." *Iskhod k Vostoku,* Sofia 1921, pp. 86-103. Translated by Kenneth Brostrom.

assets are always more complex than those of the lower stock. Since any asset from the lower stock may inspire the creation of an asset in the upper stock, and since the masses constantly introduce into their everyday life assets borrowed in simplified form from the upper stock, there is normally a process of exchange and interaction between the upper and lower stories of any culture. This interchange is increased by the fact that a nation's ruling elite is not a constant, unchanging quantity. It "rules" only as long as it maintains its prestige—that is, the ability to inspire imitation both literally and in the sense of "sympathetic imitation" (respect and obedience). However, over time this prestige may be lost and acquired by some other social group that previously belonged on the lower stories of the culture; this new aristocracy will bring many assets from the lower stock into the upper story of the cultural edifice.

In addition to this endogenous interaction between a culture's upper and lower stories, both levels are also nourished exogenously by borrowings from foreign cultures. The foreign source from which the upper story is drawing cultural assets may differ from the foreign source that is nourishing the lower story. If the borrowed assets are not incompatible with the general psychological makeup of the nation and are organically reworked during the process of assimilation, then a certain equilibrium will be reestablished between the upper and lower stories owing to the natural process of internal exchange between them. However, this equilibrium may not be established, and a cultural rift will form between the upper and lower stories and national unity will be destroyed. This always indicates that the source of the foreign influence was incompatible with the national psychology.

In considering Russian culture specifically, we must first develop a precise description of the ethnographic character of its upper and lower stories and understand clearly the links between its constituent parts and foreign cultures. The Slavic element was unquestionably of fundamental importance in the formation of Russian nationality. We can arrive at some notion of the characteristics of our earliest Slavic ancestors only through linguistic data. As we know, "Proto-Slavic," the ancestor of all the Slavic languages, descended from the Proto-Indo-European language, which has been reconstructed by comparative study of all its descendants. The hypothesis of a completely homogeneous Indo-European was abandoned long ago; linguists agree that dialects were already present in the protolanguage and that over time the differences between them became more pronounced, leading eventually to the disintegration of the protolanguage and the transformation of its dialects into separate languages.

To say that Proto-Slavic is a descendant of Indo-European is tantamount to saying that in the latter there existed a Proto-Slavic dialect which was eventually transformed into a separate *language*. The reconstructible features that differentiate this Proto-Slavic dialect from or connect it with other Indo-European dialects constitute the earliest information we have about the ancestors of the Slavs. It appears that the Proto-Slavic dialect and those closest to it, the Baltic dialects, were more or less centrally located.[1] Adjoining it on the south were the Proto-Illyrian and Proto-Thracian dialects, about which we know very little. To the east of the Proto-Slavic dialect was a uniform group of Proto-Indo-Iranian dialects that were alike in many details of pronunciation, grammar, and lexicon. Lastly, to the west was the group of West Indo-European dialects (Proto-Germanic, Proto-Italic,[2] and Proto-Celtic) which were much less homogeneous than the Indo-Iranian dialects, but which were still united by many common features in pronunciation, grammar, and lexicon.

[1]Included in the Baltic group are the closely related Lithuanian, Latvian and Old Prussian languages, the last of which died out in the seventeenth century.

[2]The Italic languages include Latin and several other related languages of the Apennine Peninsula, the principal ones being Umbrian and Oscan.

Owing to its central position, Proto-Slavic resembled the Proto-Indo-Iranian dialects in certain features and the West Indo-European dialects in others, and sometimes functioned as an intermediary between them. With respect to pronunciation, the Proto-Slavic dialect shared several common consonant changes with the Proto-Indo-Iranian dialects and perhaps only a few similarities in the pronunciation of certain vowels with the West Indo-European dialects. And because consonants are more striking to the ear than vowels, one must suppose that Indo-European as pronounced by speakers of the Proto-Slavic dialect must have sounded more like the eastern (Proto-Indo-Iranian) dialects than the western. With regard to grammar, no particular affinities between Proto-Slavic and Proto-Indo-Iranian have been observed. But even the links between the Proto-Slavic dialect and the West European group had more to do with the common loss of some old grammatical categories and the merger of once distinct forms than with the creation of new forms. Generally speaking, the Proto-Slavic dialect and the closely related Proto-Baltic dialects represent a completely distinct, unique grammatical type.

The study of lexicons is of enormous importance in determining the relationships between contiguous dialects and languages. Unfortunately, when we are dealing with the earliest periods we have no objective method for distinguishing borrowed words from cognates. Nevertheless, in some instances borrowing seems less likely than relationship. In examining a series of words and roots common to the Slavs and the Indo-Iranians but unknown in other Indo-European languages (except, in part, the Baltic), we find prepositions such as the Slavic *kъ* 'to,' *radi* 'for the sake of,' *bezъ* 'without,' *sъ* 'with' (both as a preposition and verbal prefix), the pronouns *ovъ* 'that,' *onъ* 'he,' *vьsь* 'all, whole,' the conjunction *a* 'and, but,' the special negative particle *ni* (cf. especially *ničьto* 'nothing' and Avestan *naēčit*), the adverb *javě* 'clearly,' the particle *bo* 'for,' all of which almost certainly belong to the stock of cognate, and not borrowed, words. With no other Indo-European dialect do the

Proto-Slavic and Baltic dialects exhibit detailed similarities in the area of such dependent "little words" (so characteristic of and important to every language). This allows us to assume an especially close bond between the Proto-Slavic and Proto-Indo-Iranian dialects. Among the other lexical elements common to these two dialectal groups are many words that could have been borrowed very easily from dialect to dialect on the basis of their semantics. Such words are very typical.

A whole group of these words pertain to religion. Slavic *bogъ* 'god,' *svętъ* 'holy' (where the *a* in Russian *svjat* comes from Old Slavic nasalized *e*), and *slovo* 'word' are usually cited (after the work of the French scholar Antoine Meillet) as words comparable to Old Iranian *baga-*, *spǝnta*, and *sravah-*. It is noteworthy that these correspondences exist only between Slavic and Iranian (Indian is not involved, and only the second of these three words is known in the Baltic languages). It is appropriate to recall here that the Indo-European word *deiwos*, which means 'god' in other languages (Latin *deus*, Old Indian *deva-*, Old Icelandic *Týr* 'name of god,' pl. *'tīwar*, etc.), in the Slavic and Iranian languages denotes an evil mythological being: Avestan *dāeva-*, Modern Persian *dēv* (cf. *Asmodev*), Old Russian *divъ* (in *The Lay of the Host of Igor*), South Slavic *diva* 'witch,' *samodiva*; in addition *divьjь*, *divъ* 'savage, barbaric.' With regard to the Iranians, this semantic change is usually explained by the reform of Zarathustra (Zoroaster), who recognized Ahura Mazdah (Ormazd) as the one true god and then declared all other gods to be demons; consequently, the term *dāeva-* came to mean 'demon,' while 'god' was denoted by other words (among them *baga*). One must assume that the ancestors of the Slavs participated in some way in the evolution of religious ideas which ultimately led to Zarathustra's reform among their eastern neighbors, the ancient Iranians.

Under these circumstances, Meillet's hypothesis regarding the identity between the Slavic verb *věriti* and Avestan *varayaiti*, which also means 'to believe' but originally meant 'to choose,' is most plausible; according to the teaching of Zarathustra, the one who believes rightly is the one who has made the correct "choice" between the god of goodness (Ormazd) and the god of evil (Ariman). These similarities in the religious terminologies of the Proto-Slavic and the Proto-Indo-Iranian dialects illuminate several other lexical correspondences between them. For example, Slavic *zovetъ, zъvati* 'call' has a parallel (in addition to the Baltic languages) only in Indo-Iranian, where the corresponding verb has a special technical usage meaning 'to summon god.' Slavic *sъdravъ* 'healthy' has a more or less precise parallel only in Old Persian; and we remember that health is the most frequent concern in prayers. Slavic *bojati sę* 'to be afraid' occurs (in addition to Lithuanian) only in Old Indian; it can easily be placed in the general context of religious terminology. The fact that Slavic *šujь*, adj. (a synonym for *lěvъ* 'left') has parallels only in the Indo-Iranian languages gives rise to some interesting considerations: a superstitious attitude toward the left side is well known, as is the custom of using special words to denote frightening ideas (so-called verbal taboos). In general, one can say that terms in one way or another associated with religious experience account for a very significant portion of the lexical correspondences between Proto-Slavic and Proto-Indo-Iranian.

Specific correspondences between Proto-Slavic and the West Indo-European languages are different in nature. Such correspondences may be more numerous than those with Proto-Indo-Iranian, but they do not include any of those intimate little words (conjunctions, prepositions, etc.) that play such a vital role in everyday language. The most prominent words here are those with technical meanings related to economic activity. Among nouns, *sěmę* 'seed,' *zrъno* 'grain,' *brašъno* 'food,' *lexa* 'furrow,' *jablъko* 'apple,' *prasę* 'piglet,' *bobъ* 'bean,' *sěkyra* 'ax,' *šilo* 'awl,' and *trudъ* 'toil'—all have exact parallels (beyond the Baltic languages) only in the Celtic, Italic, and Germanic languages. The same is true of the verbs *sějati* 'sow,' *kovati* 'forge,' *plesti* 'weave,' and *sěšti* 'cut, carve, cut off.' The adjective *dobrъ* 'good' (German *tapfer*, Latin *faber*, from Indo-European *dhabros*) originally had no ethical meaning and denoted a purely technical "virtue," that is, dexterity, or fitness for particular work. A sense of the old social *mores* is conveyed by the words *gostъ* 'guest' (German *gast*, Latin *hostis*), *měna* 'exchange,' *dlъgъ* 'duty' (known only in Slavic, Italic, and Germanic), and perhaps by the word *dělъ* 'portion,' which has an exact parallel only in German *Teil*.

Other words encountered only among the Slavs and Western Indo-Europeans are less characteristic since they denote features of the natural environment, and their widespread usage is explained by common geographic conditions (*more* 'sea,' *mъxъ* 'moss,' *drozdъ* 'thrush,' *osa* 'wasp,' *srъšenъ* 'hornet,' *elъxa* 'alder,' *iva* 'willow,' *sěverъ* 'north'); or they denote parts of the body (*lędvьę* 'loins,' *brada* 'beard'). Both of these categories are represented in the stock of Slavic and Indo-Iranian correspondences (Slavic *gora* 'mountain'/Avestan *gairi-*/ Old Indian *giríṣ*; Slavic *griva* 'mane,' *usta* 'mouth,' *vlasъ* 'hair'/ Old Indian *grīvā́* 'back of the neck,' *oṣṭhas* 'mouth,' Avestan *varesa* 'hair').

It is very likely that, in addition to these ties with the East and West, the Proto-Slavic dialect had certain connections with the South, at least with the Proto-Thracian and Proto-Illyrian dialects, and with the dialect from which the Albanian language later developed. Unfortunately, Albanian is a highly mixed language as we know it; foreign elements from the Greek, Turkish, modern Slavic, and Romance languages are much more numerous in its lexicon than the indigenous, of which very few remain. The languages of the ancient Thracians and Illyrians are almost completely unknown. Consequently, we can say nothing definite about the nature of the connections between the Proto-Slavic dialect and its southern neighbors.

Toward the end of the Indo-European era (that is, as the Proto-Slavic dialect was becoming an independent language), the Slavs were confronted with the need to make choices among these ties to the East, the South, and the West. We have seen that the Slavs were drawn to the Indo-Iranians "spiritually," and "physically" to the Western Indo-Europeans owing to geographical and economic circumstances. After the final separation of Proto-Slavic from the other branches of the Indo-European family, the ancestors of the Slavs continued for quite some time to be strongly influenced by the Western Indo-Europeans, who had already separated into three linguistic groups: Germanic, Celtic, and Italic (from which the Romance languages developed). The oldest Romance and Germanic elements entering the Common Slavic proto-language were related to the same semantic categories as the lexical items common to the Proto-Slavic and West Indo-European dialects earlier. They referred primarily to tools and the like, to trade and government, and to weaponry. Later, Christian terminology entered this language, at first by a rather circuitous route, from the Greeks and Romans via the Germans (cьrky 'church,' postъ 'fast') or via peoples speaking Romance languages (križь 'crosier,' krьstъ 'cross,' kumъ 'kinsman') and later, directly from the Greeks.

Finally, in the period since the era of Common Slavic unity, the Slavs have separated into three groups—the West, South, and East Slavs—each of which embodies, as it were, its own "orientation." Thus the cultural physiognomy of Slavdom was predetermined when the ancestors of the Slavs were still part of the common mass of Indo-Europeans and spoke a dialect of the Proto-Indo-European language, for the central location of the Slavic tribes inclined them at various times to the east, to the west, and to the south. Later these tendencies became differentiated in connection with the division of Slavdom itself, so that each of its three branches preserved *one of these tendencies*.

The West Slavic lands adjoined the Romano-Germanic world. True, this world did not consider the West Slavs equal members of the family and subjected them to Germanization and wholesale slaughter. At one time these Slavs occupied the entire eastern half of present-day Germany, all the way to the Elbe and to the Fulda (in Hessen); but now, of this large area, only Poland, the Czech lands and a small Lusatian island surrounded by Germans remain. Nevertheless, the West Slavs assimilated

Romano-Germanic culture more or less completely, and they participated as far as possible in its development, despite their unenviable position in a world where they were not considered "family." The intellectual revolution that marks the beginning of the "new history" of the Romano-Germanic world was advanced to a significant degree by the work of two West Slavs—the Czech Jan Hus and the Pole Nicolas Copernicus.

The South Slavs found themselves in the Byzantine sphere of influence, and together with the other peoples of the Balkan Peninsula they created a special "Balkan culture," which was Hellenistic in its upper stories. Because the roles of the various ethnic sources that created this culture have not been sufficiently studied, a detailed ethnological description of its lower stories is not yet possible. The spirit of Byzantine culture was being thoroughly assimilated by the South Slavs, at least until the Greek Phanariots began their chauvinistic intrigues (during the era of the Turkish occupation) and tried to impose mechanically what was being spontaneously assimilated.

The cultural orientation of the East Slavs was much less clearly defined. Since they were not located near any of the centers of Indo-European culture,[3] they could choose freely between the Romano-Germanic West and Byzantium, both of which they had come to know primarily through Slavic intermediaries. The choice was made in favor of Byzantium, and the results initially were very good. Byzantine culture was developed and enriched on Russian soil. Everything that came from Byzantium was thoroughly assimilated and could thus serve as a model for the creative efforts that shaped these elements to satisfy the requirements of the national psychology. This was particularly true of the religious culture, of art, and religious life.

[3]The Northern Iranian (Scytho-Sarmatian) tribes, which inhabited Southern Russia at one time, disappeared rather quickly; some of them were assimilated by the East Slavs, and some were driven out or swallowed up by Turkic nomads. The modern Ossetians are the last remnant of the Scytho-Sarmatian tribes.

Conversely, everything received from the West was not assimilated, and failed to inspire national creativity. Western products were imported and purchased, but not reproduced. Skilled artisans were not hired to teach Russians but to fulfill commissions. Occasionally books were translated, but they did not initiate a corresponding growth in the national literature. We are concerned here with general trends, not details. There are of course many exceptions to this general rule; on the whole, however, things Byzantine were unquestionably assimilated more easily and thoroughly in Russia than things Western. It cannot be argued that this is the result of superstitious misoneism. In this very "superstitiousness" there was an instinctive revulsion against the Romano-Germanic spirit and a recognition by Russians of their inability to create in this spirit. In this regard, the East Slavs were true descendants of their prehistoric ancestors—those speakers of the Proto-Slavic dialect of the Proto-Indo-European language who, as comparative lexical studies show, had no feeling of spiritual kinship with the West Indo-Europeans and who were linked religiously with the East. This psychological trait was suppressed among the West Slavs by continuous, direct contacts with the Germans; among the East Slavs it was perhaps intensified by intermarriage with the Ugro-Finns and the Turks.

This situation changed radically owing to the reforms of Peter the Great. Russians were supposed to be imbued with the Romano-Germanic spirit immediately and to be creative in this spirit. But they were incapable of fulfilling this task quickly. If Russia before Peter the Great could be considered the most gifted and productive successor to Byzantium culturally, after he initiated the Romano-Germanic orientation she found herself at the tail end of European culture, in civilization's backyard. Certain basic motive principles of European spiritual culture (e.g., European legalism) were poorly assimilated by the Russian elite, and not at all by the masses. The absence of several fundamentally important Romano-Germanic psychological traits was apparent at every turn. And so the number of genuine contributions by Russian genius to "the treasure house of

European civilization" remained negligible compared to the mass of foreign cultural assets mechanically transplanted to Russian soil. Efforts to rework Romano-Germanic cultural assets and to display originality and individual creativity within the boundaries of particular European forms were common in Russia, especially in the realm of spiritual culture. However, only a few exceptional geniuses were successful in creating works that were acceptable not only in Russia but in the West. The overwhelming preponderance of activity was always on the side of simple, almost mechanical adaptation and imitation.

Whenever a talented or brilliant Russian artist tried to create within the framework of European culture something national and original, he usually introduced a Byzantine, a "Russian," or an "eastern" element (especially in music) that was quite alien to the Romano-Germanic world. A native Romano-German will respond to such works as exotica that can be admired from a distance but not absorbed and experienced. At the same time, such hybrid works cannot be viewed as truly original, and a sensitive Russian will always detect something false in them. This falsity is the product of a flawed understanding of what is essentially Russian, as well as of a disharmony between form and content.

In the final analysis, and despite all the protestations of the Russian intelligentsia (in the broadest sense of the term), two abysses dug by Peter the Great—the first between pre-Petrine Rus' and post-Petrine Russia, and the second between the masses and the educated elite—remain open and gaping. Not even the spiritual perspicacity of great artists could throw bridges across these abysses, and the music of Rimsky-Korsakov differs fundamentally from a genuine Russian folk song, just as the paintings of Vasnetsov and Nesterov differ from a genuine icon.

Such then is the state of the upper story of the edifice of Russian culture. The life of the Russian cultural elite was always associated with traditions that were received first from Byzantium, and then from the Romano-Germanic West, and more or less thoroughly assimilated. It is true that these foreign traditions worked their way downward from the elite into the masses. The traditions of Byzantine Eastern Orthodoxy had a great impact on the masses and colored all aspects of the spiritual life of the people. But contact with the life of the Russian masses so altered Orthodoxy that its Byzantine traits were greatly suppressed. Western culture affected the Russian masses much more superficially and never touched the depths of the native soul. The result was a profound disharmony between the upper and lower stories of the edifice of Russian culture, unlike the situation after the assimilation of Byzantine culture by the elite.

However, the cultural and ethnographic composition of Russian national life consists not only of the Byzantine and Romano-Germanic traditions. It is widely believed in educated Russian society that the unique characteristics of this life can be described as Slavic. This is incorrect. From an ethnographic point of view, the culture (meaning the stock of cultural assets that meets the physical and spiritual requirements of a particular milieu) of the Russian people is an absolutely singular entity that cannot be accurately identified with any broader cultural zone or grouping of cultures. Generally speaking, this culture comprises its own special zone and includes, besides the Russians, the Ugro-Finnic peoples and the Turkic peoples of the Volga Basin. Moving to the east and southeast, this culture merges almost imperceptibly with the Turko-Mongolian culture of the steppes, which links it in turn with the cultures of Asia. In the west there is also a gradual transition (via the Belorussians and Ukrainians) to the culture of the West Slavs, which borders on the Romano-Germanic and "Balkan" cultures. But these links with other Slavic cultures are not very strong, and they are counterbalanced by strong connections with the East. Russian national culture is closely associated with the East in a whole set of issues, so that at times the boundary between East and West passes exactly between the Russians and other Slavs. On certain issues the South Slavs and Russians are closely related, not because both groups are Slavs but because both have experienced strong Turkic influences.

This trait of Russian national life is clearly evident in folk art. Many Great Russian songs (including the most ancient, ritual and wedding songs) are composed in the so-called five-tone or Indo-Chinese scale (that is, like a major scale minus the fourth and seventh tones).[4] This scale is used (in fact, it is the only one) by the Finnish and Turkic tribes of the Volga and Kama Basin, and also by the Bashkirs, the Siberian Tatars, the Turks of Russian and Chinese Turkestan, and by all Mongols. Apparently this scale once existed in China as well; in any case, Chinese music theory assumes its existence, and Chinese musical notation is based upon it.[5] At present this is the predominant scale in Thailand, Burma, Cambodia, and Indochina. So we have here an unbroken line from the East that stops with the Great Russians. Among the Ukrainians the five-tone scale is found only in a very few ancient songs, and among other Slavs there are only isolated instances of its use. It is unknown among the Romano-Germans and is encountered again only in the far northwestern part of Europe, among the British Celts (the Scots, Irish, and Brythons).

Rhythmically the Russian song is fundamentally different not only from the Romano-Germanic but from the songs of other Slavs (if only because three-four rhythm is unknown—the rhythm of the waltz and the mazurka). The Russian song differs from the Asian in that most Asians sing in unison. In this respect the Russian song is transitional: the vocalization of the

---

[4] For readers unfamiliar with music theory, this scale obtains if one plays only the black keys on a piano. Rachmaninov's romance "The Lilac" is one of the "cultured" works familiar to the Russian public which were composed using this scale.

[5] In performance, a transposition occurs, so that a scale with four tones is produced. For example, a melody represented by the scale do, re, mi, sol, la, will replace both sol and la with la-flat, for sol an octave higher than for la.

Russian chorus is polyphonic; unison singing is not rare, but a "lead voice" is mandatory in certain kinds of choral songs.

Another type of rhythmic art—the dance—is distinctive in the same way. Romano-Germanic dances are characterized by the obligatory presence of "cavaliers" and "ladies" dancing together and holding each other, which permits them to make identical rhythmic movements with their feet only. Russian dances are in no way comparable: couples are not obligatory, and even if two people are dancing, they may be of the same sex and may dance in turn rather than simultaneously; and they do not hold one another. Consequently, rhythmic movements can be executed not only with the feet but with the arms and shoulders. The foot movements of the men differ from those of the women; they are characterized by the way they alternate heel and toe. Distinctive, too, is the effort to keep the head motionless, especially among the women. The men's movements are not defined in advance, and there is much room for improvisation within the boundaries of a particular rhythm; the gait of the women is highly stylized. The dance motif is a short musical phrase, whose rhythm is quite distinct but open to variation. All these features can be seen in the dances of the eastern Finns, the Turkic peoples, the Mongols, the peoples of the Caucasus Mountains (however, dances with couples who hold one another are found in the northern Caucasus), and in the dances of many other "Asian" peoples.[6]

Unlike Romano-Germanic dances, in which (with their minimal technical requirements) constant contact between the man and woman introduces a distinct sexual element, Russian-

[6]In addition to the "solo" dances of the type described here, the Russians also practice a choral dance. It is very different from such dances among other Slavs, the Romano-Germans, and several eastern peoples. Strictly speaking, the Russian circle dance is not a dance at all, because none of the participants executes "steps," and no one is obliged to move his or her feet to the rhythm of the music. It is really a kind of "game," or a ritualistic act in which the choral singing is most important.

Asian dances are more like competitions in agility and in the rhythmic discipline of the body. The force of the rhythm is intensified by the participation of spectators, who instinctively stamp their feet, whistle, and shout. Similar dancing is found among the Spanish, but in all probability it is traceable to eastern (Moorish and Gypsy) influences. As far as the other Slavs are concerned, they do not resemble the Russians in the art of dancing; only the Bulgarian *ruchenitsa* is reminiscent of the Russian-Asian type, doubtlessly because of some eastern influence.

Great Russian national culture has its own unique style in the area of ornamentation (wood fretwork, embroidery); this art has connections with the Balkans through the Ukrainians and with the East through the Ugro-Finns. There is apparently a complex pattern of intersecting influences here that requires scholarly attention. Unfortunately, our understanding of ornamentation is still rudimentary, and we have not worked out a classificatory system that would allow us to establish the degree of relatedness among various ornaments. Thus we cannot specify the differences between Russian ornamentation and those of the West Slavs and Romano-Germans, even though these differences are palpable.

The folk literature of the Great Russians is original. The style of the Russian fairy tale has no parallels in the folk literatures of the Romano-Germans or the other Slavs, although there are analogues among the Turkic peoples and those of the Caucasus. The fairy tales of the eastern Finns are completely under Russian influence as far as style is concerned. Russian folk epics are related in subject matter to the "Turanian" East and to Byzantium, as well as to the Romano-Germans. But their form is completely original, they display no Western features; one can only note that they have peripheral connections with the epos of the Balkan Slavs and significant connections with the steppe epos of the Tatar Horde.

The material culture of the Russian people is predictably very different from the culture of the steppe nomads and related much more closely to the cultures of the South and West Slavs. One thing is certain: with regard to material culture, the Great Russians and most of the Finnic peoples (excluding nomads) constitute a coherent whole. Unfortunately, there have been very few detailed ethnographic studies of the material culture of the Russian people; dilettantism characterizes most of those that exist. It is embarrassing to admit that the material culture of the Finnic peoples is far better understood, thanks to the efforts of Finnish ethnographers. But the relative roles of the Ugro-Finnic and East Slavic elements in the formation of what can be called a Russo-Finnish culture have not yet been established. It is generally believed that the Ugro-Finns had the greater influence in the world of fishing, and the East Slavs in housing construction. Russian and Finnish clothing display certain common features (bast sandals, the so-called Russian blouse, and types of feminine headwear) that are unknown among the Romano-Germans and the other Slavs (bast sandals are encountered among the Lithuanians). But here, too, the historical connections among these elements have not been fully explored.

Thus from an ethnographic point of view, the Russian people are not purely Slavic. The Russians, the Ugro-Finns, and the Volga Turks comprise a cultural zone that has connections with both the Slavs and the "Turanian East," and it is difficult to say which of these is more important. The connection between the Russians and the Turanians has not only an ethnographic but an anthropological basis: Turkic blood mingles in Russian veins with that of the Ugro-Finns and Slavs. And the Russian national character is unquestionably linked in certain ways with the "Turanian East." The brotherhood and mutual understanding that develop so quickly between us and "Asians" are rooted in these invisible racial consonances. However, the Russian national character is still quite distinct from that of the Ugro-Finns and the Turks; it resembles not in the least the national characters of the other Slavs. Numerous traits that the Russian people value highly in themselves have no equivalents in the moral makeup of the other Slavs. The contemplative tradition and devotion to ritual in Russian piety are linked historically to Byzantine traditions; they are alien to the other Orthodox Slavs, and they connect Russia with the non-Orthodox East. The exuberant daring prized by the Russian people in their heroes is a virtue that comes from the steppes; it is understood by the Turkic peoples but is quite incomprehensible to the Romano-Germans and the other Slavs.

Any attempt to erect a new Russian culture must take into account the unique psychological and ethnographic composition of what is natively Russian, because it is this that must serve as the first story of the edifice of Russian culture. To ensure the stability of the edifice and prevent any discontinuities or gaps between the upper and lower stories, these stories must correspond with one another. Such stability existed as long as the edifice of Russian culture was capped with a Byzantine cupola. But when the upper story of the Romano-Germanic structure began to replace this cupola, the harmony between the parts of the edifice and its stability were lost; the upper stories began to lean and sway, and finally collapsed. And we—the Russian intelligentsia—after wasting so much energy in our attempts to shore up a Romano-Germanic roof that broke away from Russian walls for which it was never suited—we stand in amazement before these massive ruins and wonder how we can build a new roof according to the same old Romano-Germanic model. Any such thoughts must be rejected outright. In order for Russian culture to become firmly established on Russian soil, its upper story must be, at the very least, something other than Romano-Germanic.

A return to Byzantine traditions is obviously impossible. It is true that these traditions have not been swept away by Europeanization in one part of the edifice of Russian culture, the Russian Orthodox Church, which has shown itself to be amazingly resilient. When everything else was being destroyed, it not only failed to collapse, but it regained its original form by rebuilding itself according to the ancient model inherited from

Byzantium. In the future, the Byzantine element in Russian culture, which has its roots in the Church tradition, may even be strengthened. But it is of course impossible to imagine the complete reconstruction of Russian life according to ancient Byzantine principles in their pure form. And this is so not only because two and one-half centuries of compulsory Euro-peanization did not leave Russia unscathed, but because of past experience: when in the seventeenth century Patriarch Nikon decided to strengthen the Byzantine element in Russian life and to bring Russian worship closer to its Byzantine model, that model was perceived by many Russians as something alien, and it led to the Schism. Later the schismatics turned the blade of their protest against Europeanization. The yearning of the Russian national spirit for an original culture has been embodied since that time in the Russian Schism—a yearning that is perhaps misdirected and futile, since it can claim only a lower but no upper story. Nevertheless, one senses in the twists and turns of the Schism the presence of the Russian spirit's healthy national instinct protesting against the foreign upper story, artificially imposed on Russian culture. It is therefore extremely important that Emelyan Pugachev stood under the banner of the Old Belief and rejected the "pagan Latins and Lutherans"; but he did not consider it reprehensible to unite with the Bashkirs and other adherents of not only non-Orthodox Eastern Christianity but of the non-Christian faiths of the East.

Guidelines for constructing the edifice of Russian culture must be discovered in these subconscious sympathies and antipathies of the Russian national spirit. We profess Eastern Orthodoxy, and this faith, while conforming to the traits of our national psychology, should be at the very center of our culture, from there influencing many aspects of Russian life. In addition to this faith, we have received many cultural traditions from Byzantium, which people once knew how to develop and adapt to Russian traditions. Work in this direction should continue.

But this does not exhaust the matter. Not everything should be put into a Byzantine framework. We are Russians, not

Greeks; in order for Russian culture to be completely "ours," it must be closely linked to the unique psychological and ethnographic characteristics of Russian national life. Here one must bear in mind the special properties of Russianness. We have often heard that it is Russia's historical mission to unite our Slavic "brothers." But it is usually forgotten that our "brothers" (if not in language or faith, then in blood, character, and culture) are not only the Slavs but the Turanians, and that Russia has already consolidated a large part of the Turanian East under the aegis of its state system. Attempts to Christianize these "foreigners" have met with very little success. Therefore, if the upper story of Russian culture is to be in harmony with the singular nature of the ethnographic zone comprised by Russian national life, this culture must not be based exclusively on Eastern Orthodoxy but must also manifest those traits of the underlying national life that can unite into a single cultural whole the diverse tribes are linked historically with the destiny of the Russian people. This does not mean of course that bast sandals and the five-tone scale must become integral parts of the upper story of Russian culture. It is impossible to predict or prescribe in advance the specific forms a new Russian culture might display. But any difference between its upper and lower stories must reflect not their conflicting orientations toward two different ethnographic zones, but a contrast in the degree to which elements of a single culture have been reworked and elaborated. Russian culture, understood as a cultural edifice under construction, must rise up harmoniously from its foundations in Russian national life.

4 The Russian Problem*

The "restoration of Russia," as Russian political emigrés imagine it, would be nothing less than a miracle. One beautiful morning we will all awaken to discover that everything now happening in Russia (as we picture it) has simply been a bad dream, or that it has all disappeared with a wave of a magic wand. Russia will again be a great power, feared and respected by everyone, and offered the most tantalizing political and economic alliances as assistance during the "interregnum"; her only task will be to choose with complete freedom the best form of government for herself, and then to live happily ever after, bringing fear to her enemies and glory to herself. What would this be, if not a miracle?

It is impossible to deny that miracles sometimes occur, and they will again. But is it really possible to use a miracle as the basis for political calculations? Can one introduce a miracle as one element (and an indispensable one at that) into realistic political formulations? After all, by its very nature a miracle is unexpected and inaccessible to foresight and prior calculation. When a serious, realistic politician develops his plans for the future, he must take only real possibilities into account. If he believes in miracles and wants to be especially cautious, the most he can do is consider how to act if a miracle should suddenly occur. This is all he can do. But a politician who does not take real possibilities into account and bases his plans

*Originally as "Russkaia problema," *Na putiakh*, Berlin 1922, pp. 294-316. Translated by Kenneth Brostrom.

exclusively on a future miracle can hardly be called realistic. In fact, one might ask whether "politician" is the appropriate term for such an individual. And yet, all our emigrés are like this. Realities do not interest them in the least; they seem not to notice them. The miraculous restoration of Russia is for them the alpha and the omega, the immutable goal and the point of departure for all their plans, projects, and formulations. This blind confidence in an inevitable miracle would be understandable if we were dealing with mystics of some sort. But we are discussing practical men of action, whose orientation is toward real facts. So what is the problem here—a blindness that prevents them from seeing undeniable realities, or fear of looking these realities straight in the face?

II

There are truths that are accepted more or less by everyone. War, revolution, and Bolshevik experimenters have brought Russia to a state of such complete economic collapse that she will be able to recover only gradually, over a long period of time—and *only* if she receives extremely vigorous, active assistance from abroad. Because the Soviet government is concerned first of all about its own survival, it has created a regime against which the hungry, disarmed population can mount at best only small, local revolts that are suppressed forcefully or terminated by an "internal explosion," thanks to the ingenious use of propaganda and provocation. Effective anti-Bolshevik operations are impossible without active, long-term foreign support. A voluntary relaxation of the Soviet system is possible only if the Soviet government can find some new way to guarantee its inviolability—for example, a completely secure, reliable agreement with foreign nations, without whose assistance the overthrow of this government is impossible in any case. Therefore, the creation of living conditions in Russia that are to any degree tolerable, that guarantee the security and the material needs of the population, are possible only with foreign assistance (i.e., foreign intervention).

By "foreigners" we of course mean the "great powers" that fought the World War. We now know exactly what they are. The War washed the powder and rouge from the face of humane Romano-Germanic civilization, and the descendants of the ancient Gauls and Teutons have now shown the world their true visage—a savage beast, hungrily gnashing his teeth. This beast is the true *Realpolitik*. He is quite different from our own "representatives of the spirit of community." He does not believe in miracles and he laughs at ideas. Just give him plunder and food—the more and the tastier, the better. If you don't give, he will take; this is why he has technology, science, culture—and above all, battleships and cannons.

This is the nature of the foreigners without whose help the "restoration of Russia" is impossible. They have made war upon one another to achieve world domination. The world was to be divided among them or bestowed upon a single victor. But neither goal was achieved. Russia in her vastness (comprising one-sixth of the earth's surface) does not belong to any of them. As long as she remains undivided and outside the control of any of the Romano-Germanic beasts, we cannot view the World War as ended. This is the essence of the "Russian problem" for the Romano-Germans. They look upon Russia as a potential colony. Her vast dimensions disturb them not in the least. In terms of population, India is larger than Russia, but England has snapped up the entire country. Africa exceeds Russia in size, but it has been divided among several of the Romano-Germanic states. The same will probably happen to Russia. Russia is a territory on which certain things grow and within which such and such minerals are available. The fact that people inhabit this territory is a matter of indifference—they will be studied by ethnographers. Generally speaking, it is territory that is of interest in politics; populations come into the picture only as sources of labor.

Can one possibly suppose that these foreigners will bow politely and step aside after they have helped Russia to recover and stand on her own two feet? Such a scenario can be imagined as a miracle, but if one views the world in terms of real possibilities and probabilities, one must admit that such a turn of events is absolutely impossible. The Romano-Germanic states that will give aid to Russia (or more precisely, will be giving aid, since protracted assistance will be required) will do so not out of philanthropic conviction; they will try to arrange matters so as to make Russia their colony in exchange for their help. At present it is difficult to foresee which of the Romano-Germanic states will manage to do this. It could be England, Germany, or America; or perhaps a consortium of these states will divide Russia into "spheres of influence." The only thing one can say with confidence is that Russia will not be annexed, and she will not be added to the list of some state's colonial possessions. Russia will be left with only the shadow, the appearance of independence. A government will be formed that is unconditionally subservient to the foreigners; it will enjoy the rights once enjoyed by the governments of Bukhara, Siam, and Cambodia. Whether this government consists of S.R.'s [Socialist Revolutionaries], Cadets [Constitutional Democrats], Bolsheviks, Octobrists, or reactionaries will not be important. The only important requirement will be this: that it is a fictitious government.

This is the realistic conclusion that emerges from a dispassionate examination of the current state of affairs. The restoration of Russia is possible only at the cost of her independence.

III

As very realistic politicians, the Bolsheviks must take into account the inevitability of this foreign yoke. The Russian policies of the foreign powers all boil down to a desire to create a compliant Russian government from Lenin's party; for their part, the Bolsheviks sometimes play give-away and sometimes show their claws. Consequently, the process is moving slowly. It is unquestionably more advantageous to "tame" the Soviet government than to overthrow and replace it with some new government. The foreigners will embark upon the overthrow of the Bolsheviks only after they are convinced that "taming" them is impossible. This is why the equivocal tactics of the Soviet government are winning time. But no matter how protracted this situation proves to be, only two alternatives ultimately confront the Soviet government: either become a government subservient to foreigners like the governments of Cambodia and Bukhara, or relinquish their positions to another, equally subservient government consisting of representatives of other political parties. If the Bolsheviks nevertheless consider it advantageous to impede this process, then they do so because they are still placing all their hope on one last throw of the dice—the much-touted world revolution.

World revolution, a communist seizure of power in all the Romano-Germanic countries, is the only thing that can save the Soviet Russian government from perishing or from subjugation to the "bourgeois" governments of the West. It is difficult to say how well-founded the Bolshevik hope for a world revolution is. At present everything is apparently going well in the Romano-Germanic countries, and the workers' movement has seemingly entered a "safe" channel. But no one knows how stable this state of affairs is, or whether it might change quickly, especially if the tense international situation were to lead once again to armed conflict. To assess the claims of the Bolsheviks, it would be necessary to have in hand a great deal of factual data which no one possesses other than those same Bolsheviks, who have gathered information about preparations for communist revolts in all the countries of the world. Clearly, it is impossible to agree unquestioningly when the Bolsheviks confidently predict world revolution, since they may simply be indulging in wishful thinking. However, there is also no way to refute their claims.

It is worth asking whether a world revolution would substantially change the future that now confronts Russia. If the Bolsheviks are awaiting deliverance through world revolution, they do so because they see the greatest danger from foreigners not in the political and economic enslavement of Russia, but in the fact that the guardianship of "bourgeois" Romano-Germanic governments would interfere with their efforts to realize the ideals of a communist social order in Russia. It is true that world revolution would eliminate this danger. But for us noncommunists, the destruction of the communist order can hardly be considered a "danger"; this is why we are interested in one question only: Will world revolution eliminate the danger of Russia's enslavement by foreigners? The answer to this question must be an unqualified no.

Socialism and communism are products of Romano-Germanic civilization. They presuppose specific social, economic, political, and technical conditions which exist in all the Romano-Germanic countries, but not in "backward" countries—that is, in countries which have not yet assimilated the Romano-Germanic civilization. If a communist revolution were to occur throughout the world, then the Romano-Germanic countries (which currently stand at the "summit of progress") would doubtlessly turn out to be perfect examples of communist government. They would continue to "set the tone," to play the leading role. Having exhausted herself in efforts to establish socialism in extremely inhospitable conditions where the social, economic, and technical prerequisites necessary to achieve this goal are absent, "backward" Russia would find herself in a state of complete subjugation to these "leading" communist states and would endure unbridled exploitation at their hands. If the population of Russia now suffers and lives in poverty in large measure because an enormous portion of Russia's national wealth is being wasted on communist propaganda and support of workers' movements abroad, what will happen when preserving the well-being of model communist states in Europe depends on the sweat and blood of

Russian workers and peasants? And when the "specialists" controlling the exploitation of "backward natives" devoid of "class-consciousness" are themselves foreign representatives of these same model communist governments?

Thus, world revolution will not change in any essential way the gloomy prospects confronting Russia. Without it, Russia will become a colony of the bourgeois Romano-Germanic countries, and with it, a colony of Communist Europe. But a colony she will be in either case. The page of history on which "Russia, a Great European Power" is inscribed has been turned once and for all. Russia has now entered a new epoch in her life, the epoch marking her loss of independence. In the future, Russia will be a colony similar to India, Egypt, and Morocco. This is the only possibility that actually exists for her, and every realistic politician ought to deal with it to the exclusion of all others—unless a miracle occurs.

IV

Russia's entry into the family of colonial possessions is occurring in reasonably auspicious circumstances. Recently the prestige of the Romano-Germans has declined noticeably in their colonies. Everywhere, despised "natives" are slowly raising their heads and beginning to criticize their masters. Of course, the Romano-Germans have only themselves to blame for this. During the World War they spread propaganda in their enemies' colonies, thereby discrediting one another in the eyes of the "natives." They taught these "natives" military skills and forced them to fight against Romano-Germans during the War, preparing them for victory over the "race of the masters." They created among these "natives" a class of intellectuals with a European education and then showed these people the true face of European culture, which could only produce disillusionment. Efforts to achieve liberation from the Romano-Germanic yoke are evident in many colonies now; and if these efforts sometimes find expression in senseless, easily suppressed armed uprisings, there are others that show signs of being very serious national movements. In the misty distance, vistas of the imminent liberation of oppressed humanity from the yoke of the Romano-Germanic predators seem to be unfolding. One senses that the Romano-Germanic world is growing decrepit, and its rotten teeth will soon be incapable of tearing and chewing the delicious flesh of enslaved colonies.

In such circumstances, the addition of an immense country like Russia to the roster of foreign colonies—a new colony accustomed to an independent existence and to viewing the Romano-Germanic states more or less as equals—may provide a critical impetus to the emancipation of the colonial world from Romano-Germanic oppression. Russia can assume leadership in this worldwide movement immediately. One must admit that it was the Bolsheviks whose experiments forced Russia inexorably into the ranks of the colonial countries, who also prepared Russia for her new historical role as the leader in the liberation of the colonial world from the Romano-Germanic yoke.

From the very beginning of their efforts to spread communist propaganda among Asians, the Bolsheviks have encountered the following difficulty. Pure communism had few adherents anywhere owing to the absence of the appropriate social and cultural conditions. On the other hand, propaganda directed against the Romano-Germans and their culture was unusually successful. Communist propaganda was perceived as a nationalistic attack upon Europeans and their lackeys. "Bourgeois" was understood to mean a European merchant, engineer, or functionary; or it could refer to a native exploiter or a Europeanized member of the local intelligentsia who had assimilated European culture, donned European dress, and lost his ties to his own people. The Bolsheviks were not altogether unhappy about this confusion, because it provided them with an opportunity, created as it were by deception, to use for their own purposes the unrest present in large portions of the population of Asia. Nevertheless, communist internationalists could not encourage this misunderstanding of their propaganda and allow it to shape any national movement that was to be carefully planned and based in theory. Consequently, in most Asian countries the situation has not moved beyond this state of confusion, in which elements of communism and Marxism are combined with misoneism, Europhobia, and nationalism in a fantastic and generally shapeless conglomeration.

Nevertheless, the task has been accomplished. Many Asians now associate the Bolsheviks and Russia with the idea of national liberation and with protest against the Romano-Germans and European civilization. This is the view of Russia found in Turkey, Persia, Afghanistan, India, and to some extent in China and in other East Asian countries. This view is shaping Russia's future historical role—not as a great European power but as an immense colonial country leading her Asiatic sisters in their common struggle against the Romano-Germans and European civilization. Russia's only hope for salvation lies in a victorious conclusion to this struggle. Formerly, when Russia was still a great European power, it was possible to say that her interests coincided with or departed from the interests of one or another of the European states. Now such statements are senseless. Henceforth the interests of Russia will be inseparably linked with the interests of Turkey, Persia, Afghanistan, India, and perhaps with those of China and the other countries of Asia. An orientation toward Asia is becoming the only possible orientation for the true Russian nationalist.

V

If the populations of a significant number of Asian countries are prepared to accept Russia in her new historical role, Russia herself is not prepared for this at all. Most of the Russian intelligentsia continue to bow down slavishly before European civilization and to view themselves as citizens of a European nation; they strive to imitate native Romano-Germans and dream that Russia will one day resemble the Romano-Germanic countries culturally in all things. A conscious desire to be separate from Europe is found in only isolated individuals. If disenchantment with the French and English is observable in some Russian refugees and emigrés, this generally reflects a purely personal sense of injury resulting from the many insults and humiliations visited upon them by the "allies" during their evacuation or later in the refugee camps. Quite often this disenchantment with the "allies" leads to exaggerated admiration of the Germans. Thus, the Russian intellectual still continues to bow down before the Romano-Germans (if not before these, then those), and the possibility of assuming a critical attitude toward European culture does not arise.

In such circumstances, the foreign yoke may prove fatal to Russia. Many members of the Russian intelligentsia who exalt the Romano-Germans and who view their own motherland as a backward country with "much to learn from Europe" will enter the service of the foreign oppressors without a twinge of conscience; and they will assist in the subjugation and enslavement of Russia, not out of fear, but as a moral duty. Moreover, the arrival of the foreigners will be associated at first with some improvement in the material conditions of life, and superficially the independence of Russia will appear unaffected; at the same time the Russian government, seemingly independent but in fact subservient to the foreigners, will be obviously liberal and progressive. All of this will partially conceal the truth from some segments of the ordinary masses and will simplify the rationalizations and moral compromises made by the members of the intelligentsia who serve the foreign oppressors.

This is a very dangerous path in the long run—first, collaborative efforts with the foreigners to help the starving, then service (of course, in minor positions) in the offices of foreign concessionaires, then in the management of the foreign "Control Commission for the Russian Debt," then in the foreign counterintelligence associated with that Commission, and so on.

Working for foreigners is not actually a great danger, and in itself does not deserve condemnation, especially since it will often be unavoidable. Most damaging of all is providing moral support to foreign domination, and given the present orientation of the Russian intelligentsia, the majority of them will certainly provide such support. It is this that is so deeply alarming. If unflagging moral support is given to the foreign yoke by the majority of a Russian intelligentsia that continues to bow down before European culture, seeing in it an ideal model which must be copied, then Russia will never throw off this yoke and fulfill her new historical mission—to liberate the world from the Romano-Germanic predators. Her mission can be completed only if a radical shift occurs in the consciousness of Russian society, if it distances itself from Europe, affirms its national uniqueness, strives to create its own national culture, and rejects European culture. If such a reversal occurs, victory is assured, and every service rendered to the foreigners, as well as physical subjugation by them, will be no cause for alarm. But if this does not happen, Russia will perish ingloriously and forever.

VI

We have examined the possible futures that lie before Russia. What then should Russians do now, at least those people who thirst for action and yearn to help Russia improve in some way, if not her present, then her future? What realizable tasks confront them? Should they do everything possible to undermine Soviet power and the economic reconstruction of Russia? We already know that both are possible only if Russia is enslaved by foreigners. Should we then facilitate this inevitable process? Should we deliberately "bring" the foreigners to Russia?

This is a task which even the most pragmatic of politicians would refuse to undertake. And what does "bring the foreigners" actually mean? They will come to Russia when they find it profitable and convenient, and they will be guided in doing so by practical considerations. The supplications of Russian emigrés will not hasten the process, because the foreigners do not act out of compassion but out of self-interest. They will come to Russia only if they can guarantee their own safety from the adverse consequences this step might entail: from international complications provoked by division of the "Russian bequest," or from revolutionary outbreaks at home. No amount of effort on the part of Russian emigrés will have any effect until a safe method is found for interfering in Russian affairs. When the political leadership of some Romano-Germanic state has discovered this method, the intervention will occur without any pressure from the Russian emigration. Which is to say that the Russian emigration is entirely powerless in this matter, and all its efforts here are a waste of time.

Should we prepare ourselves to participate in the future government apparatus of a "restored" Russia that is "liberated from Soviet power"?

But we already know what kind of government this will be. Superficially it will be Russian, but in fact, the instrument of foreign colonialist policies. Who will find work in such an apparatus congenial? Perhaps those moved by petty ambition and the attributes of power, however fictitious? Or perhaps unprincipled adventurers who dream of their own success at the price of personal disgrace and the destruction of their country? Such people have always existed, and they always will. It is not for their sake that I am writing all of this. Let them prepare for their future labors; it is impossible to stop them. But let no one be deceived—they are *traitors!*

However, there are also honorable, idealistic people who will want to enter this foreign-dominated future Russian government in order to free Russia from the foreign yoke by a combination of hard work and Machiavellian resourcefulness.

The image of Ivan Kalita's determined, methodical efforts to unify Russia while humbly swearing allegiance to the Tatar Horde probably arises like a polestar in the imaginations of these idealistic people. But Ivan Kalita was an independent prince who was not constrained by governmental structures and influential colleagues. Tatar ambassadors and control commissions were not looking over his shoulder; they simply arrived in force occasionally to collect their tribute, which was paid quickly and punctually; otherwise they left their vassal alone to do as he pleased. The position of an honorable man will be much more difficult in the government of the future, after Russia is enslaved by the Romano-Germans. He will be forced to share power with a group of ambitious Russian rogues and scoundrels, each of whom will happily destroy a colleague by discrediting him in the eyes of the omnipotent foreigners. What is more, the foreigners will maintain a careful surveillance of the government's activities through their official representatives and spies. In such circumstances, the efforts of a new Ivan Kalita can scarcely be effective. Most important, if there is no moral resistance to the foreigners in Russian society, such efforts are doomed to complete failure from the outset.

There remains the question of preparing ourselves for purely technical work directed toward the restoration of transport and the circulation of goods, the regulation of finance, and so on, all of this occurring under foreign domination. This context will make all such technical work abhorrent, for it will be carried on in close cooperation with foreigners, and inevitably will lead to the establishment of Russia as a colonial nation. As long as this new phase in the history of Russia remains unrecognized by honorable Russians or they refuse to admit its existence, the thought of technical work directed toward national restoration occurs naturally and does not elicit psychological resistance. However, insofar as this thought is fundamentally disconnected from the true situation, it can only be viewed as a futile dream. But when people eventually realize that they are working not in a miraculously restored great Russian state, but in a colony

controlled by foreigners, they will simply throw up their hands
and lose interest in technical work.

VII

Thus, any kind of political or apolitical activity directed
toward the restoration of the Russian state is futile and should
therefore be rejected by the Russian emigration. However, it
does not follow that Russian emigrés can give themselves up to
idleness or forget about Russia and immerse themselves in their
private affairs. On the contrary, the possible futures now
confronting Russia permit no Russian who understands them to
remain indifferently serene. But the activities of the Russian
intelligentsia, and of the Russian emigration in particular, must
follow a path altogether different from the one that guided
them in the past.

As we have argued, Russia's future under foreign domination
depends to a large degree on the ability of the Russian
intelligentsia to muster the necessary spiritual resistance to that
foreign control. For this to happen, a revolution in Russia's
social consciousness and attitudes must occur, since our
contemporary Russian intelligentsia is not inclined psychologically to resist the foreigners in any way. This indicates a
direction for the activities of the Russian intelligentsia. The
center of gravity must shift from the techniques of state-building
and from political work to the development and consolidation
of a unique national culture and of a world view appropriate to
it. We must accustom ourselves to the idea that the Romano-
Germanic world, together with its culture, is our most
implacable enemy. We must topple and crush under foot the
idols of the Western social ideals and prejudices that have
guided the thought of our intelligentsia to the present moment.
Once we have freed our thought and our attitudes toward life
from their oppressive European blinders, we must draw out of
ourselves, out of the treasure-trove of our Russian national

spirit, the elements necessary for the creation of a new world view. It is in this spirit that we must nurture the next generation. After we have completely abandoned our idolatry of Western civilization, we must use every means possible to work for the creation of an independent national culture shaped by this new world view, which will be validated by this culture. In this immense, all-encompassing task, there is a place for everyone, not only for theoreticians, thinkers, artists, and scholars, but for technicians and ordinary citizens as well. A revolution in world view is the only duty that confronts *everyone*.

This is a vital, fundamental task for the entire Russian intelligentsia. If it is not successfully completed, Russia will never be liberated from slavery. At present, intellectual efforts in this direction are being made by a few people, but this is not enough; such efforts must become universal. By their very nature these efforts must be made primarily in Soviet Russia. And it would seem that such efforts are being made. Letters arriving from there frequently contain indications of profound shifts and changes in the world views of the most diverse people, and of their thirst for a creativity permeated with a completely new spirit. However, these same letters also indicate that intellectual labors of this sort have been driven underground and smothered. Above all else, the Bolsheviks want to indoctrinate everyone with their outworn, vulgarly simplistic world view, which cannot satisfy any thinking person; they fear every manifestation of free thought, obstruct the exchange of non-Marxist ideas, and thus hinder the intellectual and moral rebirth of the Russian intelligentsia. Because they have their own, extremely limited understanding of what the culture of a communist state should be, they try to suppress utterly every effort in the direction of a truly national cultural creativity.

These inauspicious circumstances in Soviet Russia make the efforts of the Russian emigration especially important. We Russian emigrés are not oppressed by the Soviet censors, and we are not required to be Marxists. We can think, say, and write what we like, and if any of our ideas elicit repressive actions against us wherever we happen to be living, we can always move. So it is our duty to carry out the immense cultural task that is so often beset with insuperable difficulties in Russia. This task is immeasurably more important than the futile political bickering and squabbling that now engrosses our public figures. If the Russian emigration truly wants to play an honorable role in the history of Russia, it must cast aside this worthless political gamesmanship and take up the task of restructuring our spiritual culture. Otherwise future historians will rightfully pronounce a harsh sentence upon us.

Sofia,
September 1921

5 The Temptation of Religious Union*

The existence of several Christian Churches, each of which calls itself Christ's only true Church and denies the others the right to this name is the greatest temptation for every believing Christian. The temptation becomes all the more dangerous because the Prince of This World in the guise of socialism, Christianity's enemy, in striving to create a godless state and deprive people of religion, attempts to use the division of the Churches in his interests. Wherever possible, anti-Christian, socialist, or half-socialist governments fight the Church dominant in their countries, seek support in the other Christian Churches, and set one Church against another, according to the principle "divide and conquer." It is only natural that many believers find the idea of the unification of the Churches quite palatable. At first sight, this idea seems pleasing to God and informed with the true Christian spirit of love and reconciliation, which lends it great moral glamour and puts the proponents of division and religious isolation at a disadvantage. They appear narrow-minded, dogmatic, and prone to fanatic obscurantism. But at closer inspection the picture changes. If we give the idea of the unification of the Churches more thought, we will realize that its piety is questionable and its Christian spirit is illusory.

When an outsider, a nonbeliever, makes it his business to preach the unification of the Churches, his idea obviously contains nothing Christian or valuable for religion. Such a

*Originally as "Soblazny edineniia" in *Rossiia i latinstvo*, Berlin 1923, pp. 121-140. Translated by Anatoly Liberman.

person seeks unification for reasons alien to Christianity, be they politics or some other earthly, human, transient expedience. And indeed for real politics the unification of the Churches would be most desirable. A nonbeliever, who is, however, a convinced opponent of socialism and communism, would like to enlist Christianity among his allies in the struggle against a common enemy; such a politician regrets the fact that division into separate Churches physically weakens Christianity, for division means internecine strife. He does not care to know why the Churches are so bitterly opposed to each other and would be happy to see them united. For him who stands outside any Church, Christianity, and perhaps any religion, the unification of the Churches is as desirable as the notorious unification of all "state-oriented elements of society," and of all bourgeois parties, with their fighting and bickering about petty programmatic issues at a time when it would be much wiser to lay aside insignificant differences and form a "single," "antisocialist," or "anti-Bolshevik" front against a common enemy.

The unification of the Churches can also seem attractive to a nonbeliever standing outside one of the Churches, a died-in-the-wool anti-Semite, who regards the unification of all Christians as a powerful weapon against worldwide Jewish domination. Finally, many a nationalist among peoples torn by confessional differences may wish for the unification of the Churches, in order to strengthen his people's national unity and increase their power of resistance in the struggle for their ideals. Beyond doubt, from the standpoint of such politicians and of common sense, the idea of unification has a good deal to recommend it. But it is equally clear that a believing Christian will not share such views. For a believing Christian the Church is not simply one of many factors of social or political life. For him the Church is something eternal, whose fate he cannot discuss in terms of the transient interests of international politics or social and national struggle. To be sure, the Church is not indifferent to the vicissitudes and results of this struggle, but a believer and an unbeliever have opposite views on the relation between the interests of the Church and interests of this struggle.

The Church will welcome and bless a life style that will allow it to successfully carry out its task of saving souls; it will be overjoyed to see the broad masses renounce godless and irreligious doctrines and leaders. But it cannot, for the sake of transient earthly well-being, give up its dogmas and its structure, which it regards as the divinely established foundations of the Church edifice rather than as time-honored relics bequeathed to it by history. To give up its indispensable dogmas and statutes would mean to kill the Church, to make it a false institution, and such an act could not be compensated for by any earthly benefits. Besides, a Christian believer has his own historiography based on divine revelations and prophesies, and from the standpoint of this historiography a Christian and a politician have a dissimilar perspective on social, political, national, and racial struggle. Such concepts as struggle, defeat, and victory are treated differently by a believer and by a political outsider, and their ideas of expedience are also different. They speak at cross-purposes when it comes to the unification of the Churches and will never reach an agreement. The two points of view are incompatible. A believer should once and for all give up a political or any other earthly, transient (even if expedient) approach to this problem.

For a believing Christian the question of the unification entails a number of irreconcilable internal contradictions. Indeed, even to discuss this question, a believing Christian should place himself outside any Church and look upon himself as a judge of the Churches. Such a situation contradicts the basic principles of belonging to a Church. Someone who belongs to a church, who recognizes that he is a branch capable of bearing fruit only on a vine, that he has value only insofar as he is a member of the Church, suddenly places his mind above the wisdom of the Church. Even though this withdrawal from the Church is temporary, conditional, and imaginary, it contains the anti-Christian spirit of human pride directed against the Church. To find a way of unifying the Churches means to eliminate the differences between them, which is possible only if some of the opinions separating the Churches are declared erroneous. But where are the criteria for such a declaration? What should guide me in settling the differences? The word of God, a free interpretation of the Holy Writ? But then the believer begins to address God without an intermediary and rejects the Church as an obstacle hindering his communication with God. If this is possible in one situation, then why not in all? In such a case no Church is needed, and the whole problem becomes moot; at best it has some interest from the point of view of political expedience.

However casuistic the foregoing argument may seem, it is not irrelevant. All attempts to talk about the unification of the Churches from the point of view of "pure," "nonconfessional" Christianity are fundamentally contradictory, for even asking this question conceals the negation of its idea, namely, the idea of the Church. These attempts deny the Church and are permeated with the anti-Christian spirit of arrogance and the self-assertion of the human mind. The same spirit is felt in such widespread statements as "the barriers between the Churches do not reach Heaven"[1] and the like. Such statements presuppose that the Church is a superfluous structure, a hindrance; the center of gravity is shifted to the individual believer, who appears capable of judging the errors of all Churches and rectifying them with his own mind.

Given such a view of an individual believer, it will be more natural to abolish all Churches as antiquated, misleading relics rather than unifying them. And if a believer standing on such a nonconfessional platform keeps insisting on the unification of the Churches and on seeking practical ways for achieving this end, he apparently means that he does not need any Church,

---

[1]This statement has been mistakenly ascribed to Metropolitan Philaret, but it belongs to Bishop Platon of Kiev, who made it as "vindication" when on an inspection tour of his diocese he was "embarrassed" by a Catholic priest

but other simple-minded people, in their weakness, cannot do without a Church, and for their sake the many existing Churches should be replaced with a new one, if possible without the drawbacks and errors made by the separate Churches. Needless to say, this arrogance has nothing to do with Christianity.

However, the "nonconfessional" approach can sometimes go together with the recognition of the Church; it is typical of those believing Christians who deny the fact of the division of the Churches. According to this approach, there was no division; the Pope and the Patriarch of Constantinople, both ambitious, power-hungry men, simply quarreled one day. There is allegedly no heresy in either Catholicism or Orthodoxy, for no heresy of which the Churches accuse each other has been officially condemned by any Ecumenical Council; consequently, all these "heresies" are only different opinions, and there is nothing wrong in any of them. The Universal Church is still undivided, as evidenced by the fact that the rituals performed by bishops and priests of either domination are recognized by both Churches. For example, when Catholics become Orthodox, they are not rebaptized; if they are married, they are not rewed; if they have taken holy orders, they are not reordained, nor is another laying on of hands required. So (these people say) one can very well be a Christian in general and stay in the fold of the Universal, Ecumenical, Apostolic Church, without being Orthodox or Catholic.

This argumentation is debatable from both a historical and a canonical point of view. I would only emphasize its factual untenability. The division of the Churches is an incontestable fact. For a united Church to exist, it is not enough to have an idea of unity; a common life is also necessary. But there is no common life. There are two absolutely independent lives. We do not have two parts of one Church making up a single living whole; rather we see before us two separate living organisms, each of which calls itself a Church and teaches in its own way. The imaginary "Christian in general, belonging to the Church, but neither Catholic nor Orthodox, is unthinkable. If he stays outside both, he apparently looks upon each of them as false and denies the existence of a true Church on earth; consequently, he has left the fold of the Church. Belonging to a "nonconfessional Church" remains a *contradictio in adjecto* and, not unexpectedly, leads to a crying internal contradiction: what began as an argument for the unchanged existence of the Universal Church ended as negation of the true Church; what began as a desire to stay in the fold of the Ecumenical Church ended as an act of excommunication from any Church.[2]

Thus, the nonconfessional approach to the unification of the Churches is fraught with internal contradictions. However, this fact has no practical significance, for the problem will be solved (assuming it can be solved) by representatives of denominations, that is, of the Churches, at their Council, not by nonconfessional Christians. How then should a person sharing the confessional point of view regard this question—I mean a person belonging to one denomination and sincerely convinced that his Church is the only Church of Christ? Such a Christian will look upon any other denomination as heresy, at best as schism, and can imagine the unification only as the conversion of the heretics and schismatics, with their subsequent incorporation into the one true Church—his own. But this approach makes unification impossible, because every Church that considers itself true will reason in the same way. For the Church to deviate from such a position would mean to doubt that it is true and infallible. The Church can meet heretics at a Council only to expose them, to witness their repentance, and take them into its fold. But it will not allow heretics to teach it,

---

[2]A perfect illustration of this statement is the autobiography of a priest named Tolstoy (if memory does not fail me, it was published in *Byloe* for 1916 or 1917 [see index]), an active proponent of the view of the still extant Universal Church. He wished to remain in the fold of the Church without fully committing himself to either Catholicism or Orthodoxy; as a result, he found himself outside the Church.

unless it agrees to admit its own heresy, which is of course out of the question.

None of this should be treated as an expression of stubbornness, inflated ambition, a desire to protect one's prestige. Such criteria are applicable to individuals, not to the Church. An individual, a member of the Church, who wants his ideas to spread, may only submit them to a Council of the Church to which he belongs and let the Church judge them. And if the Church condemns his ideas, he will have to give them up, for his teachings have been proven false, heretical, and he cannot remain a member of his Church if he persists in them. If such a person, despite condemnation, does not recant, he could be accused of stubbornness, pride, undue ambition, and above all, of disobedience; excommunication would be an appropriate punishment for him.

But the situation changes completely when our subject is the Church. At that imaginary Council it will meet heretics, outsiders. Their judgment means nothing to the Church, and since the Church differs from a private individual in being infallible and in having the right to judge (note that these are the Church's inherent features; without them there is no Church), the predicates of pride, ambition, and stubbornness are inapplicable to it. It cannot let heretics judge its teachings. At the Council it itself will judge heretics, accept in their teachings what is consonant with its dogmas, and reject the rest. But for this to happen, the heretics must recognize the right of the Church to judge them. And herein lies the most insurmountable difficulty.

At the Council that is expected to accomplish the unification of the Churches, each Church will try to judge the other ones as heretical and will not subject itself to judgment. This is the principal difference between our imaginary Council and any other. At any other Council, all the members have the same point of departure, namely, the authority of the Church to which they belong. The opponents defend their arguments in the hope of making them part of the Church doctine, and the

Church examines them and formulates its view, which, once it has been accepted, becomes obligatory for all. At our imaginary Council, nothing of the sort happens, for it will not consist of members of one Church united by obedience to its authority; participants will be two (or more) independent Churches, and each will consider itself true and look upon the other members of the Council as excommunicated heretics.

Nothing will change even if all the members of the Council happen to share the nonconfessional approach. We have seen that this approach leads to negation of true Church, to recognizing all Churches as equally false, that is, to one's voluntary excommunication from the Church. Under such circumstances, the members of the Council would have to treat themselves as heretics, and the main prerequisite of success—a single authority—would still be absent.

A Council convened to unify the Churches could attain something only if one Church or several Churches surrendered to another or if the Churches met as partners with equal authority. In both cases the Council would look more like a gathering of laymen, a peace conference, a congress at which enemies try to come to terms, a meeting of reconciliation, and the like. The surrender, the capitulation of one Church, cannot be considered even as a theoretical possibility. It would mean conversion of a whole denomination to some other, but conversion is thinkable only as an individual act, an event affecting a single person. It has happened before that a bishop would change his denomination and part of his flock would follow him, but only part, not the whole of it. The aforementioned capitulation would have similar consequences: the head of the Church, the bishops, and some priests and laymen would leave their Church and change their denomination, but if even a handful of people refused to follow them, the Church would survive, and neither a formal nor an actual unification would occur.

The second case seems especially attractive and natural to outsiders, to those who do not belong to any Church, but it cannot satisfy a thinking Christian. When the negotiating sides are two opposed organizations of laymen, two countries, or employees and employers, they try to reach an agreement by mutual concessions and compromises—a tug of war depending on the balance of power and material interests; justice and morality are insignificant in this struggle and are chiefly called upon to influence public opinion. This is to be expected, for there is no supreme judge standing above the two sides at such negotiations. When two negotiating countries turn to an arbiter, they do not seek a supreme being: each side looks for an ally, that is, for an entity of the same order as they are, and a third party can play the role of an arbiter only because it has no vested interest in the cause. But even this arbiter will be guided by the power game and material interests rather than by abstract principles, and if the negotiating countries disagree with the arbiter's decision, they may make their own solutions or simply stand up and leave. Similar relations obtain when employers and employees turn to the government for assistance.

If the Christian Churches should meet as equal partners to discuss their unification, they will end up in exactly the same position as the one described above; only no arbiter will be found unless they decide to turn to the assistance of Moslems, Jews, or Buddhists! Mutual concessions and compromises will be dictated by the partners' relative strength and "interests," but since the main dogmas, sacred canons, and statutes are at stake, the negotiations will degenerate into an unworthy bargaining over principles and sacred objects. As soon as we imagine such negotiations and compromises (for instance, "take our Filioque but give us the infallibility of the Pope" or "we will give up the immaculate conception, but you must give up the eucharist in two kinds," and the like), we will realize that the only result of this procedure will be a temptation for the believers. Such a unification will be tantamount to the moral death of all Churches.

Both possibilities of the unification of the Churches by *human means*—capitulation and compromises—presuppose special historical conditions. The capitulation would be thinkable only in case one Church (or all Churches except one) were cornered by a godless government or a government supporting the other Church. As for negotiations, the "balance of power" that would determine the entire procedure would also reflect the circumstances under which the Churches function in different countries, so that the Churches would become political factors, obey the temporary, transient conditions of political life, and renounce their role, which is atemporal and not of this world.

Any believer who is accustomed to look upon the Church as the Bride of Christ and a ladder connecting man to his God, rather than as a "factor" of political and social life, will never agree to bringing the Church down to earth in this manner and will never accept the changes in the dogmas, canons, and hierarchy that will result from the "balance of power," once the "Churches" have been reduced to mere political factors. They will regard the dignitaries of their Church who will succumb at that imaginary Council to compromise or surrender and sign the act of unification as private individuals, as people who have yielded to earthly temptations, abused their power, and betrayed the Church. And one can be certain that the quasi-Church which will emerge as the result of such negotiations will be in the believers' eyes not the true Church but the fruit of a mortal sin.

This is the main point! A unification dictated by political contingencies and presupposing either the humiliation of one of the Churches or concessions in matters of principle will arouse the discontent of some members of one or several Churches and will at the very least leave many Christians dissatisfied. These people will not recognize the unification and will consider themselves as belonging to the old Church (in their opinion, the only true Church) and look upon the advocates of the new, quasi-united Church as apostates. However diplomatic the terms of the unification might be, the compromise or the capitulation (in any case, the transient character of the act) would be too obvious for the authority of the new, unified Church to overcome the efforts at secession on the part of the members of the old Church. No matter what the new "united" Church should do, all its persecution and anathema will not prevail against the proponents of the old, steadfast, unwavering true Church, whereas the "united" Church will become a new denomination based on compromise with heretics and schismatics.

Thus the unification by human means will not abolish the former multitude of Churches, will not diminish the number of Churches that lay claim to being true; it will only add to them one more uniate Church also calling itself the single Holy, Ecumenical, Apostolic, Universal Church. Will all of this contribute to the well-being of Christianity, will it reinforce Christianity in its struggle with external enemies? No! On the contrary, it will only weaken Christianity physically and morally. For even if the number of Christians who refuse to join the new uniate Church and remain true to their old Church happens to be small, the importance of their dissent will not be diminished by this fact; in questions of faith and truth the number of believers plays no role: there were more Arians than Orthodox, and yet they were heretics; in the beginning there were, and there still are, more pagans and atheists than Christians, and yet they are what they are: pagans and atheists.

At first sight so pleasing to God and conducive to the good of Christianity, all attempts at the unification of the Churches will have consequences deleterious to Christianity. The contradiction between the pious exterior and the baleful nature of the idea of unification by *human means* points clearly to its anti-Christian origin. It is no wonder that this idea so often finds favor with outsiders, with people not belonging to any Church. On closer scrutiny, one sees in it the intrigues of the wily enemy of Christ's faith, Satan, who puts on the guise of Christian piety to tempt even the faithful sons of the Church. If such a unification ever takes place, it will happen in the kingdom of the

Antichrist, and those who will stay away from it will be the few righteous ones prophesied in the Scriptures.

A true unification of the Churches cannot be achieved by human means alone. It can happen only by Divine Providence, as a miracle. And we believe and know that this miraculous unification of all Christians into one flock with a single Shepherd will indeed occur in the last days, when all the prophesies have been fulfilled, when all that is hidden has become known, and all doubts have been dispelled. But we do not and cannot know what concrete forms this miraculous, true unification of the Churches will take.[3] A miracle cannot be predicted, and God's ways are not our ways. But we must believe that in the last days the Churches will be united, and this miraculous true unification will in principle be different from what can be accomplished by human hands under the leadership of the Antichrist, the false unifier.

What practical consequences follow from the above? First of all, every believing Christian who is aware that there is no salvation outside the Church must belong soul and body to the Church that has revealed itself to him as true. He must belong to it not because his parents baptized him there when he had no choice; it is the inner unity with the Church that matters. And his belonging to the Church should find its expression in his active participation in Church life to the best of his abilities, rather than in a statement in his passport. If a Christian detects faults and imperfections in Church life, he must do all he can to improve the situation. A Christian, an Orthodox Christian as well, has every opportunity for that; even a layman can influence the organization of the Church by participating in the life of his parish and his district. If his efforts fail, a true son of the Church should not lose heart and remember that the path to salvation is narrow and difficult. In any case, shortcomings in Church life and imperfections of the clergy should not make a believer doubt the true nature of the Church and seek a path to salvation

[3]A curious sample of lay theologians' guesses on this subject is Vladimir Solov'ev's famous tale *On the Antichrist*.

outside it. Such doubts and such strivings are from the Devil, who wants to bring a believer to self-excommunication, close to him the only path to salvation, and see him go into perdition. A true Christian sees that besides his own true Church of Christ, there are other "churches" in the world which lay claim to being universal and that many people belonging to them are undoubtedly true Christians who have gone astray through ignorance or under the pressure of historical circumstances; he must grieve for them and constantly pray that God should convert these lost Christians and bring them into the fold of the true Church. But we must always remember that the unification of all true Christians in one Holy, Ecumenical, Apostolic Church cannot be accomplished by human means; it will be achieved by the will of God, as a miracle, in the last days. Any other unification of the Churches by human means will be a false step pleasing only to the enemy of Christ's faith, the Antichrist. A Christian should qualify such endeavors as a Satanic temptation and resist it.

The Holy Orthodox Church has always had its eye toward the Lord; it has not looked aside, not cared about its power on earth, and has not bowed to the human mind. It also demands from its members that they not rely on their power on earth and on their mind. If all Churches displayed the same humility before God's might, the same love of God, and boundless loyalty to him, they would lead believers to the same goal, to God, and would lead them there by a straight path, without squandering their energies and frittering away their time on extraneous tasks. And the closer we are to this single goal, the closer all Christians will be to one another. For only in the love of God are people united, and only on this love does the Christian love of one's neighbor rest. And only such a gradual coming together through the pursuit of a common goal, which is God, only a common love of God coupled with humility and renunciation of worldly vanities can prepare the way for the complete amalgamation of all true Christians that will come to pass miraculously in the last days by the will of God.

We, weak people, have no other means to achieve this goal; nor is anything else required of us. We the Orthodox know that our Church leads us along the true path. Let us put our trust in its guidance, make its spirit our own, and follow it without looking aside. Let us resist the temptation of power on earth, the temptation of the omniscient human mind, and the temptation to solve the fortunes of Christianity by human means. Let us be humble and entrust ourselves unconditionally to the beneficial authority of the Holy Orthodox Church, which knows the true path to God. And may other Churches follow its example. They will merge with it miraculously, by the will of God, in the last days.

Editorial Addenda

Fragments and section summaries from N. S. Trubetzkoy's "The Religions of India and Christianity" (1922)[4]

I. When one begins to speak about the exodus to the East, about facing the East, one runs the risk of being misunderstood. Such statements can be interpreted as an appeal to assimilate one of the "Oriental" cultures or at least part of these cultures. And since the most conspicuous difference between any "Oriental" culture and the culture of the West lies in the religious sphere, the appeal to face the East can be taken for one's gravitation toward some "Oriental" religion.

In our transitional epoch marked by the disappointment in what seemed to be the inviolate achievement of European culture, disoriented people, who feel that a radical change is needed but are unable to tell what should be changed, often look in the direction of the East. They hope to carry out a synthesis between Christianity and "Oriental religions." This trend is old; it sprang up in the West, chiefly in the Anglo-

[4]Originally as "Religii Indii i khristianstvo," in *Na putiakh,* Berlin 1922, pp. 177-229.

Saxon countries, where Christianity, unencumbered by belonging to the Church and by dogmas, has long since degenerated into sheer hypocrisy. The passion for theosophy came from there and infected the Russian intelligentsia, whose ties with the Church are weak, whose knowledge of Orthodoxy is meager, and which has always been in the habit of satisfying its religious needs everywhere except Orthodoxy—a source declared unfit by definition.

Few are attracted by the religions of the "Far East." The religion of China, based on the veneration of dead ancestors and on the cult of demons and forces of nature, is too alien to our religious psychology. We marvel at the equanimity of the Chinese, their lack of fear of impending old age and death, their indifferent, even businesslike attitude toward death, and we may sometimes envy these traits. But all of this is absolutely alien to us; we realize that their religious psychology is a product of millennia of spiritual development which has nothing to do with us, so none of us is going to turn Chinese.

Roughly the same can be said about Islam. We admire the spiritual discipline of the Moslem world, its magnificent unity, the inner coherence of its world view, in which the law, religion, and realities of daily life form an indissoluble whole. But when we open the Koran to find in it an answer to our religious searchings, we feel disappointed. The dogmas of Islam appear elementary, shallow, and trivial, its morality strikes us as crude and primitive, and none of us can become a faithful Moslem.

But the so-called mysticism of the East, that is, the religious, philosophical, and mystical systems of India and Sufism, has a tremendous appeal to every Europeanized Russian intellectual. Theosophy derives from this mysticism and attempts to synthesize it with Christianity, cabala, and all kinds of magical and mystical teachings related to cabala.

The craze for "Oriental mysticism" is rooted in two misunderstandings. In the first place, this mysticism comes to us from proselytizing theosophic treatises, which are either devoid of any methodology or, what is even worse, are written in a pseudoscientific way. Besides that, people who study the "mysticism of the East" and who want to synthesize it with Christianity have a very vague idea of Christianity and divorce it from the historical Christianity as it is revealed in the works of the great saints and the Fathers of the Church. Since they are not well versed in the Christian teachings, they overlook the fundamental differences between these teachings and the systems of Oriental mysticism and philosophy; they overrate the chance and superficial similarity of detail, which they take for inner identity. That is why in examining the "mysticism of the East" one should treat it from a reliable historical perspective and assess it from the standpoint of the Christian dogmas explained to us by the Holy Fathers and the Apostles.

[*Editor's section summaries. II.* Satan is a real person, the leader of the whole legion of devils. Revelations can come from God and from the Devil, and most of the revelations received by the mystics all over the world are of Satanic origin. *III.* Only those "gods" to whom men pray for morally valuable gifts can be treated as the indistinctly realized elements of a truly divine image. All other recipients of worship are devils. *IV.* In the Vedic period, Indians worshipped the great gods who were (contrary to popular belief) unconnected with natural phenomena. The most outstanding figures of that pantheon are Varunas and Indra. Varunas is the creator of the world, and he laid down the laws of morality; he is the only incorruptible god. Indra is the embodiment of brute force, greedy for sacrifices. *V.* From the point of view of Christian theology only Varunas is a divine image; all the other "gods" are devils. Varunas and Indra could not coexist as equally important gods, and in the later parts of the *Rig-Veda* we see the victorious Indra. The defeat of Varunas determined the entire subsequent development of Indian religious thought. *VI.* With the ousting of Varunas, the world, devoid of justice and reason, appeared to Indians as a place in which every "god" pulled his own way and could disrupt the natural course of events. The supreme beings had to be propitiated, and therefore the knowledge of rituals came to the foreground (old Brahmanism). Worship began to be regarded as a tool for achieving miracles. The gods themselves turned into priests, and men vied with them for accumulating magic force. Man aspired to become God. Religion almost lost its function, and life emerged as the reign of chaos; but since the world is apparently governed by laws, a divine substratum of the universe was invented (Brahma). At first Brahma was a nonanthropomorphic substance, a reservoir of being, a surrogate of the absolute God. The idea of transmigration of souls is a logical continuation of the doctrine of Brahma. Karma (i.e., the ability of every living creature to predetermine the subsequent incarnation of its soul) has little to do with morality, for this concept was mainly used to justify division into castes. *VII.* The next stage in the development of the Indian religious thought is characterized by attempts to break away from the senseless cycle of being, with souls constantly changing their bodily integuments. The greatest philosophers did without the idea of the Divine and without morality. *VIII.* (An overview of Buddhism). For a true Buddhist, love, charity, and compassion are a psychophysical exercise and the result of the atrophy of all feelings (on the way to nirvana one can easily sacrifice himself for others). Buddha taught that since the old gods had not reached nirvana, people could rise above the gods. In this pronouncement dethronement of the gods reached its culmination. *IX.* The idea of nirvana, that is, of spiritual suicide, became possible only because Indra had defeated Varunas, the creator of the world, the guardian of morality. The devil left his imprint on the concept of nirvana, on the immeasurable pride of Buddhism (man is declared to be above the gods and the master of his fate and of his role in the cosmos), and on the doctrine of love and forgiveness as a psychophysical exercise required for spiritual suicide. *X.* Hinduism (or new Brahmanism) sought to find a more tenable system of ideas for the ordinary man. Its gods are Vishnu and Siva, surrounded by lesser divinities. "In Hinduism everything impresses, everthing appeals to the imagination. The architecture of its temples is glorious and grotesque, the service is magnificent, the statues of the gods and goddesses are monstrous and fantastic. Equally colorful, fantastic, and grotesquely confusing are its myths, which resemble a tropical forest, all overgrown with lianas. It is these traits that allowed Hinduism to defeat Buddhism: the popular mind was more susceptible to bright colors and monstrous images than to the philosophizing of the Buddhist monks, who over time turned into the most detestable breed of mealy-mouthed hypocrites" (220). *XI.* From a Christian point of view the entire history of Indian religious thought has been dominated by Satan. *XII.* No synthesis between Indian mysticism and Christianity is possible. *End of editor's summaries.*]

Concluding paragraphs of section XII. Attempts to combine God with the Devil will always seem blasphemous to a Christian. This is not what we mean when we speak about "facing the East". No, Russia does not need a new faith. Eastern Orthodoxy, which is the purest type of true Christianity, which has succeeded in protecting itself from the Satanic temptation of power on earth, as we see it in Catholicism, and from the temptation of pride, as we see it in Protestantism, with its adoration of the human mind and rebellion against authority, this Eastern Orthodoxy must remain the treasure that we have to cherish and for whose gift Russia should incessantly thank the Almighty. We will not exchange our faith for any other religion, be the spirit of Satan manifest or hidden in it.

But if we have no need to learn a new faith from the non-Christian East, we can borrow something from its religious life, namely, its attitude toward religion. This religion may be a Satanic pseudodoctrine from our standpoint. What matters is that its adepts treat it as one should treat a true religion. We Christians know and often repeat that earthly life is transient, that its blessings are vanities and that faith and the salvation of one's soul are more important than our daily cares. Yet the people among us who translate these words into actions and put the salvation of their souls above everything else are exceptions, and we marvel at them. But in India, in periods of catastrophic dearth so typical of that country, entire villages die of starvation and leave their herds of cows untouched, for no one will slaughter them despite the famine: such is the power their religious laws prohibiting people to eat the flesh of their cattle! The conviction that the salvation of one's soul is the only important matter, more important than all earthly riches and even life itself, is a mechanical formula for us. Among Christians it has become a guiding principle for a few, whereas in India everyone obeys it, and therefore it is a motor of their social life.

This is what we have to learn! We must keep intact the dogmas of our faith, Eastern Orthodoxy, and make faith the center of our existence as it has happened in India. We must learn to live according to our faith and look upon it as the determining factor in our daily life, rather than as a set of abstract formulas. And only when this active attitude toward our Russian faith becomes habitual to most Russians, can we hope to create a new national Russian culture, for great cultures are always religious, while irreligious cultures fall into decay. But such a shift in the attitude toward religion is the personal task of every individual, and the creation of the national religious culture is contingent on a change of mind in each of us. This dependence of the communal on the individual, of the external (i.e., culture) on the internal is perhaps the main difference between the "Oriental" solution of life problems and the "Western" one.

6 At the Door: Reaction? Revolution?*

In political and cultural life, *left* and *right* are relative concepts. Everything depends on the starting point. A leftist ideal always looks back on a certain ideological *status quo*, which presents in relation to it, a rightist ideology. This original ideological *status quo* can survive even after the leftist ideal has emerged victorious and materialized as sociopolitical reality: the relation between *left* and *right* will not be affected, and the rightist ideology, even in opposition rather than serving as the protector of the existing order, will still be rightist, i.e., reactionary. Strictly speaking, the rightist ideology is always based on the immediate past and the modern state of things interests it only insofar as this state is an immediate continuation of the past. Rightist ideology is hostile to change not only when change is a figment of leftist imagination but also when it has become reality. The leftist ideals that become reality remain leftist as long as they appear new: only as long as the idea of their novelty is preserved will their defense remain a leftist cause and the right wing fight them. But a stage can be reached when the novelty of these ideals becomes so weak and so vague that their defenders will turn from left wing ideologists into conservatives and their opponents will begin to attack the once leftist ideals as outdated, worthless, and in need of replacement. Because their own new ideals will not signify a return to the *immediately* preceding *status quo*, their defenders will now be in the left wing, and the former leftists in the right, conservative wing.

*Originally as "U dverei. Reaktsiia? Revoliutsiia?" *Evraziiskii vremennik* 3, 1923, pp. 18-29. Translated by Anatoly Liberman.

In European life, the growth of new ideals pushing old ones into the outdated *status quo* has, on the whole, proceeded along a straight line so far. Therefore, the terms *right* and *left* were at any given moment appropriate. Each new ideal was indeed more "to the left" than the immediately preceding one, because it went further in the same direction, leaving the initial *status quo* more and more behind in politics; democracy—socialism—communism, constitutional-parliamentary-Soviet, constitutional monarchy—democratic republic—Soviet Federal Socialist Republic—all these triads of ideals are points on a line going from right to left. But one can imagine rectilinear movement that has reached its limit, i.e., a wall blocking further progress. In this situation, the next new ideal using the immediately preceding *status quo* as its point of departure will not be more to the left (for this is physically impossible) but somewhere beyond the straight line on which leftist and rightist ideals have heretofore been placed. All this holds for theories of national relations, religious convictions, and so forth, just as well as far socio-political theories.

When one looks at political, social, and cultural life in Europe and Russia, one cannot avoid the conclusion that the "leftist" ideologies which have so far determined this life have not only lost their freshness, but have become eroded and worn out and acquired a patina of dogmatism and protective obscurantism. This is equally true of the countries that have long since implemented "leftist" political ideals and enjoy "progressive" reputations and of the young republics that have recently become "progressive." The laws of "the protection of the republic" and constant fear of "counterrevolution" are typical modern phenomena testifying to the loss by the once leftist ideologies of their former youthful freshness and vigor. Modern leftist theories and practice are informed by a strange dogmatism and fear of novelty, i.e. with features characteristic of conservative and reactionary ideologies. Leftism smacks of officialdom and, what is more important, of decrepitude. Those who sincerely believe in leftist ideologies are usually old, or they belong to a bygone generation. Leftist declarations from those who are really modern sound like an official lie sanctified by higher authority, a lie in which the speakers themselves have no faith.

The deterioration of the once leftist ideologies should have resulted in the rise of new, even more radical ones. But the extreme leftist ideas invented by peoples and partly realized in Russia, for instance, are the limit of leftism, beyond which movement in the same direction is impossible: these ideas already signify a certain *reductio ad absurdum*, an approach to the point in which plus infinity becomes minus infinity. It is no wonder that in search of a way out of this impasse our contemporaries look to the right rather than to the left. We are living at a strange time when "children" either lack principles altogether or are more to the right than "fathers." Yet a mere turn to the right can under no circumstances offer a way out of our predicament. History never moves straight back; besides, the former ideological *status quo*, the starting point of the former leftist (now obscurantist) ideologies, is devoid of vitality and has been left behind. If people no longer believe in the once so attractive "leftist" ideals, if the theoretical foundations of these ideals seem to smack of officialdom and be made up of cliches and platitudes, the same is true of the "rightist" ideologies to which modern people turn in despair now that leftism has lost its appeal. The very fact that at one time (indeed, at a very recent time, when from the cultural point of view the situation did not differ from ours) the rightist ideologies failed to defend themselves, to satisfy our contemporaries, and to stop them from moving left is clear evidence of their impotence.

It would be absurd to refer to the blindness of "progressive society" that failed or refused to appreciate the salutary essence of the rightist ideologies: had these rightist ideologies been strong and full of vitality, a spontaneous rejection of them would have been unthinkable. Only people with a short memory can idealize the recent past, but, since the average human memory is not so short, the illusory character of this idealization very soon becomes evident. The fact remains that when the rightist ideologies ruled our society, many people lived better than now, and still most were dissatisfied not only with life but also (most importantly) with these ideologies, and in search of more satisfactory ideologies they veered to the left. Now no one believes in the leftist ideologies, and many live worse than before. It follows that the way chosen by the majority was wrong, but we must not return to the unsatisfactory situation which engendered the desire to change the old ideologies and forms of life. A return to the "rightist" ideological *status quo* which was tested and found unsatisfactory can be understood only as an attempt to play the entire game again, to return to the initial point and after having realized that the "leftist" path is wrong, to try another path. But then the rightist ideology is not an ideal in the proper sense of this word; however, to show people the way out of their impasse, one needs an ideal rather than a mere admission of the fact that they have run up against a wall.

The spontaneous movement to the right, modern man's instinctive desire to return to the "good old days," is only a sign of despair. This mindset is bred by a strong sense of disappointment with the present state of affairs and idealized recollections of the recent past; there is no clear, conscious ideology in this blend. The ideological poverty of the contemporary rightist movement is apparent to any impartial observer. Furthermore, the theoretical concepts characterizing some forms of the rightist movement contradict the basic spirit of any truly rightist ideology. The right wing has so long rubbed shoulders with the leftists that it seems to have caught the attitudes that are the foundation of leftist ideologies.

The examples are plentiful. Monarchists among the Russian emigrés have the same trust in the magical saving force of legal formulas that have always characterized the leftist ideologies; the difference is that the leftists believed in democratic republic, universal suffrage, and so forth as a source of happiness for all, whereas the rightists expect similar results and equally soon from the restoration of monarchy. And because the rightists look on monarchy as a complex of legal norms that work like magic independent of time, place, and personalities, monarchism naturally turns into legitimism. And herein lies the ideological contradiction of the entire approach. Insofar as the head of state is viewed as the sum of legal rights to ascension to the throne, the monarch will not be a living personality concentrating the national will but an algebraic sign. Such a view would be natural for a republican or a populist parliamentarian for whom the head of the state is a mere signing machine in human form, but it is hard to relate such a mechanization of monarchy to the genuine monarchist spirit.

The mechanical legitimism permeating the mentality of the leaders of the modern rightist movement bears witness to the ideological helplessness, the ideological poverty of reaction as a movement straight back: these leaders have only idealized recollections of the recent "good old days." Therefore, it is natural that the leaders of the right are people more prone than others to idealize the recent past, i.e., people who lived especially well and have lost a great deal. In such circumstances it is also natural that those who are not inclined to idealize the recent past (because their memory is good or because their past was not particularly glorious) stay away from the rightist movement and associate it with the fleshpots, so to speak.

And yet, although the forms of the rightist movement received from its leaders are devoid of ideological content and barren, there is something sincere and healthy in the shift of the younger generations to the right; they act spontaneously, little interested in why they do so. This spontaneous shift conceals an unconscious, instinctive readiness for a new ideology, which alone can take us out of the leftist impasse. The reactionary statements and formulas pronounced in this connection are far from new and only a surrogate of the yet unexpressed and unconscious genuinely new ideology of the future. The familiar phraseology is the result of inertia, of the inability to go beyond the plane of traditional political thinking on which rightism and reaction are opposed to leftism and "progressiveness." Our instinct tells us that the ideology we unconsciously search for lies very far from the extreme left end of the chain of the requisite sociopolitical and socioethical ideologies, but since only this chain is given to us, we involuntarily turn our glances to its extreme right end. However, the cause of this mistake is obvious: we are accustomed to the chain, or straight line, on which all the previous ideologies and formulas called upon to shape sociopolitical life, culture, and *mores* have hitherto been situated from right to left. In actual fact, the spontaneous shift of the younger generation to the right stems from the instinctive, subconscious striving for something new rather than old, and "the old guard" sustained only by recollections of the recent past is constitutionally unable to grasp the meaning of this movement and to lead it.

The ideology of the future does not lie on the familiar straight line. It may well be that if we project the new ideology onto this line, the resultant point will be somewhere in its right sections — hence the optical illusion of those who know only the traditional straight line. But the essence of the new ideology which makes it novel, vital, and stimulating cannot be reduced to the fact that its projection is situated to the right of the extreme left point of the rejected ideological chain. This ideology lies on a *different plane.* That is why it is *not reactionary,* it does not signify a return to the recent past; it appeals for a sharp change of direction, for a leap onto an absolutely new plane. It is now a commonplace that there can be no complete return to the past. We hear this statement from leftists and rightists alike. But made by people whose thinking is limited by the old and hopelessly exhausted ideological chain, it sounds nostalgically trivial: the coveted future is visualized by them as a compromise between various old ideologies, a recombination of elements borrowed from various old "programs" and trends; needless to say, this recombination remains on the same exhausted ideological line. Contrariwise, those who reject the whole antiquated ideological line fill the declaration about the impossibility of returning to the immediate past with an entirely different meaning and represent the future as a new organization of life. And this is the only way out of the impasse of our time. The past has been used up, tested to the very end, and hopelessly compromised. We want something really new, we need essentially new elements, not a recombination of old pieces.

Nothing is absolutely new in history. Historical development is unthinkable without historical memory, and this memory provides models and inspiration for new forms. But the rejection of the exhausted "rightist" and "leftist" ideologies does not amount to historical amnesia. On the contrary, those who keep plowing the same ideological ground can be said to possess a short memory: their recollections do not transcend the familiar ideological line; with regard to Russia, they do not go beyond the eighteenth century. Every radical innovation, every new (revolutionary) ideology presupposes a very old historical recollection. It is essential that this recollection be indeed *very old*, that it refer to the time long gone, rather than to the comparatively recent past that attracts the conservative ideologies—reactionary, i.e., backward-looking in the true sense of the word.

The French Revolution, the classic example of a social cataclysm, was permeated with recollections of the Roman republic. Innovation consists in the rejection of the immediate, recent past, not of the past in general; the near past is discarded while remote epochs are used as an ideological model. These *very ancient* elements discovered in the depths of historical memory appear new and revolutionary because they have been transplanted into a new context. In such circumstances, mechanical reproduction of the remote past, i.e., mechanical restoration, is impossible just because this past is so remote. Elements of the remote past, removed from the historical perspective and transplanted into a modern context, take on a new life and begin to inspire original forms of creativity.

Old should be distinguished from *ancient*. A modern painter looks at banal, sentimental icons of the previous century and dismisses them as trash, as completely outmoded, but an Old Russian icon can strike a spark of genuine admiration in him, and he can create something really new, which need not be restoration or even a stylization. A modern painter (if he is a real painter, not a copyist) will never paint like an Old Russian master. The reason is not only that he is a representative of a different culture but also that, despite his admiration for Old Russian painting and his possible indebtedness to it in the future, his starting point is nineteenth century painting, an art which was unknown to an Old Russian master and which leads to a quite different, fundamentally new attitude toward Old Russian icons.

Similar psychological processes are also possible in other areas of art and in ideology. A new ideology, whose starting point is a series of immediately preceding ideologies, can find its inspiration in the remote depths of historical memory and remain new in principle, for elements of antiquity will appear in it in an absolutely new aspect; even if this aspect is distorted from a historical perspective, it will be valuable from the point of view of our time. Any "revolution" (understood as a radical change in the world view) fights the *immediate* past; it cannot be a "restoration," but it can and often does strive for the "restoration" of antiquity.

So the ideals that can take us out of the modern impasse lie outside the plane on which the "rightist" and "leftist" ideals have been situated until now. The feeling that these ideals are to be found somewhere to the right of the familiar leftist ideals is based on an optical illusion, on the habit of projecting everything onto one straight line. The instinctive desire to move back is the result of misunderstanding; there is no salvation in the recent past, and we can only jump over it, to discover sources of inspiration in the remote past and create something really new. What we need is not reaction but a real revolution, i.e., an upheaval in our consciousness.

We have trodden the European ideological path, the straight line from left to right, to the end; not only does it lead to a cul-de-sac, it does not have a single point at which one can stop. The whole of it must be abandoned, once and for all, and a new path should be sought. We Russians must first and foremost give up the European forms of political thought, stop worshipping the (alien) idol of "the form of government," and renounce the belief that a certain ideal legal system will by itself, automatically guarantee common welfare; in a word, we must stop viewing human society as a soulless mechanism, even though all modern sociopolitical ideologies are based on this view. The ideal of the future must be sought in the spirit that creates and cements government through *mores* and a stable ideology, not in perfect legislation. The main task of our time is not to multiply legal speculations but to create a stable spiritual basis and implement it in everyday life.

A longing for a new ideal that conceals salvation in it fills one with anxiety and tension. It is impossible and dangerous to be content with surrogate of the cast-off formulas of reaction. We must realize that this approach is wrong and strain our hearing not to miss the new word. This word must be and will be said. Collective forebodings do not deceive, and collective effort, with God's help, can work wonders.

We are standing at the door. Knock and it shall be opened unto you.

7 The Tower of Babel and the Confusion of Tongues*

Apart from the punishment for man's first Fall in the persons of Adam and Eve, the Holy Scriptures tell us of yet another consequence of the collective transgression of all mankind, namely, the confusion of tongues that ensued as a punishment for the building the Tower of Babel.

The "confusion of tongues," that is, the establishment of a multiplicity of languages and cultures, is depicted in the Scriptures as a divine curse, analogous to the one of "eating bread in the sweat of thy face" imposed on mankind in the person of Adam. Both curses are realized as a natural law against which mankind is powerless. The physiological nature of man and of the world surrounding him is such that nourishment cannot be obtained without physical work, and the laws governing the evolution of peoples entail the emergence and preservation of national distinctions in language and culture. Whatever devices human beings may invent to minimize physical labor, its complete elimination is impossible. And no matter how much we may struggle to counteract the multiplicity of national distinctions, they will always exist. Physical labor is so intimately connected with the normal functioning of the human organism that its absence is harmful, and those who need not do physical work for their daily bread engage in artificial substitutes for manual labor—calisthenics, sports, walking, and the like. In similar fashion, the dialectal division of language and culture is so organically linked with the existence of the social organism

*Originally as "Vavilonskaia bashnia i smeshenie iazykov." *Evraziiskii vremennik* 3, 1923, 107-124. Translated by Kenneth Brostrom.

that any attempt to abolish national diversity would lead to cultural impoverishment and extinction.

Labor as such, in its pure form, is never pleasurable. Any pleasure associated with it is found only in attendant feelings—in awareness of one's own strength and ability, in one's interest in the immediate result of one's work, in competition, in the anticipation of rest, and so on. The fewer these feelings, the more clearly labor stands out as suffering. Whenever there is a need to transform labor into a punishment, those entrusted with the task attempt to deprive labor of anything that might relieve its painfulness and conceal its true nature: "hard labor" is a most appropriate term. As a special grace, God endows certain individuals with strength and success in their physical work. But even these divine gifts alleviate the pain of labor only when man is aware of and rejoices in them as gifts, for labor remains labor, that is, suffering.

Thus labor in and of itself is suffering, and the necessity of labor remains an eternal curse—divine retribution for the Fall of man. Dialectal division and a multiplicity of national cultures entail no suffering, even though they may well serve as an obstacle to the realization of human strivings and "ideals," and lead to war, ethnic hostility, and the oppression of one community by another. The difference between the law of the division and multiplicity of national cultures and the law of obligatory physical labor stems from the fact that the latter law is a punishment inflicted upon mankind for its original fall from grace, whereas the law of division is, according to the Bible, not so much a punishment as God's response to the building of the Tower of Babel, God's divine establishment, aimed at preventing similar attempts in the future.

Even if we disregard the historical basis of the Biblical account of the Tower of Babel, we must acknowledge its profound inner sense. The Holy Writ depicts mankind speaking one language, that is, a linguistically and culturally homogeneous mankind, and it turns out that this single, universal culture, devoid of national characteristics, is extremely one-sided: an enormous development of science and technology (which is indicated by the project of the tower) is coupled with spiritual emptiness and moral decay. The result is excessive arrogance and pride, whose embodiment is the godless and senseless project. The Tower of Babel was a marvel of technology, but not only did it lack religious content; its purpose was downright blasphemous, and God, wishing to prevent the realization of this plan and to put a stop to the self-aggrandizement of mankind, confounded the languages, and established for all time the law of national division and the multiplicity of languages and cultures. This act of divine Providence implies that godless, self-sufficient technology, which found its ultimate expression in the project of the Tower, is the unavoidable result of a homogeneous culture without national differentiation and that only national cultures can be free from the spirit of empty pride and can lead mankind along paths pleasing to God.

The internal connection between the building of Babel and the concept of a homogeneous, universal culture is apparent. Culture is the ever-changing creation of the collective activity of past and present generations and everything it produces is expected to satisfy the material or spiritual requirements of either the whole community or of some of its members. Therefore, within a given community, culture always levels individual distinctions. In cultural products that receive wide recognition, the overly individual features of their creators and the overly individual tastes of separate members are effaced. This is the consequence of the mutual neutralization of polar, maximally opposed, individual distinctions. As a result, any culture bears the imprint of an average psychic type occurring in the given social milieu.

The greater the individual distinctions among the members of a social and cultural whole, the more diffuse and indeterminate, the more "impersonal" becomes the median type embodied in its culture. If we were to imagine a culture whose creator and bearer were all of mankind, its diffuseness would be maximally great. In such a culture, only the psychological elements common to all people would find their embodiment. People's tastes and convictions are different, and individual variation in such matters is enormous; however, logic is the same for all, and requirements for nourishment, for means of saving labor, and so on are also more or less the same for all. Therefore, in a homogeneous culture, logic, rationalistic science, and technology will always predominate over religion, ethics, and aesthetics, and the intense development of science and technology will be accompanied by spiritual and moral decay. Logic and technology not ennobled by probing spiritual depths deprive man of higher interests and obstruct his path to self-awareness; they only confirm him in his arrogance. A homogeneous, universal culture inevitably becomes irreligious and theomachic, and turns to the building of its Babel. On the other hand, in a national culture spiritual needs and predispositions, aesthetic tastes and moral aspirations—in short, everything related to people's moral and spiritual life—is held in high esteem. The entire spiritual aspect of such a culture, imbued with its own unique national psychology, is organically close to its bearers. The embodiment in culture of the spiritual experience of kindred natures facilitates for individual members the attainment of personal self-awareness.[1] Therefore, elevating, morally positive values can arise only in such a culture.

While acknowledging the positive aspects of national culture, we should, however, reject the idea of national division in excess of a certain organic limit. National division is in no way equivalent to the anarchic fragmentation of national and cultural energies, to reducing the whole to ever smaller units, as we can see if we examine the darker aspects of such fragmentation.

The law of the heterogeneity of national cultures limits mankind: human thought proves to be circumscribed not only by its own peculiar nature, its inability to transcend space, time,

---

[1]See our article "On True and False Nationalism" [no. 2 in this collection].

and "categories," its inability to shake off the blinders of sensual experience but also by the fact that any person is capable of fully assimilating only the products of the culture to which he belongs himself or of the cultures nearest to his own (this is especially evident when the division of cultures degenerates into fragmentation). The law of the heterogeneity of national cultures makes communication between representatives of different peoples difficult, and, given a certain disparity between cultures, even impossible. But alongside these negative consequences, the law of the heterogeneity of national cultures (insofar as national and cultural division does not exceed its organically imposed limit) also has beneficial consequences for mankind; as pointed out, various peoples produce morally positive and elevating cultural values only thanks to this law. So we should be aware of our national limitations and reconcile ourselves to them.

If people's wish to lighten their physical labor and diminish its application is natural and entails nothing essentially sinful, the wish to destroy the variety of national cultures and create a unified, universal culture is always sinful. It leads to the establishment of the human condition which the Scriptures depict as directly preceding the building of Babel, a condition that leads toward a new attempt at constructing the Tower of Babel. Every International is by its very nature atheistic, antireligious, and suffused with the spirit of human arrogance.

Herein is the chief sin of contemporary European civilization, which attempts to level and abolish national distinctions and introduce everywhere uniform *mores*, socio-political structures, and conceptions. It breaks down the individual spiritual foundations of each people, but it fails to replace them with new spiritual foundations and imposes only external forms of daily life resting on a material-utilitarian or rationalistic basis. European civilization causes unimaginable devastation in the souls of Europeanized peoples; it destroys their ability to create spiritual values and instills in them indifference and cynicism. Enormous greed for material goods and sinful arrogance accompany the progress of this civilization. It is making its way inexorably, toward a new Babel.

From the moment Romano-Germanic culture began to parade as the universal civilization of mankind, technology, rationalistic science, and an egoistic, utilitarian world view gained a decisive advantage over everything else, and such a relation of elements in culture is only increasing with time. Nothing else could possibly occur: the Japanese and Germans will find common ground only in logic, technology, and material interest, while all other elements and mainsprings of culture must gradually atrophy. It would be an error to assume that, thanks to the leveling of cultures brought about by the abolition of their spiritual dimensions, barriers between peoples will likewise be abolished and communication among them eased. The "brotherhood of nations" purchased at the price of the spiritual depersonalization of all nations is a despicable fraud.

No brotherhood is achievable when its cornerstone is formed by egoistic material interests, when technology, by its very existence, introduces worldwide competition and militarism and the idea of international civilization promotes imperialism and schemes for world domination. The abolition of culture's spiritual dimension or its demotion to secondary status leads only to moral degradation and to the development of personal egoisms, which increases, rather than decreases, the difficulty of communication among people and deepens hostilities among social groups even within a single people. Such are the consequences of striving toward an international and universal culture; obviously, this striving is unacceptable to God and sinful.

The variety of national cultures and languages is a consequence of the law of division. The effect of this law manifests itself most clearly in language. Every language is divisible into dialects, dialects into local vernaculars, and so on. Every dialect, aside from possessing certain features unique to itself, also possesses a number of features common to all dialects of the given language; it shares certain features with one of its neighboring dialects, other features with another, and so on. Between neighboring dialects we find transitional dialects that combine features of both. Language is a continuity of dialects, gradually and imperceptibly merging into one another.

Languages in their turn combine into families and fall into branches, sub-branches, and so on. Within a family, individual languages are related as dialects are within a language, that is, every language, aside from possessing features unique to itself and features characteristic of the entire branch, also possesses certain features uniting it with another language, other features uniting it with still another language of the same branch, and so on; between related languages we often find transitional dialects. Separate branches within a family are related as languages within a branch. There is no essential difference between the concepts of branch, language, and dialect.

When all the units of a linguistic whole are so close to one another that communication among its speakers poses no problems, they are referred to as local dialects, their groups as dialects, and the whole (i.e., the totality of all such divisions) is called a language. But when representatives of individual dialects cease to understand one another, subdialects are renamed languages, their groups branches, and the totality of branches becomes a language family. Therefore disputes often occur over whether a unit is a language or a dialect and whether a group of borderline, transitional dialects belongs to one or the other of two neighboring related languages; in most cases such disputes cannot be resolved by linguistic means alone.

This is what happens to *genetically* related language units, that is, units derived historically from dialects of the once undivided protolanguage (family, branch, subbranch, and so on). However, in addition to genetic grouping, we can observe grouping of neighboring languages not derived from the same source. Several languages belonging to a single geographic and cultural-historical region often exhibit similar features and this resemblance is conditioned by prolonged proximity and parallel development, rather than by common derivation. For groups formed on a nongenetic basis we propose the term language unions.[2] Not only separate languages but even families can form language unions; in such cases several genetically unrelated families belonging to a single geographic and cultural-historical zone are united by common features and form a union of language families.

For instance, the Finno-Ugrian-Samoyed (or Uralic), Turkic, Mongolian and Manchurian language families share a number of common features and form a single union of Uralo-Altaic families, though modern linguistics denies their genetic kinship. The division of nouns into grammatical genders and the ability of roots to modify, insert, and drop the vowel in the production of new forms, (cf. Russian *soberu* I will gather, *sobrat'*, perfective, to gather, *sobirat'*, imperfective, 'to gather,' *sobor* 'assembly, cathedral') mark the Indo-European, Semitic, Hamitic, and North-Caucasian families as members of the union of Mediterranean families, to which in all likelihood some extinct languages of the Mediterranean basin also belonged.[3] Such unions of genetically unrelated language families occur all over the world. It often happens that a family or an isolated language belongs to two unions or vacillates between two neighboring

[2]A striking example of a language union in Europe is provided by the Balkan languages: Bulgarian, Romanian, Albanian, and Modern Greek. While belonging to different branches of Indo-European, they are nevertheless united by a number of common features and correspondences in their grammatical structure.

[3]The Indo-European language family, which belongs, on the whole, to the Mediterranean union, shares some features with the Uralo-Altaic union (cf. the absence of prefixes); but in several instances it exhibits a striking resemblance to the Uralic languages (the Finno-Ugrian-Samoyed family). The isolated languages of Eastern Siberia (Yenisei-Ostyak, Gilyak, Yukagir, and the so-called Kamchatka languages, that is, Kamchadal, Chukchi, and Koryak) form a kind of transitional link between the Uralo-Altaic and the North American (Eskimo-Aleutian) union, and so on.

unions, playing the same role transitional dialects play in a genetic classification of languages.

In view of both means of grouping languages—genetic (according to language families) and nongenetic (according to language unions), we can say that all the languages of the world form an uninterrupted network whose links merge into one another—something like a rainbow. Because this rainbowlike network is continuous and transitions within it are gradual, the overall system of the languages of the world, for all its motley variety, constitutes a whole, obvious though it may be only to a scholar. Thus in the area of language the law of division leads not to anarchic fragmentation, but to a balanced, harmonious system, in which every component, however small, preserves its unique individuality, and the unity of the whole is attained not by the leveling of its components but by the continuity of the rainbowlike network.

The distribution and interrelation of cultures do not coincide with the groupings of languages. Native speakers of the same branch, let alone the same family, may belong to different cultures. A case in point is the Hungarian (or Magyar) people. The closest relatives of the Magyar language are Vogul and Ostyak (in northwestern Siberia), but Hungarian and Vogul-Ostyak cultures have absolutely nothing in common. While the distribution and interrelation of cultures are based on the same general principles as the interrelation of languages, the unit of culture corresponding to a language family is of far less consequence than the one corresponding to a language union. The cultures of neighboring peoples always exhibit comparable features. Therefore, among such cultures we find certain cultural-historical "zones." For instance, Asia falls into zones of Islamic, Hindustani, Chinese, Pacific, Arctic, steppe region, etc., cultures. The boundaries of these zones intersect one another, so that cultures of a mixed, or transitional, type emerge. Separate peoples and their subgroups appropriate definite cultural types and contribute to them their own individual traits. As a result, we have the same rainbowlike network, unified and harmonious by virtue of its continuity and infinitely varied by virtue of its differentiation.

Such are the consequences of the law of division. Despite their apparently anarchic variety, national cultures preserve their uniqueness and constitute an uninterrupted, harmonious unity, a whole. National cultures cannot be synthesized by sacrificing their individual features, because their coexistence secures the unity of the whole. As with everything natural, proceeding from the laws of life and development established by God, this picture is majestic in its incomprehensible and inexhaustible complexity and in its complex harmoniousness. The effort to destroy it by human hands, to replace the organic unity of living, dissimilar cultures with the mechanical unity of one impersonal culture that leaves no room for the manifestation of individuality and is miserably abstract—such an effort is unnatural and blasphemous.

In light of the worldwide significance of Christianity, it appears that we should not condemn as godless all attempts at the cultural unification of mankind and the creation of a homogeneous culture. For those who see in Christianity only one of the many religions of the world, a product of certain historical and cultural conditions, there is no problem, for they equate Christianity with other cultural products and regard it as part of the general cultural scheme. In such a case, no special universal significance can be ascribed to Christianity. But for those who accept Christ as the Son of God incarnate and Christianity as the only true religion, Christ's words "Go ye therefore, and teach all nations, baptizing them in the name of the Father, and of the Son, and of the Holy Ghost" (Matt.28:19) seem to refute the thesis that the cultural unification of mankind is a godless cause. However, there is no contradiction here.

By acknowledging Christianity as absolute truth founded on divine revelation and given to people by means of God's direct interference in the historical process, we have rejected any view of Christianity as a product and element of culture. Preaching

Christianity does not constitute the introduction into culture of some new element. Unlike Judaism, which is linked with a certain race, or Islam, which is linked with a certain culture, or Buddhism, which is in principle opposed to any culture, Christianity is above race and culture, but it does not abolish either their variety or their individual character. The acceptance of Christianity entails the renunciation of many elements of national pagan culture and its transformation. However, the concrete forms of this transformation vary and depend on the cultural-historical ground on which Christianity falls; uniformity in this matter, far from being obligatory, is even impossible. Christianity is a leaven that can be added to all kinds of "dough," but the results of its fermentation are contingent on the "dough." Therefore the above-mentioned rainbowlike network of the uniquely individual national cultures would preserve its design even if all nations of the world embraced Christianity.

Christianity does not call for the leveling of national and cultural differences or for the creation of a homogeneous, universal culture. Christianity, being a divine institution, is changeless. In the historical process, Christian dogmas do not undergo modification: they are merely *revealed*. Culture, on the other hand, is a human enterprise. It is subject to historical modifications, the laws of evolution, and, above all, the law of division. A single, unified Christian culture is a *contradictio in adjecto*. There *must* be several Christian cultures. Each people, once it accepts Christianity, has to transform its culture in such a way that its elements can conform to Christianity and that not only its own, national, spirit but also the Christian spirit can permeate it. Christianity provides a stimulus to cultural creativity by setting it new tasks. All Christian peoples are called upon to reconcile their cultures with the dogmas, ethics, and canons of the true Christian Church, to create temples and forms of divine service and its accouterments capable of evoking Christian moods in worshippers, and every people *must* accomplish these tasks in its own way, for Christianity to be accepted organically and become merged with the national psyche.

None of this precludes the influence of one Christian culture on another. Such influences can also be observed among non-Christian cultures; they follow from the essence of the development of cultures and in the natural course of events do not result in the leveling of national distinctions. What matters is that one culture should not suppress another, that cultural borrowings undergo organic assimilation, and that out of native and foreign elements a new, unified whole, fully compatible with the national psyche, be formed. The Christian Church is indivisible. Its unity presupposes interaction among local churches. However, interaction is possible even without cultural unity. The unity of the Church is expressed in the universality of the Holy Scriptures, Holy History, dogmas and canons, but not in the artistic and legal forms by which they are adapted to the life of each people. Attempts to restrict these forms and abolish national distinctions among peoples belonging to a single Church, but not to exactly the same culture, are prompted by superstition and ritualism and always prove unproductive. We Russians have suffered bitterly from such an attempt under Patriarch Nikon, leading in religion to the Great Schism, and in national life to the weakening of the resistance of the Russian cultural and national organism, which prepared the way for the devastation of the Petrine era.

For a Christian, Christianity is not bound up with one particular culture. It is not an *element* of any culture but a *ferment* added to various cultures. The cultures of Abyssinia and medieval Europe are entirely dissimilar despite the fact that both are Christian. If we examine the history of the dissemination of Christianity, we will find convincing evidence that this dissemination succeeded only in those places in which Christianity was accepted as a ferment, rather than an imported element of a ready-made foreign culture. Christianity happened to be organically and fruitfully assimilated only where it effected a reshaping of the local, national culture without abolishing its individuality. Contrariwise, one of the strongest hindrances to its acceptance has always been the mistaken identification of Christianity with a foreign culture.

Although the rejection of Christianity by a certain people has its profound, perhaps even mystical or providential causes, in most cases it can be accounted for by the fact that missionaries preached not Christianity but some Christian culture. Orthodox missionaries made the same mistake: it is an open secret that missionary work within Russia served as an instrument of Russification, and outside its borders, as a tool for the expansion of Russia's political influence. The same is true, and to an even greater degree, of non-Orthodox— Catholic, Protestant, and Anglican—missionary work. Romano-Germanic missionaries look on themselves primarily as carriers of a definite culture. Their activities are connected with "spheres of influence," colonization, Europeanization, civilization, concessions, trading stations, plantations, and so on. Missionaries appear not as God-sent messengers of divinely revealed truths, but as agents of colonial policy or as representatives of the "interests" of some world power or another.

In preaching not Christianity but Catholicism, Protestantism, or Anglicanism, that is, these deviations from Christianity that took root in Romano-Germanic culture and remain intimately linked with it, missionaries simply preach that culture. The success of their mission is naturally assessed by the capacity of any given people to "become a part of European civilization." And because in that civilization Christianity has long since receded into the background and been drowned out by Babel-constructing tendencies, the newly converted "natives," who have assimilated Christianity from the perspective of European civilization and as an element—moreover, not the most important one—of that civilization, prove to be poor Christians unable to create anything new. Missionaries convert not peoples capable of reshaping their national cultures in a Christian spirit but rather separate individuals, who by the fact of their conversion cut themselves off from the main trunk of their native cultures and become agents of the economic and political ambitions of a foreign power.

So Christ's precept to teach all nations, baptizing them in the name of the Father, and of the Son, and of the Holy Ghost remains unfulfilled because Christian missionary work was turned into an instrument of Europeanization, into a means for the establishment of a homogeneous, universal culture, whose godless essence we have attempted to illuminate in the foregoing discussion. The wish to level national distinctions cannot be justified by references to the need for Christian missionary work; on the contrary, this work proves fruitless and ineffectual precisely because it is a vehicle of leveling, anti-Christian interference in human culture.

8 The Legacy of Genghis Khan:

A Perspective on Russian History Not from the West but from the East[*]

I

A point of view generally accepted in history textbooks, namely, that the foundations of the Russian state were laid in so-called Kievan Rus', can scarcely be accepted as correct. That state, or rather that group of more or less independent principalities subsumed by the name Kievan Rus', in no way corresponds to the Russian state which we presently consider our motherland. Kievan Rus' was a group of principalities governed by the princes of the Varangian dynasty and located along those rivers that connect in an almost unbroken line the Baltic and the Black seas. The *Primary Chronicle* identifies the geographical essence of this state quite correctly as "the path from the Varangians to the Greeks." The area of Kievan Rus' did not comprise even a twentieth part of modern Russia. Kievan Rus' was not identical in its territory with so-called European Russia, nor was it the most significant part of the territory of European Russia in political and economic terms. The Khazar state (located along the lower reaches of the Volga and on the Don River) and that

*Originally as *Nasledie Chingizkhana: vzgliad na russkuiu istoriiu ne s Zapada a s Vostoka*. Berlin 1925. Translated by Kenneth Brostrom.

of the Bulgars (located on the Middle Volga and along the Kama) existed during the same era as Kievan Rus', and they were very likely more significant economically and politically. None of these principalities, whose settlements were located along and bound to one river basin or another, could become a state in the political or economic sense. Across the path to the Black and Caspian seas lay the vast steppe, and over it wandered warlike nomads whom no one could subjugate completely, and who made every effort of the settled states toward dominion and expansion impossible. This is why no powerful state could emerge from Kievan Rus'.

The notion that the present Russian state is somehow the continuation of Kievan Rus' is incorrect. Kievan Rus' could not extend its territory, nor could it strengthen the internal power of the state; although bound to a system of rivers, it was unable to control it. The lower and most important part of this system, which lay in the steppe, was forever open to attack by the nomads—the Pechenegs, the Cumans, and so on. The only path open to Kievan Rus' was that of decay, of fragmentation into petty principalities constantly warring with one another, devoid of any higher conception of the state. Any state is viable only when it can respond successfully to the challenges posed by the geographical nature of its territory. The challenge confronting Kievan Rus' was to maintain trade between the Baltic and the Black Sea, but it could not do so, and was thus nonviable. Every nonviable organism disintegrates. The only path open to the individual river towns and principalities of Kievan Rus' was that of "self-determination" and internecine strife. They were incapable of regarding themselves as parts of a single state entity, because this entity could not accomplish its geo-economic mission and was therefore devoid of meaning. It is clear that contemporary Russia did not arise and could not have arisen from Kievan Rus'. The only thing shared by Kievan Rus' and the Russia that we consider our motherland is the name "Rus'"; but the geographical and political-economic content of this name has changed completely.

Let us ask in the words of an ancient chronicler: "Whence cometh the Russian land, and how hath the Russian land arisen?" We will try to answer this question by investing the notion of the "Russian land" with a new, contemporary, geographic, economic, and political content.

A glance at a historical map reveals that at one time almost all the territory of the present-day U.S.S.R. constituted a part of the Mongolian empire founded by the great Genghis Khan. Several parts of prerevolutionary Russia that were incorporated during the post-Petrine period—Finland, Poland, and the Baltic provinces—never entered into the empire of Genghis Khan, and, characteristically, they have fallen away from Russia, because they have no natural, historical, or state connection with her. Other areas that by mere chance did not become parts of the Mongolian empire but that, owing to geographic or ethnographic considerations, had natural connections with this empire and were later incorporated into prerevolutionary Russia, have remained in the U.S.S.R. And if several of them (e.g., Bessarabia and the eastern borderlands of Poland) have been torn away, this is a temporary phenomenon; sooner or later nature will have its way. The incorporation into the Soviet Union of Khiva and Bukhara, which preserved an illusory independence during the reigns of the last Russian emperors, and the proclamation of a Soviet republic in Mongolia extend and strengthen the historical connections between Russia and the empire of Genghis Khan. Following the same line of reasoning, one can predict with confidence the future incorporation of Chinese Turkestan.

In historical perspective the present-day state that is called either Russia or the U.S.S.R. (its name is not the issue) was once part of the great Mongolian empire founded by Genghis Khan. But one cannot equate Russia with the empire of Genghis Khan. Almost all of Asia was incorporated into the empire of the great

Mongolian conqueror and his immediate heirs. But no matter how much Russian influence has penetrated China, Persia, and Afghanistan, these countries have not become parts of Russia, and if Russia were to incorporate them into herself, she would indeed alter her historical physiognomy. Russia's historical heritage includes only the fundamental nucleus of Genghis Khan's empire, not its entirety. This nucleus is characterized by specific geographical features that distinguish it from the remaining parts of the former Mongolian empire.

Geographically, the territory of Russia, understood as the nucleus of the Mongolian empire, can be defined in the following manner. A long, more or less uninterrupted zone of unforested plains and plateaus stretches almost from the Pacific Ocean to the mouth of the Danube. This belt can be called the "steppe system." It is bordered on the north by a broad zone of forests, beyond which lies the tundra. In the south, the steppe system is bordered by mountain ranges. Thus there are four parallel zones stretching from west to east: the tundra, the forests, the steppes, and the mountains. In the meridional direction (i.e., from north to south or south to north) this system of four zones is intersected by a system of great rivers. This then is the essence of the geographical configuration of the land mass under discussion. It lacks both access to the open sea and the ragged coastline so characteristic of Western and Central Europe and East and South Asia. With regard to climate, this land mass is distinguished from both Europe and Asia proper by a set of characteristics associated with the term "continental climate": extreme variations between summer and winter temperatures, a distinct isotherm and wind direction, and so on. This land mass differs from both Europe and Asia proper and constitutes a separate continent, a separate part of the earth, which in contrast to Europe and Asia can be called *Eurasia*.

The population of this part of the earth is not homogeneous and comprises several races. The difference between the Russians and the Buryats or the Samoyeds is very great. But a series of intermediate, transitional links exists between these extremes. With regard to anthropological facial type and build, there are no striking differences between the Great Russian and the Mordvin or the Zyryan. Likewise, no striking transition exists between the Mordvin and Zyryan and the Cheremiss or the Votyak; as representatives of a type, the Volga-Kama Finns (the Mordvins, Votyaks, and Cheremiss) are very similar to the Volga Turks (the Chuvash, Tatars, and Meshcheryaks). The Tatar type gradates into the Bashkir and Kirghiz type, from which, by way of similar gradual transitions, we pass to what is, properly speaking, the Mongolian-Kalmyk-Buryat type.

Eurasia represents an integral whole, both geographically and anthropologically. The presence within it of geographically and economically diverse features, such as forests, steppes, and mountains, and of natural geographical connections between them makes it possible to view Eurasia as a region that is more or less self-sufficient economically. By its very nature, Eurasia is historically destined to comprise a single state entity.

From the beginning the political unification of Eurasia was a historical inevitability, and the geography of Eurasia indicated the means to achieve it. In ancient times only the rivers and steppes served as paths of communication. The forests and mountains were not suited to this, while the tundra was a region inhospitable to the development of any human activity. We have already seen that the numerous great river systems within the territory of Eurasia are oriented in a north-south direction, while the single steppe system passes across the entirety of Eurasia from east to west. Consequently, there was only one path of communication between east and west, while there were several between north and south (all the riverways between north and south intersect the steppe road between east and west at some point). Therefore, a people that gained control over one of the river systems became the master of only one specific part of Eurasia, but a people that gained control of the steppe system became the master of Eurasia. In mastering the segments of the river systems located in the steppes, they subjugated each of these systems in its entirety. Only a state that controlled the entire steppe system could unite all Eurasia.

Within the territory of Eurasia there were originally tribes and states with a settled life style along the rivers, and steppe tribes with a nomadic life style. Conflict between river and steppe was inevitable, and it is indeed a predominant feature of the ancient history not only of Kievan Rus', but of the other Eurasian river states (e.g., the Kingdom of the Khazars and of Khorezm). In the beginning the nomads were divided into many tribes, each of which remained within a defined area of the steppe; only when some tribe penetrated an adjacent area would conflict break out between neighboring tribes. At that time the river states were able to oppose the steppe people quite successfully. The constant threat of nomadic raids on the river settlements and the never-ending danger that trade along the rivers would be interrupted made normal development impossible for the river states. But they continued to exist and to struggle with the nomads, although not always successfully.

The situation changed radically when Genghis Khan subjugated the nomadic tribes of the Eurasian steppe and transformed the Eurasian steppe system into a single, all-encompassing nomad state with a superb military organization. Nothing could resist such power. All the organized states within the territory of Eurasia lost their independence and became subject to the ruler of the steppes. Thus Genghis Khan was successful in accomplishing the historical task set by the nature of Eurasia, the task of unifying this entire area into a single state, and he accomplished this task in the only way possible—by first unifying the entire steppe under his power, and through the steppe, the rest of Eurasia.

However, Genghis Khan subjugated not only Eurasia but also most of Asia. In conquering Eurasia and unifying it into a single state Genghis Khan was accomplishing a historical task set by nature itself; but the same cannot be said about the conquest of parts of Asia proper. The conquest and unification of Eurasia was ultimately to its benefit; the conquest of parts of Asia proper was destructive, and for them, ruinous. Neither China nor Persia stood in need of political unification from without. These were countries with ancient national, political, and cultural traditions, and with well defined spheres of cultural influence. To be sure, Genghis Khan introduced elements drawn from these old Asiatic cultures into his newly created Eurasian state. He utilized the cultural riches and influence of China, Persia, and India, not only without submitting to their political power but while making them subservient to himself. Consequently, Eurasia received certain benefits from this process. But the process was very damaging to Asia; the Mongolian conquest tore into the historical life of certain parts of Asia, deprived them of their independence, and interrupted their cultural development for a very long time. Ultimately, the Mongolian conquerors could not occupy old Asiatic states, enjoy all the benefits of their culture, and still remain culturally autonomous forever. Inevitably they were assimilated by the local populations and accepted their traditions. When the Mongolian empire disintegrated, each state again became what it had formerly been.

Although Genghis Khan apparently attached greater importance to the conquest of China and of Asia proper than he did to the subjugation of Eurasia, he fulfilled a valuable historical mission only in Eurasia. This is why, in defining the historical essence of the Russian state in terms of its occupation of all, or almost all, of the territory of Eurasia, I identified it with the nucleus of Genghis Khan's empire. Eurasia is a geographically, ethnographically, and economically integrated system whose political unification was historically inevitable. Genghis Khan was the first to accomplish this unification, and after him the consciousness of its necessity penetrated every part of Eurasia, although not always with the same degree of clarity. In time the unity of Eurasia began to break up. Instinctively the Russian state has striven and is striving to recreate this broken unity; consequently, it is the descendant of Genghis Khan, the heir and successor to his historical endeavors.

Genghis Khan was not only a great conqueror; he also had a genius for administration. And like all state administrators of his caliber, he was governed in his activities not only by the narrow, practical considerations of the moment, but also by certain higher principles and ideas that formed a harmonious system. As a typical representative of the Turanian race he lacked the ability to formulate this system clearly in abstract, philosophical terms; but he was fully aware of it, completely at one with it, and each of his actions, each order or decision, flowed logically from it. On the basis of the few surviving statements made by him and the general nature of all his ordinances, we can reconstruct his system and give it the theoretical formulation that Genghis Khan himself did not and could not provide.

Genghis Khan made certain moral demands upon his subjects, from the highest of the nobles and military leaders down to ordinary soldiers. The virtues he valued and encouraged most were loyalty, devotion, and steadfastness; the vices he particularly despised and hated were treachery, treason, and cowardice. These virtues and vices were the indicators he used to divide all people into two categories. For one type, material well-being and safety are more important than personal dignity and honor; this is why such people are capable of cowardice and treachery. When such a person submits to his leader or master, he does so only because he is aware of a certain force and power in this leader that could deprive him of his well-being, or even of his life; and he trembles before this power. He sees nothing beyond his master, and he is subject to him only on a personal basis and out of fear—that is, he is subject not to his master but to his own fear. In betraying his master, such a person thinks he is liberating himself from the only person who has power over him. But in doing this, always from fear or greed, he remains the slave of his fear, of his attachment to life and to material well-being, and he becomes even more deeply mired in his slavery. Such people are base, craven, they are slaves by nature. Genghis Khan despised them and destroyed them without mercy.

On his path of conquest, Genghis Khan had to overthrow or depose a large number of kings, princes, and rulers. Among the retinues and nobles of such rulers there were almost always traitors and turncoats who facilitated the victories and successes of Genghis Khan through acts of treachery. But Genghis Khan rewarded none of them for their services. To the contrary, after every victory the great conqueror ordered the execution of the nobles and courtiers who had betrayed their masters. Their treason was a sign of their slavish psychology, and there was no place for people of this mentality in Genghis Khan's empire. This is why, after the conquest of each new kingdom or principality, Genghis Khan gave lavish rewards to all those who had remained faithful to the former ruler, even when their loyalty had become disadvantageous and dangerous, and he brought them into his own retinue. By their loyalty and courage these people had proved that they belonged to the psychological type upon which Genghis Khan wished to base his state system.

The kind of people valued by Genghis Khan placed their honor and personal dignity above safety and comfort. They did not fear a man with the power to deprive them of their lives or their wealth; they feared rather the commission of an act that could dishonor them or diminish their personal dignity in their own eyes rather than in the eyes of others (because they did not fear the censure and mockery of others, just as they did not fear others in general). They were governed in their behavior by a special code, a body of rules setting out the actions that are permissible and impermissible for any honorable, self-respecting person. They valued these rules more than anything else, and they honored them in a religious manner, as something divinely ordained and inviolate; to break them meant to despise oneself—which for such people would be worse than death. In respecting themselves, they also respected others who adhered to the same internal set of rules, especially those who had demonstrated their unshakable loyalty to these rules in action.

In bowing down before the dictates of their inner moral code and in viewing deviations from this code as a loss of face and of personal human dignity, such people were necessarily religious. They perceived in the world an order wherein everything has a specific, divinely ordained place with attendant duties and obligations. When a man of this psychological type obeys his immediate superior, he obeys him not as a person but as part of a specific, divinely ordained hierarchy. He obeys in the person of his immediate superior a subordinate of a more highly placed superior, who is in turn a subordinate of an even higher superior, and so on, up to the supreme earthly ruler, who is also thought of as a subordinate not of a man, but of God. Thus, a man of this type always looks upon himself as part of a hierarchical system, and he is subordinate ultimately not to a man, but to God. Betrayal and treachery are psychologically impossible for him; in betraying his immediate superior, he is not liberated from the judgment of superiors more highly placed. And even if he has betrayed all his earthly superiors, he still cannot escape heavenly judgment, he still cannot escape the sanctions of the divine law that is so actively present in his consciousness. A consciousness of the impossibility of escaping the sanctions of the superhuman, divine law, a consciousness of one's own natural and inescapable legal accountability imparts to such a man the steadfastness and composure of fatalism. It is precisely to this human type that Genghis Khan himself belonged. Even after he conquered everyone and everything and became the all-powerful ruler of the largest state that ever existed on earth, he was constantly and acutely aware of his subordination to a higher will, and he looked upon himself as an instrument in the hands of God.

Having divided human beings into two psychological categories, Genghis Khan made this division the cornerstone of his state organization. He controlled those with the psychology of slaves the only way they can be controlled, by material rewards and fear. The fact that the vast territory of Eurasia and part of Asia were unified into one state and that safety along the Eurasian and Asian trade routes and the regulation of finances were guaranteed created such beneficial economic conditions for the inhabitants of Genghis Khan's empire that their efforts to achieve material well-being could meet with complete success. On the other hand, the might of his unyielding, unconquerable army, which was unconditionally loyal to him, together with the merciless cruelty of his punitive methods, forced everyone who was preoccupied with his own physical existence to tremble before him. Thus, people with the psychology of slaves were completely under Genghis Khan's control. But he did not allow them to come near administration. The entire military and administrative apparatus consisted only of people of the second psychological type; they were organized into a well-ordered, hierarchical system, at the summit of which stood Genghis Khan himself. And if his other subjects saw only oppression and terrifying power in Genghis Khan, the people in the administrative apparatus saw him first of all as the most brilliant representative of the psychological type characteristic of them all, and they revered him as the heroic embodiment of their personal ideal.

As Genghis Khan applied his theory of the state to concrete situations, as he implemented it in the real conditions of conquered countries, he was guided by the conviction that people possessing the psychological traits valued by him were to be found primarily among nomads, while settled societies generally consisted of people with the psychology of slaves. And indeed, the nomad is far less attached to material possessions than the townsman or peasant. Being by nature averse to sustained physical labor, the nomad places little value on physical comfort and is accustomed to limiting his needs without considering this limitation an especially onerous deprivation. He is not accustomed to struggling with the forces of nature for his subsistence, and thus looks upon his own well-being fatalistically. The nomad's wealth consists of his livestock. If this wealth is to be destroyed by disease, there is absolutely nothing he can do to prevent this misfortune. Even now it is difficult to combat epizootics, and at that time it was quite impossible. Livestock could be taken by an enemy, but by the same token one might be able to seize the enemy's livestock the next time around. Both possibilities depended upon one's prowess in battle, and also upon the existence of friendly and hostile relations governed by customary law and by a sense of decency and honor. For this reason the nomad placed special value on a man's military prowess and on his willingness to keep his word or an agreement. These factors created conditions congenial to the development of the psychology that Genghis Khan considered especially valuable.

These characteristics were reinforced among the nomad aristocracy by clan traditions and by an intense awareness not only of personal but of family honor, by a consciousness of one's responsibility to both ancestors and descendants. It is therefore not surprising that Genghis Khan drew most of the human material for his military and administrative apparatus from the ranks of the nomad aristocracy. Yet he was not guided by class prejudice; many who were appointed by him to important military positions came from the least prominent clans, and some of them were formerly "common" shepherds. What mattered to Genghis Khan was not whether a man belonged to a particular class or level of nomad society, but his psychological type. Genghis Khan found people of the psychological type necessary to him primarily among the nomads, and he understood very clearly the connection between this psychological type and the nomadic life style. Therefore, the most important instruction passed on by him to his heirs and to all the nomads was that they should preserve their nomadic life style and avoid becoming a settled society.

As regards the scorn that Genghis Khan felt for settled societies, in which he recognized people with the craven psychology of slaves, he was to some degree correct when one considers the settled societies he had to deal with. The settled Asiatic kingdoms of that time were dominated from top to bottom by the spirit of the slave; greedy devotion to material wealth not always honorably acquired, haughty and insulting treatment of inferiors, and servile groveling before superiors characterized the social life of these states, just as unprincipled careerism and treachery characterized their political life. The division of people into two different types, a division Genghis Khan placed at the foundation of the state system he was building, could not be found in these states, since their administrative apparatus was maintained exclusively by means of physical terror and material gain. So Genghis Khan was able to locate suitable human material for the military and administrative apparatus of his state only among the nomads; in settled communities he could find only "specialists" in finance and in office management. The distinguishing feature of Genghis Khan's state, then, was the fact that it was governed by nomads.

Another important feature of Genghis Khan's state was the place given to religion. Being himself a deeply religious man who was constantly aware of his personal connection with the divine, Genghis Khan considered this kind of religious feeling an indispensable condition for the frame of mind he valued in his subjects. In order for a man to fulfill his duties fearlessly and unconditionally, he must believe firmly—not theoretically, but intuitively, with his whole being—that his personal destiny, like the destinies of others and of the entire world, is in the hands of a higher being, a being infinitely high and beyond all criticism. Such a being can only be God, not a man. A disciplined soldier who can obey a superior as willingly as he gives orders to a subordinate, who never loses his self-respect and therefore is able to respect others and to elicit their respect, is by nature capable of submitting only to the authority of an immaterial, transcendent first cause—in contrast to a slave, who submits to the authority of earthly fear, earthly prosperity, earthly vanity. And being convinced that all this was true, Genghis Khan regarded only those people who were sincerely and deeply religious as valuable to his state.

In approaching religion from what was, in essence, a psychological perspective, Genghis Khan did not compel his subjects to accept any specific religion with a formulated dogma and liturgy. There was no official state religion in his empire, and among his soldiers, generals, and administrators could be found Shamanists, Buddhists, Moslems, and Christians (Nestorians). The only important consideration for Genghis Khan was that his subjects actively sense their complete subjugation to a transcendent, supreme being—in other words, that they be religious, that they confess some religion or other. This religious tolerance can be attributed in part to the fact that Genghis Khan was himself a Shamanist; that is, he confessed a religion that was rather primitive, lacking any dogmatic formulation, and uncommitted to proselytism. But his religious tolerance was in no way the result of passive indifference or apathy, since the identification of his subjects with some religion was of primary importance to him. He was not passive in his toleration of various religions in his state; rather he gave his active support to all of them. And this support, affirmation, and elevation of religion were as vital to Genghis Khan's state system as his affirmation of the nomadic life style and his placement of power in the hands of the nomads.

Thus, in accordance with Genghis Khan's state ideology, the power of the ruler must rest not upon some ruling class, estate, nation, or official religion, but upon people of a specific psychological type. The highest positions in his state could be occupied not only by aristocrats but by persons of humble origin. The rulers belonged to various Mongolian and Turko-Tatar tribes, and they were adherents of various religions. The important consideration was that they should belong in their personal character and manner of thinking to the psychological type described above. The practical implementation of these ideas in the countries constituting Genghis Khan's empire produced a ruling class recruited from among the nomads, each representative of which was a zealous adherent of some religion, while all religions were encouraged.

IV

I have discussed at length the ideological foundations of Genghis Khan's empire and attempted to disclose the essence of his theory of the state in order to refute the misguided view of this leader as nothing more than an oppressor, a conqueror, and a plunderer; this view has its origins in historical works influenced by the one-sided and tendentious attitudes of chroniclers who were his contemporaries and representatives of the various settled societies conquered by him. Genghis Khan was the bearer of an important, positive idea, and the desire to create and organize, not the desire to destroy, was predominant in his activities. This must be remembered when we approach Russia as the historical heir to Genghis Khan's state.

However, let us return to a question of fundamental interest to us, the origins of the Russian state. It is not enough to state that the geographical territory of Russia more or less coincides with the nucleus of Genghis Khan's empire, for it still remains unclear how the empire of the great Mongolian conqueror came to be replaced by the Russian state.

The destruction of the independent feudal principalities of Rus' by the Mongolian invasion and their incorporation into the Mongolian state undoubtedly caused a profound upheaval in the hearts and minds of the Russian people. Their anguish and their keen awareness of the humiliation suffered by Russian national pride merged with a strong new impression engendered by the grandeur of a foreign conception of the state. All Russians were disoriented, the abyss seemed to yawn before them at every step, and they began to search desperately for some solid ground. An eruption of acute spiritual tumult and turmoil was the result—complex processes whose significance is generally undervalued.

The hallmark of this period was the extraordinarily vigorous development of religious life. For ancient Rus' the period of Tatar rule was above all else an epoch of religion. The foreign yoke was perceived by the religious mind as God's punishment for past sins; the reality of the punishment reinforced the consciousness of the reality of the sin and the reality of a vengeful Divine Providence, and it confronted every person with the problem of individual repentance and purification through prayer. The flight to monasticism and the creation of new monasteries and convents took on the character of mass movements. The intense religious orientation of the inner life of Russians suffused every product of the spirit, especially art, with its colors. This period is associated with feverish creative activity in all areas of religious art; icon painting, church music, and religious literature reached new heights (the oldest specimens of religious folk poetry appeared at this time). This powerful upsurge in religious life was a natural accompaniment to that revaluation of values, to that disillusionment with life, which were caused by the calamity of the Tatar invasion.

At the same time, a fiery devotion to the national ideal arose as a reaction against the depressing awareness of national humiliation. The Russian past began to be idealized—not the recent past of the feudal principalities, the darker sides of which had led to the defeat on the Kalka river and were thus all too obvious—but a more distant past. This idealization is evident in such works as "The Tale of the Destruction of the Russian Land" [Slovo o pogybeli russkiia zemli] and in the *byliny* [heroic songs], which, as we now know, were reworked during this very period. In the folk consciousness, this idealization of Rus' and of ancient Russian heroism transformed minor princes and their retainers into all-Russian heroes, and their adversaries— unimportant leaders of Cuman raids—into Tatar khans commanding numberless hordes; such idealization strengthened the national pride that was swelling in opposition to the foreign yoke. Together with the emergence of this spirit of national military heroism there developed another conception of heroism fostered by the religious revival, a heroism that was ascetic and sacrificial, that found real embodiments in Russian monks and in the martyrs executed by the Horde. This contemporary and local Russian heroism merged in the Russian mind with traditions of ancient, non-Russian, Christian heroism. Thus, in reaction to the despair occasioned by total defeat at the hands of the Tatars, a wave of heroism—primarily religious but also nationalistic—was growing and gaining strength in Russian hearts and minds.

These positive expressions of national sentiment in Russia's reaction to the Tatar Yoke were accompanied by others more negative, and their existence and pervasiveness should not be minimized or ignored. The humiliation of Tatar rule caused many Russians from various levels of society to lose their pride in Russia and even their sense of duty and dignity. It is likely that instances of such moral degradation were more common than contemporary historical accounts would lead us to believe. Contemptible sycophancy and obsequiousness in relations with the Tatars, efforts to extract as much personal profit as possible from the Tatar overlordship, even at the price of treason, humiliation, and moral compromise—these things unfortunately existed, and in significant measure. There were unquestionably traitors who did not balk at religious conversion to further their careers. Consequently, examples of spiritual selflessness and heroism were offset by examples of abject moral degradation; the exalted national religious fervor of some existed side by side with the spiritual bankruptcy and servility of others. Epochs of this sort, with their soaring flights and steep declines, epochs characterized by extreme psychological contradictions that reflect a profound shock to a nation's spiritual life—such epochs create an atmosphere congenial to the emergence of a new national type; they are harbingers of the birth of a new era in the nation's history. For all their infectiousness, instances of moral degeneration still remained matters of personal conscience during the epoch of Tatar rule, while the religious and national revival of this period became a universal social phenomenon and a powerful factor in the development of a national identity and a national culture.

Such was the spiritual and psychological atmosphere created in Old Rus' by the Tatar Yoke. It was in this atmosphere that the underlying historical direction of the epoch was defined—the absorption of the Tatar conception of the state and its application to the conditions of Russian life.

Historians usually pass over or ignore this process. They describe Russia during the period of the Tatar Yoke as if no Tatar Yoke existed. The fallacy of this perspective in historical writing is obvious. It would be absurd to write a history of the Riazan region outside the context of general Russian history. It is equally absurd to write the history of Russia during the period of the Tatar Yoke ignoring the fact that Russia was then a province of a larger state. Nevertheless, to the present day Russian historians have proceeded in exactly this manner. Consequently, the influence of the traditions of the Mongolian state on Russia has remained unexplained. For example, we know beyond all doubt that Russia was drawn into the financial system of the Mongolian state. The contemporary Russian language contained numerous words borrowed from Mongolian or Tatar that related to finance, indicating that the Mongolian financial system not only took root in Russia after it was introduced, but that it outlived the Tatar Yoke (e.g., *kazna* 'treasury,' *kaznačej* 'treasurer,' *den'ga* 'half-kopeck piece,' *altyn* 'three-kopeck piece,' *tamožnja* 'customs office').

In addition to finance, one of the basic tasks of every large, properly organized state is the establishment of a postal system and other means of communication within its territory. In this area the pre-Mongolian, independent principalities of Rus' were at the lowest level of development. The Tatars brought Russia into the Mongolian state network of postal roads; and the Mongolian system for organizing the mails and other means of communication, based on a statewide "postal obligation" [*jamskaja povinnost'*] (from the Mongolian word *iam* 'posting station'), continued to exist in Russia long after the Tatar Yoke.

If there exist undeniable historical connections between the Russian and Mongolian state systems in such important branches of state activity as the organization of finance, the mails, and the means of communication, then it is natural to assume the existence of such connections in other areas—in the structure of the administrative apparatus, in the organization of the military, and so on. If Russian historians would only abandon their preconceived and absurd indifference to the fact of Russia's participation in the Mongolian state and examine the history of Russia from another perspective, the origins of many aspects of the state *mores* of so-called "Muscovite Rus'" would present themselves in an entirely new light. Russia's inclusion in the Mongolian state system could not be a matter of form only, simply the extension to Russia of the system of government as it existed in the other provinces and regions of the Mongolian empire; the spirit of the Mongolian state system must also have been absorbed by Russia to some degree.

It is true that, for reasons to be discussed below, the ideational foundations of this state system gradually began to crumble and disappear after the death of Genghis Khan. It is also true that the Tatar rulers and officials with whom the Russians had to deal were in most cases very far from measuring up to the ideals of Genghis Khan. Nevertheless, certain traditional ideas continued to exist within the Mongolian state system, and beyond the imperfections of its implementation there glimmered the state ideal, the fundamental design created by the great founder of the nomad state. And the spirit of Genghis Khan associated with the Mongolian state system, a spirit permeating and audible within it like a musical overtone, could not remain unnoticed and was certain to touch the souls of the Russians. In comparison with the extremely primitive notions of the state typical of pre-Mongolian Rus', the Mongolian conception developed by Genghis Khan was grand, and its grandeur was bound to impress the Russians deeply.

Thus the Tatar Yoke gave rise to a rather complex situation. As Russia acquired the techniques of the Mongolian state system, she also appropriated its spirit, its underlying design. Although this state system and its fundamental ideas were perceived as foreign and hostile, their grandeur, especially in comparison with the primitive insignificance of pre-Mongolian Russian conceptions of the state, made such a powerful impression that reactions of one sort or another were inevitable. The fainthearted simply bowed down and tried to find a personal niche for themselves. But bolder spirits could not reconcile themselves to this situation; the unprecedented religious revival and the birth of a new national self-awareness, of a heightened sense of national dignity, did not permit them to bow down before the might of a foreign state or before a foreign idea of the state. Yet this idea attracted them irresistibly and often filled their thoughts. It was necessary to find a way out of this painful dilemma. And find it they did, thanks to the religious revival.

The Tatar conception of the state was unacceptable to the extent that it was foreign and hostile. But the great idea possessed an irresistible power of attraction. Consequently, the Russians had to do away with what was unacceptable, what made it foreign and hostile. In other words, it had to be separated from its Mongolianism and associated with Orthodoxy, so it could be heralded as one's own, as Russian. In doing this, Russian national thought turned to Byzantine-Greek political ideas and traditions that provided material useful in the religious appropriation and Russification of the Mongolian state system. The ideas of Genghis Khan, obscured and eroded during the process of their implementation but still glimmering within the Mongolian state system, once again came to life, but in a completely new, unrecognizable form after they had received a Byzantine Christian foundation. In the Russian mind they acquired all the intensity of the religious fervor and national self-affirmation that distinguished the spiritual life of this era. They acquired unprecedented vividness and freshness, and with such contours they had became genuinely *Russian*. This is how the miraculous transformation of the Mongolian conception of the state into the Orthodox Russian conception occurred.

This miracle is so out of the ordinary that many would prefer to deny it. Nevertheless, it is a fact, and the psychological interpretation of this miracle offered above provides it with a satisfactory explanation. In any case, let us remember that Russia had come to know Orthodox Byzantium long before the Tatar Yoke and that during the time of the Yoke the grandeur of Byzantium was in eclipse. Yet for some reason it was during the period of Tatar rule that Byzantine state ideologies, which formerly had no particular appeal in Russia, came to occupy a central place in the Russian national consciousness. It follows that the grafting of these ideologies onto Russia was not motivated by the prestige of Byzantium, and that they were needed only to link an idea of the state, Mongolian in origin, to Orthodoxy, thereby making it Russian. So it was that this idea was absorbed, an idea which Russians had encountered in real life after their land was incorporated into the Mongolian empire and became one of its provinces.

V

The center of the process of inner rebirth was Moscow. All the phenomena brought into existence by the Tatar Yoke resonated there with exceptional force. It was in Moscow and in the Moscow region that the positive and the negative spiritual processes characteristic of this era were most strikingly evident. Instances of moral degradation, unprincipled opportunism, humiliating servility vis-à-vis the Tatar regime, and careerism stained by treason and crime were not unusual there. But it was also in the Moscow region that religious feelings were afire and at white heat. The embodiment of this fervor was Sergius of Radonezh, founder of the St. Sergius Trinity Monastery, the principal center of the religious revival during the Tatar rule. The assimilation of the techniques of the Mongolian state system and of the Tatar life style proceeded at an especially rapid pace in Moscow. This is why Russians in this area assimilated more easily and quickly the spirit of the Mongolian state, that is, the ideational legacy of Genghis Khan. It was also Moscow and the Moscow region that exhibited particular interest in Byzantine state ideologies. Every manifestation of the complex psychological process that culminated ultimately in the transformation of the Mongolian state system into the Russian had its center in Moscow.

The Grand Princes of Moscow gradually became the living bearers of the new Russian state spirit. It is difficult now to judge to what degree they were conscious "gatherers of the Russian land." Initially they may have simply adapted themselves to the Tatar regime as they strove to extract as much personal profit as possible from it; they may have been governed by self-interest and not by any patriotic considerations. Then, after assimilating a larger vision of the state but perhaps still viewing Russia as merely a province of the Mongolian Empire, they began to work with the Tatars. Finally, they began to work with conscious intent against the Khan of the Golden Horde, striving to usurp his place—first, with regard to Russia, and later, with regard to other lands under the control of the Golden Horde. Certain centralist traditions doubtlessly existed in the house of the Suzdal princes from which the Muscovite princes sprang, but they would not have been sufficient to transform the Muscovite princes into the "Tsars of all Rus'." This transformation became possible owing to the psychological process which, as we have seen, led to the emergence of the Russian state ideology. In addition, the Muscovite princes (to the extent that they were loyal servants) enjoyed the full patronage and support of the Horde, which could only welcome the administrative centralization of its Russian province. Whatever the case, the political unification of Russia under the power of Moscow was a direct result of the Tatar Yoke.

The expression "the overthrow of the Tatar Yoke," which occurs in old textbooks of Russian history, is conventional and imprecise. There never was, strictly speaking, a genuine overthrow of the Horde by military force. After the battle of

Kulikovo Field, Russia continued to pay tribute to the Tatars for a long time and so remained a part of the Mongolian Empire. It would be more accurate to call Ivan III's refusal to pay tribute to the Tatars the "overthrow of the Yoke," but this event attracted little attention and had no military consequences. Nor was the title of Tsar, which Ivan III assumed, considered anything out of the ordinary by the Tatars; the rulers of some of the larger areas within the Mongolian Empire had long since assumed the title of khan or tsar while preserving their political connections with the empire. The important historical moment was not the "overthrow of the Yoke" nor the separation of Russia from the power of the Horde, but the extension of Moscow's power over a large part of the territory once under the control of the Horde—in other words, *the replacement of the Tatar khan by the Muscovite tsar, together with the transfer of the center of political power to Moscow.* This took place during the reign of Ivan the Terrible, after the conquests of Kazan, Astrakhan, and Siberia.

It is a remarkable fact that a folk tradition understands these events in precisely this way. Ivan III's name disappeared quickly from the popular memory. His refusal to pay tribute to the Tatars is reflected in one relatively late *bylina* put together from parts of other, more ancient songs. This is the "Bylina about Vasilii Kazimirovich." Ivan III's name is not mentioned in it, and in its place one encounters the traditional *bylina* formula "gentle Prince Vladimir." The setting is moved to Kiev, thus relating the action to that semifabulous, legendary, historically indeterminate, distant antiquity where all the events of the "pre-Muscovite" period flow together in the folk imagination. Ivan III's refusal to pay the tribute is given a typical folkish twist in this *bylina*: not only do the ambassadors of "gentle Prince Vladimir" refuse to pay the tribute to the Tatars, but they inspire such fear in the Horde that the Tatars begin to pay tribute to Vladimir. This anticipation of a historical fact, namely, the subjection of the Horde's territories to the power of Russian rulers, indicates that the Russian national consciousness considered the cessation of tribute payments to the Tatars insufficient; it was not content with the separation of Russia from the Horde, but demanded the opposite—unification of Russia and the Horde under the power of a Russian tsar. Therefore the popular memory retained only the name of Ivan the Terrible, who realized this demand, and it celebrated him not in the *byliny*, but in historical songs, where it is typical of the folk tradition to begin the "Moscow period" with his reign, that is, with the foundation of a historical, rather than a legendary or fabulous, Russian state: "Stone Moscow arose, the great and terrible tsar Ivan Vasil'evich arose."

Thus, the external history of the "rise of Moscow," or of the beginnings of the Russian state, can be depicted in the following manner. The Tatars looked upon the Russia they had conquered as a single province. From the perspective of the Tatar state system, the financial and administrative unification of the Russian province was much to be desired. The Muscovite princes took this task upon themselves, and in doing so they were champions of the Horde's political strategy and agents representing the central Tatar government. The Muscovite princes prospered greatly in these endeavors, and they won the unswerving trust of the Tatars and made themselves indispensable to them. They were transformed into the permanent, hereditary governors of the Russian province of the Tatar Empire, the equals of the other provincial khans and rulers, from whom they differed only in their nonnomadic origins and their non-Islamic faith. Gradually all these provincial rulers who called themselves tsars and khans (including the Muscovite tsar) became so emancipated that their connections with the central government became purely nominal or disappeared altogether, while the central government had ceased to exist. But the consciousness of a state entity lived on, as did an awareness of the need to reunify the uncoordinated provinces of the former Tatar state, now separated into independent kingdoms.

This task had to be accomplished by one or another of the provincial rulers. The Tatars failed to do so, and it was completed by the only non-Tatar provincial overlord, the

Muscovite tsar. From that moment he ceased to be the ordinary ruler of a single, independent province; he ceased to be a separatist and became the representative of central state power, the restorer of the unity of the Tatar state system. The phrase "gatherers of the Russian land" does not capture the importance of the Muscovite tsars. While they were "gathering" (i.e., while they were restricting themselves to the unification of *Russian* lands administratively and financially, while they were collecting tribute from them for the Tatar treasury and imposing on them the Tatar state system), they were merely provincial governors, local agents of the central Tatar government. Even when they revolted against this power, they did not overstep the boundaries of provincialism. They became genuine rulers of a state only when they abandoned the "gathering of Russian land" for the "gathering of Tatar land," that is, when they decided to subjugate the separate, uncoordinated parts of the northwest *ulus* [administrative territory] of the Mongolian Empire.

However, the external history of the formation of the Muscovite state system becomes comprehensible only in the light of its internal, psychological, and ideological history. Without the profound spiritual rebirth that swept over the Russian nation as one product of its reaction to the Tatar Yoke, Russia would have been completely assimilated and would have remained one of the many fragments of Genghis Khan's empire. If among the provincial rulers of the Mongolian Empire *only* the Muscovite tsars aspired to control the entire Eurasian territory once united by Genghis Khan, if they alone had both the external and the internal strength to realize this aspiration, and if in assimilating the legacy of Genghis Khan Russia retained her national identity and even strengthened it, then this occurred because (owing to the psychological processes described above) it was in Russia alone that the spirit and ideas of Genghis Khan underwent a religious transformation and emerged in a revitalized and genuinely Russian form. It was in this crucible of national religious feeling that the northwest *ulus* of the Mongolian Empire was fused into the Muscovite state, replacing the Mongolian khan with the Orthodox Russian tsar.

VI

The rise of Moscow and the formation of the Russian state system were consequences of psychological processes set in motion by the Tatar conquest of Russia. To some extent, however, the transfer of political power in Eurasia from the Tatars to the Muscovite tsar was also caused by processes at work among the conquering Mongols and Tatars themselves.

Soon after the death of Genghis Khan, the imperfections and impracticability of some of the great conqueror's plans and ideas became evident. One very important imperfection in Genghis Khan's system was to be found in the connection between the state and religion. Religion was one of the foundations of his state system, but no logical connections were developed between the dogmas of any particular religion and the organization of the state. Genghis Khan's power as the chosen one, ordained by the God of Heaven (Tengri), was mystically sanctioned only from the perspective of Shamanism, a religion that was formless dogmatically, uninterested in proselytism, unaggressive in spirit, and therefore unable to compete with the other religions of Asia and Eurasia. It was psychologically impossible to turn to Shamanism from Islam, Buddhism, or Christianity. Indeed, when a Shamanist with genuine religious inclinations encountered other religions, he was easily convinced of their superiority and was likely to convert to another faith. And after converting, he could not avoid seeing his former fellow believers as primitive heathens abiding in darkness. Thus the religion of the Supreme Khan, the only religion that provided his power with a mystical sanction, was an inferior faith to many of his subjects. Gradually all the highest ranks and most of the members of the nomad ruling class converted from Shaminism to either Buddhism or

Islam, while Shaminism remained the religion of a small number of tribes with no important role in the state.

From the perspective of Buddhism or Islam, the power of the Supreme Khan was without religious foundation. Islam recognized the religiously sanctioned power of the universal sovereign of all true believers, the Caliph, the descendant and heir of Mohammed, the greatest of all prophets. But it was impossible to associate the conception of the Caliph with the supreme ruler of the empire founded by Genghis Khan: neither Genghis Khan nor any of his offspring could be viewed as descendants and heirs of Mohammed or as rulers having some inner connection with Islam. Moreover, Islam has its own elaborate system of criminal, civil, and public law, which corresponded hardly at all with the law code that Genghis Khan bequeathed to his descendants. Consequently, the rulers in various parts of the Mongolian Empire who accepted Islam could either reject some of the precepts and official regulations of Genghis Khan and adhere to Islamic law in governing or be bad Moslems. So no lasting fusion between the predominant religion and the Mongolian state system occurred in the Islamic provinces of the Empire. In such countries the state system lost its "planetary" nature, since it could not merge with the ideal Islamic state sanctified by religion, the universal kingdom of the Caliph. And there were many Islamic countries in the empire of Genghis Khan, they were of great importance, and Islam spread from them ever faster and farther.

It was somewhat easier to reconcile the Mongolian state system with Buddhist ideas: with its man-centeredness and doctrine of the transmigration of souls, Buddhism left open the possibility of declaring the Supreme Ruler of the Mongolian Empire the earthly incarnation of Buddha. This could happen only after doing some violence to orthodox Buddhist dogma, but a measure of violence was unavoidable in harmonizing Buddhism with the requirements of a nomadic life style, which was irreconcilable with several of Buddhism's guiding principles (e.g., vegetarianism). A form of Buddhism adapted to the life

style and world view of the nomads, with a strong admixture of
Shamanism (so-called Lamaism), did in fact become the religion
of many tribes within the empire founded by Genghis Khan,
including the Mongols, the tribe of Genghis Khan himself. And
with time the state idea came to be more firmly established in
the Buddhist parts of the Empire. But Buddhism failed to
spread throughout the Empire and displace Islam. Moreover, by
its nature Buddhism is incapable of maintaining (much less
enhancing) the level of state-oriented and military activity,
without which the state inevitably weakens and passes into
decline. Therefore, the conversion of many subjects to
Buddhism in Genghis Khan's empire did not resolve the
problem created by the absence of a strong, religiously
formulated sanction for the Mongolian state system.

Genghis Khan's conception of the guiding role of the nomads
was also bound to suffer a certain amount of damage. It was
inapplicable to the ancient Asiatic countries conquered by
Genghis Khan, since the nomads there adopted a settled life
style, assimilated the local culture and local traditions of
government, merged with the indigenous ruling class, and
finally disappeared within it. The history of these states then
continued along its former path after the temporary
interruption of the Mongolian invasion. But the nomads were
unable to carry out the precepts of Genghis Khan even in the
countries of Eurasia, where the supremacy of the nomads
seemed predestined by geography itself, where the Mongolian
invasion was not an accidental episode, and where it introduced
something fundamentally new and positive. The ruling nomads
were certain to be corrupted by a position that gave them
unlimited power over a settled population they had been taught
to despise as natural slaves controllable only through terror.
Moral degeneration could be avoided only through exceptional
awareness of duty and through constant reinvigoration of
personal heroism and of the memory of Genghis Khan's idea of
the state. But it was impossible to maintain this exalted vision in

daily life, and moral degeneration inevitably infected the nomad rulers.

The national and religious revival, which intensified in Russia during the Tatar rule and led to the emergence of a religiously sanctioned concept of a national state, was contemporaneous with the opposite psychological process in the ruling circles of the Tatars—the weakening of the ideological and moral foundations of the Mongolian state system. And when the separate provinces of the erstwhile Mongolian Empire (among them Russia) began to acquire an ever-increasing degree of independence, only in the Russian province ruled by Moscow had the idea of the state acquired a new religious, moral, and national foundation. It is therefore not surprising that the Prince of Moscow began to enjoy a certain moral prestige among the Tatars themselves, and this long before the so-called overthrow of the Tatar Yoke. Tatar nobles and highly placed officials living among the Russians gradually ceased to treat them with contempt; they were then inspired by the national religious revival themselves, and converted to Orthodoxy. Instances of the conversion of representatives of the Tatar ruling circles to the Russian faith and of their entry into Russian service became commonplace, and the Russian ruling class began to admit Tatars in great numbers. The importance of this phenomenon is usually underestimated. Historians lose sight of the fact that every such "conversion" presupposes a profound spiritual upheaval. Only the extraordinary force of the religious fervor everywhere present in Russian society at that time could induce a Moslem, and a Tatar into the bargain, to change his faith. The newly converted Tatars who joined the ranks of the Russian ruling class had immense importance for Russia: they were representatives of the noble nomad type that Genghis Khan regarded as the backbone of his state; they contributed greatly to the formation of this new state and became reliable supports for the emerging Russian state system. They brought with them the traditions and practices of the Mongolian state system and strengthened in their own persons the Russian state's connection as heir apparent with the Mongolian state. Thus the transformation of the Muscovite Grand Prince into the successor of the Khan of the Golden Horde and the replacement of the Mongolian state system by the Russian were the results of two parallel psychological processes, one occurring in a Russian milieu and the other in the Tatar ruling circles.

VII

The Russian state system that arose as successor and heir to the state of Genghis Khan rested upon a strong religious cultural foundation. Every Russian, regardless of his occupation and individual circumstances, belonged to the same culture, professed the same religious convictions, the same world view, the same moral code, and was guided in his behavior by the same traditional life style. The differences between separate classes were economic rather than cultural. They signaled quantitative, not qualitative distinctions in the spiritual and material values that determined people's world view and life style; they indicated the degree to which each person had realized a single cultural ideal in his life. The boyar dressed more richly, ate better, and lived more expansively than the peasant, but the cut of his clothes, the composition of his diet, and the structure of his house were in principle the same as those of the peasant. Aesthetic tastes and intellectual interests were the same for all, but some had an opportunity to satisfy them more fully than others. The foundation of everything was religion, the "Orthodox faith." In the Russian mind this "faith" was not an aggregate of abstract dogmas, but rather an all-encompassing, internally consistent way of life. Russian faith and Russian *mores* were inseparable from one another. There was nothing in everyday life and in the culture that was morally or religiously neutral. To be an Orthodox believer meant not only confessing certain dogmas and fulfilling the moral directives of the Church, not only repeating prescribed prayers, performing prescribed liturgical gestures, and attending religious services, but also eating prescribed food on specific days, with or without meat, wearing clothing of a specific cut, and so on. Faith entered into *mores*, *mores* into faith; the two merged into a single entity, into a coherent system of *religious living* (*bytovoe ispovednichestvo*).

The ideology of the state was also an organic part of this life style, for it, like everything else in Russian life, was inseparable from the religious world view. This ideology placed the tsar, who was viewed as the embodiment of the national will, at the head of the state. As the man embodying the will of the nation, the tsar was understood to bear moral responsibility before God for the sins of his nation; this is why his reign was viewed as a kind of heroic moral feat. In accordance with Christian teaching, such spiritual heroism is inconceivable without prayer and without God's help; this is why the tsar appeared to be the bearer of a particular kind of divine grace, for whose presence in him it was fitting to pray publicly. As every person, from the Christian point of view, is given the task of living according to God's commandments and of realizing God's will in his or her own life, so, too, is the nation. And since the life and all the actions of the national whole are shaped and directed by the tsar as the embodiment of the national will, the tsar must be the champion of God's commandments in the life of the nation. The ideal tsar was understood to be the intercessor for his people, their representative before God, and the instrument for implementing God's commandments in the life of the nation, the anointed one of God before the people.

Because the nation whose will the tsar embodied was not a supernatural entity and because the gifts of grace given the tsar through anointment and elevation to the throne freed neither him nor the nation he represented from the sinfulness inherent in human nature, it was recognized that both the tsar and his nation could stray from the one true path and fall into sin. And as each individual was warned against sin by the voice of conscience, so, too, was the tsar obligated to guard against falling into sin by listening, in his private life and in acts affecting the entire nation, to the voice of conscience—his own conscience and the conscience of the nation embodied through the Church in the person of the patriarch. Although he stood first among the laity and was the highest embodiment of the national will, the tsar was nevertheless mortal and limited by his human nature, and he was therefore not omniscient.

Even with the best of tsars, agents of state power could be guilty of abuses outside the tsar's knowledge. The "unfaithfulness" of individual agents of state power, unavoidable from the perspective of the Christian conviction that human nature is morally imperfect and that "the world abides in evil," was not thought to contradict the principle that the tsar strives to establish "faithfulness" on earth in all his actions: the agents' abuses were explained by the natural fact that the tsar did not know about them. The elimination of such abuses could therefore be achieved only by informing the tsar about them, for he was the natural and sole earthly protector of his subjects. At the same time there was a strong belief that no matter how effective the process of informing the tsar about abuses might be, their complete and final elimination (including the possibility of their reappearance) could never be achieved, for "the world abides in evil," human nature is imperfect, and no human ingenuity can correct this imperfection. The only kingdom of perfect faithfulness was the Kingdom of Heaven; no earthly kingdom could ever achieve this ideal, it could only strive after it. And the path to the ideal was to be found not in the perfection of the external forms of life within the state but in the inner struggle of every person to achieve moral self-perfection, a struggle that was valuable and useful only to the extent that it was voluntary and not the result of external compulsion. This struggle was not possible through human effort alone; one also needed help from God gained through prayer, fasting, and everything that constituted religious living.

In looking at the life of the state from the perspective of his religious world view, the Orthodox Russian citizen did not deceive himself with idle fancies about the possibility of achieving within the state structure ideal solutions for all problems; he was fully conscious of the limited results possible in this direction. In transferring the center of gravity to ethics, he acknowledged that the basic cause of the "unfaithfulness" of the agents of the state resided in their moral imperfections; and uprooting this unfaithfulness was looked upon as an ethical problem and not as a matter of juridical or political reform. A person with a strong desire to be moral could achieve this goal if he subordinated his fleshly nature to his will, lived according to the Law of God, and called upon God for His ever-present help. Likewise, the nation could achieve the greatest victories over discord (the foundation of which is sin) if it remained committed to living according to God's Law, and if its will, embodied in the tsar and responsive to the voice of conscience embodied through the Church in the patriarch, were to have unlimited power over all the earthly activities of the nation and over the organs of government. From the perspective of Old Russian ideology, the best political order achievable on earth (less than the kingdom of perfect faithfulness possible only in Heaven) results when the tsar possesses unlimited power, when he is fully informed about everything occurring in his state, when a religious life style prevails throughout the nation, and when the tsar listens to the voice of the Church. The efforts of separate estates to limit the power of the tsar were considered sinful; they were analogous, on the level of personal life, to the efforts of the various passions to limit and subjugate the will of the individual human being.

The Russian state system and the supreme power of the Russian tsar rested upon an ideology that was inextricably linked to the Russian religious world view and the Russian way of life. The power of the tsar was supported by the nation's religious attitude toward life, just as this attitude found support in the tsar. The tsar realized most completely the Russian religious life style in his personal life, and in this regard he served as an example, he "set the tone" for the entire nation. The tsar was the most devout of all the Russian laity, and in his private domestic life, he was the most typical Russian. The life style of the tsar was the Russian life style in a distilled and ideal form, practiced, so to speak, with all the stops out. Other members of the Russian laity measured themselves against this model, each to the limit of his abilities and his position in life.

The Russian people of this time did not separate life style and culture from faith; they perceived all three as a single, undifferentiated, religious way of living called the Orthodox faith, and they equated "Russian" with "Orthodox." They did not consider the linguistic and physical characteristics of Russians to be essential. What was essential for the Russian was his Orthodox faith, that is, his religious way of living. A person from another country or ethnic group was perceived as foreign only to the extent that he deviated in his convictions and behavior from the Russian religious life style; a person who was purely Russian in origin could evince the same kind of deviation after falling into heresy or sin. A connection was established in the Russian mind between the ideas of foreigner and sinner. "Foreign" was not an ethnographic but an ethical notion. As a result, genuine, conscious nationalism or chauvinism could not exist. No efforts were made to Russify by force the non-Russian tribes and peoples incorporated into the Muscovite state; on the contrary, all of them enjoyed a considerable degree of national autonomy.

With regard to non-Orthodox religions, the government adhered to principles that followed logically from recognition of Orthodoxy as the one true faith. The conviction that Orthodoxy was the only direct continuation of the teachings of Christ, the only true Christianity, and that Christianity was the only continuation and the consummation of the Old Testament prophecies forced Russians to look upon Judaism (which accepted the Old Testament but rejected Christianity) and upon all non-Orthodox Christian teachings that accepted Christ but deviated from Orthodoxy as heresies. The government could not allow such religious doctrines to be practiced freely: every heresy (i.e., conscious rejection of a divine truth well known to the heretic) was a sin, a crime against divine truth; and the government was obliged to struggle against sin and crime.

Relations were quite different with religious doctrines that had no connections with Orthodoxy in their fundamental ideas and that encroached upon no part of the divine revelation whose full disclosure was present, according to Orthodox belief, only in Orthodoxy (Islam, Buddhism, and various forms of paganism). The heretic saw the light, but did not want to walk to it; this was his sin. The pagan did not see the light, and was walking in darkness because of his ignorance. If there was any sin in this (sin in the sense of capture by Satan), then it was a venial sin, excusable on grounds of ignorance. Consequently, such religions should not be subject to persecution. The obligation of the Orthodox Christian toward such religions was to convert, to enlighten those walking in darkness. But the state, the secular authority could not take this evangelical burden upon itself. This was the business of the Church, which the government should not hinder but help, and not by forceful means: the enlightenment of those walking in darkness was an undertaking motivated by love, and where there was love there was no place for force. So the attitude of the government toward religions not based upon Old and New Testament revelation was one of cautious tolerance. Such religions were not persecuted or insulted, but measures were taken to permit the voices of Orthodox preachers to reach the hearing of those "who because of ignorance are walking in darkness," so that Orthodoxy might appear in their eyes to be a religion more worthy than their own, and they might be led to a conscious recognition of its superiority. The instructions sent by Ivan the Terrible to the Most Venerable Gurii of Kazan clearly reflect this point of view; and the subsequent mass conversion of Tatars to Orthodoxy (including the ruling circles of the Tatar nation) witnesses to the correctness of this course of action.

VIII

Despite the large differences between the ideological foundations of the Muscovite and Mongolian state systems, there is an inner kinship between them. Good reasons exist for considering the Muscovite state system the successor to the Mongolian system not only with regard to territory and certain peculiarities of state organization, but in its ideological content. Both were based on a life style that was bound up with a specific psychological orientation—the nomadic life style in the empire of Genghis Khan, and the Orthodox way of living in the Muscovite state. In both, the supreme head of state was the most brilliant representative, the exemplar of the ideal form of that particular life style. In both, discipline within the state depended upon the universal subordination of all citizens and of the monarch himself to a transcendent, divine source; the subordination of one man to another and of all persons to the monarch was understood as a consequence of universal subordination to the divine source whose earthly instrument the monarch was. In both, the absence of attachment to earthly goods, freedom from the tyranny of material prosperity, together with unshakable devotion to a religiously conceived notion of duty were recognized as virtues.

The basic distinction between them has its origin in the differing contents of their religious ideas—Genghis Khan's eclectic Shamanism and the Orthodox Christianity of the Muscovite state. Because the diffuse and dogmatically unformulated Shamanism of Genghis Khan gave way in the Muscovite state to Orthodoxy with its formulated dogma, certain essential aspects of the political-ideological system had to change, for it could now be linked more closely to the religious foundation. The nomadic life style in the system of Genghis Khan (which was bound up with ethnographic and geographic rather than religious conditions) was replaced in the Muscovite state by Orthodoxy, that is, by the organic fusion of a life style with a specific religion, the whole being essentially independent of ethnographic and geographic conditions. Instead of the complete religious tolerance that ultimately undermined the religious foundation of the ideological and political system, a limited religious tolerance was practiced in the Muscovite state; this tolerance was in harmony with the dogmas of the fundamental religious idea and with the principle that the state ideology should derive from the religious. In practice this limited religious tolerance could not harm the purely secular state system, because none of the peoples of the Eurasian world professed the religious doctrines that were excluded from toleration as heresies.

The features distinguishing the Russian ideological and political system from that of Genghis Khan are those that made the Russian state system superior to the Mongolian. As we have seen, the weakness of the Mongolian system was to be found in the absence of a strong link between the state ideology (entirely religious in nature) and the dogmas of a specific religion, in the disparity between the system's broad sweep and the primitive formlessness of Shamanism, and in the impractical dream of staking everything on the ethnographically and geographically limited, historically transitory nomadic life style. The Muscovite state system was also free from another defect of Genghis Khan's system, namely, its claim to supremacy over the old Asiatic kingdoms. Laying claim to territory that can be conquered but not controlled always weakens a state. Genghis Khan's Pan-Asiatic imperialism led to the cultural subjugation of the nucleus of his empire by the conquered territories and created disharmony between the centers of power and the centers of culture. In its subordination to Moscow, the Eurasian world achieved for the first time a cultural self-sufficiency equivalent to the self-sufficiency of the old Asiatic kingdoms, of China and of Persia. And this cultural self-sufficiency gave the state strength, stability, and the power to resist. It is remarkable that even during the period of the Time of Troubles and the

Interregnum, not one territory willingly fell away from the Muscovite state.

IX

One important problem unknown to the Mongolian Empire confronted the Muscovite state system—defense against the West. All of the Ukraine and Belorussia, which had belonged to Eurasia and Russia from time immemorial, was under the control of Catholic Poland, Europe's outpost in the East; and it was only with the greatest difficulty that a part of these lands was reunited with the Eurasian world under the control of Moscow. But Poland was not without competitors. In the northwest, there was increasing danger of a Swedish invasion, while other European countries not immediately bordering on Russia were greedily reaching out for the wealth of Russia-Eurasia through maritime trade. National defense was a necessity, but one that implied another—the need to acquire Western military and industrial technology. The situation was complex and difficult. Russia had to borrow and learn certain things from Europe but avoid falling into a state of cultural and spiritual dependence. Inasmuch as the peoples of Europe were not adherents of Orthodoxy but called themselves Christians (i.e., from the Russian point of view they were heretics), the spirit of Europe and of European civilization was perceived by Russians as heretical, sinful, anti-Christian, and satanic. Contamination by this spirit was a very great danger.

The Muscovite tsars were aware of the complexity of this situation, and they turned away from the path of technological apprenticeship. They limited themselves in this direction to half measures; they invited European specialists, craftsmen, and instructors to work in Russia, but kept them isolated and watched them closely to prevent excessive fraternization with Russians. This certainly was no solution to the problem. Sooner or later it would be necessary to begin borrowing European technology in earnest, while taking decisive measures against contamination by the European spirit.

It was Peter I who decided to borrow European technology. But he was so carried away by this undertaking that it became almost an end in itself for him, and he took no measures against contamination by the spirit of Europe. The task was accomplished in the worst way possible, and with catastrophic results: external power was purchased at the cost of Russia's complete cultural and spiritual enslavement by Europe. In borrowing Western technology to strengthen Russia's external power, Peter I subjected Russian national sensibilities to the most terrible humiliations and destroyed the foundations on which Russia's internal power and might rested. He destroyed the patriarchate, which was so important to the ideological and political system; he destroyed the habits of religious living in the ruling class; and he terminated the tsar's role as the archetypal bearer of this ideal life style. He shook the moral foundations as well: blasphemy (the "General Synod of Wags and Drunkards") became a pastime at court, and the replacement of the chaste Old Russian style in women's clothing by European dress— shameless from the Russian point of view, with its deep décolletage—was carried out coercively, just as the Russian boyars were coerced into appearing at the notorious *assemblées* and compelled to behave there in a disgraceful manner.

The foundations of Russian life were not only overturned, but they were replaced by their opposites: in living openly with his German mistress without marrying her, in fathering children by her, and, as a finishing touch, in crowning her the "Empress Catherine," the tsar provided an example of unbridled licentiousness rather than behaving as the exemplar of the Orthodox life style. The whole of this religious life style gave way among the upper classes to one that was cosmopolitan, irreligious, European, and purely secular. The Church was now headed not by a patriarch who embodied the national conscience, but by a synod that was humiliatingly subservient to the government and prohibited from raising its voice with authority. All of this was allegedly offset by the fact that Russia had become a great power; she was extending her borders and possessed such military might that foreigners were trembling before it. As for the people, the disreputable image of the tsar was supposedly offset by the fact that the "tsar-carpenter," the "tsar-craftsman" worked like a common laborer, cursed like one, and even beat windy, arrogant courtiers with a club.

This spectacle could awaken only disgust in any Russian in whom national, religious, and moral principles were strong. Only the foreigners invited by Peter to work in Russia or Russian opportunists—unprincipled careerists motivated by petty vanity or easy profit—could follow Peter's lead. The famous "fledglings from Peter's nest" [Pushkin] were for the most part inveterate swindlers and crooks, who stole far more than government officials in the past. The circumstance that, as Russian historians have noted with sadness, "Peter had no worthy successors" was in no way accidental: no worthy Russian could have sided with Peter.

It is true that Peter's grand design was born of patriotism, but a patriotism that was unique and unprecedented in Russian experience. He did not care about the genuine, historical Russia, because he had a passionate dream of creating from Russian material a great European power that would resemble other European countries in every way, but surpass them in territorial size and military might. His attitude toward the Russian material from which he had to create this great power reflected hostility, not love, for he had to wage a never-ending, stubborn war against this material, which naturally resisted his efforts to squeeze it into the mold of an alien ideal. This explains the paradox characteristic of all Peter's activities: his fiery, self-sacrificing love for his country ("And of Peter know that life is not dear to him, but only that Russia should be happy") was inseparable from his conscious, malicious desire to humiliate national sensibilities and to mock traditions sacred to every Russian.

The borrowing of European technology was historically inevitable because of the need for a national defense, but the forms it took during Peter's reign did not correspond to this need and even contradicted it. No foreign conquest could have destroyed the national culture of Russia to the extent that Peter's reforms did, even though they were originally intended to protect Russia from foreign conquest. The explanation for the disastrous direction taken by these reforms resides not in historical necessity but in Peter's character. His activities inevitably promoted to the highest civil and military offices the type of individual who was hostile to the genuine national element in Russian life; this corrupted the upper strata of society, making a change in course impossible even after his death. There were too many people with a personal stake in the new regime, and the military and the government were in their hands.

X

Thus, Peter set the tone for the entire course of Russia's subsequent history. He initiated a new period, the era of antinational monarchy. The bases of Russian life were radically altered. Since the ideological foundations of the former Russian state system had been overturned and trampled upon, the new state system had to depend exclusively upon power. Serfdom and military organization had existed in Russia previously, but she became a genuinely feudal and militarist nation only after the beginnings of Europeanization. The new ideology was one of unadulterated imperialism in all matters, including culture; while an alien civilization was being implanted in Russia, in foreign policy enthusiasm for foreign conquest reigned supreme. Thus, the paradox that characterized all of Peter's activities was preserved in this ideology.

Not Russians but foreigners, native Europeans, would find it most congenial to view Russia and the Russian people as material for the creation of a powerful European state, to despise as barbaric everything that had been Russian from time immemorial, and to scorn the Russian people as half-civilized dolts who had to be taught to be Europeans with a club. So it was natural that foreigners began to enjoy the special favor of Russian monarchs; they were everywhere present in the government apparatus and the highest echelons of the army, and the official history of this period exalts the pure-blooded German, Catherine II, above every other monarch after Peter I. Since these Europeans were by their nature the most appropriate champions of the course now established in Russia, it was they who created an atmosphere to which the native Russian ruling class gradually yielded. Its essence was the loss of the feeling of organic connection with the Russian soil, with the Russian "material." In such conditions patriotism was replaced by devotion to one's career, to social position, and in the best of cases, to the person upon whom this position depended—to the monarch, to the ruling dynasty, or to individual representatives of this dynasty. The monarchs understood this and strove to surround themselves with people personally devoted to them, which caused the center of gravity to shift to court relations. The resultant situation produced intrigues, struggles among cliques at court, favoritism and, as a consequence, "palace coups." The monarchs' efforts to find support in groups of people personally devoted or obligated to them led not only to favoritism but also to a constantly growing body of privileges for the land-owning aristocracy, who constituted the personnel of the government apparatus and the military elite. And these privileges were granted at the cost of oppressing other classes, especially the peasantry.

The process of Europeanization continued unrelentingly. It came from above; that is, Europeanization originally spread only through the upper levels of society, and then it moved down the social ladder, encompassing in ever-widening circles the other strata of the nation's social structure. Destruction of the spiritual foundations of the national culture together with engraftment of disparate, external features of European culture constituted the first stage of Europeanization; this was followed by the gradual engraftment of European spiritual culture. Between the beginning and end of this process there must have existed a long period characterized by a complete absence of spiritual culture. One after another all the strata of the Russian national social structure passed through these stages, the entire protracted process lasting several generations. The high aristocracy acquired a European veneer during the reign of Peter I, but they did not begin to assimilate the spiritual foundations of European culture until the end of the eighteenth century. The lesser aristocracy became Europeans in spirit somewhat later; and so on.

As a result, social differences within the Russian nation were deepened by differences in spiritual culture and patterns of behavior. This was not a matter of simple, hierarchical distinctions within a single culture; one culture was being replaced by another, which created a transitional stage of culturelessness. The malignancy of the ruptures between social strata was exacerbated by the legal codification of the privileged status of certain strata and the disenfranchisement of others. Moreover, "leaps" across the cultural chasms separating social strata were accomplished by individuals, not by entire social groups, so levels of culture never corresponded fully to the legally established social structure, and social privilege did not go hand in hand with the degree to which European spiritual culture had been assimilated. Finally, these circumstances gave birth to acute dissension between generations and opened up chasms of misunderstanding between the old and the young, between fathers and children. In a word, the process of Europeanization destroyed every aspect of national unity, it gouged deep wounds in the nation's body, it spread discord and hidden enmity everywhere. Deepest of all was the gulf between the common people, whose lives were shaped by the debris of the old national culture, and the strata of society that had begun to be Europeanized. In the relations between them, the social element got mixed up with the national cultural element: for the common people, the *barin* [master] was not only a representative of the ruling class but a bearer of a foreign culture; for the person who was in some way Europeanized or at least touched by Europeanization, the *muzhik* was not only a representative of the disenfranchised class, but a benighted savage as well. In one way or another, no one living in Russia during the era of Europeanization felt entirely "at home"; some lived under a foreign yoke, as it were, while others lived as if in a land they had conquered or in a colony.

The disfigurement of the Russian led to the disfigurement of Russia. Loss of the national physiognomy led to disintegration of the national personality, to forgetting the historical essence of Russia. In such circumstances Russia could not continue along the natural path of historical development preordained by geography itself. Post-Petrine Russian history is defined in its entirety not by movement along this path but by unwarranted departures from it for the sake of mistaken ideas about Russia's destiny. In both domestic and foreign policy, the antinational Imperial Government has been guided not by Russia's own historical traditions but by European models.

When Europe was pursuing the policies of dynasticism, which viewed the territory of the state as the private property of a specific dynasty and provoked the most unnatural alliances and wars with countries that were not even neighbors, the same view of politics was adopted by Russian monarchs. Russia was drawn into this senseless foreign game and began to take part in absurd, unnecessary, and unnatural military campaigns in countries not even contiguous with her and of no possible interest to her. Natural geographical conditions in Western Europe (the mountains, the jagged coastline, the presence of the ocean, and the impossibility of feeding its population from the land alone) made the impulse toward the open sea natural, because the sea allowed Europe to develop colonial trade. In imitation of the European powers, Russia also adopted this direction in foreign policy, although her own geography was quite different and confronted her with different historical tasks. Russia was also prepared to go to war for ideas, for abstract principles, but ideas that were always foreign, that had been created and assimilated by other major (invariably European) powers. During the reigns of Alexander I and Nicholas I, Russia went to war to strengthen the feudal monarchies and the principle of legitimacy in Europe; then she went to war "for the liberation and self-determination of small nations" and for the creation of small "independent" states, and in the last war, "for the overthrow of militarism and imperialism." Russia invariably accepted these ideas and slogans at face value, even though they were invented merely to conceal the greedy, predatory schemes of the European powers. Consequently, she was always finding herself in absurd situations.

Having lost altogether its sense of history, its ties with Russia's historical past, and any genuine feeling for Russia's national essence, the Imperial Government constantly tried to justify its policies by referring to historical traditions and to the national character of Russia. This led to the creation of a deceitful official ideology, a bureaucratic lie, which the Imperial Government sometimes believed quite sincerely. The drive "toward Constantinople and the straits"—strongly supported in Russia by foreign diplomats who were trying to use Russia as an instrument to weaken Turkey—was justified (aside from the theory that every European power must have "an exit to the sea") by references to the campaigns of Oleg, Igor, Sviatoslav, and Vladimir. In the process it was forgotten that Rus' at the time of Oleg was not what is now called Russia. For a state occupying the basins of the river system between the Baltic and the Black seas, for a state whose *raison d'être* was control of the waterway "from the Varangians to the Greeks," campaigns against Constantinople had a meaning altogether different than they had for a continental state extending not from north to south, but from east to west. For a long time relations between

Turkey and Russia-Eurasia, the heir of Genghis Khan, were disrupted in the name of a task supposedly bequeathed by Oleg.

Likewise, the partitioning of Poland (an episode typical of European dynastic politics, for it enlarged most advantageously the territories of two European powers bordering on Russia) was justified by references to the fact that Poland was historically Russia's enemy. But Poland had been Russia's enemy primarily as the spearhead of an invasive movement by European civilization and Catholicism. The partitioning of Poland further strengthened the two countries bordering on Russia that represented the imperialism of European civilization in its extreme form; it also caused Galicia, which comprised with its East Slavic population a natural geographic extension of Eurasian territory, to fall under the control of one of these countries; finally, it placed the Ukrainian population of Galicia under the control of the Catholics.

Pan-Slavism was an equally mendacious, supposedly nationalistic ideology which was fraught with serious consequences; it was supported, sometimes even sincerely, not only by the Imperial Government but by part of the intelligentsia. In essence this ideology was as foreign to and had as few connections with historical Russia as the ideologies of enlightened absolutism, liberalism, socialism, and so on.

The same loss of an awareness of Russia's historical essence, the same obtuseness regarding national traditions combined with an artificial, deceitful, ostensibly nationalistic pathos can be observed in domestic policies. It will suffice here to discuss two areas only—relations with the "indigenous peoples" and with the Orthodox Church. Following the example of other European states, which pursued a policy of assimilation at home and abroad in their attempts to achieve the cultural denationalization of subject peoples, the Imperial Government strove to "Russify" every region with a non-Russian population. This policy represented a complete betrayal of every Russian historical tradition: ancient Rus' never practiced forcible Russification. If various Finnic tribes that once constituted the native population of a significant part of Great Russia became completely Russified in antiquity, this happened naturally, without force or oppression, without declaring war upon national characteristics, and without the artificial inculcation of the Russian language in the schools. If the Tatar mirzas who accepted Orthodoxy were Russified while in the Russian service, this also happened quite naturally, without force. In any case, as they merged with the Russian tribe, the Russified Turanians imparted their own characteristics to the Russian people and introduced them into the Russian national psychology, so that together with the Russification of the Turanians there occurred a simultaneous "Turanianization" of the Russians. From the organic merger of these two elements there arose a unique, new entity, the national Russian type, which is in essence not pure Slavic but Slavo-Turanian. The Russian tribe was created not through the forcible Russification of "indigenous peoples," but through the fraternization of Russians with those peoples. And whenever the Russian people have been left to their own devices, they have continued the national tradition of fraternization, even during the imperial era. Artificial, government-inspired Russification was a product of complete ignorance about the historical essence of Russia-Eurasia, the result of forgetting the spirit of her national traditions. Consequently, this apparently nationalistic policy did great damage to Russia's historical interests.

The antinationalism of the Imperial Government's policies was most evident in the relations between the government and the Russian Orthodox Church. Insofar as the voice of the nation's conscience was heard in the Church as one manifestation of the national character, the antinational Imperial Government was bound to deal with the Church in a hostile manner; policies that induced the government to ignore the individuality of the Russian nation, to view it merely as material for the creation of a great European power led in time to the conclusion that this individuality must be completely suppressed. Accordingly, the government made every effort to render the Church mute, resorting finally to persecution at the slightest manifestation of an independent spirit. The ideals borrowed from the West (imperialism, militarism, chauvinism, and state-worship) were alien not only to the national element in historical Russia but to the Christian Church as well. For all these reasons the Church was an inconvenience for the government. However, the debris of the ideology of tsarist authority upon which pre-Petrine Rus had depended continued to exist among the people; and since this ideology was closely associated with the Church, the government did not dare to launch an open campaign against it.

The upshot was a hypocritical compromise. The Imperial Government created the impression of giving the Church its full support, and constantly emphasized its union with the Church. But because it was in essence alien to the real spirit of the Church, the government struggled implacably against every manifestation of this spirit and used every means to ensure the complete subjugation of the Church to state authority. Members of the hierarchy and the priesthood who did not wish to submit or who manifested the spirit of the Church in too independent a manner were systematically removed from office. The reestablishment of the patriarchate and the convocation of local Church councils were topics not open to discussion. The Church Synod, which consisted of bishops appointed by the government, was actually run by a secular official, the *Oberprokuror*; likewise, authority in the local dioceses was in the hands of the consistory officials, while the bishops received only *pro forma* veneration. Through its governors the government kept close watch over the activities of the bishops, archbishops, and metropolitans, and they were replaced and exiled to monasteries or to remote, "safe" dioceses for the smallest deviations from the prescribed course of action.

This enslavement of the Church was gradually killing its spirit, which continued to flicker, but only feebly, as it was hypocritically smothered by the "Orthodox" Russian government. Imitating the European powers, the government tried to infect the Church with the spirit of imperialism and chauvinism with which it was itself saturated. And when the people could no longer find in the Church the responsive national conscience they had found there in the pre-Petrine period, and they veered off into sectarianism or the Old Belief, the government used harsh reprisals and police harassment against the sectarians and schismatics. A situation was created in which the Church found itself being defended by the police. Everything possible was done not only to bureaucratize the Church and deprive it of its spirit, but to make it unpopular among the masses. This was persecution of the Church at its most malicious, the more so because it was concealed behind a facade of piety that was supported in the highest circles.

XI

Such were the consequences of Russia's deviation from her historical path. And these consequences were logically inevitable. After setting for itself the goal of creating a great European power from Russian material, the government was certain to look upon Russia not as a living personality, but as inert material. It was certain to place itself in opposition to Russia and to do whatever was necessary to smother all manifestations of Russia's individuality, to mangle and disfigure the national physiognomy. No government could last long after it had demonstrated open hostility toward the historical essence, the living personality of Russia; and since it could infect only a very small number of Russians with ideals alien to the Russian spirit (imperialism, mindless chauvinism, militarism), it had to lie and invent deceitful official slogans and ideologies that allegedly proved the hereditary link between itself and historical Russia and justified the established direction of its policies. But official lies could not deceive the nation for long.

After it had placed itself in opposition to a Russia it viewed as inert material, the government was certain to incur universal hatred. This happened inevitably, fatefully, and could not have been otherwise. In its attempts to build a great European power out of Russian material, the Imperial Government had to graft European civilization and European culture onto Russia. Educated Russian society assimilated a variety of European ideas in the process of Europeanization, but not always those that were agreeable to the government. The government was partial to the ideas of imperialism, militarism, bellicose chauvinism, and capitalist exploitation, while educated society was attracted to liberalism, parliamentarism, democracy, various "freedoms," socialism, and the like. Several parties formed, each of them wanting to shape the Russian material according to one European idea or another—but not according to the ideas that appealed to the government. Nevertheless, there was an essential kinship, a single, fundamental characteristic shared by all these parties and the government: utter indifference to Russia's individuality, the view that Russia was inert material from which an edifice had to be erected according to some borrowed European idea.

The European ideas themselves were diverse; some Russians were partial to one idea, others to another, and the government to a third. Both the government and the various parties comprised by Russian educated society wanted to make a European state from Russian material, but each understood "European state" in its own way. This is why struggle and a general atmosphere of enmity were inevitable. But enmity against the government was especially bitter, because among all the plans for the creation of a European power from Russian material, only the government's was making any progress. For other parties, the overthrow of the government thus became the starting point, the first step on the path to realization of their own ideal. This was logically inevitable. Once the government had introduced two principles—ignoring the individuality of historical Russia and constructing from Russian material an edifice that conformed to an alien European ideal—it became possible for any group of Europeanized Russians to dream of building its own edifice from that same material.

The government preferred not to argue about which ideal was best. To have done so would have necessitated conducting the argument in terms of the degree to which a given ideal was "European" (i.e., the degree to which it corresponded to the spirit of European civilization) rather than in terms of the degree to which a given ideal was applicable to Russian realities (this perspective would have contradicted its basic view of Russia as inert material from which virtually anything could be made). If the argument had been conducted on this plane, the government would have been compelled to admit that its ideal was the worst. The lifeblood of the great European powers is moved only by militarism, imperialism, and capitalist exploitation, but the hypocritical profession of entirely different ideals is still considered "good taste" there. Not wishing to enter into this debate, the government could only persecute educated society and uproot every European idea in conflict with the direction of its own policies. This created an obvious internal contradiction (the government of a European power appeared to be struggling against Europeanism while desiring to remain in the "Concert of Europe") and exacerbated the conflict by intensifying the hostility and restiveness of everyone in educated society.

Such were the relations between the Imperial Government and educated society (i.e., the Europeanized part of the nation). As far as the "common folk" were concerned (i.e., the non-Europeanized part of the nation), to the degree that they held onto fragments of the national, pre-Petrine Russian culture, the post-Petrine state system was completely alien and incomprehensible to them. Since the sole link between the pre-Petrine and post-Petrine state systems was the authority of the tsar, this element alone was understandable to the most "benighted" (i.e., those least touched by Europeanization). It was therefore natural that a certain cult of the tsar should exist among these people, to whom notions formed during the pre-Petrine era were still attached by inertia. But this cult was based on illusion and self-deception, since the monarchs of the post-Petrine era were quite different from their predecessors. What is more, the ideology of tsarist authority during the pre-Petrine era was part of a general political and ideological system that was inseparable from Old Russian religious living as a whole—a life style systematically destroyed by the government during the post-Petrine era.

Torn from its proper context, the ideology of tsarist authority could continue to exist among the people only through inertia, as a relic of antiquity. As the people lost more and more of their connections with the national past because of the ceaseless efforts of the government to create a great European power from Russian material, and as they were drawn into the current of elementary Europeanization through military service, factories, seasonal work, schools, and the like, and came into close contact with the realities of the new state system, they began to forget the old ideology of tsarist authority, and the image of the tsar lost its special aura. Ultimately, a large group came to exist between "educated society" and the "common folk," between the Europeanized and non-Europeanized parts of the nation; they were the "quasi-intelligentsia," who despised the foundations of the old national life style, but who also hated with increasing intensity the nation's upper strata. This group was not yet saturated with European culture, but it had managed to assimilate a few simple European ideas in a rather elementary form; these were the ideas they preached to the people. The government was able to combat the successes of this propaganda only with repression and the police; but in doing so it only managed to set everyone even more vehemently against itself by becoming the undisguised enemy of the entire nation.

The revolution and overthrow of the Imperial Government became inevitable. In all its activities, the government was preparing the way for revolution; it dug its grave with its own hands. And this happened not because the Imperial Government was especially stupid or lacking in foresight. The wisest of governments could not have acted differently, and the most farsighted could only have postponed the revolution, not prevented it. At issue here was the very essence of the task the Imperial Government had set for itself: any government that abandoned the path of history for an alien path (reshaping the Russian material to create a great European power) was certain to find itself locked in struggle with that material; and eventually this struggle was certain to culminate in an uprising of the nation against the government.

The World War served as an impetus. Initially it appeared that the Imperial Government had succeeded at last in contaminating much of educated society with its ideals of imperialism and bellicose chauvinism. But the enthusiasm was only temporary. Soon the struggle between educated society and the government was renewed, and the masses joined it on the side of society. The inevitable, long-gestating revolution finally took place, and the Imperial Government was overthrown. Immediately a question arose: Who would replace it—that is, which of the other, familiar European ideologies would now take the lead in the demolition and reconstruction of Russia? The struggle among the various parties of the intelligentsia did not last long. Victory was claimed by the party that stood for the European ideal which was at once the most difficult to achieve and the most seductive. Russia now entered a new period in her history, that of the Soviet system and the supremacy of communism.

XII

We must now try to answer the following question: Is this new period truly new—as new, for example, as the post-Petrine period was in relation to the pre-Petrine; or is it merely a new phase, a new stage in the post-Petrine period?

Examination of the present situation in the U.S.S.R. from this viewpoint leads to ambiguous results. On the one hand, the Soviet government, which was brought to power by a popular revolution that signaled the complete repudiation of past policies, is striving to alter fundamentally the course established by the defeated antinational monarchy. In the area of foreign affairs we note the rejection of the false ideas of the Slavophiles and of Pan-Slavism, as well as the rejection of all efforts to imitate the imperialistic pretensions of the "great" European powers. With regard to the East, a correct attitude has been adopted, one that corresponds to the historical essence of Russia-Eurasia: for the first time Russia recognizes herself to be the natural ally of the countries of Asia in their struggle against the imperialism of the countries of European (Romano-Germanic) civilization. Russia has now begun for the first time to speak to Asians as equals, as comrades in misfortune, and has abandoned the role of arrogant culture-bearer and exploiter—one that did not suit her at all. In the eyes of Asians, this role placed Russia in the ranks of the Romano-Germanic predators and oppressors whom Asia has always hated and feared.

In domestic affairs it is worth noting the repudiation of Russification, a policy alien to the historical character of Russia which was adopted by the government of the antinational monarchy only in imitation of the European powers. Official recognition of the national rights of the peoples that constitute Russia-Eurasia and cession of a high degree of autonomy to each of them (limited only by the need to preserve the unity of the state) are consonant with a proper understanding of the historical essence of the Russian state system, which was created by both Russians and Turanians. Also worth noting is the effort to destroy the cultural gulf between the highest and lowest strata of the nation and to draw into active cultural and governmental work groups in the population that have never been thus employed in the past.

Despite all this, it is clear that the Soviet government is completely controlled by the recent past and is continuing the old course, although in a new form. No matter how one looks at it, the most important figures in shaping Soviet policy are representatives of that ideologically denationalized and

Europeanized intelligentsia to which the era of the antinational monarchy gave birth. The influx of "new forces" from the broad democratic strata of society could not alter this state of affairs, since the representatives of the masses who took part in the revolution were precisely those who had lost the last vestiges of the national culture, but who had acquired only a smattering of European ideas (such people are said to have "class-consciousness"). Finding themselves in the world of the intelligentsia, such expatriates from the people had nothing to teach, inasmuch as they were the ones being taught. Consequently, the atmosphere in the ruling circles was entirely the creation of the intelligentsia.

Thus, the activities of the Soviet government represent what is essentially a continuation of the course chosen by Peter I. Once again the government sees in Russia only material for erecting an edifice whose plan has no connection with the Russian soil, since this plan has been borrowed directly from Europe. The ideal of Peter I and the rulers who succeeded him was the creation from Russian material of a great and powerful European state which was in every way the equal of its European peers; the present government is striving to create from this same Russian material the socialist state that has long been the dream of European socialists. In both cases the ideal is foreign, and its connection with the Russian material is artificial; for both it is necessary to demolish everything to achieve the ideal, and to struggle with the Russian material, which resists efforts to force it into a foreign mold.

The practical consequences have been identical in both cases. In foreign affairs, the accomplishment of Russia's historical tasks continues to be stymied by an utterly superfluous, costly, and pragmatically unjustifiable involvement in the affairs of other European countries for the sake of principles alien to historical Russia. Formerly Russian rulers entered into various "holy alliances," and they wasted vast amounts of money and sometimes human lives; at the very least they exposed the country to the constant danger of war, all for the sake of

supporting foreign thrones and buttressing the power of
foreign monarchs and the European legitimist principle of
monarchy—a principle that had nothing in common with the
Old Russian monarchic idea. Nowadays senseless sums of
money are being wasted on communist propaganda in Europe
and America; foreign labor unions, communist parties, and
strikes in foreign lands are subsidized, just as the courts of petty
Balkan monarchs were subsidized in the past. Hence the
constant danger of conflict with foreign governments.

All of this is done in the name of an international proletarian
solidarity that is every bit as illusory as the international
solidarity of monarchs upon which the idea of the Holy Alliance
was based during the reign of Alexander I. Or they are done in
the name of socialism, communism, Marxism—ideas as non-
Russian, as dissociated from historical Russia, as were the
monarchic legitimist, feudal ideas for which the Russian
emperors of the post-Petrine era exhausted themselves in
Europe. As the salons of Petersburg and the Imperial Court
were at one time a refuge for various German princes who had
lost their thrones or for high-born political emigrés who had
been expelled from various European countries, so the U.S.S.R.
is now becoming a refuge for a variety of political adventurers
and unsuccessful revolutionaries from all the corners of Europe.
As in the past, these foreigners do very well for themselves in
Russia. A typical example is provided by the Baltic provinces,
which were conquered by Peter I in order to bring Russia closer
to Europe. They avenged themselves upon Russia by inundating
the ministries, the navy, the guard regiments, governorships,
and the Imperial Court itself with German pettifoggers,
martinets, and dignitaries who spoke Russian badly but held the
Russian people in profound contempt. Presently the Baltic
provinces are again supplying us with the same kind of
administrative personnel—formerly German barons, but now,
Latvian communists.

We can see the continuation of the pretensions of the post-
Petrine era in domestic politics as well. It is difficult to make a

European of a "Russian fool"; first one must knock the foolishness out of him with a club and force him to forget his national identity. This is why Peter I and his successors were masters at insulting the Russian past and Russian national sentiments, at trampling upon the foundations of Russian life, including the moral and religious, that had evolved during the course of Russian history. All of this has continued into the present. Current Soviet policies are reminiscent, sometimes in minor details, of the policies that Peter I and his successors once imposed on the Russian nobility. The difference is merely one of scale, inasmuch as Peter I limited himself to making Europeans of the nobility, assuming that this class would continue the task of Europeanizing the other levels of society. But the Soviet government has taken the Russian masses themselves in hand. However, if one ignores this difference in scale, the analogy is striking. The attention lavished upon youth, the antireligious performances, the preaching of sexual licentiousness, and the war against shame—all of this was implemented two hundred years ago by Peter I, but only within the relatively restricted circle of the aristocracy and nobility; now these ideas are being imposed upon the general population.

Nor is the campaign against the Russian Church a new phenomenon. Through the institution of the Holy Synod and the office of the *Oberprokuror*, Peter I struck a blow against the Russian Church that was far more destructive than the arrest of the Patriarch by the Soviet government. Catherine II closed eighty percent of the Russian monasteries, appropriated a comparable portion of the Church's property, and left Bishop Arsenii Matseevich, who had stubbornly resisted her anti-Church policies, to rot in prison in Revel. In this she anticipated the campaign of the Soviet government against the Church. A detailed examination of the history of the Russian Church during the period of the Synod and *Oberprokuror* will reveal how systematically the government of the antinational monarchy made war on the Church; it is distinguished from the Soviet government in this regard only by its greater tact, hypocrisy, and careful planning.

Thus the Soviet government has shown itself to be not an opponent, but a conscious, active partisan of the antinational policies of Europeanization characteristic of the post-Petrine monarchy. And no matter how strange or paradoxical it may seem, the reason for this is the Soviet government's devotion to communism. If it were to reject communism with its European origins, the connection between it and European civilization would be severed, and the task of strengthening and developing the national historical life of Russia could begin. This would truly be the beginning of a new era in Russian history. It would be an era characterized by intentional achievement of national historical tasks and the creation of a new culture not according to alien European models or prescriptions, but from within, and in harmony with national historical tasks and the special traits of the real Russia. Russia would not be viewed as faceless, inert material, but as a living personality seeking embodiment in its own culture. But this has not happened. Russia remains on the perilous path that the zealot Peter I set her upon long ago. Russia has remained a province of European civilization. What is more, Russia is a laboratory for risky experiments that test in real life the journalistic theories of European dreamers—experiments from which Europeans shield their own "valuable" human material.

It is natural, therefore, that Europeans should look approvingly upon the intentions of the Soviet government, and that they should criticize Soviet reality only to the extent that these intentions have not been fully realized, or realized unsuccessfully. Foreigners who visit the U.S.S.R. poke fun at the "Russian savages" after their return home, but they still approve the laudable intention of the rulers of Russia to give these savages an injection of European civilization. Despite the commercially unprofitable presence of a communist government in Russia (its socio-economic experiments hinder importation of European goods in large quantities), Europeans are reconciling themselves to this inconvenience. They still consider the existence of a communist government in Russia profitable for themselves, because it is carrying out the task of Europeanization there. In destroying the spiritual foundations and national uniqueness of Russian life, in propagating there the materialist world view that shapes both Europe and America, and in nurturing Russia on theories with deep roots in the soil of European civilization, the communist government is consolidating Russia's position as a province of European civilization and confirming the spiritual conquest of Russia by Europe, a conquest whose foundations were laid by Peter I. This, in the final analysis, is clearly profitable for Europeans.

The secret dream of every European is to strip away the uniqueness of every nationality on earth, to destroy all distinct national cultures and casts of mind with the exception of the European, which is essentially a national culture itself (it was created by the peoples of a single Celto-Germanic race who have represented a self-contained whole similar to that found in certain areas of China during the entire course of their common history). But this culture wants to be considered universally human. The realization of this dream, the propagation of this "universally human" (i.e., Romano-Germanic) culture throughout the world, would transform all the world's peoples into second- and third-rate Europeans; only native Europeans would be first-rate (i.e., speakers of the Romance languages and the Germanic and Anglo-Saxon peoples)—those for whom this "universally human culture" is also a national culture. Europeans would then be preeminent throughout the world.

Since this is the ultimate imperialistic goal of European civilization, it is a matter of indifference to Europeans how it is achieved. This is why they look upon the Russian communist government as an ally in their enterprise. Only one activity of the Soviet government is genuinely disliked by Europeans—communist propaganda in their colonies and in Asia. This propaganda frightens them not because it is communist, but because it may ignite nationalistic feelings among these peoples

and encourage them to reject European civilization in the name
of nationalism. Thus the only activity that alienates the
Europeans from the Soviet government is the one in which the
Soviets are fulfilling the historic task of Russia (instinctively
rather than consciously). The real enemy of pan-European
imperialism, the imperialism of European civilization, is not
communism—born of European civilization and organically
linked to it—but historical Russia, Russia-Eurasia. From its very
essence Russia-Eurasia will inevitably resist Europeanization
despite all the efforts of its rulers, be they kings or communists.

The communist government has proved to be an active
partisan of the Europeanizing traditions of the old antinational
monarchy. It has not broken with the past, but is completely
controlled by the infamous "legacy of Peter the Great."
Moreover, it is continuing the work of Peter I on an even
grander scale and with greater zeal than all the post-Petrine
monarchs. No abrupt turning point such as the one during
Peter's reign has occurred in Russian life under the Soviets, but
only an abrupt acceleration, and always in the same direction. If
one condemns this direction and perceives in the revolution the
elemental desire of historical Russia to change it, then one must
also see that the Soviet government has not yet faced up to the
tasks that the revolution set for it. The government has not
liberated Russia from the yoke of European civilization; on the
contrary, it has directed its efforts toward strengthening this
yoke.

XIII

Let us glance briefly once again at the outline of Russia-
Eurasia's historical development as it has been presented in the
foregoing argument.

The Eurasian world represents a self-contained geographical,
economic, and ethnic whole distinguishable from both Europe
and Asia proper. It is the natural environment itself that teaches

the peoples of Eurasia to recognize the need to form a single state and to create their own national cultures while working cooperatively with one another. The political unification of Eurasia was first accomplished by the Turanians in the person of Genghis Khan; these Turanian nomads were the first bearers of the idea of a common Eurasian state system. Later, the Turanians' statist zeal degenerated as a national religious revival spread rapidly among the Russians, and the idea of a common Eurasian state passed from the Turanians to the Russians, who became its inheritors and bearers. It was now possible for Russia-Eurasia to become a self-contained cultural, political, and economic region and to develop a unique Eurasian culture.

But in neighboring Europe the spirit of imperialism, of conquest and empire, had begun to develop with increasing rapidity. European civilization, preoccupied with technology and the external organization of life, was devoting ever greater amounts of energy to expansion. It was mandatory that Russia-Eurasia be protected from this danger in the West, which was threatening her cultural, economic, and political independence. Consequently, some of Europe's technological advantages had to be assimilated. But this assimilation quickly became an end in itself for the rulers of Russia-Eurasia. They forgot that borrowing European military and, to some extent, industrial technology was necessary only to defend Russia from a foreign cultural influence, and they became preoccupied with the process of borrowing itself. Once seduced by European civilization, they were carried away by a vain desire to transform Russia into a state exactly like European states, and they dreamed of standing on an equal footing with the rulers of the most powerful European nations. So the foreign danger, the repelling of which had motivated importation of European technology, was not repelled at all, but introduced into Russia by Russians. Russia was on her way to becoming a province of European civilization, and the imperialism of this civilization achieved one success after another there. Rather than technology, Russians began to borrow the European way of thinking—a way congenial to a completely different psychological type. The Russian ceased to be himself. But he did not become a European, he simply became a freak. As a consequence, social relationships among Russians were distorted; deep abysses appeared, separating some Russians from others, and existing social bonds were broken.

The two-century-long rule of the antinational monarchy, which turned every stratum of the population against itself, led to the revolution. But the revolution changed nothing, since the crew that rose to power was itself contaminated by the poisons of European civilization. Their propagation in Russia of a world view that is a fully developed product of the European spirit and European civilization reveals Europeans to be an instrument serving the imperialism of European culture, mistakenly understood by them as the culture of "mankind." Thus it is that after the revolution Russia has not become her true self, she has not been liberated from the spiritual yoke of European culture, and she cannot create her own unique national culture freely—a culture based not on the psychological characteristics of a generalized European type but on those of the Russian, the Eurasian.

It will be Russia's responsibility in the future to arrive at last at a conscious understanding of her true nature and to return to the achievement of her own historical tasks. Russia must understand that the ominous military and economic power of European states, which caused the prerevolutionary antinational monarchy to militarize and Europeanize Russia, and the bourgeois capitalist order, whose defeat is the postrevolutionary communist government's justification for collectivizing Russia, are all organic aspects and natural manifestations of European civilization, which is the principal enemy of historical Russia. Russia must understand that it is senseless to struggle against these manifestations, since the enemy is European civilization as a whole, especially the spirit of this civilization. She must understand that the methods utilized in this struggle cannot embody the spirit of European civilization. Otherwise the struggle will be useless.

The post-Petrine antinational monarchy erred when it identified a single, well-defined danger in the military and economic power of individual European states and hoped to oppose this danger with comparable Russian military and economic power; to this end it brought to Russia and began to cultivate there the spirit of European militarism, imperialism, and pseudo-nationalism (i.e., arrogant chauvinism)—a spirit entirely alien to Russia. The postrevolutionary government erred when it perceived a single, well-defined danger in the bourgeois capitalist order; in order to overcome this danger, it began to cultivate in Russia the world view of economic materialism, which is equally European and alien in spirit. And it is striving to realize ideals of social life that are the creations of European theorists and therefore completely alien to Russia. Once it is understood that both of these errors lead to the spiritual enslavement of Russia by European civilization, to the disfigurement of historical Russia's true nature, the only sensible course will be to reject every manifestation of the European spirit and to begin the final battle against European civilization as a whole. This battle must be conducted while an independent and self-sufficient Russian-Eurasian culture is created on foundations altogether distinct from the spiritual bases of European civilization.

There is no reason to lose hope that Russia will again find—and not in the remote future—her own true historical path. At the present moment, both hatred of Europeanism and efforts to repudiate it unquestionably exist in elemental forms among the most diverse groups of the population of Russia-Eurasia. It is true that many identify the object of their hatred with the bourgeois capitalist order in contemporary Europe, and they do not understand that the world view of socialism and economic materialism, which places itself in opposition to this bourgeois order, is actually an integral part of Europeanism, that it is the spawn of the spirit of European civilization. But this way of looking at things is not fixed forever. Sooner or later it will be replaced by another, more conscious, consistent, and radical repudiation not only of specific expressions, but of the very essence, the spirit of European civilization. And repudiation of this foreign spirit will allow Russia-Eurasia to find her own true nature.

XIV

No matter how strange it may seem, it is precisely now, when the Russian government is directing all its efforts toward the propagation of a world view created by typical representatives of the European spirit and toward the restructuring of Russia according to theories created by European writers—it is precisely now, despite all of this, that the elemental, national uniqueness and the non-European, half-Asiatic face of Russia-Eurasia is becoming more visible than ever. It is surfacing everywhere, despite all the internationalist and antinational bric-a-brac, despite all the pretensions of this final proclamation of a "universally human" (i.e., European) civilization—everywhere we can see the genuine Russia, historical Russia, ancient Russia, not an invented "Slavic" or "Slavo-Varangian" Russia, but the real, Russo-Turanian Russia-Eurasia, heir to the great legacy of Genghis Khan. Various Turanian peoples—the Tatars, Kirghiz, Bashkirs, Chuvash, Yakuts, Buryats, and Mongols—have begun to speak in their own languages (now recognized as official languages) and to participate on an equal footing with Russians in building a common state system. In Russian physiognomies, which formerly appeared purely Slavic, one is beginning to notice something Turanian. In the Russian language itself one is beginning to hear new sound combinations that are also "barbarous," also Turanian. It seems that once again, as if it were seven hundred years ago, one can smell everywhere in Russia the odors of burning dung, horse sweat, camel hair—the smells of the nomad camp. And hovering over all Russia is the shade of the great Genghis Khan, unifier of Eurasia.

The legacy of Genghis Khan is inseparable from Russia. Whether Russia wants it or not, she remains forever the guardian of this legacy, and her historical destiny has been shaped by this fact. Even during the period of the antinational monarchy, when both the government and educated society strove to make a European power of Russia, and everything they did reflected a shame-filled aversion to the natural bond between Russia and Asia—even then Russia was compelled by the very nature of things to continue the historical enterprise of uniting Eurasia into one state—the enterprise of Genghis Khan. The annexations of the Crimea, the Caucasus, the Transcaspian region, and Turkestan, and the formation of closer links between Eastern Siberia and Russia were all steps along the path toward reunification of the scattered parts of the Eurasian *ulus* of Genghis Khan's empire, while the colonization and cultivation of the steppe, its transformation from a nomad camp into a tilled field, consolidated the transfer of the Eurasian state idea from the Turanians to the Russians.

Although the government, in trying to imitate the "great European powers" in all things, was prepared to implement a policy of forcible "assimilation" that would strip the newly acquired regions of their cultural identity (as Europeans do in their colonies), the Russian masses sensed instinctively the true task of Russia and adopted a policy of fraternization with non-Russian populations, borrowing various customs and practices from them. Special mixed life styles developed in the newly annexed regions, life styles that in time could have served as the basis for a whole spectrum of Eurasian cultures, variations on a single, general Eurasian type. It was the efforts of the Russian elite (both educated society and the government) to possess a culture indubitably European that interfered with this process.

The same process, Russia's instinctive return to her natural historical path, can be observed at present. Although the communist government looks to the West, to the proletariat of "civilized countries," and cherishes ardent hopes that the European and American proletariats will recognize them as true kinsmen, Russia is still being forced, by the very nature of things, to deal more and more with Asia and to put into practice in her internal development that fraternization with the peoples of Eurasia which is an inevitable consequence of the historical mission of Russia, the political unifier of Eurasia and the heir and descendant of Genghis Khan. The gravitation of the various peoples of Eurasia toward a common state structure that unites them into a single family compels them to look upon the Russian state as their own, as theirs by birth. The plowing of the nation's entire social landscape, which has brought to the surface layers previously far below, is bringing ever closer an opportunity to create a new culture or a whole spectrum of related cultures on the basis of the customs and world view of the masses, both of which were until recently subjects fit only for ethnographic study. Once again, however, this opportunity is being frustrated by the stubborn desire of the managers of cultural life to have a European culture, perhaps not identical in every detail with the contemporary culture of the peoples of Western Europe, but still corresponding to the dreams and theories of European sociologists and writers. Consequently, it will be a culture permeated with the spirit of European civilization.

Despite the stubborn war which the ruling circles (distinctions here are unimportant: formerly the monarchists, now the communists) have waged against the essence of Russia-Eurasia for over two hundred years, Russia-Eurasia has never ceased striving to be herself, striving to reenter her natural historical path despite the long detour through Western European models and doctrines. This instinctive striving must become conscious at long last. The future Russia-Eurasia must consciously repudiate the spirit of European civilization and build its own state system and culture upon completely different, non-European foundations.

It is impossible to predict exactly what this state system and culture will be. But the legacy of Genghis Khan, which has been continuously present in Russia since it was first embraced by pre-Petrine Muscovy, will shape her future as it has her past; and this makes predictions to some degree feasible. In international relations, the future Russia, the conscious custodian of Genghis Khan's legacy, will not try to become a European power; on the contrary, she will completely dissociate herself from Europe and European civilization. Remembering the lessons of the past, she will follow developments in European technology and adopt what is needed. But she will constantly protect herself against the adoption of European ideas, the European world view, and the spirit of European culture. She will not involve herself in European affairs, she will not side with any factious party or ideology in the countries of Europe, and she will consider no European social group a loyal ally. In particular, while continuing the struggle against international capital as an important feature of European civilization, she will not consider the European proletariat a reliable ally; she will take into account the fact that, although this proletariat is also struggling against capital, it will cease to struggle when international capital yields to it a portion of the profits gained from exploiting "uncivilized" countries. The complete destruction of international capital and the interruption of its exploitation of "uncivilized" or "half-civilized" countries (precisely what Russia's goal must be) is as unprofitable and unacceptable to the European proletariat as it is to the European bourgeoisie.

On the other hand, in her relations with countries and peoples outside the boundaries of European civilization, the future Russia should be guided by a sense of solidarity, recognizing that they are natural allies who are equally interested in overcoming the imperialism of European civilization. Russia should avoid attempts to annex any country not located within the geographical boundaries of Eurasia, remembering the damage that such annexations once did to Genghis Khan's enterprise. At the same time, Russia should

support both cultural and vigorous trade relations with these
non-Eurasian, purely Asiatic countries. From bitter experience
Russia knows more about Europe than they do; she should
unite them in opposition to European civilization, forewarn
them against the invasive spirit of Europeanism in its diverse
manifestations, and help them to create and develop their own
national cultures.

Domestically, the future Russia should never forget the past.
This does not mean the past should be resurrected; that is
impossible and unnecessary. But certain principles that
organized life in the time of Genghis Khan and in pre-Petrine
Muscovite Rus' can be placed at the foundation of future
development. The most important is a close connection between
the *mores* of private life, the state system, and religion. The
godless, antireligious state is a European invention that depends
on the spirit of European civilization. It is true that Europeans
take great pride in this invention and consider it a sign of
progress. But this is how Europeans evaluate all the products of
their civilization. They reason in the following way: Everything
invented by Europeans that conforms to the general spirit of
their culture is good and "progressive," while everything not
invented by Europeans is good only to the extent that it
resembles some European invention. But when one reasons
objectively, resists European self-adulation, and remembers that
the antireligious state has never existed in the history of any non-
European people, one is led to the conclusion that this state
system is unnatural and freakish, contrary to normal human
nature; and if it does not contradict the human nature of
Europeans, then this is so because their natures are abnormal
and degenerate. A healthy human being is always religious. And
it is untrue that religion is a private, individual matter. In reality
religion always has been, is now, and always will be the concern
of the whole nation. The peoples of Eurasia have always been
religious. The fact that some have fallen away from religion can
be attributed to the crippling influence of European civilization
and ideas. Russia-Eurasia can recover her true nature and

become her true self only after returning to religion and strengthening the religious dimension of her life.

This does not mean that it is necessary to recreate the union between the state and the official church that existed in Russia before the revolution. Quite the opposite is true. This union stifled Orthodoxy, it deprived the Russian Church of its capacity to develop, and it aimed to transform the Church into a branch of the police—a pattern that is antithetical to the spirit of a genuinely religious state system. This union, which led to the subordination of the ecclesiastical hierarchy to the state and to the imposition of state censorship on free expressions of the religious spirit, does not conform to the principle of a close relationship between the state and religion that lies at the foundation of every genuine Eurasian state structure. But other ideas about the relationship between religion and the state familiar from European practice are equally unsatisfactory (e.g., separation of church and state, subordination of the state to an ecclesiastical hierarchy, a pact between the state and an international ecclesiastical hierarchy).

All of these schemes are permeated with the spirit of European civilization, a spirit that is crippled in the realm of religion. They are based on an abstract conception of church and state as two separate organizations with different personnel, while in real life church and state are made up of living people, and what is more, of the same people. The people in the church and in the state are not two separate entities but one. Free will and conscience exist in every human being; they are not different entities, but different qualities, different capacities of the same person. In a normal, rational, decent person there is no discord between will and conscience, but rather a certain harmony. The same should be true of the state system and religion. Lifeless, official religiosity is analogous to the subordination of conscience to the will; struggle between church and state is analogous to the struggle between conscience and will. But the subordination of the state to the ecclesiastical hierarchy is not analogous to subordination of the will to conscience. In this case the state and the ecclesiastical hierarchy can be thought of as two separate entities; the result is the subordination of the will of one entity to the conscience (and, consequently, the will) of another.

The problem of the mutual relations between the state system and religion is of fundamental importance to Russia-Eurasia, since, as I have argued, Russia-Eurasia can become herself only after she has become religious. The solution to this problem is to be found not in legislation but in the warp and woof of everyday life. There was no official religion in the empire of Genghis Khan, nor was there subordination of the state to any ecclesiastical hierarchy; but the state system of Genghis Khan was nevertheless deeply religious. Similarly, in pre-Petrine Rus' the faith was not official and subservient, nor was the government subordinate to the power of the Church. Nevertheless, the old Muscovite state system was religious.

In both systems this problem was resolved not in the realm of politics and legislation, but in the realm of life style and psychology. Every one of Genghis Khan's warriors swore allegiance not only to his superior (and through him, to his superior's superior, and so on, up to the Supreme Khan), but also, and above all else, to a higher religious principle. And every warrior knew that his superior swore allegiance to that same religious principle, and his superior's superior, and so on, up to Genghis Khan himself. This allegiance to religious principle on the part of the warrior, his superior, and of Genghis Khan himself was not merely *pro forma*, it was not merely an aspect of their service; it also existed beyond the boundaries of their service, at the center of their everyday lives. The life of nature, human destiny, and the customs that guided human life were understood as elements in the orderly movement of things preestablished by a transcendent, Supreme Being. The state system was understood as part of this natural order. The same attitude toward these matters can be seen in pre-Petrine Rus', despite the enormous differences between it and the nomad state of Genghis Khan. If Russia-Eurasia wants to become her true self once again and not a misshapen image of European civilization, she must recreate these same conditions. Externally these conditions need not resemble either pre-Petrine Rus' or the empire of Genghis Khan, but the principle underlying the structure must be the same. For this is the true, underlying principle of every genuine Eurasian state system.

Thus, the path along which Russia-Eurasia must pass to reach what is genuinely her own, the path to her own true nature, has been traced by her past. This is not a path into the past, but forward, toward something genuinely new, toward something extraordinary. Russia's task is to create a completely new culture, her own culture, which will not resemble European civilization. What is happening in Russia at present only appears to be new and unprecedented. In actual fact, it represents destruction and not creation; and this destruction is permeated with the same old spirit, the spirit of Peter I, of Catherine II, and of the nineteenth-century intelligentsia, which was seduced by the superficial allure of European civilization and ideas. Genuine, constructive creation remains in the future. It will be possible only when the attractions of European civilization and of ideologies invented in Europe have been exhausted once and for all, when Russia ceases to be a distorted reflection of European civilization and finds her own unique historical nature, when she becomes once again herself: Russia-Eurasia, the purposeful heir to and bearer of the great legacy of Genghis Khan.

9 Pan-Eurasian Nationalism*

I

Before the revolution Russia was a country in which Russians were recognized as the official owner of the entire state territory. In this respect no distinction was drawn between provinces with an indigenous Russian population and those with an indigenous non-Russian population: Russians had the status of owner and master everywhere, and non-Russians that of household members.

The revolution changed this situation. In the natural process of anarchic disintegration, Russia would have broken into separate parts if the Russian people had not preserved the unity of the state by sacrificing their position as the state's sole master. Owing to the implacable logic of history, the former relations between the Russians and non-Russians underwent a change. The non-Russian peoples of the former Russian Empire acquired a position they had not held earlier and Russians found themselves not the single ruler but one *people* among a number of others. However, since they surpass their neighbors in population and possess an old tradition of state government, they still play, as they should, the leading role among all the peoples of the state. Yet they are no longer masters among household members; only first among equals.

Everyone who has occasion to reflect seriously upon the future of our motherland should take into account the new

*Originally as "Obshcheevraziiskii natsionalizm." *Evraziiskaia khronika* 9, 1927, pp. 24-31. Translated by Kenneth Brostrom.

status of the Russians, for it is neither temporary nor transient. The rights with which the non-Russian peoples of the U.S.S.R. are now endowed cannot be taken away. Any attempt to rescind or even restrict them will meet with the fiercest resistance. If at any time the Russians were to undertake such a forcible repeal or restriction of the rights of the other peoples, they would be engaged in a hard and protracted struggle, in perpetual, total war open or hidden. Russia's enemies would of course welcome such a war in their struggle against the encroachments of Russians; some peoples that have gained self-determination would find support and allies among foreign powers, all the more so since from the moral point of view the position of Russians trying to repeal or restrict the national prerogatives of the other peoples would be most disadvantageous—practically indefensible. So immoral would be any attempt to wrest away the rights of the non-Russians that it would prove unpopular first and foremost among the Russians themselves. It would signify, whatever the results, that Russians had abandoned their feeling for state government in favor of chauvinistic self-affirmation, which in and of itself would be a sign of the state's imminent collapse. Any repeal or restriction of the rights gained by the peoples of the former Russian Empire in the course of the revolution is therefore out of the question. The Russia in which Russians were the sole master has now receded into the past. Henceforward Russians will enjoy the same rights as all other peoples inhabiting the country and taking part in its government.

The change in the role of Russians in the state presents a number of problems for Russian national self-awareness. Formerly, *the most extreme* Russian nationalist was nonetheless a patriot. Now, the state in which Russians live is no longer their own exclusive property; at the moment *exclusive* Russian nationalism disturbs the equilibrium of the constituent elements of the state and leads to the disruption of national unity. An *excessive* increase in Russian national pride will now set other peoples against Russians and isolate them. Whereas in the past even extreme Russian national pride was a factor supportive of the state, now that pride raised to a certain degree can prove to be an antistate factor, threatening state unity rather than contributing to it. Given the current role of Russians, extreme Russian nationalism can lead to Russian separatism, which formerly would have been inconceivable. An extreme nationalist, whose aim is that Russians should be the sole master in their own state, come what may, and that the state itself should belong to the Russians as their full and undivided property—at present such a nationalist must reconcile himself to a "Russia" that would lose all the "outlying provinces" and have borders coinciding approximately with those of the exclusively Great-Russian population up to the Ural mountains; a radically nationalistic aim could now be realized only within such narrowed geographic boundaries. From the modern point of view an extreme Russian nationalist turns out to be a separatist no different from any Ukrainian, Georgian, Azerbaijanian, etc., nationalist-separatist.

II

Formerly the basic factor serving to knit the Russian Empire into a single whole was the ownership of its entire territory by a single master—the Russian people ruled by its own Russian tsar; now that factor has been abolished. Is there another capable of knitting the state together? The revolution proposed the realization of a certain social ideal as such a unifying factor. The U.S.S.R. is not merely a group of separate republics, but a group of socialist republics striving to realize the same ideal of social organization, and it is the common ideal that unites them into a single whole.

A common social ideal of the separate parts of the U.S.S.R., the common direction they follow, is indeed a unifying factor of great force. Even if that ideal changes with time, its very presence and movement toward it along a common path will still underlie the state unity of the peoples and regions now

united in the U.S.S.R. But is this factor sufficient for the
unification of various peoples into a single state? From the
circumstance that the Uzbek Republic and the Belorussian
Republic are guided in their domestic policy by the effort to
realize the same social ideal it does not follow that both should
be incorporated into a single state. Nor does it follow that they
will not be on bad terms or engage in military conflicts. Clearly,
a common social ideal alone is insufficient, and something else
must counterbalance nationalist centrifugal ambitions of the
separate parts of the U.S.S.R.

In the contemporary U.S.S.R, such an antidote to nationalism
and separatism is class hatred and the proletariat's consciousness of solidarity in the face of ever-present danger. In each of
the peoples forming the U.S.S.R. only the proletarians are
recognized as full-fledged citizens, and the Soviet Union itself is
composed not so much of peoples as of proletarians. Having
seized power and now exercising its dictatorship, the proletariat
of the various peoples of the U.S.S.R. feels constantly threat-
ened by its enemies, both internal (since socialism has not yet
set in, and in the "transitional" period one must concede the
existence of capitalists and the bourgeoisie even within the
U.S.S.R.) and external (the rest of the world still ruled by
international capitalism and imperialism). And so in order to
defend its power against the machinations of its enemies, the
proletarians of the peoples of the U.S.S.R. have no other choice
but to unite into a single state.

This view of the meaning of the U.S.S.R.'s existence allows
the Soviet government to combat separatism: separatists want to
disrupt the unity of the country but the proletariat needs that
unity for defense; consequently, separatists are enemies of the
proletariat. For the same reason it also becomes possible and
necessary to combat nationalism, since the latter can easily be
construed as latent separatism. Besides, according to Marxist
doctrine, the proletariat is devoid of nationalistic instincts,
which are attributes of the bourgeoisie and a product of the
bourgeois order. The struggle against nationalism is achieved by

refocusing popular attention away from national onto *social* emotions. Consciousness of national unity, the prerequisite of any nationalism, is undermined by an intensified class struggle, while most national traditions have been compromised by their links with the bourgeois order, with aristocratic culture, or with "religious prejudices." The pride of each people is flattered somewhat by the fact that within the bounds of the territory it occupies its language is given official status, administrative and other positions are filled by people from its own milieu, and more often than not the region itself is named for the people inhabiting it.

The factor uniting all parts of the U.S.S.R. into a single state is once more the presence of a recognized sole master; but formerly that master was the Russian people governed by its tsar, whereas now the master is considered to be the proletariat of all the peoples of the U.S.S.R. governed by the Communist Party.

III

The deficiencies of the present solution are obvious. It is not only the fact that the division into proletariat and bourgeoisie is for many peoples of the U.S.S.R. untenable or insignificant and artificial; more important is the fact that this solution is provisional. Indeed, the state unification of peoples and countries in which power has been seized by the proletariat is expedient only at the present stage of the proletariat's struggle with its enemies. For that matter, the proletariat itself as an oppressed class is, according to Marxism, a temporary phenomenon. The same applies to class struggle. The unity of the state appears to rest not on a permanent but on a temporary and transient basis. This gives rise to an absurd situation and numerous abnormal phenomena. To justify its existence, the central government has to inflate artificially the danger facing the proletariat; it has to create objects of class hatred in the form of the new bourgeoisie, to stir up the proletariat against it, and so on. It has to keep convincing the proletariat that its position as sole master is highly unstable.

It is not my purpose to criticize the Communist conception of the state as such. The idea of the dictatorship of the proletariat will be examined here in only one of its aspects, namely, as a factor serving to unify the peoples of the U.S.S.R. into a single political whole and to oppose nationalist and separatist movements. And just in this aspect the idea of the dictatorship of the proletariat, however effective it has proved until now, cannot guarantee a stable and permanent solution of the problem. The nationalism of the peoples of the U.S.S.R. grows stronger as they become accustomed to their new status. The development of education and literacy in the national languages and the preferential appointment of natives to administrative and other positions are intensifying national distinctions among the regions, and are creating in native intellectuals a jealous fear of "alien elements" as well as the desire to shore up their own positions more firmly. At the same time class barriers within each individual people of the U.S.S.R. are breaking down and class antagonisms are fading, which creates most favorable conditions for the rise in each people of its own nationalism with a separatist tendency. In the face of this, the idea of the dictatorship of the proletariat turns out to be powerless. A proletarian, once risen to power, finds himself possessed of nationalistic instincts (and occasionally at quite a powerful dosage) that, according to Communist doctrine, should be absent. And the interests of the world proletariat, it appears, will move such a proletarian in his new position of power to a much smaller degree than is assumed by that doctrine. Consequently, the idea of the dictatorship of the proletariat, the proletariat's consciousness of solidarity, and the whipping up of class hatred should eventually prove to be ineffective means of combatting the nationalist and separatist ambitions among the peoples of the U.S.S.R.

IV

The current principle of state unification for the former Russian Empire follows logically from the Marxist dogma of the class nature of the state and from the characteristically Marxist disregard for the national substratum of statehood. Adherents of this dogma have of course no other choice but to replace the domination of a single people with the dictatorship of a single class, that is, to substitute a class substratum for a national substratum of statehood. Everything else follows quite naturally from this substitution. In any case, the Communists are far more consistent than the democrats who deny a single national substratum of Russian statehood but advocate a broad regional autonomy or federation *without* a class dictatorship, though under such conditions the existence of a unified state is impossible.

For the separate parts of the former Russian Empire to continue as parts of a single state there must exist a single substratum of statehood—a nation (ethnicity) or a class. The class substratum can unify the separate parts of the former Russian Empire only temporarily. A stable and permanent unification is therefore feasible only on the basis of an ethnic (national) substratum. Before the revolution, Russians formed such a substratum. But there is no return to the situation in which Russians were the sole owner of the state territory, and, clearly, no other people can play such a role. Consequently, *the national substratum of the state formerly known as the Russian Empire and now known as the U.S.S.R. can only be the totality of peoples inhabiting that state, taken as a peculiar multiethnic nation and as such possessed of its own nationalism. We call that nation Eurasian, its territory Eurasia, and its nationalism Eurasianism.*

V

Any nationalism derives from an intense awareness of the
individual personal nature of the given entity and affirms its
organic unity and the uniqueness of its people, group of
peoples, or part of one people. However, there are no (or
virtually no) perfectly monolithic, or homogeneous peoples in
the world; in any people, even a very small one, there will exist
several tribal subgroups, sometimes rather sharply distinguished
from one another by language, physical type, temperament,
customs, and so on. Similarly there are no (or virtually no)
entirely unique, isolated peoples: every people belongs to some
group of peoples with which it is linked by certain general traits.
Moreover, one and the same people will often belong to one
group by one set of criteria and to a different group by other
criteria. The unity of an ethnic entity is inversely proportional
and its uniqueness directly proportional to its magnitude; only
the smallest ethnic entities (some tribal subgroup within a single
people) approach total homogeneity and absolute unity, and
only large ethnic entities (for example, a group of peoples)
approach total uniqueness. Nationalism inevitably departs from
the actual heterogeneity and nondistinctiveness of the given
ethnic entity, and, depending on the degree of departure,
various sorts of nationalism can be distinguished.

Every nationalism contains both centralist elements (the
affirmation of unity) and separatist elements (the affirmation of
uniqueness and distinctiveness). Inasmuch as ethnic entity is
included into another (a people is included in a group of
peoples, but itself includes several tribal or regional subgroups),
there may exist nationalisms of various amplitudes, of various
breadths. These nationalisms are also "included" within one
another like concentric circles, in accordance with those ethnic
entities upon which they are oriented. The centralist and
separatist elements of the same nationalism do not contradict
one another; however, the centralist and separatist elements of

two concentric nationalisms are mutually exclusive: that is, if ethnic entity A is "included" as a part of ethnic entity B, the separatist element of nationalism A and the centralist element of nationalism B are indeed mutually exclusive.

For the nationalism of a given ethnic entity not to degenerate into pure separatism, it must be combined with the nationalism of a broader ethnic entity. With regard to Eurasia this means that the nationalism of every individual people of Eurasia (the contemporary U.S.S.R.) should be combined with Pan-Eurasian nationalism, or Eurasianism. All citizens of the Eurasian state should not only realize that they belong to a given people (or to a given subgroup of a given people) but also that that people belongs to the Eurasian nation. And their national pride should find satisfaction in both aspects. The nationalism of these peoples should have a corresponding foundation: Pan-Eurasian nationalism should arise as a broadening of the nationalism of each people of Eurasia, as a merging of these individual nationalisms into a whole.

VI

Among the peoples of Eurasia there have constantly existed (and there are easily established) fraternal relations which presuppose the existence of unconscious mutual attractions and sympathies (cases of the reverse, that is, of unconscious repulsion and antipathy between two peoples of Eurasia are quite rare). However, unconscious feelings alone are insufficient. The brotherhood of the peoples of Eurasia must become a significant fact of their consciousness. Each people of Eurasia must be conscious of itself first and foremost as a member of that brotherhood. The consciousness of belonging specifically to the Eurasian brotherhood of peoples must become stronger for each member than the consciousness of belonging to any other group. Any individual people of Eurasia can of course be included in some other, not exclusively

Eurasian group according to certain criteria. For instance, by linguistic criteria Russians belong together with the Slavic peoples, Tatars, Chuvash, Cheremiss, and others belong to the so-called Turanian peoples; by religious criteria Tatars, Bashkirs, Sarts, and others belong to the Moslem peoples. But these links should be less strong for them than links uniting them as the Eurasian family: Eurasianism, rather than Pan-Slavism for Russians, Pan-Turanianism for Eurasian Turanians, or Pan-Islamism for Eurasian Moslems, should become predominant. These "pan-isms," by intensifying the centrifugal energies of particular ethnic nationalisms, emphasize the one-sided link between the given people and certain other peoples by only a single set of criteria; they are incapable of creating any real, living and individual multiethnic nation. But in the Eurasian brotherhood, peoples are linked not by some one-sided set of criteria, but by their common historical destiny.[1] Eurasia constitutes a geographical, economic, and historical whole. The destinies of the Eurasian peoples have become interwoven with one another, tied in a massive tangle that can no longer be unraveled; the severance of any one people can be accomplished only by an act of violence against nature, which will bring pain. The same holds for the ethnic groups forming the basis of Panslavism, Panturanianism, and Pan-Islamism. Not one of them is united to such a degree by a common historical destiny. Not one of these "pan-isms" is pragmatically as valuable as is Pan-Eurasian nationalism. That nationalism is not only pragmatically valuable; it is nothing less than a vital necessity, for only the awakening of self-awareness as a single, multiethnic Eurasian nation will provide Russia-Eurasia with the ethnic substratum of statehood without which it will eventually fall to pieces, causing unheard-of suffering in all its parts.

For Pan-Eurasian nationalism to function effectively as a unifying factor for the Eurasian state, it is necessary to re-educate the self-awareness of the peoples of Eurasia. To be sure, such a re-education is already being carried out by life itself.

[1]See the article by Prince K. A. Chkheidze in *Evraziiskaia khronika* 4.

The mere fact that the Eurasian peoples (they alone in the whole world) have for a number of years been together living under and overcoming the Communist regime—that fact alone is responsible for a thousand new psychological, cultural, and historical links among them; it compels them to perceive most clearly their common historical destiny. But this is not enough. The individuals who have already fully recognized the unity of the multiethnic Eurasian nation must spread their conviction— each in the Eurasian nation in which he or she works. And here is an untapped mother lode of work for philosophers, journalists, poets, novelists, artists, musicians, scientists, and scholars. It is necessary to re-examine a number of disciplines from the point of view of the unity of the multiethnic Eurasian nation, and to construct new scientific systems to replace old and antiquated ones. In particular, one needs a new history of the Eurasian peoples including the history of the Russians.

In the midst of these efforts to re-educate national self-awareness with a view toward establishing the symphonic (choral) unity of the multiethnic nation of Eurasia, it can well be that the Russian people will have to exert itself more than any other. In the first place, Russians will have to struggle more persistently with the old points of view that shaped Russian national self-awareness outside the real context of the Eurasian world and isolated Russians from the general perspective of Eurasian history. Besides, Russians, who before the revolution were the sole master of the entire territory of Russia-Eurasia and are now the first (in population size and significance) among the Eurasian peoples, should naturally provide an example for everyone else.

The Eurasians striving to re-educate national self-awareness work in singularly difficult conditions. They cannot do anything openly on the territory of the USSR, and in emigration most people are unable to realize the objective results of the revolution. For them, Russia is still a territory conquered by Russians and belonging to Russians on the basis of full and undivided ownership. They are unreceptive toward Pan-

Eurasian nationalism and the idea of a unified the multiethnic Eurasian nation. They look upon the Eurasians as traitors who have substituted the idea of Eurasia for the idea of Russia. They fail to understand that it is not Eurasianism but life itself that has brought about the "substitution"; they do not understand that nowadays their brand of Russian nationalism is simply Great-Russian separatism, that the purely *Russian* Russia they would like to "revive" is possible only after the separation of its "outlying provinces," that is, within the bounds of ethnographic Great Russia. Other emigré movements attack Eurasianism from the opposite point of view; they demand the rejection of national uniqueness and believe that Russia can be organized on the basis of European democracy without a single national or class substratum. As the representatives of the abstract Westernizing attitudes of the old Russian intelligentsia, they do not understand that the first prerequisite for the existence of a state is its citizens' consciousness of their membership within a single whole, within an organic unity which can only be based on ethnicity or class, and that at present only two alternatives are possible—either the dictatorship of the proletariat or the consciousness of the unity and uniqueness of the multiethnic Eurasian nation and Pan-Eurasian nationalism.

10 The Ukrainian Problem*

The Petrine reforms established a distinct boundary between two epochs in the history of Russian culture. At first glance it would seem that a complete break with tradition occurred during Peter's reign, that the cultures of post-Petrine and pre-Petrine Russia have nothing in common, and that no links exist between them. But impressions of this sort are generally erroneous. Careful examination of periods in the history of any people will disclose the illusory nature of such putative breaks and reveal the presence of initially imperceptible links between the two epochs. Such is the case with the post-Petrine and pre-Petrine cultures.

It is common knowledge that historians of Russian culture point to numerous phenomena linking the post-Petrine and pre-Petrine periods in Russian culture in support of the claim that conditions favorable to the Petrine reforms were created by specific currents in pre-Petrine culture. A glance at the links identified by historians leads to the following conclusion: It is possible to speak of a complete break in tradition only if one restricts the meaning of the term "Russian culture" to its Great Russian variant. No abrupt break in tradition occurred in West Russian (specifically Ukrainian) culture during Peter's reign. And to the extent that Ukrainian culture began to penetrate Muscovy before Peter's reign, giving rise there to cultural developments congenial to itself, it can be argued that the ground was prepared in Great Russia for the Petrine reforms.

*Originally as "K ukrainskoi probleme," *Evraziiskii vremennik* 5, 1927, pp. 165-184. Translated by Kenneth Brostrom.

During the course of the fifteenth, sixteenth, and the first half of the seventeenth centuries, the cultures of Western and of Muscovite Rus' developed in directions so different that the breach between them ultimately became very wide. At the same time, a vivid awareness of all-Russian unity and of the Byzantine cultural legacy they shared contradicted the opinion that these two cultures were completely independent of one another and strongly supported the view that they were two "variants," two individualizations of a single all-Russian culture. After the annexation of the Ukraine, the question of the merger of these two variants of Russian culture arose. However, the question was posed in a form that was rather demeaning to the national pride of both the Great and the Little Russians.[1] It was not so much the merger of these two variants of Russian culture that was being considered as the abolition of one of them as "ruined," and the preservation of the other as "true" and genuine. The Ukrainians believed the Muscovite variant had been ruined by the illiteracy of the Muscovites; they reproached them for their lack of schools and boasted about their own handling of educational matters. The Muscovites for their part considered the Ukrainian (generally, the West Russian) variant ruined by the heretical influence of Polish Catholicism. Reasonable people may have understood that both sides were both right and wrong, that Great Russians needed to organize more schools, and the Ukrainians needed to get rid of many traits acquired from the Poles. But there were few reasonable people, while the majority on both sides was intransigent. In effect, the question came down to this: Which of the two variants of Russian culture ought to be accepted in its entirety, and which rejected? The government—that is, in the final analysis, the tsar—had to resolve this issue.

[1]We use the terms "Little Russian" and "Ukrainian," although in every case it would be more correct to say "West Russian." During the era under discussion there was no difference between Little Russians and White Russians [Belorussians] from the upper strata (in the cultural sense) of West Russian society.

The government sided with the Ukrainians, which was perfectly correct from a political point of view. The inevitable anger of the Great Russians would lead to local uprisings at worst, but Ukrainian dissatisfaction could have seriously impeded or even halted the ongoing reunification of the Ukraine and Great Russia. However, after siding with the Ukrainians, the government took only the first steps toward recognition of the "correctness" of the Ukrainian variant of Russian culture. Of course, these were crucial steps involving the "correction" of the liturgical books (i.e., replacing the Muscovite redactions of these books with the Ukrainian) and the other Nikonian reforms. In this particular area, unification was total, that is, the Great Russian was replaced by the Ukrainian. But in other areas of culture and life this unification was not achieved until the reign of Peter. The unadulterated West Russian variant of the culture reigned in the Ukraine without any Great Russian admixture, while in Great Russia there was a mix of the Muscovite and West Russian cultures. Certain representatives of the upper classes (the contemporary "Westernizers") went rather far in accepting the invasion of West Russian elements into Great Russian culture, while others (the contemporary Muscovite nationalists) tried to maintain the purity of the Great Russian tradition.

Tsar Peter set himself the goal of Europeanizing Russian culture. Only the West Russian, Ukrainian variant of Russian culture could be used in accomplishing this task, for it had already absorbed certain elements from European culture (in its Polish variant) and was showing a tendency toward further evolution in this direction. The Great Russian variant of Russian culture, owing to its pronounced Europhobia and tendency toward self-contained autonomy, was not only valueless for Peter's goals, but it interfered with their achievement. So Peter attempted to uproot and destroy the Great Russian variant completely, and he established the Ukrainian variant as the sole expression of Russian culture, making it the starting point for future development.

Thus the old, Great Russian, Muscovite culture died during the reign of Peter. The culture that has existed in Russia since his time and continues to develop there is a direct, uninterrupted continuation not of Muscovite, but of Kievan, of *Ukrainian* culture.

This can be observed in every branch of the culture. Let us use literature as an example. The *literary language* used in belles-lettres and in religious and scholarly literature in both Muscovite and Western Rus' was Church Slavonic. But the variants of this language used in Kiev and Moscow before the seventeenth century were not altogether identical in lexicon, syntax, or stylistics. During the patriarchate of Nikon, the Kievan variant of Church Slavonic replaced the Muscovite in the liturgical books. Later the same process could be observed in other types of literature. In short, the Church Slavonic that served as the basis for the "Slavo-Russian" literary language during the Petrine and post-Petrine eras was the Kievan variant of Church Slavonic.

A rich *poetic (verse) tradition* existed in Muscovite Rus', but it was largely oral. Only a few written works of poetry have come down to us, but extrapolating from them (e.g., "The Tale of Misery-Luckless-Plight" [Povest' o Gore-Zloshchast'i]), we can formulate a rather precise description of the characteristics of this tradition. Its language was a relatively pure Great Russian with a few Church Slavonic elements, and it was embellished with certain traditional poetic conventions. Its meter was neither syllabic nor tonic, for it relied upon the metrical principles of the Great Russian folk song. In Western Rus', a different, bookish poetic tradition developed; because of its association with the Polish tradition, it was based upon syllabic meter and the use of rhyme. These "verses" [virshi] were written in Church Slavonic and in the Russo-Polish (or more precisely, Belorussian-Polish) jargon that served in Western Rus' as the language of conversation and business among the upper classes of Russian society. This West Russian poetry made its way into Great Russia before the reign of Peter (of course, in Church

Slavonic—that is, in the all-Russian literary language of the time). Poems of this sort by Simeon Polotskii were popular, to cite one example. Local imitators of this kind of poetry also began to appear in Moscow (e.g., a certain Sil'vestr Medvedev). After the reign of Peter, Russian poetry of the old Great Russian type retreated once and for all "into the people." Among the upper strata of society (in the cultural sense), there henceforth existed only one poetic tradition, which traced its origins to West Russian syllabic *virshi* written in Church Slavonic.

Narrative prose existed in both Muscovite and Western Rus', but the overwhelming Polish influence in Western Rus' thwarted development of an independent tradition. Consequently, narrative prose there consisted almost entirely of translations. But the prose tale existed as an independent tradition in Muscovite Rus'. During the seventeenth century this tradition became especially vigorous and began to show promise of a bright future (e.g., "The Tale of Savva Grudtsyn"). But West Russian translated tales flooded into Muscovite Rus' all during the seventeenth century, and Russian narrative prose in the post-Petrine era is closely associated with this West Russian tradition. The native Muscovite tradition perished before it was able to reach its full development.

In all likelihood, *oratory* existed in Muscovite Rus'. The style of Archpriest Avvakum's works is distinctly oratorical, and despite its apparent ingenuousness, it implies the existence of an old oral tradition in homiletics. But this tradition had nothing in common with the scholastic rhetoric cultivated in Western Rus' by the monastic schools and the Mohyla Academy. Moscow came into contact with this Ukrainian homiletical tradition long before Peter, and during his reign the prominent Ukrainian orators Feofan Prokopovich and Stefan Iavorskii consolidated the final triumph of this tradition. The roots of Russian rhetoric (both secular and religious) during the post-Petrine era are found in this Ukrainian tradition, not in the Muscovite, which perished altogether, leaving only the few traces in the works of Old Believer writers like Avvakum.

Finally, the *drama* existed only in Western Rus' during the pre-Petrine era; there was no independent dramatic tradition in Moscow. On rare occasions the dramas of Ukrainian writers (e.g., Simeon Polotskii) were staged at court. Russian drama during the post-Petrine era is genetically linked to the Ukrainian school dramas. We can see, then, that in all its branches post-Petrine Russian literature was a continuation of the West Russian, Ukrainian literary tradition.

We can observe the same pattern in other kinds of art: in vocal (primarily religious) and instrumental music, in painting (where the Great Russian tradition was continued only by the Old Believers; post-Petrine icon painting and portraiture derive from the West Russian tradition), and in church architecture (i.e., the only architectural type in which certain design characteristics are recognized as the "Russian style").[2] This convergence with West Russian traditions and repudiation of Muscovite traditions are observable not only in the arts but in every other aspect of the intellectual and spiritual culture of post-Petrine Russia. Attitudes toward religion and the direction of ecclesiastical and theological thought were bound to merge with the West Russian tradition after its version of the liturgy was recognized as correct during Nikon's patriarchate, and after the Mohyla Academy became the all-Russian wellspring of the highest spiritual enlightenment, which meant that for an extended period of time the majority of the Russian hierarchy were products of this academy. The post-Petrine tradition in education (the schools, the spirit and content of the curriculum) was also West Russian. Finally, the attitude toward old Great Russian culture prevalent during the post-Petrine era was typically West Russian in its origins. It was the accepted thing (and it still is) to repeat opinions about this culture that had been voiced in the seventeenth century by "learned" Ukrainians.

[2] For more on the West Russian tradition in Russian architecture, painting, and sculpture during the post-Petrine era, see P. N. Savitskii, "Great Russia and the Ukraine in Russian Culture," *Rodnoe Slovo*, No. 8 (1926).

II

It is evident, then, that at the turn of the eighteenth century *the intellectual and spiritual culture of Great Russia was Ukrainianized*. The differences between the West Russian and the Muscovite variants of Russian culture were eliminated through the eradication of the latter. Now there was only *one* Russian culture.

Whereas the culture of the post-Petrine era was West Russian, or Ukrainian, in origin, the Russian state was historically Great Russian, so the center of culture had to move from the Ukraine to Great Russia. Consequently, this culture lost over time any specific Great Russian or Ukrainian identification and became *all-Russian*. Its future development was determined in large measure by this shift from a limited, local identification to one that was all-embracing and national. The West Russian variant of Russian culture was formed during a period when the Ukraine was a province of Poland, while Poland, in a cultural sense, was a province (a remote province) of Romano-Germanic Europe. Because this West Russian variant of Russian culture became the all-Russian culture after Peter, it also became willy-nilly the culture of the *capital*, while Russia herself began to aspire to a place among the most important parts of "Europe." This is how Ukrainian culture moved, as it were, from an insignificant provincial town to the capital. So it had to change its distinctly provincial characteristics. It strove to free itself from everything that was specifically Polish and to replace it with corresponding elements from the basic Romano-Germanic cultures (German, French, and so on). Thus, Ukrainianization became a bridge to Europeanization.

The linguistic basis of the culture was also changing. Formerly, a special conversational and commercial Russo-Polish jargon had existed alongside literary Church Slavonic in the West Russian upper classes. After the Ukrainian variant of Russian culture became all-Russian, this jargon, which was an emblem of provincialism and of the Polish yoke, was obviously doomed. The Great Russian commercial and conversational language, which had developed in the environment of the Muscovite bureaucracy, was strongly affected by this Russo-Polish jargon, but finally overcame it and became the sole language of business and conversation among the upper classes in the Ukraine as well as in Great Russia. The close connections that developed between this language and Church Slavonic, which continued to serve as the literary language, were characterized by a kind of osmosis, a mutual saturation; the conversational language of the upper classes became strongly "Church-Slavonicized," while literary Church Slavonic became strongly Russified. Ultimately, both merged into the contemporary Russian language, which is at once the literary and the commercial and conversational language of all educated Russians—in short, the linguistic basis of Russian culture.

The cultural Ukrainianization of Great Russia and the transformation of Ukrainian culture into the all-Russian culture led quite naturally to the loss of its specifically Ukrainian provincial character. But it could not become specifically Russian, because, as we have said, the continuity of the Great Russian cultural tradition had been finally and irretrievably broken, and only the chancellery language of the Muscovite bureaucrats remained. The generalized all-Russian quality of post-Petrine, "Petersburg" culture derives from this fact. This emphasis on the generalized and all-Russian led in practice to repudiation of the specifically Russian, that is, to national self-renunciation, which was certain to provoke a reaction among those with healthy national sensibilities. A situation in which everything uniquely Russian was persecuted and eradicated in the name of Russian grandeur was so ludicrous that protest was inevitable. It is not surprising that groups appeared in Russian society which sought to affirm the uniqueness of the Russian national character and to display the Russian national physiognomy. However, insofar as these groups were opposed to the generalized character of all-Russian culture and strove to replace it with the specific and concrete, they could not avoid acquiring a distinctly regional quality: every effort to give Russian culture a more concrete, national identity had to select one of the individualizations of the Russian people—the Great Russians, Ukrainians, or Belorussians—since only Great Russians, Ukrainians, and Belorussians exist in fact, while "all-Russians" are mere abstractions. And indeed, we see that groups committed to a concrete, national Russian culture have moved along two parallel courses, the Great Russian and the Ukrainian.[3]

The close parallelism between these two courses is remarkable; it can be observed in every manifestation of either one. Beginning around 1800, we encounter numerous works in the area of literature that were purposely written in the language and style of the common people; these works form two closely parallel lines of development, one Great Russian and the other Ukrainian. Initially a humorous, parodic tendency came to the surface in both (e.g., "The Hero [*bogatyr'*] Elisei" by V. Maikov in the Great Russian line of development, and "Eneida" [*The Aeneid*] by Kotliarevskii in the Ukrainian); it was replaced by a Sentimental-Romantic tendency that laid special emphasis on the stylistics of the folk song (the major figure here in the Great Russian tradition was Kol'tsov, and in the Ukrainian, Shevchenko). In the middle of the nineteenth century, this tendency was replaced by a literature of denunciation and "civic sorrow" (a unique, aberrant Russian manifestation of European *Weltschmerz*).

The Romantic idealization of pre-Petrine antiquity, which found expression in literature, historiography, and archeology, also received its impetus from this pursuit of the concretely national, and it was simultaneously manifest in the same two parallel courses, the Great Russian and the Ukrainian. The same thing can be said about populism and the various expressions of "going to the people." Every populist (to the extent that he

[3]A Belorussian tradition has always existed as well, but it has always been less well developed.

centered his attention on a real, existing people) inevitably became a "regionalist" to some degree, and a fiery partisan of specific Great Russian or Ukrainian characteristics and *mores*.[4]

Despite the fact that attraction to the concretely national found expression during the St. Petersburg period in various forms of regionalism, in an emphasis on specific individualizations of the Russian tribe (Great Russians, Ukrainians, and so on), this phenomenon was all-Russian in nature, because its causes were all-Russian. Russia was distinguished during the post-Petrine era by the isolation of the higher strata of the culture from their foundations in the people; this isolation fostered both estrangement between the intelligentsia and the people and a yearning for their reconciliation. So the problem of cultural reform, of erecting a new cultural edifice whose upper stories rose directly from their mass foundations, was all-Russian in nature. This problem still confronts every group within the Russian tribe, the Great Russians as well as the Ukrainians and Belorussians.

III

A question arises in connection with the problem of cultural reform: Should the new, reformed culture be all-Russian, or should such a culture be rejected and a reformed culture be created for each group within the Russian tribe?

This question has special urgency for the Ukrainians. It is greatly complicated by political considerations and is usually merged with the question of the Ukraine's political status, whether it should be a completely independent state, a full and equal member of the Russian Federation, or an autonomous part of Russia. However, this connection between the cultural

[4]For the sake of brevity we refer only to the two biggest parts of the Russian tribe and territory. However, analogous phenomena arose (but less vigorously) in other, smaller areas—in Belorussia, the various Cossack regions, in Siberia, and so on.

and political is not obligatory. We know that an all-German culture exists, even though the groups constituting the German tribe are not united in a single state. We know that the Hindus have their own autonomous culture, even though they have long been deprived of their political independence. Thus the problem of Ukrainian and all-Russian culture can and must be considered apart from the question of the most appropriate political and legal relations between Great Russia and the Ukraine.

We have seen that the all-Russian culture of the post-Petrine era was seriously compromised by efforts to reform it in specific, national ways. Several partisans of Ukrainian cultural separatism have tried to argue that the culture which has existed in Russia up to the present is not all-Russian, but simply Great Russian. This is factually incorrect: I have already shown that the intellectual and spiritual Ukrainianization of Great Russia was the basis for the creation of the post-Petrine all-Russian culture and that this all-Russian culture is connected historically only to pre-Petrine, Ukrainian (West Russian) culture, and not to the old Great Russian culture that was abruptly terminated at the end of the seventeenth century. It is also obvious that Ukrainians participated actively and on an equal footing with the Great Russians not only in the genesis but in the development of this all-Russian culture; and they did so as Ukrainians, without abandoning their ethnic identity. On the contrary, they affirmed it. No one would exclude Gogol from Russian literature, Kostomarov from Russian historiography, Potebnia from Russian philology, and so on. It is simply impossible to deny the fact that Russian culture during the post-Petrine era is all-Russian and that it is not foreign to Ukrainians. If this native culture is viewed by some Ukrainians as not fully their own, and if the incompatibility between the cultural elite and the masses is obvious when this culture is juxtaposed with the thought patterns and life style of common Ukrainian people, the same phenomenon can be observed in Great Russia.

Consequently, it has causes altogether different from the mistaken belief that this culture is Great Russian.

Every cultural edifice should have two components, one oriented toward the culture's concrete, ethnographic foundations in the people, and the other toward the heights of spiritual and intellectual life. To ensure a culture's stability and vitality, an organic connection must exist between these two components, and each of them must perform its inherent function; that is, the component oriented toward the culture's roots in the people must reflect specific characteristics of its concrete ethnographic foundation, and the component oriented toward the cultural heights must be responsive in its development to the spiritual and intellectual requirements of the nation's most eminent representatives.

In the all-Russian cultural edifice of the post-Petrine era, these two components, or "stories," were unevenly developed. The "bottom story,"[5] which was oriented toward the culture's roots in the people, was very poorly adapted to the specific characteristics of the Russian ethnographic type; consequently, it functioned badly. A person "from the people" could absorb this culture only by losing his individuality completely (or at least almost completely), by suppressing in himself and losing certain traits intrinsic to the people. On the other hand, the top story of all-Russian culture, which was oriented toward the heights of spiritual and intellectual life, was developed at least to

[5]To avoid misunderstanding, we hasten to add that the terms "top" and "bottom" do not imply any evaluative judgment. Not only do we want to avoid discussing which of these stories is more "valuable," we reject the question itself as fundamentally misguided. The images of top and bottom stories depict not differing stages of cultural development or value but two different functions of a culture. Degrees of value depend only on the gifts of individual creators, regardless of whether they are working on the top or on the bottom story. The poetry of Kol'tsov is aesthetically far more valuable than the poetry of Benediktov, although Kol'tsov worked on the bottom story of the culture, while Benediktov was on the top.

the extent that it could fully satisfy the requirements of the Russian intelligentsia.

Let us now imagine what would happen if the Ukraine were to replace this all-Russian culture with a newly created Ukrainian culture. The population of the Ukraine would have to opt for one culture or the other. If the new culture were successful in adapting its bottom story to fit the specific features of the ethnographic foundation, the lower strata of the population would certainly accept it, since, as we have seen, this dimension of the old all-Russian culture was very poorly developed, and it was not adapted to specific traits of the people. In order for this new Ukrainian culture to be chosen by the upper strata of society as well (i.e., by the best educated of the intelligentsia), its top story would have to conform to their highest spiritual and intellectual needs to an even greater degree than was the case with the old all-Russian culture. Otherwise the overwhelming majority of the Ukrainian intelligentsia (including the part especially valuable from the perspective of cultural creation) would remain loyal to the old culture. An independent Ukrainian culture deprived of the collaborative efforts of this extremely valuable part of the Ukrainian people would be condemned to degeneration and death.

Looking at the question impartially, we must conclude that, however likely it is that a new Ukrainian culture would resolve the problem of conforming the bottom story of its edifice to its foundations in the people, it will never resolve even partially the other problem: creating a new top story that could satisfy the needs of the intelligentsia more fully than the top story of the old all-Russian culture did. A new Ukrainian culture would be in no position to compete successfully with the old culture in meeting these spiritual and intellectual needs. Above all, it would not possess the rich tradition of the all-Russian culture. The work of those who create the most valuable cultural assets (even when this involves creations that are in principle entirely original) is greatly facilitated by immersion in such a tradition and by using it as a point of departure.

The availability of a highly qualified group of talented people has great importance for the creation of such valuable cultural assets. It is therefore vital to the successful development of this side of a culture that the ethnic whole be as inclusive as possible. The more numerous the bearers of a culture, the greater will be the number of talented people born among them (other things being equal); and the more talented people there are, the more intense the competition will be, and the more vigorous the development of the culture's top story. Competition improves the quality of culture building. Other things being equal, the top story of the common culture of a large ethnological entity will always be qualitatively better and quantitatively richer than the top stories of the cultures that the separate parts of this ethnological entity can create, each of them working only for itself and independent of the others. Unbiased representatives of an ethnological whole cannot help recognizing this; and given completely free choice they will quite naturally opt for the culture of the ethnological whole (in our case, all-Russian culture) and not for the culture of a part of that whole (here, Ukrainian culture). It follows that the only people who could opt for Ukrainian culture are those biased in some way or limited in their freedom of choice.

Everything that has been said here holds both for creators of cultural assets and for "consumers," that is, the evaluators of these assets. By the very nature of his activity, every creator of cultural assets (if he is genuinely talented and recognizes it) strives to make the products of his creative labor accessible to as many competent evaluators as possible. And every genuine "consumer" of such assets strives in turn to enjoy the products of the creative labor of as many creators as possible. This means that both have a stake in expanding, not contracting, the boundaries of a given culture. As policy, the restriction of these boundaries is desirable only for talentless or mediocre creators who wish to protect themselves from competition (genuine talent does not fear competition!), or for narrow, fanatical, regional chauvinists who have never learned to evaluate high culture impartially, for its own sake, who can evaluate the products of cultural creativity only by the extent to which they fall within the boundaries of a particular regional variant of a culture.

As a general rule, it is people of this sort who will opt, not for the all-Russian culture, but for a completely independent Ukrainian culture. They will become the principal adherents and leaders of this new culture, and they will leave their imprint upon it, the imprint of petty provincial vanity, of triumphant mediocrity, banality, and obscurantism—not to mention the atmosphere of constant suspicion, of unending fear in the face of competition they will create. Of course, these people will try to restrict or to abolish completely any possibility of choosing freely between all-Russian and an independent Ukrainian culture. They will try to deny Ukrainians the opportunity to learn the Russian literary language, to read Russian books, to absorb Russian culture. But even this will not be enough; it will be necessary to inculcate an intense, fiery hatred of everything Russian in all Ukrainians and to sustain this hatred through the schools, the press, literature, and art, even at the cost of lies and slander, of rejecting their own historical past and trampling upon things sacred to every Ukrainian. Because if Ukrainians do not begin to *hate* everything Russian, the possibility will always remain that they will opt for the all-Russian culture.

It is not difficult to see that a Ukrainian culture created in the circumstances just described will be hopelessly enfeebled; it will not exist as an end in itself, but merely as a political instrument, serving policies that are bad, vindictively chauvinistic, provocative, and shrill. The arbiters of this culture will not be the actual creators of cultural assets but crazed fanatics and political opportunists hypnotized by their own obsessive ideas. Consequently, everything in this culture—science, literature, art, philosophy, and so on—will be tendentious, rather than valuable in its own right. The door will be thrown open to the talentless, who will win cheap glory by kneeling before the partisan

260 N. S. TRUBETZKOY

platitude; but real talents, who will not don the blinders of such platitudes, will be silenced.

Above all, one might reasonably doubt that such a culture would be truly *national*. Only genuine talents, who work in response to an irrational, inner drive, and not for ancillary political objectives, are able to embody fully the spirit of the national personality in cultural assets. But there will be no place for such talents in this malevolently chauvinistic environment. Political opportunists will be interested in one thing only—how to create their Ukrainian culture as quickly as possible, regardless of the result, just so long as it does not resemble Russian culture. This will lead inevitably to feverish *imitation*: rather than creating everything anew, is it not simpler to import existing cultural assets from abroad (but not from Russia!) after hastily inventing Ukrainian titles for them? A "Ukrainian culture" created in such circumstances would not be an organic expression of the unique essence of the Ukrainian national personality, and it would be scarcely distinguishable from the "cultures" presently being cobbled together by various "new nations"—the supernumeraries at the League of Nations. Such a culture would combine a demagogic emphasis on a few isolated, haphazardly chosen, and generally nonessential aspects of the folk life style with the negation in practice of the deep foundations of this life style. The latest fad and "last word" from Europe (mechanically adopted and clumsily realized) will stand side by side with specimens of pitiable, shabby provinciality and cultural backwardness. All of this—with its spiritual emptiness concealed behind conceited self-adulation, shrill salesmanship, and bombastic phrases about the national culture, originality, and so on—will be simply a pathetic surrogate, not a culture but a caricature.

Such are the unsightly vistas that await Ukrainian culture if it decides to *replace* all-Russian culture, to *repudiate* it, if it enters into *competition* with it. A situation in which every educated Ukrainian must choose whether he wants to be Russian or Ukrainian will result in a selection of cultural workers that is extremely disadvantageous for the development of Ukrainian culture. By posing the question of Ukrainian and all-Russian culture in the form of a *dilemma* (either/or), Ukrainians doom their future culture to the unlovely condition described above. It follows that this formulation of the question is harmful to Ukrainians. To escape this lamentable future, Ukrainian culture must be built so that it supplements all-Russian culture, and not in competition with it; in other words, *Ukrainian culture must become an individualized variant of all-Russian culture.*

I indicated above that the bottom story of the cultural edifice (i.e., the one oriented toward its foundations in the people) must be entirely rebuilt and that Ukrainian culture can and must express its individuality in this undertaking. I have also indicated that it is impossible for Ukrainian culture to compete with all-Russian culture on the top story, where the higher cultural assets are located. A certain natural differentiation is evident here between the domains of the all-Russian and Ukrainian cultures. Of course, this differentiation has not been fully explored in the foregoing argument, because, in addition to the top and bottom stories of the cultural edifice, there must also be "middle" or intermediate stories. In any case, I have indicated the principle of differentiation itself.

IV

The same considerations must serve as the basis for differentiating between the domains of all-Russian culture and those of Belorussian, Great Russian, and the other regional cultures. As I have stated, the lack of fit between the bottom story of the cultural edifice and its foundations in the people has been a general phenomenon in post-Petrine Russian culture. In the future it will be necessary to correct this inadequacy, to harmonize the part of Russian culture oriented toward the people with Russia's concrete, individual, national characteristics. A closer fit between the culture and the people will guarantee the uninterrupted participation of "representatives of the people" in cultural construction. Since this part of the culture is to be adapted to *specific* characteristics of the Russian people, it is natural that this undertaking should be strongly differentiated along regional and tribal lines. The "Russian people in general" is an abstraction; in fact there are only Great Russians (the Northern and Southern Great Russians, the Pomors, the Volga Russians, Siberians, Cossacks, and so on), the Belorussians, and the Little Russians, or Ukrainians (with their subgroups). The bottom story of the cultural edifice must be adapted to fit the individual subgroup of the Russian people in each region (the specific, regional, individualized variant of the Russian national personality). Consequently, the Russian culture of the future must be sharply differentiated along regional and territorial lines; instead of the abstract, bureaucratically faceless homogeneity of the past, a rainbow of brightly rendered regional hues should appear.

It would be a great mistake to regard the development of these local cultural variants as the sole or principal goal of cultural activity. One should not forget that every culture must have, in addition to a part oriented toward its popular roots, another part oriented toward the spiritual and intellectual heights. Woe to the culture in which the latter is poorly developed, so that its cultural elite is compelled to meet its intellectual needs not with native assets but with those of a foreign culture! This is why the cultivation and development of the aspects of a culture oriented toward the people must be accompanied by hard work in the area of "higher" cultural assets. And if the very nature of the work done on the bottom story of the edifice of Russian culture requires differentiation according to individual Russian tribes and regions, the work done on the top story requires (again, by its very nature) the cooperative efforts of all the Russian tribes. Whereas regional boundaries are natural and essential to activities on the bottom story in order to achieve the optimal adaptation of a culture to the specifics of its ethnographic foundations, such boundaries on the top story are artificial, superfluous, and harmful. The very essence of this part of a culture requires a range of activity that is as broad as possible, and any use of regional boundaries to limit this scope will be perceived as unnecessary interference by both the creators and the consumers of cultural assets. Only fanatical regional chauvinists and creative mediocrities who fear competition can desire the erection of regional boundaries in this area of culture. If regional boundaries become established not only on the bottom but on the top story of the cultural edifice to please these creative lightweights and the half-baked consumers of their cultural assets, the result throughout the country will be an atmosphere of such suffocating, stagnant provincialism and triumphant pettiness that every genuinely gifted and intellectually mature person will flee to the capital, and ultimately the cultural workers indispensable to the work carried out on the bottom stories of the cultural edifice will no longer be available and at their posts in the provinces.

Thus a regional and tribal differentiation of Russian culture should not extend to the very top of the cultural edifice, to cultural assets of a higher order. There must be no tribal or regional boundaries on the top story of Russian culture in the future; this is what will distinguish it from the bottom story, where tribal and regional boundaries should be well developed and clearly outlined. Of course there should be no distinct boundary between these two stories; they should fade gradually and imperceptibly into one another. Otherwise the culture will not be a *single system*; that is, it will not be a culture in the true sense of the word. The regional boundaries, clearly outlined in the lower part of the cultural edifice, will gradually become less apparent as one moves higher and farther away from the culture's popular foundations; and at the very top of the cultural edifice these boundaries will not be evident at all.

It is important that there be constant interaction between the top and the bottom of this edifice. That is, the newly created assets accumulating on the top story should manifest the general direction which is characteristic of the regionally differentiated and individualized assets being created on the bottom story. Put differently, if the cultural creations of the regional individualizations of Russia were brought together, thereby neutralizing specific, local features and emphasizing those they have in common, they should then manifest the general spirit of the cultural work being accomplished on the top story. The functions, forms, and dimensions of regional boundaries should be determined by the necessity of ensuring constant interaction between the top and bottom of the cultural edifice: these boundaries must safeguard each regional individualization of the culture without interfering with the mutual interaction between the top and the bottom of the cultural edifice. It is obviously impossible to regulate all of this with precision. Regional boundaries will be more important in dealing with some questions and less important with others. Above all, the rationale behind these boundaries should be understood correctly, and they should not become ends in themselves.

In order for Russian culture to be a single system, despite the regional and tribal differentiation of its bottom part, one condition must be met: there must be a single organizing principle at the foundation of the single top story and of all the regional variants on the bottom story in the edifice of Russian culture. The Orthodox faith is such a principle; it is the native inheritance of all the Russian tribes, it is deeply embedded in the soul of the people and at the same time capable of becoming the foundation for those cultural assets intended for bearers of the high all-Russian culture. At one time this principle was the lifeblood of Russian culture, and this is why the West Russian and Muscovite variants of Russian culture were capable of reunification. Subsequently, the blind adulation of secularized, godless, anti-Christian European culture[6]

---

[6]European culture was Christian in its entirety (or at least it wanted to be Christian) only during the Middle Ages; since the so-called Renaissance it has placed itself in opposition to Christianity. It was this form of the culture, standing in opposition to the Church and ultimately to all religion, that was assimilated by Europeanized Russia after Peter.

characteristic of the post-Petrine era undermined and almost destroyed this ancient principle of Russian life among the nation's cultural elite without replacing it with anything else. To the extent that the elite's cultural attitudes penetrated the masses with this rejection of Orthodox principles, it brought spiritual devastation upon them.

The best representatives of the common people and the intelligentsia were painfully aware of this spiritual emptiness; this is why religious quests, often taking the most paradoxical forms, are a characteristic feature of the life of both the common people and the intelligentsia during the entire post-Petrine era. Such quests could not be successful as long as Russian culture was essentially outside religion, and the Church, which had been placed in a subordinate position by the state, was outside the culture (or at least outside the mainstream of high, all-Russian culture). So these religious seekers wandered hither and yon, and only a few of them "discovered" Orthodoxy by accident during their wanderings. Now, after the years during which communism has been in power, when the spiritual emptiness of this secular (and thus antireligious) culture has been fully exposed and reached its nadir, a decisive reaction is bound to occur, with God's help. Ideally, Russian culture should become religious from top to bottom. Orthodoxy must penetrate not only the life of the people but every part of the edifice of Russian culture, up to its very top. Only then will every Russian find complete peace of mind and the fulfillment of his deepest spiritual needs in Russian culture; only then will Russian culture become a single system from top to bottom, despite its external differentiation by tribe and region.

V

At the present time we see considerable enthusiasm for the regional differentiation of Russian culture. In the Ukraine, efforts to achieve complete cultural autonomy hold sway. In large measure this can be explained by policies of the Soviet government that pander to such sentiments in order to neutralize political separatism. The majority of the most accomplished Ukrainian intellectuals are prevented from playing a decisive role in cultural work, a situation aggravated by an influx of Galician intellectuals, whose national self-awareness has been completely perverted by long association with Catholicism, by Polish servitude, and by the atmosphere created by the provincial, separatist, nationalistic (linguistic) wrangling so typical of the former Austro-Hungarian Empire. With regard to the Ukrainian population in general, some groups endorse Ukrainianization not so much because of the specific ways in which it is implemented but because it appears to be directed toward separation from Moscow—from communist Moscow. Thus cultural separatism in the Ukraine is nourished by the anticommunist ("petty bourgeois" in Soviet terminology) attitudes encountered in certain Ukrainian circles. These attitudes have no inherent, logical connections with cultural autonomy; on the contrary, under the old regime they served as a bulwark of centralism. Besides, creative activity on the top story of the culture, where all-Russian unity can and must be especially manifest, is now hampered and artificially constrained by the political hegemony of communism, which does not allow outsiders to create cultural assets but is itself incapable of creating the kind of assets that could satisfy a developed mind and spirit.

Of course the principal explanation for the enthusiastic reception of Ukrainianization is the appeal of novelty and the fact that those afflicted with Ukrainomania, who have long been suppressed and forced underground, now possess complete freedom of action. Be that as it may, much can be observed in this area at present that is unquestionably bizarre. Ukrainianization is becoming an end in itself, giving rise to inefficient and wasteful expenditures of national energies. In the future, life will make its own corrections and cleanse the Ukrainian movement of those elements of caricature that the fanatics of cultural separatism have brought to it. Much that has been and is being created by these ardent nationalists is doomed to destruction and oblivion. But the appropriateness of creating a special Ukrainian culture that does not coincide with Great Russian culture is beyond question. A properly developed national self-awareness will show the future creators of this culture its natural boundaries, as well as its true essence and most basic task: to become *a special, individualized, Ukrainian variant of all-Russian culture*. Only then will cultural work in the Ukraine be altered in a way that will allow the best representatives of the Ukrainian people to participate in it happily and willingly.

This will happen when pandering to the egoistic instincts and to undisguised affirmations of man's biological nature has been removed from the foundation of national life in the Ukraine (as well as elsewhere in Russia-Eurasia) and replaced by the *primacy of culture* and by personal and national *self-awareness*. Eurasian-ism calls all Russians to the struggle for these ideals—not only Great Russians, but Belorussians and Ukrainians as well.

11 On the Idea Governing the Ideocratic State*

It is one of the fundamental theses of Eurasians that modern democracy must give way to ideocracy. Democracy presupposes the selection of the ruling echelon according to its popularity in some circles, and the main forms of selection are an election campaign in politics and competition in economy. Ideocracy presupposes the selection of the ruling echelon according to its faithfulness to a single common governing idea. The democratic state has no convictions of its own (for its rulers come from various parties) and cannot lead the culture and the economy; therefore it tries to interfere as little as possible in both ("freedom of trade," "freedom of the press," "freedom of art," etc.) and lets such irresponsible factors as private capital and the press rule the society. Contrariwise, the ideocratic state has its own convictions and its own governing idea (whose bearer is the ruling echelon united in a single ideological state organization) and must itself organize and control all aspects of life. It cannot allow the interference of any irresponsible factors over which it has no control (especially private capital) in politics, the economy, and culture; for this reason the ideocratic state is by definition partly socialist. Can any idea become a governing one and, if not, what requirements must the idea of a truly ideocratic state meet? We will not find a clear answer to this question in Eurasian literature. The determining feature of ideocratic selection must be not only a

*Originally as "Ob idee-pravitel'nitse ideokraticheskogo gosudarstva," *Evraziiskaia khronika* 11, 1935, pp. 29-37. Translated by Anatoly Liberman.

common world view but also one's readiness to sacrifice oneself to the governing idea. This element of self-sacrifice, this realization that one is always in the forefront and has a heavy burden to carry is necessary to offset the privileges connected with belonging to the ruling echelon. In the eyes of their compatriots rulers must enjoy moral prestige. Selection for government service is inseparable from moral prestige in all societies, but it is especially great under ideocracy because the readiness to sacrifice oneself for the idea is one of the main features by which its rulers are selected. Consequently, the governing idea must be worthy of a sacrifice and the sacrifice must be viewed by all citizens as a morally valuable act.

Since selfishness and greed are looked upon as immoral or at best as of small moral value, neither can form the basis of the governing idea. But nothing will change even if "expanded" selfishness or greed take their place. Whether my goal is well-being and profit for myself or for myself, my family, and my companions, egoism will be egoism and greed will be greed, and no moral value is attached to them. Sacrificing my personal selfishness for that of my biological or social group is meaningless, or it stems from my low animal instincts, for this is exactly what animals do. Man, on a certain level of development, cannot treat such behavior as morally valuable. He regards as valuable only a sacrifice for a "common cause," i.e., a sacrifice justified by the welfare of the whole rather than of the one segment to which he who has made the sacrifice belongs.

What is then the whole for whose sake one can make a morally valuable sacrifice? Obviously, it cannot be a class, for by its nature a class is only a part of the whole; besides, since class membership is determined by common economic interests, any activity directed toward enriching it at the expense of other classes is an expanded form of greed. Nor can a nation be viewed as a whole in the above sense of the word. A nation is an ethnic, and consequently biological, unit. The difference between a class and a nation is one of degree, not of principle. And if doing something for one's family, insofar as the results are detrimental to others, is considered a form of immoral expanded egoism, service (however selfless) to the interests of one's own nation, insofar as it is detrimental to other nations, must be viewed in the same light. So neither the well-being of a class nor the well-being of a nation can be the content of the idea governing an ideocratic state, and if modern ideocracies choose as their idea the dictatorship of a class or nationalism, it happens because in these states only the form, not the content is ideocratic and they replace the ideocratic content by ideologies corresponding to other forms of organization, i.e., to democracy.

It is fully appropriate to advance slogans like "everything for my class" or "everything for my nation" under democracy, with its focus on individualism and a clash of egoisms at home and abroad. Under ideocracy such slogans are anachronisms, and attempts to make them sound "tenable" are naive and doomed to failure. It cannot be proved that one nation or one race is better than another. But equally absurd are the arguments called upon to demonstrate the superiority of the proletariat over the other classes, especially when a good half of those who insist on this superiority are themselves not proletarians. Even if the proletariat were indeed a bearer of the socialist idea, this fact would not mean anything, for socialism is neither absolute good nor the content of ideocracy, nor its goal, but only its logical consequence.

But if neither a class nor a nation is a whole for which one can be asked to make sacrifices, the same holds true for "mankind." Every creature reveals itself to the investigator in opposition to other creatures of the same order. The class has certain contours, a certain individuality, inasmuch as it is opposed to other classes; a nation is likewise opposed to other nations. But what is mankind opposed to? Not to other mammals, one should suppose! But if so, this is a zoological unit for whose sake one can make sacrifices only "to preserve the species," obeying a rudimentary animal instinct rather than a moral duty. If mankind is not opposed to anything, it does not possess the main features of a living personality, it has no individual being and can under no circumstances serve as a stimulus of moral behavior.

So not a class, not a nation, not mankind. But between a nation, which is too concrete, and mankind, which is too abstract, exists the concept of a separate world. The totality of nations inhabiting an economically independent (autarkic) place of development and tied together by common history and fate, by common work on the creation of one culture and one state, rather than by race—this is the whole that meets the aforementioned requirements. It is not a biological unit because it is a whole made up of many tribes and the bond connecting its members is not of an anthropological nature. Efforts directed toward the welfare of this whole do not stem from expanded greed, because, since this place of development is autarkic, its welfare can do no harm to other human groups. And yet this whole is not a vague, impersonal mass like "mankind." It has the features of an individual being, as any subject of history does. Service to such a variety of "concrete mankind" inhabiting a separate world has as its proviso the suppression of personal, class, and national egoism and of all kinds of egocentric self-aggrandizement. However, it does not exclude the support of each nation's individuality; it even insists on such support, for national individuality within the framework of an autarky carries no destructive potential.

The feeling that one belongs to a multinational whole has among its constituents the feeling that one belongs to a definite nation within this whole. The readiness to sacrifice one's personal and family interests for the sake of the whole, based as it is on a higher status of social ties in comparison to ties of a biological nature, results in a similar attitude toward one's nation: the features common to a given nation and the other inhabitants of the same place of development are valued higher than the features common to this nation and one's brothers in blood and language not belonging to one's place of development (the primacy of spiritual, cultural kinship and of common fate over biological kinship).

So we see that the idea governing a truly ideocratic state can be only the welfare of all the nations inhabiting a given autarkic separate world. Consequently, the territory of such a state must coincide with some separate world (an autarky). The other requirements associated with the concept of autarky—planned economy and the state regulation of civilization and culture—lead to the same conclusions, because these requirements can be met only in an autarkic state. And only under such conditions can the state protect itself against the interference of foreign capital.

An ideocratic state, as we see, needs an autarky. However, it does not follow that any autarky can become a true ideocratic state. A colonial empire inhabited by nations that have nothing to do with one another except for the fact of being subjugated by the same oppressor can be quite independent from an economic point of view, but it cannot become an autarky, for the economic bond connecting its separate parts is insufficient for creating a governing idea. One also needs a vivid awareness of common culture and common historical traditions, continuity in the place of development, and, above all, the absence of national inequality, a thing unattainable in a colonial empire.

It follows that not every state can become an ideocracy. And since ideocracy is the organization of the society of the future, quite soon the map of the world will undergo drastic changes. Equally serious changes will occur in the psychology, ideology, and self-awareness of all nations. Modern collectivism meets its goal halfway, as it were: man looks upon himself as a member of an organic body—be it a class or a nation—but he treats this body as a consistent individualist treats his own personality. Under ideocracy these last traces of individualism will disappear, and man will look upon himself, his class, and his nation as a part of an organic whole united by a state and performing a definite function in it. All this must not only be accepted in theory but become an inalienable ingredient of the psyche of those who will live in the ideocratic epoch of the future.

The modern ideocratic states are still very far from true ideocracy. The U.S.S.R. is somewhat closer to the goal because its territory is a potentially autarkic separate world inhabited by many unrelated nations sharing the same historical fate. But if we consider the fact that the rulers of the U.S.S.R. persist in taking the consequences of ideocracy (socialism) for its content, that education, the press, pseudoscience, and literature instill in the masses wrong notions of the nature of the present period, and that a great part of the non-Russian Soviet separatism is motivated by contagious nationalistic separatism, it will become clear that the U.S.S.R. needs a long time to reach ideocracy and will possibly suffer greatly until then.

The European ideocratic states have still farther to go. At the moment, they have been carried away by zoological nationalism and fight the idea of common European culture. Paradoxically enough, "Pan-Europeanism," which alone could have become the governing idea of European ideocracy (for no single European country can lay claim to any autarky), is now the ideology of liberalism and democracy, i.e., of ideocracy's sworn enemies. And if we add that our views on the idea governing a truly ideocratic state are irreconcilable with the colonial imperialism so manifest in the modern European ideocratic ("fascist") movements,[1] it will become apparent that Europe will reach true ideocracy only after deep and bloody upheavals.

And yet, despite the fact that the prospect of such upheavals is unavoidable in the period of transition from one type of societal organization to another, the existence of the modern ideocratic states (albeit with perverse governing ideas) is not

[1]Incidentally, the Pan-Europeans are even less willing to give up colonial imperialism. On the map of "Pan-Europe" drawn by [Richard N.] Coudenhove-Kalergi [see his *Pan-Europa*. Wien-Leipzig: Pan Europa-Verlag, 1924, at the very end of the book], Europe constitutes a tiny part; the lion's share is occupied by western and northwestern Africa (the Italian, Spanish, Portuguese, Belgian, and especially French colonies); the Dutch and French colonies in Asia are also incorporated into "Pan-Europe" on this map.

without meaning. The political experience obtained by their ruling echelons, the new forms of their sociopolitical life and *mores*—all of this will come in useful in the true ideocracy of the future and may even alleviate the birth throes that will accompany the emergence of this true ideocracy.

12 On Racism*

I

For various reasons that we will not dwell upon here, during the revolution, the Civil War, and the first period of Communism and NEP, anti-Semitism infected a fairly broad layer of the Russian intelligentsia. The fall of Trotsky followed by the elimination of some of the most prominent Jewish communists from their "commanding heights" has somewhat shaken the belief that Bolshevism is tantamount to "Jewish domination." Many Russian intellectuals both in the U.S.S.R. and in emigration who have looked closely at the events and at Jews have moved away from the anti-Semitic attitudes that until quite recently had possessed them. Nevertheless, a significant portion of intellectual and semi-intellectual Russians remain anti-Semites. Of late this Russian anti-Semitism has been intensively supported from Germany. Many Russian emigrés in Germany and in countries coming under the influence of German culture cherish hopes for the establishment of a Hitlerite order in Russia. Ideas of "racism" are being propagandized quite actively in Russian circles, hardly to the displeasure of the German government. While preparing its attack on the U.S.S.R. with the goal of seizing the Ukraine, the German general staff is interested in having as many sympathetic elements as possible both in Russia and the Ukraine. And since the idea of German rule in its pure form can attract no one except the Germans themselves (along with some self-seeking and short-sighted landowners), anti-Semitism is being promoted as a means of

*Originally as "O rasizme," *Evraziiskie tetradi* 5, 1935. Translated by Anatoly Liberman.

drawing Russians toward contemporary Germany. The Russians
and Ukrainians who have been taken in by this policy and who
are now propagandizing racist theories among their
countrymen hardly suspect that they are mere catspaws in the
hands of German imperialism, which is after only one thing —
Ukrainian black earth. But such is the fate of all agents of
foreign imperialism: most of them are unaware of what is
happening and believe that they are acting solely in the interests
of their own people.

Be that as it may, anti-Semitism of the German type is
currently being propagandized in Russian circles, and, since an
attempt has been made to draw Eurasianism into this matter, it
would not be inappropriate to discuss the issue in the pages of
Eurasian publications.

II

The arguments of the Russian anti-Semites who have
attempted to win over Eurasianism to their side amount to the
following. The native population of the larger part of the
U.S.S.R. consists of representatives of three races (according to
von Eickstedt): the East-European, the Turanian, and the
Tungusic. Highly intermixed and closely interrelated with one
another, they possess a number of common psychological traits
that have determined the history and culture of Russia-Eurasia.
Jews, who do not belong to any of these races, constitute a
foreign body in it. The psychic traits characteristic of their race
are alien to the history and culture of Russia-Eurasia and exert a
disintegrating influence upon the native population. It is
therefore necessary to prohibit Jews from holding any sort of
responsible positions whatever in Russia-Eurasia and to prohibit
the native population from entering into marriage with Jews or
with representatives of any other races foreign to Eurasia, for
example, with Negroes, Hindus, and so on (since in interbreeding, according to Mendel's laws, racial traits split but do
not cease to exist).

This argument has a scholarly ring, and its authors maintain that they are operating with "scientifically established" facts. Leaving aside the reliability of contemporary anthropology, which like the majority of sciences nowadays is undergoing a crisis (and von Eickstedt's classification in particular is not generally accepted), it should be pointed out that in this issue the decisive word belongs not to anthropology but to a different science, namely, psychology. After all, anti-Semites do not reject Jews on account of the configuration of their noses, jaws, or pelvic bones, but on account of certain psychological traits supposedly characteristic of the Jewish race. Therefore it is the correlation of certain psychological traits with certain racial characteristics that needs scientific verification.

This question is not nearly so simple as "racists" may think. For every person some psychological traits are inherited and others are acquired. We may agree that so-called talents and temperaments belong to the set of inherited, rather than acquired, traits. But it has never been proved that the direction of a talent or a temperament is also passed on. On the contrary, modern psychology of the individual and the study of the lives of outstanding figures indicate that the direction of a talent is determined by biography.

Thus, the correlation of psychic traits with heredity is far more complicated than it appears at first glance. In investigating such an intricate problem as national character, it is wrong to ascribe all traits to race, just as it is wrong to explain all the traits of an individual character by heredity alone.

III

It follows that certain traits in the Jewish national character are determined by heredity, while others are acquired. To ascertain which of them are hereditary and which are acquired, one would need a large number of experiments and systematic observations of Jews isolated from the Jewish environment since infancy and ignorant of their extraction. As far as we know, such experiments and observations have never been carried out on a large scale. Even the materials concerning Jewish cantonists [soldiers in cantonments], who, according to the idea of Nicholas I, were to be raised outside any contact with the Jewish milieu, have not been studied systematically. We are forced to draw chance observations from isolated, extremely rare cases of this sort. Generalizations based on such material are impossible.

Although the number of persons of Jewish extraction who have lost contact with the Jewish milieu since infancy is very small, the number of persons born of mixed marriages or having a single "Jewish grandmother" is considerable, and this material for psychological observations is available to everyone. True, even this question has not yet been studied, but it seems that each of us, as we observe our half-Jewish and part-Jewish acquaintances, should notice that no parallelism exists between the preservation of a physical type and typical traits of the Jewish character. Just those psychological traits which anti-Semites consider especially dangerous and harmful appear in Jews of mixed descent very rarely, and in each instance one can nearly always discover the biographical circumstances that have brought about a more intimate connection between the person in question and his or her fully Jewish relatives or the Jewish milieu. In by far the greater majority of cases, characteristics of "Jewish blood" are preserved in people of mixed descent over many generations, while Jewish character traits simply cannot be found.

This is to be explained by the obvious fact that inherited character traits are in and of themselves morally neutral, with the exception of certain pathological features, which can exist in representatives of all races and cannot be considered typical of just one of them. Heredity can account for the transmission of intellectual alertness or intellectual apathy, of an aptitude (or incapacity) for music and mathematics, of a sense of humor, and so on. But the direction of the intellectual aptitude or humor is not determined by heredity. If, however, there are in the Jewish character any traits that exercise a harmful influence on the "native population," they consist only in the direction the predispositions regularly inherited by Jews take. Since it is acquired, rather than innate, this peculiar disintegrative direction of Jewish talent, Jewish temperament, and Jewish humor bears no relation to race but is contingent on the *milieu*, i.e., on the peculiar position Jews occupy among this or that people, and on daily reality. The moment this position disappears, that is, the moment the bond between a given Jew (or half-Jew) and the Jewish tradition is severed, the innate traits of his psyche begin to develop in completely new directions.

IV

To arrive at a correct understanding of the specific direction of Jewish character traits, it should be remembered that Jews have been emigrés for some two thousand years and possess a stable emigré tradition. In examining the Russian emigration, we can easily observe in it the embryonic forms of those very psychic traits which, given "favorable conditions," will lead to typical Jewish traits. Despite their notorious internal dissension, Russian emigrés quite often show a striking solidarity in relation to foreigners. No sooner does a Russian emigré obtain a good job in some foreign establishment or business than he begins setting his countrymen up with positions there, so that in a short while a veritable "Russian domination" is achieved. Among Russian emigrés there are two ethical norms—one for "our own," the other for the native population (the Yugoslavs, the Czechs, the Germans, the French, as the case may be), just as among Jews there are two different moral codes—one for the sons of Israel, the other for goyim. To swindle an "alien," a non-Russian (a goy) is not considered reprehensible. One is not expelled from the emigré community for that; on the contrary, people who are known to be swindling the "natives" and thereby making their fortunes may even enjoy the respect of the other emigrés. But should such a man dupe one of "his own," a Russian, he will at once be expelled from the emigré community as a scoundrel and a cad. The external attitude of Russian emigrés toward the foreigners among whom they live is not merely respectful, but occasionally downright obsequious. Yet when the Russians discuss them behind closed doors, among themselves, these very foreigners turn out to be base and contemptible creatures.

Among emigrés of the older generation all this is still quite rudimentary and simple. In this respect (and in many aspects of daily life) they remind one of "small-town" Jews. But among the younger Russian emigrés one can detect a development of these psychological complexes, a development reminiscent of the psychology of Jewish intellectuals. Their self-awareness and their attitude toward the native population constitute an intricate blend of mutually contradictory emotions, attractions, and repulsions. On the one hand, they seem to be ashamed of being Russians; on the other hand, they seem to be proud of it. On the one hand, they passionately desire to be "the same as everyone else," to blend in with the surrounding foreign milieu familiar to them since childhood; on the other hand, they are as though repulsed by their surroundings and despise them. This creates in the younger generation of Russian emigrés the peculiar psychological conditions which, given a certain degree of spiritual activity in any given individual, will lead inevitably to "disintegrative", "harmful" manifestations. To reach this stage, it is sufficient that a young emigré who has grown up among a host people, speaks its language like a native, and has fully assimilated its culture, does not share its patriotic enthusiasm and regards coldly, "from an objective point of view," all that it holds most precious. Such an objective point of view always reveals the absurdity and contrived theatricality of any display of sentiment that we view as outsiders and as unsympathetic outsiders at that (compare Leo Tolstoy's favorite device of describing the external details of something he does not like and making no distinction between the essential and the nonessential). And such an attitude cannot fail to provoke irony—the bitter corrosive irony characteristic of Jews. This irony is a revenge for the fact that "they" (the foreigners, the goyim) have their own national enthusiasm, their authentic object of worship—their homeland—while the younger generations of Russian emigrés have lost all that. But this irony is also a form of instinctive self-defense: without it the emigré would have ceased to be himself and would have been fully absorbed by a foreign people.

. This last circumstance should be especially emphasized. An emigré "not of the first generation" will be able to preserve his national distinctiveness only if his psychological repulsion from surrounding people predominates in his soul over his inclination to merge with it. And the predominance of repulsion results in the cynical, ironic, disintegrative psychology we have been discussing. Is that man indeed not a "disintegrator" who lives among a host nation and has become part of its culture (not even possessing any other), but is repulsed by the elements of culture and *mores* that this nation holds especially dear and precious? The disintegrative psychology is the inevitable price the second and subsequent generations of emigrés must pay for the preservation of their national distinctiveness.

                                   V

The Russian emigration faces particularly unfavorable conditions for the preservation of its national distinctiveness. There are no insurmountable barriers that might inhibit its assimilation to the peoples with whom it now lives, and it is subject to no serious persecution by them. By contrast, the Jews, since the very beginning of their Diaspora, have been separated from other peoples by religious barriers and later suffered from all sorts of persecutions. And yet among them there have always been many whose inclination to merge with the surrounding people was stronger than their "emigré repulsion." But these people left the Jewry and assimilated to the foreign milieu; their descendants are no longer numbered among the Jews. Only those in whom the emigré psychology has proved sufficiently strong have remained Jews. Transmitting itself by tradition from generation to generation, this emigré psychology now constitutes the disintegrative element that Jews, according to anti-Semites, introduce into the life of the surrounding peoples. This psychology is not connected with race and is not passed on biologically from parent to child. It is a product of the influence of the Jewish milieu and of the similar psychological conditions in which nearly every Jew finds himself once he comes into contact with non-Jews. Among Jews heredity accounts for the transmission of mental agility, certain combinatory talents ("pushiness, shiftiness"), and a passionate temperament, that is, traits, which, were it not for the above-mentioned acquired emigré psychology, would prove not only harmless but even beneficial for peoples among whom Jews have found refuge.

VI

It would be incorrect simply to deny the existence of a disintegrative psychology among Jews, as many Semitophiles are inclined to do. A lot of Jews take pleasure in debunking the ideals of others, in substituting coldly cynical calculation for lofty, idealistic motives, in exposing the unsavory basis underlying everything elevated or sublime, in the pure negation that deprives life of meaning.[1] However, to account for this direction of Jewish behavior among other peoples there is no

[1] Jews are often reproached for "materialism." This is a groundless assertion. The typical Jew takes equal pleasure in the negation of matter and in the negation of spirit. And in contemporary civilization Jews are particularly successful when material substance is abolished and replaced with an abstract relation (be it in physics or finances). Isolated from firm ground, emigrés of two thousand years gravitate neither to materialism nor to spiritualism, but to the relational nature of things.

need to resort to the hypothesis of a worldwide Jewish conspiracy or plan executed by a secret Jewish government; the Jews' two-thousand-year emigré tradition with its inevitable psychological consequences is explanation enough. Within certain limits the disintegrative behavior of Jews can be beneficial for the peoples living with them. The dialectics of the historical process requires both affirmation and negation. No development is possible without an undermining of authorities, without destroying generally accepted traditional beliefs. Yet it must be acknowledged that the Jewish disintegrative influence usually exceeds the degree to which it could have proved beneficial and in most cases constitutes an evil. Moreover, it must be acknowledged that this disintegrative psychology constitutes an evil not only for other peoples but also for the Jews themselves, for it is a symptom of the unhealthy spiritual condition in which almost every individual Jew lives from childhood onward; it becomes an outlet for his excruciating unconscious complexes and spiritual convulsions.

Whatever is unhealthy needs to be treated, and treatment depends on a correct diagnosis. In dealing with neuroses, identification of the disease is sufficient; diagnosis alone will suffice for the patient to become deeply aware of the cause of his condition and to acquire a strong desire to struggle with it. And the Jewish disintegrative tendency is a peculiar neurosis originating from the awareness of an abnormal relation between Jews and goyim and exacerbated by the influence of a Jewish milieu suffering from the very same neurosis.

VII

How exactly to treat that neurosis is a difficult question worthy of special, thorough attention. Without altering the conditions that give rise to it, no treatment will be of any use. In any case, the measures proposed by the Russian advocates of National Socialism will not solve the problem. Instituting restrictions as of old and setting new barriers between Jews and non-Jews will only reinforce the disintegrative traits of Jewish psychology, which can eventually cause great damage to the "native population." If badly informed young Germans can consider such measures efficient, we Russians should show more foresight and remember that restrictions on Jews existed in Russia until the February Revolution and had only detrimental consequences. The prohibition of mixed marriages is still less expedient. After all, the very intention to enter into such a marriage proves that the given Jew's or Jewess's inclination to merge with the surrounding (goy) people is stronger than the repulsion from it. The prohibition would only reinforce the element of repulsion and further promote the disintegrative complexes in that individual's psychology.[2]

VIII

As for the points of the "racist" program not concerned with the Jews, it would be ridiculous for us Russians even to discuss them. Negroes have interbred with Russians very rarely; and when this has occurred, we have had no cause for complaint: Negro blood flowed in the veins of our greatest poet, A. S. Pushkin. At one time, marriages between Russian noblemen and Gypsies were not infrequent: as far as I know, their descendants did not display any particular genius, but they were in no way inferior to average Russians without admixtures of Gypsy (i.e., Indian) blood. As for marriages between Russians and Caucasian highlanders, Georgians, and Armenians, these have always had the very best results, and to prohibit them would mean to rise a sort of Great Wall of China between the Caucasus and the rest of Russia-Eurasia, to cultivate the view of the Caucasus as a colony, a view held by many pre-Revolutionary administrators but now,

[2]Addressing the Jewish question, I have deliberately left aside the religious point of view, to make my argumentation accessible even to those who do not share my religious convictions.

fortunately, abandoned. This policy could occur only to some wise German imperialist, hoping to seize not only the Russian Ukraine, but the Caucasus as well.

German racism is founded on anthropological materialism, on the belief that man's will is not free, that in the final analysis all of a man's actions are determined by his bodily characteristics transmitted genetically, and that by means of systematic interbreeding it is possible to develop a type of human being that will prove especially conducive to the triumph of the anthropological entity called a people (*narod*). Eurasianism rejects economic materialism and finds no reason to embrace an anthropological materialism, whose philosophical foundation is far weaker than that of economic materialism. In all questions of culture, which constitutes the arena of the free and purposeful creativity of the human will, the decisive word ought to belong not to anthropology but to the sciences whose concern is the human spirit—psychology and sociology.

13 The Decline in Creativity*

Every human entity—be it a separate individual or a multihuman unit, (i.e., a nation or a multinational whole)—passes through periods characterized by upsurges of and declines in creativity. They do not necessarily coincide with periods of general efflorescence and depression whose existence P. N. Savitskii tried to demonstrate in *Evraziiskaia khronika* 11, pp. 65 ff. But it is true that a rise in creativity tends to accompany a feeling of strength and self-confidence, while a decline in creativity is connected with the lack of self-confidence. Creativity (if we take this word in its broadest sense) is a barometer that reacts to the deepest processes in the subconscious long before these phenomena reach the threshold of consciousness. This fact, as is known, underlies research into the workings of the creative imagination (so-called psychoanalysis).

In this regard, a separate individual does not in principle differ from an organic multihuman entity; the difference is only in the degree of complexity. It is relatively easy to define a certain period in the life of a specific person as a rise or fall in creativity, for every person has a particular sphere of creativity, and it can always be stated whether at any given moment he or she is more or less creative. In the life of a nation everything is much more complicated; a rise in creativity in one area can coincide with a fall in another, and it is hard to determine the outcome since these areas are qualitatively different and incommensurate. Furthermore, the concept of creative decline

*Originally as "Upadok tvorchestva," *Evraziiskaia khronika* 12, 1937, pp. 10-16. Translated by Anatoly Liberman.

is not unambiguous, especially with regard to a nation. For instance, our analysis will depend crucially on whether the decline is natural or enforced, whether the output diminishes qualitatively or quantitatively, and so forth.

A natural fall in creativity can occur when a previously dominant trend has been exhausted. At some moment it becomes clear that the potential of this trend has been used up, so there is nowhere to go. The inevitable result is a certain (however short) period of stagnation; the quality of the creative output goes down, and the period will come to an end only when a new direction has been found. A temporary fall in creativity caused by inner factors does not yet mean that it has lost its regenerative power. Only if the stagnation lasts too long, can the diminution of creativity be suspected. But even such a diminution admits of more interpretations than one. It can simply be the result of temporary natural fatigue after a long overexertion of one's creative forces, but it can also be a symptom of irreversible exhaustion and atrophy.

A natural periodic fall in creativity should be distinguished from a fall reinforced by circumstances. If, under the pressure of external causes, all directions of creativity except one are prohibited, creativity limited to a single channel will soon find itself in a cul-de-sac, and stagnation will ensue; this stagnation holds no prospect of improvement because the other channels are closed. If no relief comes, creativity can die. Whatever factors may be responsible for a fall in creativity, it will be a healthy phenomenon only if it is accompanied by both a quantitative and qualitative drop. The quantitative diminution of the output is a sign of a "respite" that can be natural and even useful, though not necessarily so. But when the qualitative level of creativity goes down and its quantitative intensity remains the same or even goes up, this is a dangerous sign: we witness either the degradation of taste or lack of correspondence between the wish and the ability to create, i.e., a sort of impotence.

If one examines from this point of view the cultural life of the modern U.S.S.R., one feels a certain anxiety. Not too long ago many areas were on the rise there, but now one observes unmistakable signs of declining creativity. To be sure, as pointed out above, the nature of this decline is hard to state. Since the communist power has from the very beginning placed restrictions on culture and allowed creativity to develop in only one direction, which has now reached its end point, the stagnation has been in some measure brought on by the power itself. But the excessive display of public activity, constant bustle and hurry, demands for acceleration and record breaking speed—all this could not but exhaust the nation, and a "respite" would be a natural reaction to the earlier overtaxing of its creative forces. One can also find comfort in the fact that technical reconstruction is still in full swing there and that the decay and stagnation of culture are perhaps the consequence of the nation's forces being directed only at industry.

And yet such arguments cannot dispel the anxiety caused by the miserable state of culture in the U.S.S.R. Indeed, if the stagnation has been caused by the official policy restricting the freedom of creation, one may ask: Has this policy not resulted in the atrophy of creative abilities? People obliged to keep silent for a long time finally lose the gift of speech. Creation in the technical area is of course allowed; here restrictions have not been imposed. But is there enough independent creation even in industry? A good deal has been accomplished but independent and really new things are rare. The catchword "overtake and surpass"[1] has not yet been translated into reality, and as an industrial nation the U.S.S.R. keeps lagging behind the technically advanced countries. With regard to inventions this situation is even more evident than with regard to borrowing and learning. Therefore, the decline in creativity in the nontechnical areas in the modern U.S.S.R. cannot be ascribed to the concentration of all national forces on industrial development. Even if such a shift of focus has taken place, the

[1]The reference is to the popular slogan calling on Soviet citizens to catch up with the most advanced capitalist countries and leave them behind (*dognat' i peregnat'*). —Translator's note.

decline remains a fact, for in the technical area the modern U.S.S.R. has not made great strides either—as far as creativity is concerned.

It is, unfortunately, also impossible to look on the modern decline in creativity as a natural respite, for it finds its expression in the lowering of the *qualitative* level, not in the quantitative diminution of the cultural output. People are busy in all areas of culture, but this intensive activity is largely imitative, and the artifacts selected as models are old and unable to inspire new forms. In some epochs, ancient models do serve as a source of inspiration, and then the contemporaries speak of the "revival" of antiquity, but in reality the resultant products are absolutely new. Periods bent on "revival" usually idealize a *remote* past; because the past is so remote, creation can not deteriorate into mechanical reproduction or imitation. But people in the modern U.S.S.R. do not imitate ancient models lost in a romantic haze; they restore recent fashions, i.e., models that were interesting and vital in culture about sixty or seventy years ago. The "revival" of such a recent past against the background of the social and political upheaval that followed the Russian Revolution is a triumph of bad taste, a jarring dissonance. And, most importantly, it testifies to the inability to create "one's own" modern style.

When independent creation is renounced, when the models used are those which were considered "proper" in the "good old days," does it not mean that self-confidence and trust in one's strength have been lost? If this is so, there is every ground to feel uneasy about the future of our native land. Just now, when the international situation is steadily deteriorating and the ominous specter of a new world war hovers ever closer, the loss of self-confidence can have the most tragic consequences. It is not enough to indulge in self-praise in newspapers and at public meetings. This exhibition of superiority, this showing off cannot replace organic, subconscious self-confidence, whose true barometer is cultural creativity. And in the modern U.S.S.R. this barometer stands extremely low.

As pointed out above, a decline in creativity is a phenomenon admitting of several interpretations. The present case is particularly complex because of special relations between the communist party and cultural selection in the modern U.S.S.R. If the decline in creativity is engendered by a depression in the subconscious of the cultural echelon (and, consequently, of the entire nation), it should be treated as a menacing symptom, especially dangerous in light of the threatening international situation. But a different view of this phenomenon is also possible. Inasmuch as modern cultural obscurantism and reactionary attitudes enjoy official recognition in the Soviet Union and imitation of old-fashioned models is supported by the communists in power, we can hope that we are witnessing a reflection of the subconscious depression of modern Soviet communism, rather than of the Soviet nation. There can probably be no doubt that the Soviet Communist party has become a union of "smiling augurs," that Soviet communism has worn threadbare, and that no one believes in it. But time and life cry to be filled with ideas, and, since weathered Marxism cannot provide them, every truly original creative act inevitably "deviates" from Marxism. Unable to mine Marxism for new ideas and aware of the fact that truly original creation will inescapably result in new, i.e., non-Marxist, ideas the Soviet communist leaders support imitation of old-fashioned models, with a view to blocking original creativity.

Given this interpretation of the latest decline in creativity in the U.S.S.R., the situation appears disquieting but not hopeless. Marxism must be replaced by another governing idea. One can well understand that from a psychological point of view the modern leaders of the Soviet communist party will find it hard to take such a measure. On the other hand, the "smiling augurs" are capable of "changing the landmarks"[2] painlessly, for instance, by grafting new ideas on the old phraseology, and some timid steps have been made in this direction. Be that as it

[2]The reference is to the so-called Landmark Changers (*smeno-vekhovtsy*); see Section 2 of the postscript. —Translator's note.

may, there is no time to lose. Otherwise, the modern decline in creativity can last too long and have fatal consequences for those in power and for the country.

Postscript
N. S. Trubetzkoy and His Works on History and Politics
Anatoly Liberman*

I. Life and Work

N. S. Trubetzkoy was born on April 16 (New Style), 1890, in
Moscow to P. V. Obolenskaia and Sergei Nikolaevich Trubetskoi. His was a great name on both sides. The Trubetzkoys
belonged to the foremost aristocratic families of Russia
(Jagoditsch 1964, 12-13, mentions the standard sources on the
history of the Trubetzkoys; see also Berg 1941). Nikolai
Sergeevich's father, Sergei Nikolaevich, was a famous philosopher and the first elected rector of Moscow University. His
uncle Evgenii Nikolaevich was also a well-known philosopher
and art historian, and his other uncle, Grigorii Nikolaevich,
made a name for himself as a political scientist. Sergei
Nikolaevich (1862-1905) played an outstanding role in the
democratization of Russian life (see Schultze 1950, 299-305,
Zenkovskii 1953, ch. 27 and a book-length study of his activities
by Bohachevsky-Chomiak 1976). Unfortunately, his life was cut
short: he died less than a month after his election at the age of

*My thanks are due to Professor Ladislav Matejka, with whom I had
a stimulating discussion of my postscript in the summer of 1989, to
Benjamin Stolz and Jindřich Toman (Michigan Slavic Publications) for
their cooperation, to the Graduate School of the University of
Minnesota for a summer grant (1987), and to the staff of the
interlibrary loan division at the University of Minnesota, for almost
everything needed for this volume had to come from other libraries in
the United States and abroad. I am also grateful to Professor Magnús
Pétursson (Hamburg University), Professor Earl Jackson (University of

43; the same fatal ailment (heart disease) also killed his son, who lived to be only forty-eight.

Nikolai Sergeevich lost his father when he was fifteen and a half years old. His sister Mariia was two years older than Nikolai Sergeevich, and his brother Vladimir had turned thirteen. Ol'ga Nikolaevna Trubetskaia never forgot the late evening when they learned that her brother had suffered a heart attack in the office of the Minister of Education in St. Petersburg. Praskov'ia Vladimirovna, Sergei Nikolaevich's wife, immediately left for Petersburg. Ol'ga Nikolaevna described that evening many years later: "I ran upstairs to warn the children and tell them to bid farewell to Pasha [Praskov'ia Vladimirovna]. I can still see poor Vladimir in a long white shirt, standing in the passage room, his

Minnesota), and Mr. Toru Kato of the National Diet Library (Tokyo), who helped me locate, acquire, and read the Japanese translation of *Europe and Mankind*, to Professor Thomas Noonan (University of Minnesota), whose bibliographical suggestions were helpful to me at the beginning of my work, and to Professor Margaret Mazo (Ohio State University), who drew my attention to some of the recent literature on P. P. Suvchinskii. Professor Omry Ronen (University of Michigan) and Professor Stephen Rudy (New York University) have kindly informed me about the state of Trubetzkoy's correspondence and Roman Jakobson's archive. They confirmed my ideas generated by Jakobson's statement on the "numerous, partly extant letters in which NT primarily discussed ideological and political questions of the Eurasian movement with its passionate adherents and critics" (*LN*, v). I hope someone will collect and publish these letters. Although it was my goal to read everything that appeared in print by and on the Eurasians, some mimeographed journals and emigré newspapers have remained beyond my reach. My references do not aim at bibliographical completeness and reflect only a fragment of the material at my disposal. Especially important as sources of Eurasian bibliography are Savitskii 1931d, Böss 1961, Riasanovsky 1967, Halperin 1985, and Luks 1986. I would also like to take this opportunity to call the reader's attention to my volume of Trubetzkoy's articles on literary matters which was published by the University of Minnesota Press (Trubetzkoy 1990b).

big eyes full of mortal fear, his teeth chattering" (Trubetskaia 1953, 164).

It is hard to tell to what extent Nikolai Sergeevich's father and uncles were responsible for his future scholarly and political views, but certain influences are apparent. He grew up in a devout Orthodox family and owed a great deal to his religious upbringing. The history and meaning of Christianity interested both Sergei Nikolaevich and his son; the same can be said about the relations between Christianity and other religions. It seems that many pages written by Nikolai Sergeevich about Christianity and Buddhism were inspired by his father's books and especially by *The Doctrine of the Logos* (Sergei Nikolaevich Trubetskoi, 1906; cf. Jakobson's remarks—1939, 64, and Issatschenko 1977, 10). Nikolai Sergeevich never referred to his father's works, but once (1925, 80), while comparing the teachings of the Eurasians and the Bolsheviks, he mentioned the inner connection between the unnatural, rationalistic utopias of the Bolsheviks and their "sacrilegious renunciation of the divine logos." However, the word *logos* is not specific enough to support any conclusions.

His uncle Grigorii (see the chapter "Prince Grigorii Nikolaevich Trubetzkoy" in Nol'de 1930, 226-32) wrote a book called *Russia as a Great Power*. It was translated into German (1913), Swedish (1914), and Italian (1915; with a long introduction in French). The book is devoted to the miserable state of Russia's foreign policy and diplomacy at the turn of the century. Nikolai Sergeevich's works on political topics bear no similarity to Grigorii Nikolaevich's analysis of Russia's affairs, and in journalistic work uncle and nephew could disagree rather sharply (cf. Suvchinskii et al. 1926 and G. N. Trubetzkoy 1926), but the direction of their searching thought is the same. Nikolai Sergeevich's ideas on Old Russian art are consonant with Evgenii Nikolaevich Trubetskoi's views on the Russian icon (see E. N. Trubetskoi 1965; an English version: 1973). Evgenii Nikolaevich's articles and lectures on the pre-Petrine period and Orthodoxy and Nikolai Sergeevich's essays on Old Russian literature have the same source: both admired Old Russian art and realized that it had been misunderstood, and both tried to learn its language. The least one can say about Nikolai Sergeevich's world view is that it was formed in a highly cultured religious family with a strong interest in Russia's destiny. More specific questions will have to remain unanswered, even with regard to such seemingly obvious influences in the formation of Nikolai Sergeevich's outlook as Vladimir Solov'ev's cult among the Trubetzkoys (see Riasanovsky 1964, 217-18).

Nikolai Sergeevich did not follow in the footsteps of either his father or his uncles. A man of a different generation, he thought differently on many subjects. For example, like his uncle Evgenii, he believed that the Ukraine had no future outside the Russian state, but it is enough to compare their respective statements on this problem (Evgenii Nikolaevich Trubetskoi 1976, 142ff.; Nikolai Sergeevich Trubetzkoy 1927a and 1928) to see how far apart the two thinkers stood. Within the Moscow branch of the Trubetzkoys' large family one could find extreme conservatives as well as liberals, and in his youth Nikolai Sergeevich witnessed and participated in numerous debates. Ol'ga Nikolaevna jotted down in her journal on December 10, 1904: "Little by little, echoes of party differences begin to interfere with the peaceful and quiet flow of former social and family relations... Even the children argue and quarrel, sometimes even fight: for or against autocracy" (Trubetskaia 1953, 96). Nikolai Sergeevich probably absorbed the liberal attitudes that distinguished his father. It is characteristic that in 1929, in his discussion of Gogol's *Selected Passages from a Correspondence with Friends* and Belinskii's letter to Gogol, Trubetzkoy says that the book aroused the indignation of the entire *progressive* part of Russian society (1963, 113). Note also that he intended to dedicate the final part of his trilogy to Razin and Pugachev (see below).

In 1905, when Nikolai Sergeevich was fifteen years old, he published his first article, but his scholarly interests go back to 1903. He was a typical *Wunderkind* (cf. Tschiževskij 1938, 464), and in this respect he continued the tradition of his incredibly gifted family. Among the best pages of Evgenii Nikolaevich Trubetskoi's memoirs are those devoted to Sergei Nikolaevich's and his own study of philosophy. Quite casually he says that at the age of fifteen they immersed themselves in philosophy and were oblivious to everything else. A more or less chaotic reading of Locke, Mill, Spencer, Comte, and Darwin gave way to a systematic study of German thinkers, especially Kant and Schopenhauer. When the brothers became students, there was nothing for them to do at the University. Nikolai Sergeevich's article, published in the prestigious *Etnograficheskoe obozrenie* [Ethnographic Review], treats the Finnish song "Kulto neito" in light of the theory of survivals (see Trubetzkoy 1990b, XI-XII). His contributions to the same journal appeared regularly until the war (in 1906, 1907, 1908, 1911, and 1913). They deal with Finnish, Paleo-Siberian, Russian, and Caucasian folklore and linguistics. The most striking feature of these publications is their absolute maturity: neither their style nor their content betray the author's age. A circumstance of extreme importance in Trubetzkoy's development is the fact that the subject matter of his earliest research was the culture of small nations. Not only did he later remain loyal to some of the areas which he discovered in his youth (notably, the language and folklore of the Caucasus), but he also cured himself of the Russian and European ethnocentricity (to use his own term) that were his by education and birth.

Trubetzkoy did not go to school: his teachers were private tutors. Every year he and his relatives of the same age presented themselves only to take their examinations at the Moscow Fifth Classical Gymnasium (AN, 274; Jakobson 1939, 64). Beginning with 1904, he attended meetings of the Moscow Ethnographic Section of the Society of the Friends of Natural Sciences, Anthropology, and Ethnography, whose president was Vsevolod Fedorovich Miller, a scholar best known for his studies of epic poetry. In 1904, when Trubetzkoy had just turned fourteen, Miller was fifty-six and at the height of his fame, but his reputation did not prevent him from noticing the inquisitive boy. (To be sure, the boy had a name that opened every door.) In 1907 Nikolai Sergeevich's research into the Kamchadal language brought him into contact with the three most outstanding specialists in Paleo-Siberian anthropology—V. I. Ekhel'son, L. Ia. Shternberg, and V. G. Bogoraz. Bogoraz could not conceal his amazement when, after coming from Petersburg to Moscow he discovered his correspondent's age (AN, 273; *LN*, 443; Tschiževskij 1938, 464). In 1920, when he was already a refugee, Trubetzkoy wrote a letter to the Bulgarian historian Ivan Shishmanov (*LN*, 445-48) that contains the following passage: "You may remember the Russian boy...to whom about fifteen years ago you sent your book...with the inscription 'To a future historian of ancient Bulgarians.'" At the age of fifteen, Trubetzkoy must have been sufficiently interested in the oldest period of the Slavs to ask for and to read a seventy-page offprint in Bulgarian.

V. F. Miller pursued two lines of research—Russian epic poetry and Ossetian philology—and Trubetzkoy's lifelong interest in Caucasian culture and languages was awakened by one of Miller's presentations to the Society. It is through Miller that Trubetzkoy made the acquaintance of the ethnographer and archaeologist S. K. Kuznetsov. Both Miller and Kuznetsov died in 1913. *Etnograficheskoe obozrenie* (25, 1913 [1914], 184) printed Trubetzkoy's telegram from the Caucasus ("Unable to be in church today, I would like you to accept my sincere, heartfelt condolences in your grief") and an obituary of Kuznetsov, which, if it had been known to folklorists and anthropologists when it was written, could have been hailed as the first work of structural folklore. More about this subject is said in the volume of Trubetzkoy's literary works (Trubetzkoy 1990b, XI-XII, XV, 107-9); here I will only quote the beginning of this commemorative article (1913, 325-26), for it has a direct bearing on Trubetzkoy's education.

I met Stefan Kirovich when I was a mere fifth-grader; at that time I was very much attracted to ethnography, especially to the indigenous Finno-Ugric peoples living in Russia. Naturally, I had no erudition at that time; nor did I possess any of the skills for independent work. S. K. took great care of me. He directed my scholarly interests, told me what to read on my subject, gave me books from his rich ethnographic library, and—most important—shared with me a great deal of information from his own unpublished materials. Clearly, he himself could not profit in any way by scholarly discussions with a fifteen-year-old boy. But as a result of his kindness and readiness to help anyone who felt enthusiasm for problems dear to him and who turned to him for advice, our meetings at that time were rather frequent. He taught me to work and warned me so tactfully against overhasty conclusions (to which I, like any beginner, was inclined) that these lessons were not only useful to me but also pleasant. From that time on, I met S. K. rather often in the course of three or four years, until my scholarly interests took a somewhat different turn; then my visits became rarer. During that time I learned from S. K. a great deal. I am indebted to him for numerous valuable suggestions and especially for a large quantity of precious information. I will never forget our stimulating talks.

In 1908, Trubetzkoy entered Moscow University. The University was divided into "faculties" and departments. Students declared their major at once and had little freedom in deciding which courses to take. Trubetzkoy chose the Philosophical-Psychological Department of the Historical-Philological Faculty but felt disappointed with the courses; and much to the chagrin of those who looked upon him as a budding philosopher and successor to his illustrious father and uncle (Jakobson 1939, 67), both of whom he, incidentally, resembled very much (Tschiževskij 1938, 464), he transfered after two semesters to the Department of Linguistics (AN, 274). By that time his father had been dead for three years, but Evgenii Nikolaevich Trubetskoi taught at the University. A. V. Chicherin, a literary scholar of the older generation, heard Evgenii Nikolaevich's lectures at the Polytechnic Museum. He wrote (1985, 260): "Here, like another Zeus the Thunderer, Prince Evgenii Nikolaevich Trubetskoi tore off the veil of obscurity that hid from view the wonderful

treasures of old Russian art. In his mouth, the very word
ikonopis' [icon painting], with a strong stress on the first syllable
[instead of the second] and sharp *i*, seemed piercing and
strange." Boris Pasternak was Nikolai Sergeevich Trubetzkoy's
fellow student, and he also finished the Fifth Gymnasium. He,
devoted a few paragraphs to the Trubetzkoys in his *People and
Situations*:

> The elder Trubetzkoys, the father and the uncle of the student
> Nikolai were professors, one of jurisprudence, while the other
> was Rector of the University and a well-known philosopher. Both
> were corpulent, and like two elephants, frock coats and all,
> without waists, would mount the rostrum and in a tone with
> which one might accost a deaf-mute, in aristocratic, burring,
> imploring voices, delivered their brilliant courses. Of the same
> type were the young people [Nikolai Sergeevich Trubetzkoy, S. P.
> Mansurov, and D. F. Samarin]; these inseparable three used to
> come to the University together—tall, gifted youths, with eyebrows
> that grew all the way across the forehead, with voices and names
> that carried far...I do not know Mansurov's fate, but the
> renowned philologist Nikolai Trubetzkoy became world famous
> and died in Vienna not long ago (Pasternak 1982, 444-45; written
> in 1956; the translation is mine, cf. Pasternak 1959, 74-75).

Mansurov became a priest and died in prison after the
revolution (Arsen'ev 1959,106). D.F. Samarin, an offspring of a
distinguished Slavophile family, also died early. Jakobson (1939,
67) says that Samarin's influence on the development of
Trubetzkoy's Hegelian views was not insignificant. In matters of
history Trubetzkoy was an extreme determinist, but his
Orthodoxy can explain his teleological position at least as well as
his familiarity with Hegel. Trubetzkoy was unusually sensitive to
the vocabulary of his favorite authors, and it is not improbable
that the phonological term *Aufhebung* 'neutralization,' which he
found after a long search, is Hegel's key word transferred to
linguistics. But the difficulty is the same as with *logos: Aufhebung*
is a common word in German.

Incidentally, Trubetzkoy did not like Pasternak, whom he also remembered from the Fifth Gymnasium. He disapproved of Jakobson's comparison of Pasternak with Maiakovskii. "In my opinion, Pasternak is a star of the tenth magnitude and an epigone," he wrote as late as 1936: *LN,* 358.

Evgenii Nikolaevich Trubetskoi was the life and soul of several religious circles that flourished in Moscow at the beginning of the century. A group of about fifteen young people decided to organize a circle of their own. In 1909-1910 they met regularly and discussed "the ancient world and early Christianity," Indian mysticism, theism and pantheism, Plato, Plotinus, St. Augustine, and other subjects pertaining to religion and philosophy. Nikolai Sergeevich Trubetzkoy ("Kotia Trubetzkoy, Sergei Nikolaevich Trubetzkoy's son, later a famous philologist and a professor at Vienna"), his future wife, and a few other brilliant people were participants in those gatherings (Arsen'ev 1962, 40-41; the Samarins and the Mansurovs are mentioned in this article too; see also Fleischman et al. 1983, 250).

The chairman of the Department of Linguistics at Moscow University was V. J. Porzeziński (Viktor Karlovich Porzhezinskii), "a diligent student and an excellent teacher." "Unlike so many teachers, he knew, without forcing his own convictions upon anyone, how to convey scholarly ideas in their dynamic, rather than static form, how to give impetus to further development" (N. S. Trubetzkoy 1930/31). Hardly anyone thinks of Trubetzkoy as Porzeziński's pupil, partly because few people read Porzeziński's books nowadays. Porzeziński was fanatically loyal to Fortunatov, whereas Trubetzkoy's views were different; yet he was a pupil of the same school (compare his ironic reference to his own style: Pomorska 1977b, 235, and Trubetzkoy 1990b, ix-x); Louis Hjelmslev (1939, 56, 59) traces several of Trubetzkoy's strongest beliefs directly to Porzeziński.

Linguistics meant Indo-European linguistics at Moscow University. Although Trubetzkoy was chiefly interested in non-

Indo-European languages, he stayed in Porzeziński's department because he realized that one could learn the comparative method only from the Indo-Europeanists. According to his recollections (AN, 275), he had come to the conclusion—by the age of eighteen!—that linguistics was the only branch of "human lore" with a scientific approach and that all the other branches of this lore (ethnography, history of religion, history of culture, and so forth) would leave their prescientific, "alchemic" stage only when they followed the example of linguistics. Few people thought so in 1909.

At the University, Trubetzkoy's studies of comparative philology ran their usual course. The Department offered general linguistics, Sanskrit, Slavic, and Baltic, while Latin, Greek, and Germanic were marginal in its curriculum. He also continued his studies of Caucasian languages and folklore. In 1910 or 1911 (Trubetzkoy gives different dates in AN, 275, and in 1934, 1), Vsevolod Miller invited him to spend the summer on his estate on the Black Sea (about thirty miles south of Tuapse) to record Circassian tales and songs. The next year he went to the Caucasus again. Trubetzkoy had a phenomenal memory, but even he confessed in 1934 that details in the stories he had heard in Cherkess (Circassian) villages almost a quarter of a century earlier were getting blurred. In 1913, soon after graduation, Trubetzkoy gave three papers at a congress of Russian ethnologists in Tiflis (Tbilisi)—one on the history of religion, one on folklore, and one on grammar. At that time he was mainly interested in comparative Caucasian philology. All his drafts on this subject, together with his field notes and numerous studies of Old Indic, Finnish, and Russian versification, were lost when he left Moscow in 1917 (Jakobson 1939, 69).

Trubetzkoy graduated with a work on the expression of the future in Indo-European; in 1926 he published a fragment of it in the Kretschmer *Festschrift* (cf. *LN*, 86). In those days, the brightest graduates stayed at the University to prepare for advanced exams and eventually to join the faculty. Porzeziński expressed his opinion of Trubetzkoy in a recommendation that contained the phrases "a rich store of scholarly interests and erudition rare in people of his age," "outstanding abilities," "well-read in special literature and exceptionally hard-working" (*LN*, 487). No one had any doubts about the young man's prospects. The congress in Georgia took place in the spring, and in the autumn of 1913 Trubetzkoy went to Leipzig. Brugmann, Leskien, and Windisch—all of them luminaries of German linguistics—were among those whose lectures he heard. Many years later (1937a, 346) he wrote that Leskien had been a great scholar, a superb teacher, and a lovable man.

On his return to Moscow, Trubetzkoy married Vera Petrovna Bazilevskaia (1892-1965). It is a commonplace of biography to admire great men's wives for their patience and dedication. Even if such wives are mainly literary stereotypes of compromised femininity, what one learns from the printed sources about Vera Petrovna confirms the novelistic image. Life had little in store for her. The Trubetzkoys' first child (Aleksandr) died in infancy (1917). After the revolution she lived in exile; until 1938 her circumstances were enviable in comparison to those of most other emigrés but still very modest, and after Nikolai Sergeevich's death she led a precarious existence. But without her help, Nikolai Sergeevich, with his many devastating illnesses and failing eyesight (*LN*, passim, and Jagoditsch 1977, 23), would not have been able to work regularly. Trubetzkoy's knowledge of English was poor, but Vera Petrovna knew the language well, and he owed his familiarity with English and American sources to his wife. After the war she prepared Nikolai Sergeevich's manuscript on Dostoevsky for publication, and it appeared in Russian and German thanks to her efforts. The Trubetzkoys had three daughters—Elena (1915-1968), Dar'ia (1920-1972), and Natal'ia (1925-1982). Two of their granddaughters—Barbara (Varvara, née Issatschenko) and Sophia (née Weisel)—live in Austria (see Troubetzkoi 1976, Ferrand et al. 1984, and *LN*).

In 1915 Trubetzkoy passed his Master's exams, and in the spring of 1916, having delivered two probational lectures— "Trends in *Veda* Research" and "The Problem of the Reality of the Protolanguage and Methods of Reconstruction" (according to the rules of Moscow University, one subject was suggested to him, and the other was of his own choice)—he received the rank of *privatdotsent* and began his work at the University. G. V. Vernadsky, a future fellow Eurasian and another graduate of the Fifth Gymnasium, recalled (1970, 213) that the credits obtained by students from *privatdotsents* could be applied toward the degree only when these instructors were granted the rank of 'credit dotsents' (without this rank they were not even paid and had no hope of attracting students). Trubetzkoy's status is unclear in my sources, but it is known that in 1916/1917 he taught beginning Sanskrit, traditionally Porzeziński's course. Even at twenty-seven he suffered from poor health, and after only one year at the University he had to take a leave of absence and go to the Caucasus. There, in Kislovodsk, he met the October Revolution, and the Civil War prevented him from returning home. He never saw Moscow again. But before we trace his life abroad, two earlier events must be mentioned. One is important only in retrospect, but the other was a minor sensation at the time of its occurrence.

In the autumn of 1914, at the debates of the Moscow Folklore Commission, Trubetzkoy met Roman Jakobson (*LN*, VIII). Later, in the prerevolutionary years, they saw each other a number of times, and in 1920, when both had become emigrés, their correspondence began. One cannot overestimate Jakobson's role in Trubetzkoy's life. Trubetzkoy admired his younger friend (Jakobson was born in 1896), trusted him as much as he could trust anyone, shared all his plans with him, and treated him alone as his peer. Phonology was their common cause. Structuralism in linguistics (in its Prague guise) was born of their cooperation, and in his literary studies Trubetzkoy often followed Jakobson. In all practical matters, including the never-ending hunt for travel money, Trubetzkoy depended on

Jakobson's organizational talent. By 1938 Trubetzkoy had become famous; yet his reputation would not have survived him or it would have remained a fact of local (Slavic) importance (Baudouin de Courtenay and Shcherba are good examples of this fate) without Jakobson's unremitting efforts in the United States. At present everyone who belonged to the Prague Circle has acquired a halo, which would have been unthinkable without Jakobson. Trubetzkoy's posthumous books could hardly have appeared unless his fame had grown to such proportions. Jakobson's obituary of Trubetzkoy is the best essay written about him in any language, and the volume of Trubetzkoy's letters made public by Jakobson is a fitting monument to their friendship. In 1914 all these things would have been hard to predict.

The second event was the gauntlet Trubetzkoy threw down before traditional Slavic philology. In 1915, A. A. Shakhmatov, a great Russian linguist, published his *Outline of the Oldest Period in the History of the Russian Language*. Shakhmatov was a pupil and follower of F. F. Fortunatov. Trubetzkoy disagreed strongly with Shakhmatov's principles of reconstruction and gave a talk on this subject at a meeting of the Dialectological Commission. From his early youth Trubetzkoy knew his worth, but he was prey to insecurity, so if he could say many years later (AN, 277-278; cf. *LN*, 2) that his talk had the effect of a bomb and that it was the turning point in the development of linguistics in Moscow, one can take these words at face value: he was not prone to idealize the past. Trubetzkoy's criticism of Fortunatov's methods must also have become the turning point in his own career, because he formulated principles of reconstruction that were systemic ("structuralist," as one would call them now), and later perfected these principles and expanded their sphere of application.

The February Revolution did not interrupt the work of the University, and the faculty apparently had no premonitions of the impending catastrophe. Trubetzkoy (who was scheduled to teach the Avesta and Old Persian in 1917/1918) found it possible to take a leave and go to a spa in the south several weeks before the October events. Although uncircumspect and impractical, he had no illusions about the new regime. He did not return to Moscow and migrated slowly with the White Army. If he had stayed in Russia, he would certainly have perished as an aristocrat and as Sergei Nikolaevich Trubetzkoi's son. Lenin, who hated liberals (his main competitors in the struggle for the intelligentsia), never missed a chance to revile Sergei Nikolaevich Trubetskoi. He even wrote a derisive obituary of him in October 1905 (Lenin 1960, 333), but for some reason it was not published then and appeared in print only in 1926. Even if Trubetzkoy did not know that Lenin had called his father (in *Two Tactics* and elsewhere) "the Tsar's bourgeois flunkey" and the like, he could not doubt the fate that awaited him. His younger brother Vladimir (the "poor Vladimir" of Ol'ga Nikolaevna's memoirs), born on the last day of 1891 (S. G. Troubetzkoi 1976, 132-33, and Ferrand et al. 1984, 195, give different dates because they probably use different styles), was the only child of Sergei Nikolaevich Trubetskoi's who did not emigrate. In the Soviet Union he became a writer and published his works under the pseudonym V. Vetov (according to C. van Schooneveld, personal communication, from the initials VT) to conceal his aristocratic identity. He married and had four children. In the thirties the whole family was "suppressed." The parents and the daughters perished in prisons and concentration camps (*LN,* 291 and 305). Trubetzkoy's sister Mariia Sergeevna (1888-1935) emigrated to France. His uncle Grigorii Nikolaevich settled in Vienna even before Nikolai Sergeevich, but his uncle Evgenii Nikolaevich died of typhus in Novorossiisk in 1920, shortly before the last major White armies left Russia (his family moved to Paris).

In 1918 Trubetzkoy fled from "the scholarly wilderness" of Kislovodsk to Tiflis and then to Baku. Two and a half years later he wrote to Jakobson:

> During my wanderings in the Caucasus I came to Baku in March 1918, just at the time of "the rebellion of the Muslims

against Soviet Power," or, to be more exact, during that short
time when the Armenians were slaughtering Tatars. I was alone
there, had no means of subsistence, caught typhus, and after the
hospitalization got a permit to leave with great difficulty. I did
not have a single acquaintance there, but I remembered that
when we last met you told me that you intended to go to Baku,
and I set off in search of you. But...my attempts to find you were
unsuccessful (*LN*, 4; see also Kretschmer 1939, 343) (all such
passages are given here in my translation).

Ragged and exhausted, he reached Rostov-on-Don. At the
local university he was appointed *privatdotsent* and chairman of
the Department of Comparative Linguistics, and he taught an
introduction to linguistics, comparative Indo-European
phonetics and morphology, and beginning Sanskrit. The Higher
Women's Courses invited him to teach the same subjects, and in
the spring semester of 1919 he also worked in Novocherkassk.
Despite the sophisticated curriculum, Rostov "had no scientific
life and no one to speak to." In Kislovodsk, Trubetzkoy began to
write a book called *The Prehistory of the Slavic Languages*, his *Anti-
Shakhmatov*, as it were, the fruit of his criticism of the Fortunatov
school. He never completed this work (though he published
numerous fragments of it as separate articles), but in 1918-1920
The Prehistory... was his main project. He went on with it in
Rostov, which was difficult, because his notes remained in
Moscow and the library of Rostov University reminded him of
the "Toricellian vacuum." He managed to write a good deal, but
Rostov was soon seized by the Red Army. On January 2, 1920, he
was evacuated to the Crimea; two months later (on March 11) he
fled from Yalta to Constantinople with a huge mass of Russian
refugees. Before his flight from Rostov he deposited his
manuscripts on the Caucasian languages at the library of Rostov
University, where they perished in the German bombardment of
the forties (*LN*, 2-3, 446-47; Simeonov 1977, 7).

From Constantinople, Trubetzkoy wrote to Ivan Shishmanov
and asked him whether there was any chance for him to find

employment in Bulgaria. For a short time Bulgaria became a "Russian Athens"; it gave shelter to about 30,000 refugees (Rimscha 1927, X), and Trubetzkoy was among them. (Although hopelessly biased, Aleksandrovskii 1969, 41-66, gives an idea of the Russians in Bulgaria in 1921-1926.) On October 10, 1920, he was nominated *docent* at Sofia University and stayed there for exactly two years. Although Sofia was a tremendous step forward in comparison to Rostov, as a scholar he again found himself in isolation. His duties were few, but his salary was far too small to support a family. He set himself a goal of publishing enough to become "visible": "then one can think of changing universities and moving somewhere—to Prague, Serbia, perhaps to Germany or even America; who cares where if one cannot go to Russia!" (*LN*, 5). In answer to Jakobson's query about his own possible employment in Bulgaria, Trubetzkoy described the situation in Sofia. This is what he wrote (the letter is dated February 1, 1921):

> At the beginning of last spring, when the first group of Russian scholars arrived here (mainly from Odessa), they were received in a most cordial way. But soon disappointment set in. Many provincial Russian professors had no scruples about bringing here the traditions of their academic intrigues and scheming; they showered the administration with their complaints, connived and plotted—in a word, behaved as is common at many of our universities. Bulgarians, new to this sort of experience, were impressed unfavorably. Also, many Russians appeared very successful in working in several places, getting privileges (even concessions) and "additional benefits," so that some managed to make 10,000 leva a month. This aroused envy. Bear in mind that Bulgarians tend to look upon Russians as a slightly superior race, and in the eyes of an average Bulgarian every Russian professor is, by definition, a celebrity; therefore students, especially at the beginning, preferred Russians, which also aroused envy. For all these reasons, the second group of Russian professors was received with much less enthusiasm. And when a few more people came (I among them), they did not want to take anyone. Several left without getting anything. Others had to fight for

several months. I succeeded in getting the majority (a very relative majority) only owing to the happy coincidence that the establishment of a chair of comparative linguistics had been debated for a long time; therefore a certain party immediately sided with me. The chair, however, was not established, but by way of compromise between the two groups, I was invited as a *docent* of Slavic philology with the privilege of teaching comparative linguistics, though the course was not called this, and Professor Mladenov, who applied for the position of ordinarius in comparative linguistics, did not get the job. I am absolutely convinced that at least this year no Russian has a chance here (*LN*, 9-10).

The Russian-Bulgarian publishing house brought out Trubetzkoy's first book *Europe and Mankind*, Herbert Wells's *Russia in the Shadows* (in Russian) with Trubetzkoy's introduction, the first Eurasian book called (in translation) *Exodus to the East*, and Evgenii Nikolaevich Trubetzkoi's memoirs. Nikolai Sergeevich Trubetzkoy was considered a "profitable" author by the publishers (*LN*, 16 and note 4).

Considering that Mladenov wanted to teach comparative linguistics himself, his attitude toward Trubetzkoy deserves the highest praise. In a recommendation based on Trubetzkoy's early articles and on the draft of *The Prehistory*, Mladenov, by that time a distinguished scholar, formed the same opinion of the young candidate as Porzeziński before him and Jagić two years later. M. Arnaudov shared Mladenov's opinion (both recommendations are given in Simeonov 1977). Also, Mladenov's analysis of Trubetzkoy's article "On True and False Nationalism" (1922; no. 2 in this book) was one of the first responses by a foreign author to Eurasian ideas (Savitskii 1931d, 6, note 5). Simeonov (1976, 44) gives June 25, 1920 as the date of Trubetzkoy's election and October 1 as the date of his official confirmation by the Council of Ministers. In his letter to Shishmanov, Trubetzkoy said that he knew Bulgarian "theoretically" and hoped to master the language well enough to be able to lecture in it (*LN*, 446). But he ended up lecturing in Russian, for students at Sofia University understood the language (Dontchev 1979,104; Simeonov 1976, 45). And there were not too many of them; for instance, in 1920 he lectured four times a week (from eight to ten in the morning!), and only three people enrolled (*LN*, 3). Apart from comparative Indo-European philology and Sanskrit, in the spring semester of 1922 Trubetzkoy taught the history of religious thought in India (Simeonov, loc. cit.); his long article "The Religions of India and Christianity" (1922b) is a by-product of this course.

To get an idea of Trubetzkoy's attitude toward the events in Russia, one should read several passages from his introduction to Herbert Wells's book.

> On arriving in Petrograd, Mr. Wells no longer feared being duped: his interpreter was a lady who had been imprisoned five times for her attempts to escape from Soviet Russia. A sober view of things suggested to Wells that such a person would not conceal the negative aspects of Bolshevism from him—to the contrary, she would depict the Soviet regime in the gloomiest tones possible. Russians would probably have come to a quite different conclusion: they would have guessed that after five prison terms this poor, intimidated woman had learned her bitter lesson and knew very well what she could and what she could not say, to save herself from the punishing hand of the Extraordinary Commission; they would have realized that she had been told that her fate, perhaps even the permission to meet her children in Estonia, depended on the measure of loyalty to the Soviet regime she would exhibit in her conversations with Wells. But such natural ideas occur to us only because we Russians are devoid of the common sense with which nature endowed Englishmen (v-vi).
>
> When he visited the House of Science in Petrograd, he was moved by the emaciated and exhausted appearance of the outstanding representatives of Russian science, who were glad to see him, as are prisoners when they see an outsider. He was especially struck by their hunger for work, by the fact that they suffer from a shortage of books and proper conditions for research. And he felt indignant...at the British blockade that does

not allow Russian scholars to get books and paper from abroad. For some reason, it did not occur to Mr. Wells that it would be much easier for the suffering Russian scholars to go abroad and that they longed for such a chance, but that at the very first attempt to escape they would share the lot of his interpreter— blockade or no blockade.

In the House of Literature and Art, Mr. Wells learned that Russian writers were not writing new books but were only translating literary works from foreign languages. He rather liked this arrangement. He did not even wonder why Russian authors had suddenly stopped writing. We would of course have suspected that they do not write anything because they do not want to lie but cannot risk telling the truth. But such ideas can come only to us Russians, because we are so spoiled. As for Mr. Wells, he did not give the question much thought; if they don't write, it's their business: perhaps they cannot get paper—as simple as that (vi-viii).

Wells is quite right in ascribing the Russian catastrophe to the collapse of the front and the *de facto* demobilization of the old Russian army in 1917. But he seems to have no idea of the role the present-day rulers of Russia played in these events. He states that under the Bolsheviks street robberies and murders have gone down drastically in comparison to the first period of the revolution. But he hardly realizes that all this happened because plunder has been regulated and monopolized by the Soviet government, because all kinds of professional criminals have been incorporated into "special" brigades, and because there are few people left to rob. (Mr. Wells would have learned a great deal worth knowing about why "unorganized" plunder has stopped from the sailor with a silver teapot who accompanied him if he had succeeded in drawing the sailor out. Unfortunately, Wells felt satisfied with the answer that the sailor had come by the pot legally and did not ask what methods of acquiring silver teapots are considered "legal" in Soviet Russia.) (viii-ix).

On the whole, Mr. Wells liked the Bolsheviks. True, they are naive and simple-minded, they love their boring Marx and believe in stories about a mysterious conspiracy of international capital, but, when all is said and done, they are nice people, and what is especially important, honest. The other Russians, however, are beneath criticism. Peasants are dumb half-beasts; intellectuals are worthless windbags, and generals, well, generals are mere brigands. The Bolsheviks are, after all, the only people one can talk to. It is inconceivable how Russia could exist before these people came to power! In any case, if some other Russians oust them, they will not achieve anything and will spend time in brawls and dissipation.

What solution does Wells offer for the Russian problem? He suggests that bourgeois states, especially America, recognize the Soviet government, give it their full support, and start trading with it through special trusts and consortiums, for the Bolsheviks—out of principle—can trade only with anonymous bodies and not with individuals. Foreign states should try to support the Russian Soviet regime, help it come into its own, and direct with their good advice the organization of communist economy, something the Bolsheviks cannot do alone because of their naivete and inexperience. Russian communists, in turn, at the sight of such benevolence on the part of bourgeois states, will stop pursuing revolution throughout the whole world, for they will realize that the well-being of communist Russia can be attained without it. In this way, paradise on earth will come: Russia will have its communism and other countries moderate liberal capitalism. *Suum cuique.*

It is hard to criticize seriously this project of the talented and productive author of science fiction. In any case, it is clear that Mr. Wells completely misunderstood both Bolshevism and, more importantly, Russia. He did not notice that communists are first and foremost internationalists, that they could not care less about Russia's interests and well-being, and that they do not need worldwide revolution to establish economic and political contacts with the West—on the contrary, they want these contacts to start a worldwide revolution. Nor did he understand that even with the blockade lifted, with transport functioning normally, and so forth, Russian towns would still starve, because hunger is the *raison d'être* and the main support of Bolshevism, without which communists will not be able to rule the population by red terror alone.

Yet the most characteristic part of this project is the view of Russia as only a geographical concept, an area that can produce and consume certain goods. In this geographical area, some people have seized power and gained control over the land's riches; these people are energetic but inexperienced, and they do not mind selling some of the riches they have appropriated in exchange for the products they need. They should be supported and helped in their attempts to mine the area in question for a maximum amount of the raw materials Europeans and Americans need. The author of the project has forgotten that the territory he describes is populated and that its population has certain traditions, desires, and requirements, both material and spiritual. He is indifferent to what the population might say, for it is suppressed anyway, and the Soviet government will have no trouble in putting down protests, especially if foreign guardians offer their services. Besides, the Bolsheviks say that the peasants like them and that uprisings are not worthy of consideration. The Russian intelligentsia is a *quantité négligeable* to a still greater extent (xi-xiv).

In some places in his book, Mr. Wells...seems to discern something, to notice behind the Bolsheviks' back some strange and wild face, the face of the Asiatic or semi-Asiatic "savage." Only his irresistible contempt for all non-Europeans prevents him from treating this face seriously. But this face is the crux of the matter. Communists try in vain to put an alien red mask of Marxism on it; this mask is artificial and insignificant. In Russia and Asia, *people's* Bolshevism is not an uprising of the poor against the rich, but of the despised against despisers. And its sharp point is directed primarily at the smug Europeans who regard the whole of non-European mankind as a mere ethnographic mass, as slaves fit only for supplying Europe with raw materials and buying European goods (xv-xvi).

Trubetzkoy's days in Sofia were numbered. Simeonov does not say anything about the deterioration of the political climate in Bulgaria, but in a letter to the French linguist Meillet of July 22, 1922, Trubetzkoy mentions a conflict between the University and the government and the persecution of Russian emigrés in Bulgaria (*LN*, 449). He resigned after two years of service, and there was a moment when it seemed that his rash move would have catastrophic consequences, because the position in Vienna on which he relied had been offered to Reinhold Trautmann, a specialist in Russian epic poetry. He wrote (August 12, 1922): "My only comfort is that they would have kicked me out of Bulgaria anyway" (*LN*, 30). However, the Austrian job materialized. Trubetzkoy went to Bled (Yugoslavia), where his family was spending the summer and where he himself worked with rare abandon, and from Bled to Vienna. In the autumn of 1922 began the most productive period of Trubetzkoy's life.

The position in Austria came about in the following way. Trubetzkoy's file was shown to the eighty-four-year-old Jagić, the former holder of the Slavic chair at Vienna; Jagić was impressed with what he saw (though there still was not much) and recommended Trubetzkoy as his successor. Every biographer of Trubetzkoy admires Jagić for his intuition and far-sightedness. Both were indeed exceptional. Jagić died in August 1923, and Trubetzkoy's obituary (1927b) reflects his reverence for the old scholar. In 1933 Trubetzkoy offered a rather ironic but typical retrospective in which he commented on his success in Vienna:

> The life of refugees has taught us that "it is indeed to Tula that one must go with one's own samovar" [carry coals to Newcastle], i.e., in Paris emigrés should open fashionable stores and night clubs, in Munich saloons, and the like. According to the same principle, Russian Slavists have the best chances in Slavic countries. Of Russian Slavists no one found employment in other countries except me, but this exception only proves the rule: I was offered the job not as a Slavist (I was not one at that moment!), but mainly as a prince, and that in Vienna, which is chock-full of its own princes (*LN*, 293).

The Slavic chair at Vienna University had been vacant for nearly four years. In 1922 it could look back upon an illustrious tradition, but nothing remained of its past glory (Issatschenko 1938, 323-24; Jagoditsch 1964, 11). There were no jobs for its potential graduates, and the best students of Slavic extraction preferred to study elsewhere. Trubetzkoy was the only Slavic scholar at the University, and he had a single assistant, Rudolf Jagoditsch. However, the choice of an assistant could not have been more fortunate. Not only did Jagoditsch develop a strong personal attachment for his mentor (who was only two years older than he), but he considered the time spent in Trubetzkoy's shadow as the happiest in his life. After the war, as the Chairman of the Slavic Department, he edited and published his teacher's books and wrote several scholarly and commemorative articles about him (see Jagoditsch 1964; 1977; and Anonymous 1972). So low had the level of Slavic studies fallen in Austria after World War I that it was hard for Trubetzkoy to decide what to do with the few students who enrolled in his courses. Prospective teachers did not need linguistic or literary theory, but Trubetzkoy's appointment was "Slavic philology and Slavic antiquities." Although he tried to live up to his standards of university education, deep in his heart he doubted whether the path he had chosen was the most beneficial for his students. Besides, he had a low opinion of his pedagogical abilities. (Teaching in German was not a problem: he spoke French, German, and—less fluently—Italian from an early age, and he had no fear of lecturing without notes.)

In a eulogy of Trubetzkoy, his pupil and one-time son-in-law Alexander Issatschenko (1938, 325) wrote about Trubetzkoy as a lecturer: "Always original, always thoroughly prepared, he led his students through the thicket of facts in such a way that the listeners themselves could draw the inevitable conclusions from what they had heard." André Vaillant (1939, 202) also called Trubetzkoy an unforgettable speaker. Trubetzkoy taught a great variety of subjects (*LN,* 488-90, gives a list of his courses and seminars)—comparative Slavic philology and the structure and history of all the Slavic languages and literatures, but only his literary courses, especially those on Dostoevsky, filled up (Jagoditsch 1977, 23, note 2). Later, when phonology gained popularity, his lectures on the phonological method, which he gave in addition to his regular courses, attracted many students, and his most eminent colleagues, such as Kretschmer, Luick, and Pfalz, made an attempt to put Trubetzkoy's discoveries to use. Trubetzkoy believed in self-study and used to say that universities are an anachronism, a relic of the pre-Guthenberg epoch (Issatschenko 1938, 327). But surely this man who had learned so much from Vsevolod Miller, S. K. Kuznetsov, and other professors in Moscow and Leipzig, must have realized that education is more than assimilating the basic facts of science and that scholars owe everything to the inspirations of their youth. Those who followed Trubetzkoy, even across the chasm that inevitably separates a genius from ordinary people, did draw their inspiration from his way of reasoning, from his attitude toward scholarship, from mere contacts with a man of his caliber. Even his occasional listeners, members of the Prague Circle, later recalled his infrequent visits as holidays (Vachek 1977a, 103-104).

Until the emergence of the Nazis, Trubetzkoy's life ran more or less smoothly (in addition to the previously mentioned sources see also Meister 1964, Jagoditsch 1965, 44-45, and Mayrhofer 1976). He was less than comfortably off, but he could work without feeling insecure. In the summer of 1923 he moved from a suburb to town and found a good apartment: "a real apartment, five rooms with all the facilities and in the very center of the town—a ten-minute walk from the University! I feel somewhat out of my element" (*LN*, 57). Although he did not have to look for additional work to support his family, they spent nearly everything he made. In 1930, when many Russians lost their jobs, the Trubetzkoys helped their friends without any hope of getting this money back, and a discount on a railway ticket from the state border to Prague could decide whether Trubetzkoy would be able to go to Czechoslovakia (*LN*, 186).

Others were much poorer; in 1926 Trubetzkoy described his financial situation as "relatively brilliant," while Durnovo (a Slavic scholar, also an emigré) did not have enough to buy a ticket from Brno to Prague. In 1933 Trubetzkoy informed Jakobson that the *Phonologische Arbeitsgemeinschaft* (Phonological Working Association) had two dollars (probably the equivalent of about twenty dollars today) in its "bank," which, as he thought, could be used for Jakobson's ticket to Vienna (*LN*, 267). During all his years in Austria the problem of travel money remained acute, and his participation in congresses depended on the resourcefulness of his wife and Jakobson (*LN*, 284). In 1936 he could not afford to come to the celebration of the tenth anniversary of the Prague Circle. But on the whole, life in Vienna must have been quite tolerable, though in 1926 he thought of the position in Prague, which he had not received, with regret (*LN* 93). As Tschiżewskij put it (1976, 17), "The old Czech scholars were at that time under the influence of Russian academic and nonacademic titles. Unfortunately, even the title Prince Trubetzkoy made no impression on academic circles, for he was young and primarily a specialist in Caucasian philology. Even later I was puzzled that they managed not to notice that he was a genius."

Since congresses, Trubetzkoy's visits to Brno and Prague, and Jakobson's return visits concerned them both, travel was discussed in great detail in their correspondence. Trubetzkoy's health was also a constant subject of discussion, but only because it prevented Trubetzkoy from working; as regards the other circumstances of Trubetzkoy's life, his letters are uninformative. A man endowed with talent for music and painting (Jagoditsch 1977, 18), he did not mention a single visit to a museum or theater. We never hear about his wife's occupations, his daughters' school, or his social connections.

Like most emigrés, Trubetzkoy belonged to two worlds. His work at the University, the education of his children, the very necessity to speak German most of the time, turned him gradually into an Austrian professor. He showed a lively interest in Austrian politics and Austrian affairs (Jagoditsch 1977, 20) but usually balked, if it was possible, at direct involvement. He was polite and withdrawn, and he did not realize how difficult it was for his students and younger colleagues to feel at ease in his presence. Because he was genuinely great, he did not have to strike professorial poses, but, all the same, people were overawed by him, and he tended to misinterpret their behavior as indifference (Issatschenko 1938; Jagoditsch 1964 and 1977). His tact, restraint, and excellent manners were not a mask, but rather an invisible wall, which, like every wall, served as a protection and a barrier. Jagoditsch wrote about Trubetzkoy:

> What I especially admired in N. S. Trubetzkoy was the natural simplicity and modest calmness of his personality. I have known few people who...were so little given to showing off, but I realized very soon that, despite all the simplicity of his deportment, I was in the presence of an extraordinary and noble man...There was no trace in Prince Trubetzkoy of the pose that scholars—consciously and unconsciously—are so apt to strike for self-aggrandizement. He seemed to know nothing about vanity, haste, and hectic work. The professional pushiness, so manifest in young and old scholars in their striving to assert themselves, was entirely alien to Trubetzkoy (1964, 18).

Jagoditsch says (ibidem, 20) that the deprivations of the postrevolutionary years, when Trubetzkoy wandered with his wife and baby through the devastated regions of southern Russia, through starving villages and typhus-infested towns, and the loss of everything—native land, status, property (he reached the Turkish coast with all his belongings in one bag), and the work of a decade—made him value the basic blessings of human existence above the all-too-human scramble for fame and money. Hjelmslev (1939, 57) says almost the same thing as Jagoditsch and in similar words: "In a strange land, Trubetzkoy, despite his broad education, remained...a stranger. Those who knew him then...will remember a man of great nobility, humane,...equally and naturally friendly with all people, modest and unassuming, but also a man who never overcame the inauspicious circumstances of his life." Jagoditsch knew Trubetzkoy very well, but he did not realize that beneath his teacher's composure, reticence, and seeming equanimity there lived a passionate, irascible man, prone to depression and nervous breakdowns, often insecure and shy. Only his family and Jakobson were aware of this aspect of his nature.

In Trubetzkoy's essays on the history of Russian self-awareness, one can find descriptions of various races. Jakobson (1939, 65) has suggested that Trubetzkoy's depiction of the so-called Turanian element, allegedly responsible for the making of the Russian type, was a product of introspection. In one of the essays ("On the Turanian Element in Russian Culture") we read:

> A typical representative of the Turanian psyche is characterized in his normal state by inner clarity and composure. Not only his thoughts but also his entire perception of reality conforms naturally to the simple and symmetrical schemes of his "subconscious philosophy," if one can put it this way. All his actions, behavior, and *mores* conform to the schemes of this subconscious system. As a result, there is no disharmony between thought and reality, between dogma and *mores*. External impressions, thoughts, actions, and *mores* merge into a monolithic, indivisible whole. Hence the clarity, composure, and self-sufficiency, as it were. In practice, such stable equilibrium—given low psychic activity—can result in complete immobility and stagnation. But this is not inevitable, for exactly the same features are also fully compatible with psychic activity. The stability and clear design of the system do not exclude creative endeavors, but they are, of course, regulated by the same subconscious foundations, so their products, without any pressure, become part of that same world outlook and *mores* and do not disrupt the system's inner congruity and harmony.

Elsewhere he points out that people of the Turanian type tend to subject reality to simple laws, and they do not ponder complex details at the expense of the overall scheme; such schemes are a spontaneous expression of subconscious impulses rather than of abstract philosophizing. The Turanian imagination produces stable and elegant edifices, indeed not too rich in colors and overtones, but impressive in their design and magnificent brushwork.

Two features are conspicuous in this description—a quest for the structural principle in all things (simple and symmetrical schemes, a stable and well designed system, elegant edifices) and the unpremeditated (spontaneous, natural) character of this quest. Anyone who has read Trubetzkoy's works—whatever their subject—will recognize their author in the "Turanian type." But in the passage quoted above something else can be read between the lines. One notices the phrase about the Turanian psyche in its normal state. In a special footnote, Trubetzkoy explains that if a representative of this type gives up the traditional, subconscious system of views and chooses another system, the result is catastrophic: the new model degenerates into a fixed idea, and such a person becomes the center of a sect whose existence undermines the whole. Since Trubetzkoy looked upon himself as a "Turanian," we can conclude that he did not give up the traditional values of his environment or choose a new system, but was forced into it; so, to use his phrase, he did not exist normally. He summed up his own mentality and the mentality of his ancestors and closest family in a masterful way (and ascribed it to the entire "Turanian" type!), but the picture he drew was not a self-portrait. Rather it was his ideal.

Trubetzkoy liked to assess himself and other people in terms of his anthropological concepts. In 1936 he asked Jakobson: "Have you received Sotavalta's book *Die Phonetik in ihren Beziehungen zu den Grenzwissenschaften* [Phonetics in its relation to other borderline sciences] and what do you think of it? A curious illustration of my description of Turanian psychology" (*LN* 373; his own opinion of the book was good—*LN,* 420). In 1931 he wrote a most interesting letter to W. Doroszewski, which opens with the following admission:

> Defining concepts is not my forte. I always try to be understood. From my own experience I know that this goal can be achieved not by definitions, but by the practical application of

concepts. Therefore I shed a few commonplaces at the beginning of my articles and try to come to the point as soon as possible. I am convinced that this way one's ideas can be conveyed much better than by wasting a lot of time and psychic energy on defining concepts...I know Baudouin de Courtenay very badly, and as for Shcherba I have read only his two dissertations...If I started discussing their work, I would have had to give a survey of their views, which would have taken me too far afield; besides, to tell you the truth, I do not like the history of science (*LN*, 227, 229).

This description of himself (cf. also *LN*, 122, on his distaste for surveys) fits his "Turanian type" rather well. Even phonology, an object of his special pride, was identified by him with Eurasian culture. Here is a passage from a letter to Jakobson, describing his trip to Paris (May 1934). Trubetzkoy's conclusions are astounding, yet thoroughly consistent with his views.

In Paris, as you know, I had to give an impromptu paper at the Société de Linguistique. Fortunately, the recollections of my talk in Vienna on [phonological] quantity were still fresh...I got away with it; they applauded, which, as I understand, is not customary there. Among the discussants were Meillet (who makes a rather sad impression), Homburger, and Vendryès (the latter spoke more than the others and, on the whole, quite sensibly). Then I met Martinet (a very young man) and Novák. On my way back from London, some Parisian Slavists invited me to breakfast... Of course we did not speak about phonology, not to spoil the appetite (incidentally, everything tasted very good). In general, linguists seem to treat phonology well, and Slavists badly. They repeat the same nonsense, attack the terminology, and so forth. Clearly, everything is rooted in personal antipathy. Despite French good manners, a personal antipathy against you could be felt several times in both Mazon's and Vaillant's words. But I must also say that on top of personal antipathy one detects a certain repulsion of the French towards the forms of Eurasian-Danubian culture that find their expression in modern phonology. That this specific overlay is rather strong in

phonology became especially clear to me in my talk with
Martinet and Novák. Novák is "an Oriental man," and all his
phonology has "an Oriental accent." People who have never
been to Russia or Slavic countries don't associate anything with
this accent. For them it is just an accent, like any other. The same
holds for an Indo-European scholar who has no personal attitude
toward Central Europe or Eurasia. But with a Slavist it is quite
different. Be that as it may, deep inside, French Slavists despise
and view as barbaric everything that is Slavic, Central European,
or Russian. Slavic scholars are all right as collectors of facts, but
when they begin to draw conclusions, their *manque de culture*
[lack of culture] and *âme slave* [Slavic soul] come to the surface,
and their results are dismissed as groundless fantasies,
sectarianism, and so forth. Therefore, a French Slavist will never
allow a Russian or a Slav to teach him, at least as long as he has
not become frenchified. This is how I explain why Slavists so
strongly resist phonology (apart from their antipathy against you
because of Dominois and Eisenmann), whereas Indo-European
scholars and other linguists have nothing against it. For the same
reason, Issatschenko, who, owing to the circumstances of his
emigré upbringing, has shed a great deal of his national and
culturally specific character and who can easily adjust to any
forms of foreign culture (who can imitate the forms of this
culture), appears more acceptable to French Slavists than
someone like Novák, who smells slightly of slivovitsa [plum
brandy] and paprika (*LN*, 300-301).

Trubetzkoy was not alone in discussing himself and phonology
in such terms. N. van Wijk, a sensitive critic and thoughtful
supporter of Prague structuralism, whose assessment of
Trubetzkoy's scholarly temperament and achievement is full of
subtle remarks, said among other things the following:

> At the same time phonology could not help raising objections
> because of the apodictic tone of its proponents and the dogmatic
> nature of its initial statements. These peculiarities stem, I believe,
> from Russian *priamolineinost'* [rigidity, inflexibility, a tendency to
> come to the point without looking right or left]; the Russian
> character, when it sees an inviting prospect, moves straight

ahead, never losing sight of the goal, contrary to Western circumspection, which prefers to look this way and that (Van Wijk 1939, 224).

Deeply religious, Trubetzkoy belonged to the kind of "Non-European" civilization that he glorified in his introduction to the course in Old Russian literature (1973), with science, religion, morality, and so on, forming part of an undivided complex. To live in God and to be moral meant for Trubetzkoy to reach the height of self-awareness and follow one's preordained way. He never lost sight of this way—for himself, for Russia, and for the rest of the world. He was far from indifferent to recognition and praise, but he could also have pursued his goal in the teeth of rejection, for, as he put it himself, "in questions of faith and truth the number of believers plays no role" (p. 127 above).

No one knows how Trubetzkoy would have developed as an individual under *normal* circumstances, but in emigration, surrounded by people of "the Romano-Germanic type," his "Turanian" ideal was hard to attain. His letters to Jakobson reveal an absolute opposite of the serene, somewhat resigned philosopher whom Jagoditsch met within the walls of Vienna University or of the model of "composure and self-sufficiency" one might expect from the author of the essays on Russian self-awareness (cf. Pomorska 1977a, Liberman 1980—my earlier analysis of the letters—and Kleiner 1985). Trubetzkoy was not a snob. He was always concerned about the feelings of those he criticized, and he was usually ready to withdraw a harsh remark if it could alienate a potential friend. Unlike the ebullient young Jakobson, he was reserved in his praise. His obituaries of Kuznetsov (1913), Jagić (1927), Porzeziński (1930-31), and Berneker (1937a) are warm, but rather dry and matter-of-fact.

Trubetzkoy could keep himself in check better than most. Even in his review of Dumézil's Caucasian works, which he considered harmful, he remained courteous. He made an exception only in the case of Marr, whom he openly called a

lunatic in need of institutionalizing. But from his correspondence with Jakobson we learn that his opinion of most linguists
was shockingly low. Words and phrases like *blockhead, fool, idiot,
bloated celebrity, utter imbecility, perfectly insane,* and the like (one
can again mention Pasternak—"a star of the tenth magnitude")
are among the most common in his letters. He kept reproaching
Jakobson for his disregard of the public and for writing works
too good for the collections and journals that published them
and too full of brilliant ideas; the material in them had not been
brought down to the level of the average linguist, who was
conservative, lazy, and unsympathetic:

> Remember that, on average, linguists are dull, hostile to
> novelties, and unused to abstractions (*LN,* 109)...Considering the
> relatively low intellectual level of an average linguist, you should
> have striven for utmost clarity and explained everything a
> thousand times...To be sure, a "thoughtful" reader will overcome
> this difficulty; moreover, except for some awkward places in the
> translation which offend the aesthetic feeling, the entire style of
> your book—nervous, hurried, and at the same time overloaded
> with thought—this style, together with the book's broken and also
> "nervous" composition, must make a strong and highly
> individual impression on the reader. One can see that the writer
> is not only rich in ideas but also endowed with temperament. But
> all this will be clear only to a thoughtful reader, and such are in
> the minority. An average linguist...will simply understand
> nothing (*LN,* 146-47, written about Jakobson's *Remarques sur
> l'évolution phonologique du russe comparée á celle des autres langues
> slaves,* 1929).

And a last sound piece of advice: "You must do your best to
avoid the drawbacks that injured your earlier works. One should
write keeping in mind the level of the average idiot, and this
always requires much more time than writing for normal,
cultured people" (*LN,* 190). Even in a letter to Meillet (1922) he
apologizes for the opening section of his article: it is elementary
(he says), but, unfortunately, one has no choice when dealing
with people like Hüsing and Marr. Curiously enough, Leonard

Bloomfield (born in 1887), who, like Trubetzkoy, spent some time in Leipzig and heard the same professors, also used to repeat what seems to have been a piece of conventional German wisdom: "Man kann sich den Leser nie dumm genug vorstellen" (There are no limits to the reader's stupidity). One is tempted to ascribe Trubetzkoy's repetitiveness to his disdain for his prospective readers.

In his letters from the thirties, despite his unconcealed feeling of satisfaction that phonology was becoming known, Trubetzkoy often complained that he was tired of repeating the same general truths year in and year out, and that the more seldom scholars meet the better. The only comfort for us "average" linguists and conference-goers is that Trubetzkoy looked upon even Otto Jespersen and Daniel Jones as mere "generals of science" and that once, in 1932, after many weeks of illness, he opened de Saussure's *Course* with the following result:

> For inspiration I have reread de Saussure, and I must say that at the second reading he impressed me much less. On the whole, there is little there that is of value; most of it is old trash. Even what is valuable is terribly abstract and unspecified. One begins to understand his pupils' direction. They hold forth on the system, but none of them (except Kartsevskii in his *Système du verbe russe*) succeeded in describing the system of a living language—French, for example (*LN,* 242).

Trubetzkoy was very suspicious. He sensed personal attacks in every vicissitude. The French were slow in accepting his article—doubtless because he was an Austrian professor. Jakobson did not answer his letter—his old friend had probably decided to move to the Soviet Union and had broken off relations that could compromise him. If even Jakobson was not free from suspicion in 1936, then who was! In despair Jakobson sent Trubetzkoy an offprint with the following dedication: "For dear Nikolai Sergeevich Trubetzkoy in token of absolute loyalty, friendship, and protest against fantastic reconstructions—do you not know me well enough?" (*LN,* 356, note 1 to no. cliv).

Impractical and unused to politicking, Trubetzkoy flooded Jakobson with requests "to order," "to see to it," "to rectify," "to make haste." He was worldly enough to realize that without organized effort phonology would remain his and Jakobson's, or at best the Prague Circle's private affair. Therefore, he corresponded not only with scholars like Meillet, Sapir, and Durnovo but also with linguists whom he considered nonentities.

Participation in every scholarly congress was planned like a military campaign: allies were recruited from every country, potential adversaries were neutralized, and the Circle's forces were deployed in an optimal way. All deviations from what he considered correct tactics aroused his anger. His scheming was usually inefficient, but he was always on guard. He endorsed Jakobson's plan to publish a book *Russian Philologists on the Czech Language and Czech Literature,* but he pointed out that it would be hard to steer clear of little esteemed Czechs and uninvited Russians. He noted that he would like to review a certain book; the book was no good, but "for diplomatic reasons" one had to praise it. Jespersen would be an ideal chairman of the meeting, for chairmen should be "generals"— well-known and *habiles* (shifty)—but Jespersen would be more useful as a discussant. H. Lindroth asked him to sign a document related to the reform of punctuation—"I reasoned thus: Since we have no one in Sweden, it is important that he like us; so I signed it without any reservation." "Don't write about Serbian verse: you will only make enemies" (the article was meant for a Bulgarian *Festschrift,* and Jakobson followed this advice!). Vachek, an ingenious and bright young phonologist, acted very rashly in criticizing Daniel Jones: it would spoil his own chances and irritate a big shot favorably disposed to the Circle. And for goodness' sake, don't allow Trnka to give his projected talk at the congress in Ghent: "As long as this paper exists...in Czech, no one reads it, but if he now translates it into English, an international scandal will ensue. He will completely compromise the 'Prague School' and phonology. We have had enough trouble with his English phonology and his ill-advised attacks on Jespersen" (*LN*, 76-77, 87, 224-25, 248, 250, 262, 425). Later Trnka saved all these letters from destruction (Vachek 1977b, 425).

Public lectures filled Trubetzkoy with fear. He always anticipated disasters and set down his every success to the politeness of the audience (in the same spirit in which he ascribed his appointments in Sofia and Vienna to chance). Here is a characteristic lament before a visit to Prague: "I have nothing to say; all summer I have been doing nothing, and it seems that I have never had such a barren period as now. So the paper will probably be very bad. This is not my usual insecurity but an actual fact based on objective evidence" (*LN*, 309, September 1934).

If Trubetzkoy's picture of the Turanian type provides us with his view of his own temperament and psyche, his idealized (and probably in part fanciful) description of Genghis Khan is valuable as an insight into what he held most sacred and most despicable in human nature. According to Trubetzkoy, Genghis Khan encouraged loyalty and steadfastness in his subjects and detested cowardice and treachery. Allegedly, he divided his retainers and servants into two categories. Some people are apt to put their own well-being above honor and obey their superiors out of fear. These are craven slaves, and Genghis Khan kept them away from governing his empire. Other people have an internalized set of moral values. Censure, mockery, even mortal danger do not determine their behavior, for they treasure honor more than success and wealth. Such people recognize a hierarchical order in the world, in which, they believe, everything has a divinely preordained place related to man's duty. They obey their superiors not as one would obey people giving orders but as members and constituents of a divine hierarchy that goes all the way to God's vicegerent on earth and God. They cannot betray their superiors, for treason will not make them exempt from higher judgment. It is such people that Genghis Khan supported. The entire context of the book on Genghis Khan leaves no doubt about Trubetzkoy's attitude toward "the great conqueror": he admired Genghis Khan and presented his moral code, his statesmanship, and his role in Russia's history in glowing colors. For Trubetzoy an irreligious world devoid of higher authority was a terrifying anomaly; when the concept of divine hierarchy is lost, the only driving force of social behavior that remains is fear, and then people become "craven slaves." One cannot avoid the impression that his description of the scum spurned by the victorious Genghis Khan was inspired by direct observation rather than by the study of history.

During his years in Vienna, Trubetzkoy worked in several areas. He wrote and lectured extensively on the history of the Slavic languages and on Russian literature, advanced and defended his ideas on the history of Russia-Eurasia, and made numerous contributions to phonology. However, the only place where he could discuss phonology at a professional level was the Prague Circle. The Circle came into being in 1926, and its activities mark the most brilliant period of European linguistics between the wars. On November 3, 1936, the Circle celebrated its tenth anniversary. This is the text of Trubetzkoy's greeting published originally in *Slovo a Slovesnost* and partly reproduced in English by Jakobson:

> I followed the development of CLP [Cercle Linguistique de Prague] from the beginning with a vivid interest, and I constantly felt intimately linked with this association. The different stages of development which I have gone through jointly with it emerge today in my memory: first the modest little meetings in its President's study, then the heroic period of preparation for the First Linguistic Congress, the unforgettable days of the Phonological Conference, and many other beautiful days which I have experienced in the company of my Prague friends. All these reminiscences are bound in my mind with an inspiring feeling, for at every contact with the CLP I felt a new upsurge of creative joy, which in my lonely work away from Prague inevitably declined. This elation and creative impetus are a manifestation

of that spirit which characterizes our association and emanates from the collective work of a close-knit group of scholars proceeding upon the same methodological path and inspired by common theoretical ideas (*LN*, 372, note 7).

The statement about the decline of creativity in Vienna (compare the title of his article 1937b, no.13 in this volume) is characteristic. In his scholarly work Trubetzkoy felt lonely and isolated. Nor were world events encouraging. Even before 1933 the situation was frightening enough. In the autumn of 1930 Jagoditsch returned from Moscow:

> His stories are blood-curdling and tragic. The most horrid thing is that the eradication of the intelligentsia has found support among the broad masses of population and is indeed "a common cause," to which everyone contributes with enthusiasm. Together with the intelligentsia, all spiritual culture is being eradicated too, and everything runs wild in all spheres; this is a spontaneous triumph of primitiveness, an organic, not an artificial triumph, so to speak. These are no longer tricky experiments of some dreamers divorced from life, but a real, genuine proletariat building not some higher culture, but a culture that it understands, a culture really proletarian, i.e., low, elementary, and wild. And this culture will be victorious, it will reign supreme in the whole world, for such is the logic of history (*LN*, 174-75).

The gloomy prospects for Europe and his own physical weakness made him work with fierce dedication. In 1935 it seemed incomprehensible to him that amid the wasteland of European life, with a global catastrophe approaching every day, an intelligent person could spend time on trivial matters. He wrote a reproachful letter to Jakobson, and nowhere else did he express his views on creativity, such as his own, with greater clarity and force.

> I will be unspeakably sorry if you allow the bustle of everyday life to engulf you, if you leave international linguistic problems

for petty provincial strife and fritter away your time on a polemic against "Weingart's party" and other similar trifles. Journalism has some attraction, which, however, on closer inspection, turns out to be sheer trumpery. "Ties with pulsating reality" are actually replaced in it by skimming over the surface of things, "many-sidedness" is replaced by lack of any sides, i.e., by spiritual vacuity. Bohemianism as a way of life so typical of journalism results in intellectual Bohemianism and kills scholarly thought. You have always been attracted by Bohemianism. When one is young, it is harmless. But sooner or later comes an age when one has "sown one's wild oats." You write that you have no new scholarly ideas, that you have dried up, that you must "betray the theme." And under this pretext you immerse yourself in the interests of *Slovo a Slovesnost*, journalism, meetings with Czech literary men about town, internecine Czech fights, and that sort of nonsense. And I think that this is what stands between you and your scholarly activities. I do not believe in your scholarly sterility. I think that *mutatis mutandis* you are undergoing the same process as I: a transition from an overlong intellectual adolescence to intellectual maturity. Maturity is not the same as old age and does not mean sterility. Not only do mature people continue their creative work: they produce the most valuable of all that they will leave to posterity. Only they create in a way different from that of the young. At first it is difficult to get used to the new method of work. It seems at first that nothing is left at all, that everything is over. A break, even a short one, alarms and arouses anxiety. But this is due to the lack of habit. Actually, there is nothing to worry about: you will keep creating but not as before. Subconsciously you are worried that things will not be exactly as they were. But let me assure you that this is not dangerous. What you lose in brilliance and showiness you will gain in the solidity of the constructions. Remember how we have created up until now. The printing press could not catch up with us: each of our works was outdated when it appeared (at least for us). One structure replaced another. This is a typically young way to create. Now, *this* has probably come to an end. But in return, things will stand solid, and there will be no need to rebuild so often. Instead of a showy creative fountain there will be a slow but mighty and broad river. At first it brings pain: What is the matter? Has youth passed and old age come? But that's just it: besides young and old age there also is maturity; besides a fountain and stagnant water there is a river flowing smoothly and evenly. One has to adjust to this thought, and everything will be all right. But if one refuses to adjust and rebels, things may go badly. If under the pretext of the cessation of your scholarly activities you devote yourself to Czech journalism, you will soon really lose your talent, degenerate, and become morally degraded. All attempts to perpetuate one's youth are senseless. Transition from youth to maturity is a law of nature, like the change of day and night, summer and winter. Each stage of human life has its pluses and minuses. Maturity is not worse than youth. But the most important thing is to be oneself. Nothing is worse than to feign youth or old age. One should behave according to one's age or rather according to the given stage of development...

I have written this sermon to you because in your last letter I detected overtones familiar to me from my own experience. But I may be wrong.

I will not force you to write Russian phonology, though at one time you forced me to work on morphology at the most desperately neurasthenic period of my life. But I believe that delays should not be too long even for technical reasons. Besides, "betraying the theme" can demoralize one if it lasts too long. Perhaps it only seems to you that you are now unable to write Russian phonology? Such things happen: one hates doing something and finds all kinds of excuses, but when one sits down to write, only the beginning is a bit hard, and then things go better and better, and finally all turns out excellently. My best works were just those which aroused almost insuperable *disgust* in me (*LN*, 312-14).

By spring 1938, Trubetzkoy's heart and eyes were failing him. Earlier, in 1933 he had passed through a severe depression which he called the most neurasthenic period of his life, and he had even gone to see a psychiatrist. "From my talks with the doctor", he wrote, "I learned many interesting things about myself and about the present-day state of medicine, especially psychotherapy—there are some analogies with linguistics" *(LN,*

278). The world outside his apartment had become a night-
mare. The infiltration of the universities by the Nazis began in
Germany and Austria at the same time. In 1934 Trubetzkoy
even tried to prevent a Nazi historian from getting a job in
Vienna (*LN,* 306). He never missed a chance to fight the Nazi
theory that the original home of the Indo-Europeans had been
in Germany. Antisemitism aroused his indignation, and he
made no secret of his feelings. His chances of survival in Europe
diminished every day, but the catastrophe happened even
earlier than one could expect. On March 8, 1938, he had to be
hospitalized. Three weeks later he returned home and wrote to
Jakobson:

> My health is gradually improving, though the process is slow.
> They discharged me, but I must spend four or five more weeks in
> bed at home and then, little by little, get used to a sitting
> position. Then I must learn to walk, etc. In a word, the doctor
> believes that, unless there are complications, I will recover by
> October. It is hard to understand what is meant by recovery. Yet
> everything depends on it. If by October it becomes clear that
> despite all efforts I will remain an invalid and a wreck unable to
> teach a full load, I will resign and spend my days in retirement in
> the province: I definitely do not want to be Chairman if I cannot
> work. If, however, by October I regain my strength—as I did, for
> instance, in 1936—all kinds of possibilities should be considered.
> By that time the general situation at the University will clear up,
> as well as the fate of the related departments. At present
> everything is up in the air, and no one knows anything for
> certain. There are rumors that Slavic Studies, Balkan Studies,
> and East European History will be reorganized and developed
> and that a large institute will be opened along the same lines as
> in Breslau. If I am bypassed, I may tender my resignation. But if
> my position remains stable and nothing is required of me that is
> beyond my strength, I will stay. As you know, back in 1936 I
> spoke to Twaddell about a trip abroad. He invited me for a year.
> In principle, I would not mind going. But again, I must be
> certain that I am not an absolute wreck, and in the near future I

cannot be certain of this. It is senseless to start anything if I remain an invalid (*LN,* 423).

Everything at the University was "up in the air" because five days after Trubetzkoy's hospitalization, on March 13, 1938, German troops occupied Austria. Soon after he was allowed to leave the hospital, the Gestapo subjected him to a long interrogation, and his apartment was searched. During the search his papers were impounded and taken to Gestapo headquarters, and there they perished during the air raids of World War II. Thus the destruction of Trubetzkoy's archives ran full circle. The documents of the Phonological Association were among those confiscated (*LN,* 423, note 1). They were never found again. Neither were Jakobson's letters to Trubetzkoy "despite some individual efforts since the war" (*LN,* vi). What little was missed by the Gestapo was published by Hagège in 1967. The search and the interrogation had a devastating effect on Trubetzkoy. Dangerous symptoms developed in his lungs. In the hospital he met his last (forty-eighth) birthday (April 16). He died on June 25, 1938. Several journals responded to his death; besides Jakobson 1939, see Isacenko 1938, Tschiževskij 1938, Kretschmer 1939 (mainly based on Trubetzkoy's autobiographical notes), Havránek 1939 (a survey of Trubetzkoy's works), Hjelmslev 1939 (a good and sympathetic analysis of Trubetzkoy's linguistic achievements), and van Wijk 1939 (original and interesting). The other obituaries are less notable; they are listed in Jagoditsch 1950 and 1965 and in Havránek 1939. The publication of *LN* makes it possible to reconstruct Trubetzkoy's biography at least to a certain extent. An almost complete bibliography of Trubetzkoy's works, including those to appear, was published in *Travaux du Cercle Linguistique de Prague* 8 (1939), 335-42. Of the forthcoming articles and books most found their way into print only years later. His announced review of D. M. Beach, *The Phonetics of the Hottentot Language* (Cambridge: Heffer, 1938), written for *Anthropos* seems to be lost; in any case, the present editors of *Anthropos* know nothing about it.

I will finish this biographical sketch of Trubetzkoy with a few passages from Tschižewskij's little known obituary (1938). (Tschižewskij 1976 does not repeat this obituary, and its focus is different; it can be added that Tschižewskij, an outstanding literary scholar, always regarded Trubetzkoy—preeminently a linguist—as his teacher: Tschižewskij 1966, 22.)

> Trubetzkoy is an example of what often enough happens in Russia: he is a combination of significance and relative obscurity. Nikolai Sergeevich was, of course, known to Russian emigrés. But he was known "by chance," just as his father had been. Prince Sergei Trubetskoy was known to all Russia as the Rector of Moscow University during the stormy and tragic months of the first Russian revolution, but few knew and appreciated him as a profound thinker and a not less profound historian of ancient philosophy (whose works have retained their importance). Nikolai Sergeevich, in turn, became known to the wide circles of the Russian public as one of the founders of "Eurasianism"; yet "Eurasianism" is typical of Trubetzkoy insofar as it expresses his original approach to every question, but not so very typical of his scholarly activities... In any case, each of his articles, each of his papers on professional problems, each talk with him, however short, left the same impression: you realized that you were in the presence of a genius who combined a rare gift for scholarly generalizations with a still rarer gift for seeing each question from an entirely original and unusual point of view...The form of Trubetzkoy's work is the best example of his logical thought. In world scholarship, few fundamental works say everything with such transparent clarity. The very abundance of his examples is specific: Trubetzkoy does not lavish on the reader hundreds of examples, dazzling rather than convincing; he restricts himself to the indispensable: the examples are borrowed from various areas, but their number is limited, and they are all unquestionable and explained to the end...Without doubt, Trubetzkoy's impact on world scholarship is only beginning...

Structuralism and phonology have carried Trubetzkoy's fame to all continents. Most national encyclopedias devote an entry to him, but they seldom discuss his extralinguistic activities. One might think that Trubetzkoy was interested only in phonetics and grammar; however, as Trubetzkoy's bibliography makes clear, and as the present collection of essays shows so convincingly, he was a scholar of very broad interests. The works included in this volume were published between the two World Wars in a very small number of copies (see the next section on the activities of the Eurasian Press) and addressed Russian emigrés of the first wave. Today they are available only at the largest academic libraries and only to those who can read Russian, a single exception being *Europe and Mankind*, which appeared in German (Trubetzkoy 1922a), Japanese (Trubetzkoy 1926), and Italian (Trubetzkoy 1982). Recently *Veche*, an organ of Russian nationalists in exile, has reprinted *Europe and Mankind*, Chapters 1-4 (Trubetzkoy 1987-88) with an editorial note (1987, 89-93). *Veche* is not the proper context for Trubetzkoy, but their reprint is the only one of its type in existence. When work on the present book was in full swing, Latislav Matejka brought out *The Legacy of Genghis Khan* in *Cross Currents* (Trubetzkoy 1990b); it appears here in a slightly revised form.

This volume features the most significant of Trubetzkoy's contributions to the Eurasian problem without pretending to be exhaustive. Some of the articles omitted have a linguistic component too specialized for a book on history and politics (e.g. the last chapter of his *On the Problem of Russian Self-Awareness*; see Trubetzkoy 1950). Others are more or less repetitive (ties between Trubetzkoy's ideas on politics, history, and literary theory are discussed in the introduction to Trubetzkoy 1990b). Our goal was to provide a representative sample of Trubetzkoy's Eurasian studies, which of course does not exclude the appearance in the future of Trubetzkoy's works on the model of Roman Jakobson's *Selected Writings*.

II. Trubetzkoy and the Eurasian Movement

Trubetzkoy formulated the ideas underlying his historical works early in life. In the preface to *Europe and Mankind* he says that only the war and the originality of his conception prevented him from publishing his conclusions long before 1920. This is what he wrote to Jakobson on March 7, 1921:

> I conceived this book long ago (in 1909-1910) as a first part of the trilogy *A Justification of Nationalism*. Part 1 was to have the title *On Egocentricity*, with a dedication to Copernicus; Part 2, entitled *On True and False Nationalism*, was to be dedicated to Socrates; and Part 3, with the title *On the Russian Element*, was meant to be dedicated to Sten'ka Razin or Emel'ka Pugachev. Now I have substituted a more attractive and significant title—*Europe and Mankind*—for the title of the first part and left out the dedication to Copernicus as pretentious. This book has purely negative goals. It does not offer any positive, concrete guidelines. It is meant only to depose certain idols and, having put the reader before the empty pedestals once occupied by these idols, make him think for himself in searching for a way out. The way out must be indicated in the subsequent parts of the trilogy. In Part 1, I only wanted to hint at the direction in which the way out can be found. I admit that I botched up my work. I wished to offer something complete and said in the last chapter more than I had to, and so said nothing. Thus I only fueled misunderstanding. The main point of the book is the rejection of egocentricity or "excentricity" (putting the center outside oneself, in this case in the West). And I have indicated the only possible solution that follows from all this (rather the direction in which it can be found), namely, a revolution in one's consciousness in the world view of the intelligentsia of the non-Romano-Germanic peoples... The essence of the revolution in one's consciousness consists in a complete defeat of egocentricity and excentricity, in giving up absolutism, and accepting relativism. This is the only safe barrier that can be put in the way of the rapacity of Romano-Germanic civilization. To understand that neither "I" nor anyone else is the

center of the universe, that all nations and cultures are of equal value, that no one is higher and no one lower—this is the only thing my book requires from the reader. But, as I have said, to understand this is not sufficient; one must feel it, pay for it with one's emotions, make it part of oneself. "The advice the pupil should learn from the teacher, but treat him critically," as you put it, resulted from an unhappy formulation and from my attempt to concentrate on an irrelevant detail. I just wanted to indicate that no culture is possible without external borrowings, but that borrowings do not necessarily presuppose excentricity. I could have left it unsaid, and I am sorry that I did say it, for it has weakened my main idea and created the impression that besides a revolution in one's consciousness I wish to offer some practical suggestions. Here I feel myself dissatisfied with the end of my book, which I wrote in a hurry and much later than the rest of it. I wanted to put the reader face to face with emptiness and make him think about the ways of filling it. But I created the impression that I am trying to fill the emptiness with some nebulous surrogate...How can this emptiness be filled? In my book I say that every value judgment is based on egocentricity and that therefore all attempts at evaluation should be banished from science. But in cultural work, in politics—in every kind of *activity* (rather than theory, like science)—one cannot do without value judgments. So some sort of egocentricity is indispensable. But it should be an ennobled egocentricity, a conscious, rather than an unconscious egocentricity, connected with relativism and not with absolutism. I find it in Socrates' principle "Know yourself," or, which is the same, "Be yourself"..."Know yourself" is a universal, absolute principle, but it is relative at the same time. And one must follow this principle, regardless of whether a separate individual or a nation is at stake (*LN,* 12-14).

Trubetzkoy goes on for several more pages, but the fragment quoted above is as good a summary of his ideas as one could wish for. Of interest also are the last paragraphs of the letter devoted to *Europe and Mankind.*

The non-Romano-Germanic peoples need a new non-Romano-Germanic culture. But the Romano-Germanic lower classes do not need any genuinely new culture; they only want to change places with the ruling classes, in order to go on doing what those classes have been doing all along, namely, controlling factories and "colored" mercenaries, suppressing the "black" and "yellow" peoples and making them behave like Europeans, buying European wares, and supplying Europe with raw materials. Their way is not our way. If they, God forbid, seize power, universal Europeanization will become inevitable. This is "the last stake"—though not for "Mankind" but for "Europe." This is "a formidable danger"—though not for "Europe" but for "Mankind."

That is why I insist that a revolution in the consciousness of the non-Romano-Germanic intelligentsia is the only way out. Without it, all that is happening now will only reinforce evil. I doubt that the masters of Soviet Russia are ready for such a revolution. Therefore, I look on everything pessimistically. The worst that can happen is a premature uprising of the Romano-Germanic lower classes connected with the transfer of the world axis to Berlin and to the West in general: after that a revolution in the intelligentsia's consciousness most likely will never take place, or, if it does, it will happen too late. But it is quite possible that the Romano-Germanic lower classes will do nothing at all, and then Russia, left for a long time with only its own resources and its Asian orientation, will either force its leaders to perform such a revolution or replace them spontaneously by others, more amenable to such a revolution. It is hard to tell what will happen; I expect the worst...

A last remark. You say that you do not believe in "the world as a reservoir of peacefully coexisting little cultures." Neither do I. If at some time my dreams come true, I can envisage the world consisting of several big cultures with "dialectal" variants, as it were. The difference from the European ideal lies in the fact that, first, there still will be several cultures, not one, and, second, that their dialectal variants will be brighter and freer. Most importantly: given true nationalism based on self-awareness and divorced from excentricity, each nation will belong to a culture not fortuitously but because it is in harmony with people's inner nature, which can find its best manifestation in this particular culture. As for the features that *must* distinguish the culture to which Russia *must* belong from European civilization, and which nations, besides the Russians, can participate in this culture—all of that I intend to discuss in the third part of my trilogy (*On the Russian Element*). Whether I will succeed in publishing the whole trilogy I cannot tell (*LN*, 15-16).

Europe and Mankind, with its emphasis on Russia's historical indebtedness to the East, on the necessity of a rupture with Europe and of siding with Asian colonies, and on the leading role of the intelligentsia in the Russia of the future inaugurated a doctrine that later came to be known as Eurasian, even though the official birthdate of Eurasianism is not 1920 but 1921, when a group of scholars published a book with a rather enigmatic title *Exodus to the East. Forebodings and Accomplishments. The Self-Assertion of the Eurasians.*

This was followed by two more collections of articles—*On the Paths. The Self-Assertion of the Eurasians*, and *Russia and Latinity* (see *Iskhod k Vostoku, Na putiakh,* and *Rossiia i latinstvo* in the bibliography). The founders of the movement were N. S. Trubetzkoy, P. N. Savitskii, G. V. Florovskii, and P. P. Suvchinskii. At different times many other scholars collaborated with the Eurasians, among them G. V. Vernadsky, R. O. Jakobson, L. P. Karsavin, V. N. Il'in, A. A. Alekseev, and D. P. Sviatopolk-Mirsky, to mention only those who developed Eurasianism in a significant way.

The terms *Eurasianism* and *Eurasianists* do not occur in *Europe and Mankind,* and the focus of the Eurasian movement in the twenties is different from Trubetzkoy's as it emerges from his first book. This change of focus is natural. Trubetzkoy himself points out that the goal of *Europe and Mankind* was purely negative and lay in the sphere of criticism and "forebodings." Before the war no one wanted to listen to him. In 1920 there were enough people disillusioned with Europe and ready to start thinking about Russia as "a world apart," a unique entity from a geographical, historical, and psychological point of view. Some of them would probably have advanced similar theories even if they had not become refugees. Trubetzkoy formulated his main theses long before the revolution, and Vernadsky also was predisposed to "Eurasian ideas" early on (Halperin 1985). The same seems to be true of Savitskii. Chance brought these people together in Sofia and Prague. Eurasia (the word was not new in Russian historiography) referred to Russia spreading over two continents; the implication was that Russia owed more to Asia and the steppe than to Europe. Below I will neither discuss the many aspects of the economic, political, and cultural theories advanced by the Eurasians nor attempt to outline in detail their activities (a task partly accomplished by Anonymous 1928, Malevsky-Malevitch 1928, Böss 1961 and 1973, and Riasanovsky 1964), but will concentrate only on some salient features of Trubetzkoy's world outlook insofar as they find reflection in his contributions to Eurasianism.

The Eurasians founded their press and published numerous collections, magazines, and newspapers, and Trubetzkoy was an active participant in them. In 1925 Trubetzkoy published his second book *The Legacy of Genghis Khan;* it came out under the initials I. R. (according to Böss's hypothesis—1961, 127–I. R. were chosen as the second letters of *Nikolai Trubetzkoy*). In 1927 he brought out three articles under one cover and called this book *On the Problem of Russian Self-Awareness;* so in a way he carried out his old plan and did write a trilogy, but not quite in the form envisaged in 1909-1910. The reception of *Europe and Mankind* has not been studied, for the emigré newspapers of that period are often hard to unearth. In Japan, as far as I can judge, no one has been sufficiently interested to look for the reviews of the 1926 translation. The Western discussants of early Eurasianism (probably all known to Savitskii 1931d) sometimes began their surveys with *Exodus to the East* and thus skipped *Europe and Mankind* (but in Rimscha's memory Trubetzkoy remained the leader of the movement—1970, 587). Those who paid attention to Trubetzkoy's book seldom went beyond short, noncommittal summaries (Stählin 1925, 242;

Abeghjan 1926; Block 1926; Rimscha 1927, 187; Leppmann 1931, 230-31, and Gorlin, 1932-1933, 281-87, are typical in this respect). N. van Wijk (1926, 237) said that the book was "read widely."

In the Soviet Union, Trubetzkoy's work was noticed at once and dismissed as a variation on the familiar themes of Spengler and others (Meshcheriakov 1921, 37-39). (Luks 1986, 379, was the first to point out that despite a number of similar motifs and the fact that Trubetzkoy wanted Spengler to write an introduction to his book, Trubetzkoy's attitude toward Europe differed from Spengler's: Spengler spoke about the decay of Europe, whereas Trubetzkoy was afraid of Europe and looked upon it as a rapacious, aggressive enemy of non-European nations.) Of the later critiques the most interesting is Zen'kovskii [1925] 167-72. According to Trubetzkoy himself (*LN*, 24 July 1921), the original edition of *Europe and Mankind* aroused written and oral controversy both among emigrés and in Russia, though nothing he heard between 1920 and 1922 made him modify his views (see N. S. Trubetzkoy 1922, 13-14; the Russian text is given in Pomorska 1977b, 236-37, but Pomorska was mistaken in thinking that the author's "postscript" written for the German translation had not been included: it is printed rather inconspicuously between Schlömer's introduction and Chapter 1).

To celebrate the tenth anniversary of their movement, the Eurasians published a collection *Tridtsatye gody* [The thirties], which opens with Savitskii's survey of responses to the Eurasians (Savitskii 1931d) and closes with his annotated "Eurasian Bibliography" (Lubenskii 1931a; Lubensky 1931b is the same in French—Lubenskii was one of Savitskii's pseudonyms: see Riasanovsky 1967, 47, note 17), in which Trubetzkoy's works (but not *Europe and Mankind*) are discussed a number of times. Savitskii's bibliography occasionally contains polemical remarks. In his discussion of *The Legacy of Genghis Khan* he calls the author's aversion to other cultures "not necessary and not fruitful" (Lubenskii 1931a, 296).

The Eurasians developed their own conception of Russian history and Russia's mission. To indicate the scope of their activities, I will reproduce the table of contents (only the chapter headings) of the brochure *Evraziistvo* [Eurasianism] (1926): 1. The harm of false ideologies and the vital necessity of a true ideology. 2. On some indispensable provisos of a true ideology. 3. Orthodoxy as the basis of [our] ideology. 4. The Russian church and Russian culture. 5. The Eurasian-Russian cultural world. 6. The unity of Eurasia. 7. Church and state as forms of personal being and their interrelations. 8. The meaning of the Russian revolution. 9. Problems of transitional periods and of the near future. 10. Problems of the new Russia.

Eurasianism started as an intellectual trend, but since Trubetzkoy, Savitskii (who assumed sole leadership in the thirties), and others had a nontrivial attitude toward Russia's past and the revolution and since they put forward a program for Russia's future, they could not avoid becoming a political organization. Their impact on Russian emigré circles was considerable, as testified by the passion with which they were criticized and by the great number of responses to their doctrine. Some of those who wrote about them in retrospect (e.g., Struve 1984, 40-49; Gul' 1984, 170-76) confirm this impression; Pletnev (1972, 257) echoed many older journalists and historians when he called Eurasianism the most interesting trend of the Russian emigration.

The first Eurasians (perhaps with the exception of Suvchinskii; cf. Vishniak 1957, 145) remained adamant anti-Bolsheviks to the end, but unlike most other emigrés they "recognized" the October revolution; they viewed it as a natural consequence of the post-Petrine Europeanization of Russia. They rejected the idea of restoration and were prepared to pick up where the Bolsheviks would leave off when they loosened their grip on power. They approved of the Soviets as a form of government, shared the Bolsheviks' attitude toward the East, and agreed with several of their historical conclusions. They also supported a planned, state-regulated economy and the rule of one party. In their polemic, they were pathetically honest. For instance, in a brochure on the wanton destruction of old buildings in the Soviet Union and the auctioning off of great Russian and West European paintings, Savitskii (1935, 36-37) praises the new exposition at the Hermitage because it is based on a historical, rather than thematic principle. Such examples are numerous.

In the early twenties, some emigrés decided to return "home." Especially famous among those who hoped to serve the new Russia were the so-called *smenovekhovtsy* (Landmark, or Signpost, Changers). The Eurasians had neither organizational ties nor an inner bond with the Landmark Changers, but, as they found a historical justification in the success of the October revolution, they thought that they too could look the Bolsheviks straight in the eyes. The GPU (a predecessor of the KGB) immediately returned the stare. The Eurasians functioned as a chain of clubs guided by a handful of active and prolific scholars. Their ideas allegedly attracted many people in the Soviet Union. The GPU supplied the Eurasians with letters from "over there," and in their innocence they published them as genuine documents. In 1926 Savitskii even took part in a Eurasian congress in Moscow (one can well imagine who filled the room), and some time later "the leader of the Eurasians in the R.S.F.S.R." arrived in Prague as a guest of the Eurasians abroad (Gul' 1984, 173; Struve 1984, 48, gives the beginning of 1927 as the date of Savitskii's "secret trip"). *Evraziia* [Eurasia], the newspaper of the Eurasians in France, became a mouthpiece of the GPU. In no. 1-2, Trubetzkoy published his article "Ideocracy and the Proletariat," but he protested the political sympathies of the editors. The newspaper extolled Marx and Lenin. The economic base and advantages of kolkhozes (collective farms) were analyzed scientifically (in 1929!). Each issue featured a certain slogan that was printed several times, and some of them were repeated from week to week, for example, "The Soviet Union is the first experiment of a supernational unity that has overcome imperialism and bound together internationalism and recognition of nationalities as living and indestructible personalities" or "The Russian revolution states the primacy of the general over the particular—an ethics based on the organizational duty of a creative, rather than consuming individual."

Trubetzkoy spent the last day of 1928 writing a letter to the Editor of *Evraziia*. Dated December 31, 1928, it appeared in no. 7 (January 5) and was later reprinted in a special brochure (Alekseev et al. 1929, 23). This is the text of Trubetzkoy's letter.

> Recently it has become quite clear that the great differences of opinion existing among the Eurasians cannot be bridged. The split is now a fact that cannot be silenced. The newspaper *Evraziia*, in the issues that have appeared thus far, has reflected almost exclusively one trend in Eurasianism, the one that attempts to replace the orthodox Eurasian ideological theses by elements of ideologies having nothing to do with Eurasianism (Marxism, Fedorovism). I recognize the split with regret, and I fear that the separate Eurasian trends can come to the opposite extremes, but I also realize that at least in the near future Eurasianism cannot restore its inner unity and equilibrium, which alone would allow me to participate in Eurasian activities. Therefore I announce my withdrawal from the newspaper *Evraziia* and from the Eurasian organization. I do not renounce my convictions expressed in my articles in various Eurasian editions,...in the collection of articles *Russia and Latinity*, and in my books...
>
> But under the existing circumstances I cannot and will not bear the responsibility for the present evolution of Eurasianism.

The central figure in the newspaper was Prince D. P. Sviatopolk-Mirsky, the author of an excellent history of Russian literature in English. He joined the Communist Party of Great Britain and wrote fiery articles against the world bourgeoisie. He glorified Marx and Marxism and found many good qualities in Soviet socialism. He must have felt deep respect, perhaps even affection for Trubetzkoy. While criticizing Trubetzkoy's theory of ideocracy, he did not mention his opponent by name, and in a series of articles on nationalities in the U.S.S.R. he never missed a chance to refer to Trubetzkoy as one of the greatest experts in Caucasian linguistics. In his article of 1927 (Mirsky 1927-1928, 312), he called *Europe and Mankind* a brilliant book. But these considerations played no role in his diatribes. The spirit of the newspaper was summed up by A. V. Sushkov in No. 34 (p. 8). His article, which also caught the attention of Böss (1960, 120), could have done honor to the Landmark Changers' newspaper *Nakanune* [On the Eve]:

> The usefulness of our work in emigration is determined first and foremost by the nature of Eurasianism, which is not a world outlook in the old, passive sense of the word, but an organized activity directed at the ideological clarification of the tasks set before the Soviets, as well as at the quick defense by all available means, wherever we may find ourselves and whoever may surround us, of the Soviet cause in its entirety...Any Eurasian living in emigration must, to the utmost of his abilities, resist all emigré actions against the Soviet Union...A conscious way from the past to the future and from emigration to the new Russia is possible only through and with Eurasianism.

The Eurasians and the Landmark Changers were often taken for close allies by emigré writers, as one can see even from such late memoirs as I. V. Gessen 1979, 201. The Eurasian groups in Brussels and Paris were expelled from the organization, but they remained active. The Brussels group even started its own mimeographed discussion journal for inner consumption (the last issue of *Evraziia* appeared on September 7, 1929, and the first issue of the Brussels *Evraziets* [The Eurasian] on June 15, 1929), and for five years it reprinted articles from *Pravda* and depicted the beauties of Socialist labor. "Comrade Shkiriatov" (one of the henchmen in Stalin's retinue) "pulls a poorly loaded wheelbarrow and looks timidly at the angry foreman who is unhappy about his 'royal' inferior." This is a quotation from no. 25 (the last one, dated June 15, 1934); the article describes the construction of the Moscow subway: Shkiriatov, Kuibyshev, and

Khrushchev have come to give a hand..."All Moscow builds the subway...God help them." Spellbound by their own rhetoric, the "reformed" Eurasians left their European homes (which they never liked) to be dragged through Stalin's machine of annihilation. Some perished despite their valuable service in the cause of the Soviet intelligence service abroad (like S. Ia. Efrón, the husband of the poetess Marina Tsvetaeva), others despite their ideological fervor (like Sviatopolk-Mirsky; among the seldom cited sources see especially Ivanov-Razumnik 1951, 22). Trubetzkoy never allowed his bitter nostalgia to blur his view of reality. For him Soviet life was a synonym for wilderness. The words *wilderness* and *wasteland* crop up in his letter about Jagoditsch and in his answers to the questionnaire of *Evraziiskie tetradi* [Eurasian notebooks] ("Does the World Move Toward Ideocracy and Planned Economy?").

"Orthodox" Eurasianism survived the split and continued into the thirties, mainly owing to Savitskii's fanatical loyalty to the cause; Trubetzkoy's short articles appeared occasionally in *Evraziiskie tetradi* almost until his death. He also published a note on autarky in the Estonian *Novaia epokha* [New epoch] (Narva, 1933). The war made Eurasian discussions impossible and useless. Trubetzkoy died. Vernadsky, Florovskii, and Jakobson emigrated to the United States (Vernadsky as early as 1927), the "apostates" returned to the Soviet Union and disappeared there. Savitskii stayed in Czechoslovakia. During the war he constantly feared reprisals from the Germans, but he was arrested by the Soviets when the Red Army occupied Prague; they first sent him to prison and then to a concentration camp in Mordovia. In 1956, not yet very old, but an invalid with no means, he returned to Prague. In prisons and camps he composed many poems, and as he had a brilliant memory, he recorded them after he regained his freedom. In 1960 a book of his poetry under one of his old pseudonyms—P. Vostokov (*vostok* 'east')—appeared in Paris. Gul' (1984, 175) reprints two of Savitskii's lyrics. A third one, addressed to Ariadna Efron (a daughter of Sergei Efron and Marina Tsvetaeva), whom he also met in Mordovia (the poem is dated June 20, 1947)—"I knew you a girl and found a prisoner"—can be found in Efron/Pasternak 1982, 180. In 1961 he was again arrested (mainly as a punishment for his foreign ties), this time by the Czechs. Fortunately, the Minister of the Interior during whose tenure he was imprisoned fell into disgrace, so Savitskii was allowed to return to Prague. The second term broke him physically. After his release he made his living by chance translations until his death in 1968 (Riha 1958, 26, note 8; Vernadsky 1968; Pushkarev 1983, 143-44; Struve 1984, 384; Gul' 1984, 175).

L. V. Karsavin, who was officially exiled to Germany in 1922 with many other luminaries (S. L. Frank, P. M. Bitsilli—both short-time participants in and later well-wishing critics of Eurasianism, G. V. Florovskii, a future Eurasianist, A. A. Kizevetter, a future trenchant critic of Eurasianism, N. A. Berdiaev, Piterim Sorokin, S. N. Bulgakov, Ia. I. Aikhenval'd, I.A. Il'in, and F. A. Stepun), also ended up in a Soviet concentration camp. He was arrested in Lithuania, where he taught theology before the war (Böss 1961, 8), and deported. He perished in 1952. Vernadsky did much to popularize the Eurasian doctrine in the United States (cf. Halperin 1983 and 1985). Jakobson, as evidenced by the tone in which he cites Savitskii in his *Dialogues* with Pomorska, always thought of him with affection, and, although in the United States he did not return to the problem of the Eurasian language union, he retained his admiration for *everything* done by Trubetzkoy; a feeling stronger than his personal dislike of Issatschenko must have moved his pen when he called the latter's attack on Trubetzkoy's Eurasian ideas (Issatschenko 1973) a mean and immature lampoon (*LN*, X).

After the war, Eurasian teachings, now an object of purely academic interest, have been discussed a number of times. Ishboldin 1946 and Orchard 1977 are articles of an informative, rather than analytical character. Eurasian politics and futurology have attracted no special attention since 1945, and only historians have argued with Trubetzkoy, Vernadsky, and their younger and less distinguished Eurasian colleagues in the profession. Controversy centered upon three problems—the prehistory of Russia, the Tatar Yoke, and the Petrine reforms. In the twenties and thirties, the Eurasian view of history (which irritated Kizevetter and Miliukov) was overshadowed by their everyday activities. Now that the Eurasian plans for the future had themselves become history, academicians could demolish Vernadsky's ubiquitous Alans and Trubetzkoy's shining Genghis Khan at leisure. Several surveys of Russian history contain chapters or sections on Eurasianism, for instance, Gapanovitch 1946, 101-8 (critical but restrained), Mazour 1958, 236-42 (friendly in tone, critical), and Utechin 1963 [1964], 256-61; cf. also Williams 1972, 258-61 (the "Scythian" background). Utechin advanced the idea that postwar Solidarism (NTS) owed much to Alekseev (which seems correct to me) and that the official Soviet conception of "the history of the peoples of the U.S.S.R." is close to the Eurasian one. In the literature known to me only Stammler (1962) has made a similar remark.

In 1947 V. A. Riasanovskii, whose stance was anti-Eurasian in every possible respect, brought out the first fascicle of his *Historical Survey*. N. V. Riasanovsky collaborated with his father and wrote several sections for his book. His own position is also anti-Eurasian and anti-Vernadsky, as one can conclude from the relevant sections in his handbook of Russian history (1984, 4th ed.; the same in the first [1963] edition and in the other two). Nicholas Riasanovsky emphasized his indebtedness to his father by dedicating his first book to him, yet he inherited from Valentin Riasanovskii not only the latter's conception of the Mongol period but also his reverence for Vernadsky. Vernadsky was one of those rare scholars who could remain friends with his opponents (cf. Halperin 1985, 90), but—and this is more important than Vernadsky's personal integrity and amiability—something in the apparently indefensible Eurasian doctrine continues to exercise its fascination upon historians. It is as though the argument can never come to an end. N. V. Riasanovsky's tone in his 1972 discussion of Vernadsky is one of deep respect, and if he had thought that there was nothing to learn from Eurasianism, he could hardly have undertaken to trace the origins of its ideas with such sympathetic interest (1964 and 1967).

A curious case is Charles Halperin. Since the completion of his dissertation (1973) he has been a prolific writer on the Tatar Yoke. He is also a dedicated opponent of the Eurasians. This is what he has to say about them:

> If the Eurasianists did not seriously influence historical scholarship, the explanation does not lie in the fact that, in Riasanovsky's label, they were "deviant" intellectuals, but rather in the simple truth that their ideas were wrong. Eurasian theory was hopelessly metaphysical, idealist, teleological and determinist. Eurasianist works were highly partisan, publicistic, unscholarly, flawed by enormous legerdemain. Eurasian politics were anti-democratic apologies for imperialism and colonialism. Eurasianism was an ideology which compensated for evidence with theory because the facts contradicted Eurasian beliefs. Erroneous theories can sometimes play positive roles in scholarship, irrespective of their falsity, but Eurasianism did not (1985, 98).

> [About Vernadsky's first books:] Their deplorable and divisive politics aside, their distorted and garbled presentation of Russia[n] and Eurasian history cannot sustain even the most elementary scholarly criticism (ibidem, 101).

> Journalistic hodgepodges of sometimes undigested and often inaccurate factual material dressed up in an elaborate metaphysics of dubious viability, they should not be treated as serious scholarly works (ibidem, 104). Vernadsky shared Eurasianism's whitewashing of Russian imperialism. He also echoed, during the 1920s and the 1930s, Eurasianism's least admirable and least scholarly dogmas—teleological determinism, messianism, social elitism, economic corporativism, religious and ethnic bigotry, and political authoritarianism (ibidem, 185).

> At times Vernadsky's Eurasianism degenerated or declined to
> an almost meaningless level (ibidem, 187).

Not even Zinaida Gippius, Khodasevich, and Spektorskii, who
accused the Eurasians of being the Bolsheviks' mercenaries or,
conversely, of living on Western money and biting the hand that
fed them, used such language. (However, it has always been
common in Soviet historiography.) I would like to quote a few
remarks by Oswald P. Backus III, to Otto Böss, a much more
restrained and sympathetic opponent than Halperin: "At times
the sharpness of the author's remarks makes it seem that he is
battling errors of the Eurasian movement. This is strange, since
the Eurasian movement is dead...By much of the tone of his
work, its very choice of words, its sharpness, the author conceals
his own objectivity. Do the circumstances of our time demand
such a tone? Can one not calmly reject the excesses of
Eurasianism and analyze it without heat?" (1961, 598, 599).
Halperin has proved to his own satisfaction that when
Vernadsky depended on Eurasian principles he produced trash.
He has also shown that despite minor deviations Vernadsky
remained a Eurasian all his life. Why then write an erudite
monograph about him? The monograph opens with a warm
biographical sketch of Vernadsky. What attraction does he hold
for such an eloquent critic?

V. Veidle (Wladimir Weidlé), a dedicated "Westernizer,"
spent two decades fighting the ghost of Eurasianism (cf. 1949,
184-91; 1956—his best book in this genre—and 1968, 17-29).
Again one feels that the Eurasian "heresy" can touch its
opponent to the quick.

The central event in the postwar assessment of Eurasianism
was the appearance of Böss 1961 (cf. also Böss 1973 on the
origin of Eurasian political economy). Böss's book is informative
and reliable, but like many other works written on the Eurasians
it overemphasizes the ideas common to the whole group (cf.
Backus 1961, 596-97) and examines their roots rather than their
place among contemporaries. Yet the "ancestors" of Trubetzkoy,

Savitskii, and others were recognized immediately, the more so as the Eurasians made no secret of their sympathies, and reprinted several books by their favorites, from Khomiakov onward. Those who compare the Slavophiles with the Eurasians invariably experience a feeling of *déjà vu* bordering on incredulity when they come across passages like the following (from a letter by the poet Fedor Tiutchev, dated approximately March 1848 and first published in 1928):

> A very great inconvenience of our position consists in the necessity of calling *Europe* what should not have had a name other than *Civilization*. This is the source of our countless follies and unavoidable misunderstanding...But I feel ever more convinced that we have already received everything our *peaceful imitation* of Europe could have done and given us. Indeed, it is not much. It did not break the ice, but it covered us with thin moss, which imitates vegetation rather well. At present no real progress can be achieved without struggle. That is why Europe's animosity is perhaps the greatest favor it can do us. Really, this is Providence. One needed this animosity, which is becoming more and more apparent every day, to make us look deep into ourselves, to become conscious of ourselves. And for society, just as for an individual, the first condition of progress is self-awareness. There are, I know, among us people who say that nothing in us is worth knowing. But then the only thing for us to do would be to stop existing; yet no one, I hope, holds this opinion (Tiutchev 1980, II, 103-4; the original is in French).

Some ties connect the Eurasians with the younger Slavophiles, and they were pupils of K.N. Leont'ev, N. Ia. Danilevskii (Trubetzkoy's way of thinking and vocabulary, down to the word *odichanie* 'running to seed, turning into wasteland,' is especially reminiscent of Danilevskii's; cf. Miliukov 1930, 226, who traced the Eurasians to the "reactionary" and "epigone" Danilevskii, and Gorlin 1932-1933, 282-83, specifically about Trubetzkoy's "types"), V.F. Ern, V.V. Dokuchaev (Dokuchaev had a strong influence on Savitskii), and several Western thinkers, notably Spengler. The Eurasians' dependence on their predecessors, which includes such verbal cliches as *self-awareness, Europe and civilization,* and *Romano-Germanic civilization* (Germanic is almost synonymous with German, for it does not include Anglo-Saxon), was noted by every reviewer of their books—friendly or hostile (cf. Zen'kovskii 1925, 120-22, 160-73, and Spektorskii 1927, who also found their "relatives" in the West). In the sixties the problem was studied in detail by Riasanovsky (1964 and 1967). But the critics and followers of the Eurasians in the decade 1921-1931 were equally sensitive to what was new in their doctrine and to its being a reaction to the war, the Bolshevik revolution, and the abnormal circumstances of emigré life.

On having read *Europe and Mankind,* Jakobson decided that the book was a response to the revolution and the postwar international situation. Trubetzkoy hastened to explain that the whole trilogy had already existed as a project in 1909-1910 (*LN,* 12, and note 1, see above). But whatever the history of Trubetzkoy's ideas, in 1921 anyone would have formed the same impression of Trubetzkoy's attack on the West as Jakobson did. Even from surveys such as Rimscha 1927 and Varshavskii 1956 it follows that some of the Eurasians' solutions were advanced by other Russian and European politicians of the postwar period. (Rimscha devotes a chapter to Trubetzkoy and his associates, Varshavskii mentions the Eurasians a number of times; see pp. 35, 39, 40, 43, 46, 51 and 90-91.) Ideocracy is a case in point. In the early twenties the word *fascism*—the movement was known only in its Italian guise—had none of the ominous connotations it acquired later. The first critics of the Eurasians were quick to point out the similarity between the Eurasian theory of ideocracy and Mussolini's practice.

F. A. Stepun, who admired the Eurasians but disagreed with them sharply, wrote in 1924:

> Against the restoration of monarchy; for the Bolshevik emotion but against communist socialism; and, first of all and the most passionate of all, against democracy—all this taken together gives us sufficient grounds to define Eurasianism as *Russian*

fascism. Additional evidence for this analogy (and my definition does not claim to be more than an analogy) is supplied by passionate imperialist nationalism, the arrogant pathos of the "great-power minority," the fashionable idea of replacing "popular representation" by the representation of professional groups, the denial of the legitimacy of popular rule and the support of the metaphysical idea of popular power that "must know its public," and the most important of all: the denial of the present and of the past for the glory of the future, represented in an ancient image: "The resurrection of great Italy," "The resurrection of glorious Rus'!" (Stepun 1924, 404).

Stepun did not change his opinion in later years (see Terapiano 1953, 57-58), and in 1925, S. I. Gessen developed Stepun's idea and gave a much more negative assessment of "Eurasian fascism" (S. I. Gessen 1925, 499). Even Berdiaev wrote in his journal *Put'* [The way] (all the main Eurasians were members of its editorial board!): "Eurasianism is first and foremost an emotional, not an intellectual trend, and its emotionality is a reaction of creative national and religious instincts to the recent catastrophe. This type of attitude can turn out to be Russian fascism" (Berdiaev 1925, 44). And he was horrified by the idea that the projected Eurasian state was an ordinary tyranny (Berdiaev 1927). Cf. also *LN*, 302, Timaschew 1929, 598, Riasanovsky 1967, 51, and Luks 1986, 387. Other critics put it more bluntly: "If the Eurasians ever come to power, they will make everybody memorize their brochures, as the Bolsheviks have done with Marxism."

In retrospect, the very idea of comparing such people as Trubetzkoy and Savitskii to fascists seems sacrilegious, but at that time such a comparison did not offend anyone. Trubetzkoy only explained that fascist and communist rule were both imperfect and immature ideocracies because they were irreligious and oriented toward materialism. Sviatopolk-Mirsky (a member of the Communist party of Great Britain!) spoke about communism *and* fascism with great approval, expressed his delight at the reorientation of the entire Eurasian movement leftward, and admired Suvchinskii for his pronouncements on "a right to dictatorship, which a ruling party acquires only by serving the ideal of social justice" (Mirsky 1927-1928, 318-19).

In the Soviet Union, the Eurasians were discussed at some length in the twenties (Trotskii even praised the word Eurasia in 1923; see Agurskii 1980, 178) and were chosen as a target for provocation. At present in contradistinction to the Landmark Changers, they seem to have been forgotten. Somewhere in the KGB lingered a memory of a successful action, for a pre-*perestroika* American club attempting to reestablish contact between emigrés and "home" was called "The Eurasian"; but, other than that, one found only formulaic statements deriving the Eurasian doctrine from the class structure of prerevolutionary Russia (in this case, an absolutely hopeless enterprise). The factual base of these statements was usually the introduction to the book *Na putiakh,* one of the versions of the Eurasian program, and Meisner's memoirs (for years there were references to the manuscript in the archives, which lent them some glamour, but in 1966 the book was published). In 1961 L. V. Danilova (p. 81) believed that Eurasianism was a popular trend in American historiography. She drew her conclusions from reading A. V. Efimov, Vernadsky, and Mazour. This is what even the privileged authors of books on early Russian emigration (i.e., people who had partial access to archives and emigré publications) used to write about this movement. V. V. Komin (1977, 100-105) concludes his brief sketch of the Eurasian doctrine thus:

> Eurasianism was a reflection of the contradictions, confusion, and despair of one part of the petty bourgeois emigré intelligentsia, which tried in vain to find a compromise between the October revolution and the old foundations of Tsarist Russia. In the thirties, a small group of the Eurasians broke with anti-Soviet ideology, recognized unconditionally the achievements of the October socialist revolution, returned home, and found its place in the construction of the new society. The others stayed away and did not give up their hostile attitude. The Eurasian

doctrine, lacking foundation and leading nowhere, ended up in the graveyard of the ideas born in the anti-Soviet environment of the postrevolutionary period (p. 105).

L. K. Shkarenkov (1981, 85-86, 154-55) concurs with Komin and suggests (p. 155) that "the Eurasian conception probably reflected, among other things, a peculiar emigré 'complex'—the desire to prove that Russia is above Europe and has a special great, messianic mission." Agurskii (1980, 98) and Halperin (1985, 95, Note 9) give a few more references to Soviet sources.

In the torrent of literature released by *perestroika* from the so-called special storage, one can also find Eurasian studies (cf. Shevelev 1990). The word *Eurasian* has gained such popularity that in discussing a new name for the U.S.S.R. A. D. Sakharov suggested *Soiuz Evro-Aziiatskikh Respublik* (The Union of Euro-Asiatic Republics). A volume of Trubetzkoy's works on history is due to appear in Moscow, but it cannot replace the bulk of Eurasian publications. Besides, Eurasianism should be examined in its broad and narrow context, and Soviet historians versed in emigré literature do not exist. Nor have they yet learned to deal with the twentieth century objectively. The newly established journal *Kontinent Rossiia* (The Continent Russia) purports to educate the public and reprint Savitskii and others. L. N. Gumilev's numerous articles and books, still published with apologetic forewords by admiring but slightly puzzled scholars, despite popular misconception, have nothing to do with Eurasianism. This is true of his programmatic works (such as 1989b) and of those bearing typical "Eurasian" titles, for instance *Ancient Russia and the Great Steppe* (1989a). Nor do they exhibit the author's familiarity with the Eurasian doctrine even in those rare cases when he refers to Savitskii and Trubetzkoy, and the few parallels ("the decline of creativity," role of geography in history, and so forth) are fortuitous.

Former Soviet scholars now working in the West also have little knowledge of and apparently no interest in the Eurasians. Mikhail Geller (Heller) added a page about them only in the second edition of *Utopia in Power* (1986, 189-90). He is sympathetic and probably follows Utekhin in saying that the Eurasians had an important influence on many emigré political groups (190). Agurskii (1980, 98) endorses the opinion of the Soviet historian N. Mamai that the Eurasians are Landmark Changers on a religious foundation, which shows how little both of them know about the subject. But to make up for this deficiency, Agurskii provides a context for the Eurasians' nationalism—a far cry from Halperin's "whitewashing of Russian imperialism" and "colonialism." He has also noticed Trubetzkoy's best article "At the Door..." (1980, 288, note 105; see the discussion of it below), and he is the only one to have done so, even though he calls Trubetzkoy "Nikita." In connection with Trubetzkoy's centennial, *Novoe russkoe slovo* published a translation of Luks's article (Luks 1990). Strangely enough, Alexander Yanov missed the Eurasians, though *Veche* did not.

Suvchinskii's activities as a patron of music, publisher, and Eurasian journalist were remembered so little after World War I (that is, outside musicological circles) that in 1961 Böss (p. 7) could not find any information about him at all. However, Riasanovsky got in touch with Suvchinskii personally. In the West, Suvchinskii's friendship with Igor Stravinsky has not been forgotten (cf. Allen 1986, 329; Amy 1986, 195, 196; and Taruskin 1987). The only recent Soviet article about him known to me (Nest'ev 1987) is based on half-truths, but it treats subjects other than Suvchinskii's contacts with Stravinsky.

The Renaissance of Eurasian studies in the Soviet Union may have an impact on scholars working in the West, and if it happens, the most natural first step will be the publication of V. N. Il'in's monograph *Po istoriosofii kul'tury (Evraziistvo)* [On the Historiosophy of Culture (Eurasianism)]; see Il'in 1980, 3.

III. Trubetzkoy as a Eurasianist

A student of Trubetzkoy's legacy is confronted with a number of questions, some of which were mentioned in the previous sections. A brief list of such questions will include the following:
(1) What were the main scholarly influences in the life of the young Trubetzkoy? How did it happen that long before he found himself in exile and before World War I, he developed a passionate resentment of things "Romano-Germanic," a resentment that acquired almost pathologically aggressive features as time went on? (2) How deep was the unity of Trubetzkoy's thought? Trubetzkoy began his career as an ethnographer with an emphasis on Finno-Ugric and Caucasian cultures. At the university he switched to Indo-European linguistics, and after his emigration devoted himself to Slavic studies. In Vienna he also developed the principles of general and historical phonology. He described speech sounds as functional units and left the physiological and acoustical properties of the signal to the natural sciences. He called such units phonemes and treated them first and foremost as members of oppositions, that is, as relational entities (for instance, t is articulated in a certain manner, but its relevant, "distinctive" features depend on the fact that it is opposed to d, k, etc., so that in a language without d the phoneme t is functionally different from t in a language in which it is opposed to d). Phonological thinking lies at the foundation of European structuralism. A phonologist is a structuralist by definition, but the last fifty years have witnessed a proliferation of structural approaches in other branches of linguistics (grammar, semantics) and in other areas of knowledge—literature, folklore, anthropology, and psychology among them. Trubetzkoy regarded Savitskii as a structuralist in geography (cf. LN, 106), even though the term itself (coined by Jakobson) became current later. The question is: How did phonology affect

Trubetzkoy's treatment of literature (both prose and poetry), history, and politics, if at all?

(3) How important were Trubetzkoy's contacts with other scholars? Although suffering from isolation, he was an active member of the Prague Circle, and he followed with interest and sympathy the development of Russian Formalism. Like the Prague Circle, Formalism advanced its own principles of analysis, and their impact on Trubetzkoy has not yet been studied in depth (see Trubetzkoy 1990b,xxv ff). As regards the study of culture, the personal share of Trubetzkoy's ideas in the Eurasian program is sometimes difficult to ascertain (cf. Wytrzens 1964), so close were his ties with the other members of the group. (4) Granted that Trubetzkoy's genius needs no proof, we still need to know how durable his contributions have turned out to be. He founded several new disciplines and offered a number of bold hypotheses. As a Eurasian, he studied Russia's relations with Europe and Asia, the role of the Tatar Yoke in the consolidation of the Russian state, and the consequences of Peter's reforms. In a polemic with other emigré writers, he defended his views on the causes of the October revolution and on Russia's future. He condemned Western democracy in favor of an ideocratic organization of society. None of the problems that attracted his attention has a "final solution." As Florovskii (1926, 129) once put it, "After all, the important thing is not what exactly the Eurasians think but what they think about—the truth they seek to detect." One would like to know to what extent Trubetzkoy's ideas are acceptable to modern scholarship and whether his prophecies have come true. What Halperin said about Vernadsky in 1985, Kizivetter said about Trubetzkoy in 1928. But Savitskii found equally harsh words for his critics (1933; an English summary in Orchard 1971).

This essay does not pretend to offer an evaluation of Trubetzkoy's achievements that will do him full justice; it is only a first draft of such an evaluation. As I have already said, the influences of other scholars on Trubetzkoy are difficult to trace. He felt an aversion to "the history of science" and disliked surveys. In his writings on phonology, he gives hundreds of references, but they are mainly to works containing the material he used, not to books of a general character, Bühler being the main exception. His statements concerning his lack of interest in other people's ideas should be taken with a grain of salt (for example, in October 1931 he wrote that his knowledge of Baudouin de Courtenay was poor, but it follows from a letter dated July 1929 that he read Baudouin's principal works: *LN*, 142 and 229, and cf. Kleiner 1985, 102). We often learn about Trubetzkoy's indebtedness to his predecessors by chance. If he had not called himself Gabriel Tarde's follower, it is doubtful that it would have occurred to anyone to connect the two names. As a folklorist he was Kuznetsov's and Vsevolod Miller's pupil. After the revolution, folklore and ethnography occupied a modest place in his activities, but his attitude toward scholarship and research were shaped by these people. His first published works testify to his knowledge of the British theory of folklore ("survivals"), and in the thirties, in retrospect, he declared himself a life-long admirer of the Finnish school. As could be expected from the author of *Europe and Mankind*, Trubetzkoy had a negative opinion of Lévy-Bruhl (*LN*, 424). In all probability, his attack on ethnocentricity and his defense of "savages" and "primitive thought" as equal in value or superior to "European thought" was a reaction against Lévy-Bruhl's teachings. Trubetzkoy's Hegelianism is a special problem (see section 1).

As a Eurasianist Trubetzkoy not only defended the "orthodox" theory from his opponents but sought the support of his closest allies. However early in life he may have formulated the principles set forth in *Europe and Mankind*, his views did not remain unchanged between 1914 and 1930, and in heavily politicized Eurasian studies certain solutions and even the use of some terms must have depended on the situation in the Soviet Union and Europe (see the remarks on fascism above) and on the attitudes of the emigré press toward the Soviet Union and its future. Trubetzkoy must have been especially sensitive to the opinions of Turkic exiles. It is hard to imagine that despite his indubitable dislike of Kerensky he did not read the latter's newspaper *Dni* (Days), or did not follow the brochures of the Committee for the Independence of the Caucasus in which the historical destiny of Turkey, Azerbaijan, and the entire Turanian race was being discussed just when he left the Eurasian organizations. The Committee's position was close to Trubetzkoy's, but he never referred to its literature (a typical specimen is Rasul-zade 1930).

In ethnography and history, Trubetzkoy was primarily interested in relations between large and small nations. His Eurasianism is, if we disregard details, a theory of nationalism. He considered linguistic and cultural diversity an immutable law, as follows from his article on the Tower of Babel (1923b, no.7 above). The main ideas of this remarkable article resolve themselves into the following. National differences will remain despite the most recent efforts to abolish them. Internationalism and Europeanization ("the brotherhood of peoples") can be bought only at the price of destroying the individual component in the psyche and culture; they result in spiritual impoverishment and social death. Culture serves many people and in doing so levels out the most salient individual distinctions. The larger the group, the less original its culture; a culture serving all mankind would reflect only those traits common to people as such, that is, merge with logic and science at the expense of ethics and aesthetics, thereby producing a "spiritual wilderness," from which the road to self-awareness is closed. Only an organic group, not too small and not too large, offers satisfactory conditions for the development of human beings.

In this article, Trubetzkoy formulated his idea of language unions and cultural zones. Eurasianism, despite its indebtedness to the Slavophiles, never shared Pan-Slav ideas. Trubetzkoy's theory of unions and zones foreshadows the Eurasian historical conception as it emerged in the mid-twenties. He does not deny the importance of genetic unity but emphasizes the role of later convergences. He also points out that it is hard to distinguish between inherited and acquired features and that languages traditionally looked upon as related could have been members of "unions" in the past. Cultural zones are formations of the same order as language unions. Here we find the earliest approach to the Eurasian concept of autarky. Trubetzkoy regarded Eurasia as an autarky and a cultural zone. The Pan-Slavic union, in the Slavophiles' program, was determined by linguistic factors; cultural and political unity was expected to be superimposed on it as a matter of course. Trubetzkoy's picture of Eurasia did not depend on the genetic unity of the languages its nations spoke. In his later investigations, he showed that *Indo-European* is nothing more than a linguistic concept and that the search for an Indo-European "people" with its own culture is a thankless enterprise.

Preservation of the constituents' relative independence within an autarky—be it a language union or a cultural zone—especially interested Trubetzkoy. In his opinion, a viable social organism must have several unifying features. For example, Eurasia is a geographical autarky as evidenced by its climate, access to the sea, the direction of the rivers, and the like. In their entirety, these traits give Eurasia its traditional character. Certain regions do not "belong" to Eurasia; even if incorporated into it, they will sooner or later fall away. Trubetzkoy usually tried to bring out the continuity and (partial) indestructibility of tradition. He approved of expansion only insofar as it preserved or reinforced the dominant features of the whole. A social organism, according to his theory, only weakens itself if it tries to absorb alien parts. Nor did he believe in mixed types (see Chapter 3 of *Europe and Mankind*), and his negative reaction to hybrids was almost instinctive: both English culture and Czech prosody aroused his suspicions (cf. Backus 1961 and Gasparov 1987, 65-67). He was against mergers if they were based on compromises: he then spoke about "the lure of the merger"—for instance, with regard to Orthodoxy and Catholicism. His contempt for Marr could, among other things, stem from the latter's theory that languages constantly cross and produce new languages. Even if Marr had been more reliable and less vicious in his Marxism, his reconstruction would have struck Trubetzkoy as preposterous nonsense.

Trubetzkoy viewed every phenomenon from a stable center; when it came to Eurasia, he spotted such a center in the Turanian element. It is no wonder that Peter's reforms stood for everything he did not like: they disrupted the age-old tradition of the Muscovite state, shifted the center, and did not take into account Eurasia's goal as it was allegedly predetermined by its geography. For the same reason he distinguished between the Communists' practice and their slogans and praised the Bolsheviks for their attitude toward the East, even though he knew very well why they were interested in the colonies of the Romano-Germanic world. He was ready to forgive Genghis Khan his atrocities: for him they were overshadowed by the conqueror's creative achievement, because he served as an active instrument in the consolidation of Eurasia. In pre-Petrine Russia he saw the development of the state idea and overlooked its barbarity insofar as he approved of its general trend.

Trubetzkoy gives the following examples of cultural zones in Asia: Muslim, Hindu, Chinese, Steppe-Pacific, and Arctic. With the exception of the Muslim zone, with its religious foundation, the others are based on geographic criteria. It was important to Trubetzkoy to prove that Russia had always belonged with the steppe nomads rather than with West Europeans. The steppe exercised a special fascination over him. He admired the moral values of the nomads and had a high opinion of their languages. In Indo-European, most grammatical relations are expressed by endings and vowel change in the root (inflection and ablaut). In the Turkic languages, grammatical formants are added, "glued" to one another, so that the word becomes longer and longer (agglutination). In December 1936 Trubetzkoy spoke before the members of the Prague Circle on Indo-European and finished his talk with a panegyric on agglutination as an ideal structure that Indo-European had never been able to acquire.

The most difficult problem for Trubetzkoy and the other Eurasians concerned the expansion of Russia in the past. According to Trubetzkoy, conquests in the West were harmful for Russia because they violated the nature of Eurasia. But eight and even five centuries ago, how could Russia's rulers know the direction in which their country had to grow? How could they choose between the East and the West? The Eurasians referred only to the rivers and the steppe.

We know from Trubetzkoy's biography that he chose linguistics as his main subject after some hesitation: his first choice was philosophy, and his first articles treated ethnography, mythology, and folklore. But by the age of nineteen he came to the conclusion that linguistics led the way in "human lore." Why did he ascribe this role to linguistics? Matejka (1987, 307-8) says that for the young Trubetzkoy linguistics was not yet an autonomous discipline but rather an auxiliary tool for analyzing non-Russian cultural material from the Russian empire. He sees the primary target of Trubetzkoy's interest in the spiritual link between Slavs and non-Slavs: "An ardent patriot, he wanted to illuminate the Eurasian roots of Russian culture and to define his intellectual position vis-à-vis Europe on the one hand and Asia on the other. He was more a culturologist than a linguist in this endeavor, although knowledge of non-Indo-European languages was essential for his quest." This is undoubtedly correct, but the question remains: If the young Trubetzkoy was preeminently a culturologist, why did he switch to linguistics?

It can be assumed that by the time Trubetzkoy transferred to Porzeziński's department, he knew what he would study there and had perhaps even familiarized himself with the rudiments of the comparative approach. Those who choose linguistics as their major nowadays are often attracted by its theoretical concepts and so-called exact method. Trubetzkoy must have shared this opinion, even though (largely owing to his own activities) the direction of linguistics and the content of its methodology have changed radically since the beginning of the century. The comparative approach opens the door to the prehistory of languages. The reconstruction of extinct forms, as it was practiced eighty years ago, was so good that we still learn from revised editions of the textbooks used by Trubetzkoy's generation. Trubetzkoy revolted against Fortunatov's school, but his rebellion did not make nonsense of the comparative method. He differed from his teachers in his views on the formation of language families and the disintegration of the Slavic linguistic unity, not in his general attitude toward comparative studies. When Marr dismissed the comparative method as antiquated, Trubetzkoy rose in its defense.

Whatever Trubetzkoy had learned about Indo-European linguistics by 1909, he recognized in it a superior tool for penetrating the past. He could have hoped to gain new perspectives on the prehistory of the Finno-Ugric, Turkic, and Caucasian languages, and to a certain extent his hopes came true. Finally, he could have expected that linguistic methodology would prove applicable to culture in general. His earliest works deal with the reconstruction of myths, legends, and rituals, and he may have felt the inadequacy of the procedures offered by the British school of folklore. His obituary of Kuznetsov confirms this hypothesis.

Trubetzkoy had a strong bent for classification and formalization. Long before he engaged in phonological oppositions and distinctive features, he attempted to describe cultural phenomena in what can be called an algebraic way. The first example of this algebra is his analysis of features A, B, C, etc. as they are displayed by cultures in contact (*Europe and Mankind*). Ten years later he "dismantled" Dostoevsky's characters as only an anthropologist or a linguist could, using exactly the same notation. Indo-European linguistics compares forms of related languages and derives the protoform. The best comparisons and the most convincing etymologies of the Indo-Europeanists display mathematical precision. Linguistics gave Trubetzkoy exposure to formalization, faced him with numerous classificatory problems, and allowed him to stay in touch with literature and culture in general. In 1908-1909 he must have begun his quest for a unified science of human lore, which continued into the twenties. Trubetzkoy gives no references to Wundt, so we do not know whether he owed anything to the idea of *Völkerpsychologie*, but on December 22, 1926, he wrote the following Wundtian letter to Jakobson:

> There can be no doubt that some parallelism in the evolution of the various aspects of culture exists, so some law governing this parallelism also exists. Thus, for instance, the entire evolution of Russian poetry, from Derzhavin [1743-1816] to Maiakovskii has inner "logic" and meaning; no moment of this evolution should be "derived" from nonliterary facts; but at the same time it is not fortuitous that Symbolism flourished in the prerevolutionary period, and Futurism at the beginning of Bolshevism. It is wrong to "explain" literature by politics (or the other way around), but the connection should be established: we need a special science that would stand outside literature, politics, etc. and study, in a synthesizing way, the parallelism of the evolution of life's various aspects. All this holds for language as well. From a subjective, intuitive point of view I am, for instance, absolutely certain that there is some inner tie between the general acoustic impression of Czech speech and the Czech psychic (even psychophysical) shape ("national character"). It is an irrational impression, but who knows that no rational law stands behind it? Thus, in the final analysis, we are quite justified not only in asking why this or that language has chosen a certain path and developed just as it did but also in asking why this language belonging to this people has chosen just this particular path of evolution (e.g., Czech has retained length, and Polish has retained palatalization). Only this is not a question for linguistics but for some other science, say, "ethnosophy" (LN, 97-98; see also Trubetzkoy 1990b, 114).

"Ethnosophy" remained a project, but in 1928 Meillet responded favorably to Trubetzkoy's suggestion concerning the mentality and language of the Turkic peoples and proposed to extend the same principle to the Indo-Europeans. Indo-European, according to Meillet, is as full of anomalous forms as

Turkic is free from them, and Indo-European chieftains also strove after autonomy and independence. The ancient Greeks allegedly preserved this mentality, and Greek shows an overabundance of anomalous forms; the Greek word retains its individual character. On the other hand, all the autonomous forms are grouped into exact, well defined classes; Greek literature and art are also characterized by the harmony and elegance of lines (Meillet 1928). These remarks were made at a meeting of *La Société Linguistique de Paris*, and Savitskii (1931a and 1931b) was delighted that Meillet had supported one of the main Eurasian ideas.

Trubetzkoy felt a strong attraction to what we now call interdisciplinary studies, and Eurasianism offered him extraordinary opportunities for developing his inclinations. In Eurasia he found a great autarky and he could examine the laws governing its history, culture, and languages. At present, hardly anyone would speak about Greek chieftains and Greek grammatical forms in one breath, but Trubetzkoy's idea of language unions and cultural zones, as well as Jakobson's discovery (1971 [=1930]) of a language union spreading over the postulated territory of Eurasia, remains a permanent monument to Eurasian endeavors in this direction (see also Savitskii 1931c on linguistic geography and *LN*, 164-71, comments on Jakobson's work).

The passage on ethnosophy quoted above explains why Trubetzkoy looked on the ability to understand phonology, with its emphasis on the systemic principle, as a manifestation of a certain (namely, Turanian) type: for him all major phenomena in society were interconnected, and if we take into account the geographical determinism of the Eurasian conception, we will see the world through his eyes—as an indivisible whole. He believed in the presence and guidance of Superior Reason and detected it in both the structure and the growth of all things. A pessimist in politics and a hypochondriac in everyday life, he was an optimist in philosophy and history. He never doubted that self-awareness is attainable and that history—far from being chaotic—is governed by laws. In his linguistic studies, he insisted on the goal-oriented development of phonemes and grammatical forms. It is not by chance that Volume 1 of Jakobson's *Selected Writings* opens with an article on the role of the teleological criterion (cf. Liberman 1987). Trubetzkoy's belief in system and Superior Reason, that is, his historical optimism was such a conspicuous feature of his personality that even his students singled it out and found comfort in it (Issatschenko 1938, 326-27; Hafner 1977, 60, 62; cf. also Timoféeff-Ressovsky 1939, 61). This "Turanian" element in Trubetzkoy's psyche keeps attracting scholars who study his life (cf. Gasparov 1987; Toman 1987).

When phonology had demonstrated its worth, Trubetzkoy could not help asking himself whether the phonological method was to any extent applicable to other areas of knowledge. Phonology concerns itself with the function of minimal units of speech and their relations. Several disciplines face *mutatis mutandis* similar problems, and the humanities occasionally borrow phonological methods or at least phonological ideas. Direct connections between phonology and literature, history, or political science are rare in Trubetzkoy's works, though he did try to draw a bridge from phonology to other sciences. Phonology needs special procedures for isolating the phoneme, and Trubetzkoy formulated a series of rules to separate a phoneme from its neighbors in the speech chain and to describe it in relation to the other elements of the system. His theory of nationalism also depends on discovering a minimal natural unit of society. Several candidates for such a unit are known, and choosing the best of them is not merely an academic problem. When Marxism gained popularity among the Russian prerevolutionary intelligentsia and later became obligatory in the U.S.S.R., the role of the main unit in post-primitive society was assigned to class, and nations were expected to disappear together with the conquered bourgeoisie. The Russian philosophers of the twenties attempted to show how counterproductive Marxist dogma was when it came to great issues of history (cf., for instance, Frank 1926, 36-37). According to Trubetzkoy, the most viable unit of human society is a historically predetermined union of nations, "a separate world," an autarky.

Trubetzkoy obviously wanted to prove his historical theses scientifically and turned to phonology for the best tools at his disposal. In his first Eurasian contributions he had already shown that the term *mankind* should be abandoned because European scholars equate mankind with the Romano-Germanic world. He also discussed *mankind* in its true meaning and rejected one culture for all people as mechanical, irreligious, and devoid of any spiritual component. Close to the end of his life he offered new arguments for his conclusion; they reflect his preoccupation with phonology. The members of the Prague Circle, following Trubetzkoy and Jakobson, viewed only those features of linguistic entities as significant which could be obtained from relations within a system. A cornerstone of their phonology is the concept of opposition. They taught that an entity not opposed to anything has no features important to the linguist; compare the case of the phoneme *t* discussed above. Inspired by such ideas Trubetzkoy wrote the following variation on his favorite theme—in defense of autarky:

> But if neither class nor nation (*narod*) is a whole for which one can be asked to make sacrifices, the same holds true for "mankind." Every creature reveals itself to the investigator in opposition to other creatures of the same order. The class has certain contours, a certain individuality, inasmuch as it is opposed to other classes; the nation is likewise opposed to other nations. But what is mankind opposed to? Not to other mammals, one should suppose. But if so, this is a zoological unit for whose sake one can make sacrifices only "to preserve the species," that is, obeying a rudimentary animal instinct rather than a moral duty. If mankind is not opposed to anything, it does not possess the main features of a living personality, it has no individual being and can under no circumstances serve as a stimulus for moral behavior (1935, 32-33, pp. 271-72, above).

Such arguments could hardly convince the uninitiated. Compare Berdiaev's indignant remark on another occasion (1925, 136): "If mankind and cosmos are not reality, all the other stages are equally unreal." The disagreement between Berdiaev and the Eurasians concerns the very essence of modern thought: relativism against nominalism. It will be remembered that the word *relativism*, though in a slightly different meaning, turns up repeatedly in *Europe and Mankind* (see also what is said below about Trubetzkoy's article "At the Door").

Trubetzkoy was not a practical politician, and his futurology may have been sheer utopia, but one cannot help admiring his extraordinarily sharp vision when he speaks about Russian and European life. One of his best political works is the article "At the Door" (1923), in which he applies his method, already familiar to him from ethnography (see his obituary of Kuznetsov, 1913: Trubetzkoy 1990, xv and 107-9) and later applied to speech sounds. He explains that things acquire their meaning only in relation to other things (cf. once again the case of the phoneme *t*); consequently, identical names can refer to dissimilar phenomena. *Left* and *right* in politics should not be associated with a set of unchangeable slogans; one and the same demand can be rightist or leftist, depending on the circumstances. He discusses a situation where a rectilinear political movement has reached its logical end, when a new ideal, viewed in relation to the preceding ideological status quo, will not be more "to the left" (because the drift leftward has exhausted its possibilities) but somewhere outside the line on which society used to project its "right" and "left" ideals. When that happens, the leftist ideology does not simply lose its freshness; it looks weathered and withered and acquires a patina of conservatism and protectionist obscurantism. At such moments leftist slogans smack of bureaucracy and, amazingly enough, of the past. They begin to sound like a hallowed lie in which even the speakers themselves have no trust. But he also warns against futile admiration of the past, against the desire to restore, after the incubus of leftism, the previous stage. The "good old ideology" proved its impotence at a time when it had to defend itself and is not worthy of restoration. The leftists and the rightists appear to be quite similar, only they expect rescue from different sources.

The "law of the exhausted straight line," as Trubetzkoy points out, is applicable not only to political doctrines but also to the doctrines governing national relations, religious convictions, and so forth. In trying to justify his own idealization of the pre-Petrine period, he says that if society returns to the past, it must be a very remote past. Here he comes close to the favorite law of the Russian Formalists—that of "the knight's move," according to which literary development proceeds not from "father to son" but sideways: "from uncle to nephew" or "from grandfather to grandchild" (see also Trubetzkoy 1990b, xxxv).

Trubetzkoy realized that the communist "ideocracy" triumphed in denial of the Marxist principle of the basis and superstructure, for dogma, not economy, determined Bolshevik policy and made the new rulers defend injurious and irrational measures. (This discovery was made again in the sixties and struck everyone as daring and new.) He did not doubt that hunger was a blessing for the Soviet government because it allowed the Bolsheviks to keep people in constant fear (see above and his letter of July 28, 1921: *LN*, 24, "Properly speaking, until now there has been no real, uncontrollable famine, just a shortage of food, which is part of the regime, used, to my mind, quite skillfully for consolidating power"). Although after the tragedy of collectivization and the great famine in the Ukraine, the role of hunger as a state-manipulated deterrent became clear to all, it was guarded in the Soviet Union for decades as the greatest national secret and was recognized only by the extreme "conservatives" in the West (despite Robert Conquest's books). Trubetzkoy explained to H. G. Wells (who, naturally, would not have listened to an emigré journalist) that street robberies had subsided under the Bolsheviks because under totalitarian regimes maraudery becomes a state monopoly.

Engrossed in his own utopia, Trubetzkoy was, however, far-sighted enough not to believe the communist promises concerning the future of the state: he insisted that the theory of a gradual weakening of the state was nonsense (it should be remembered that as late as 1920 Lenin repeated the Marxist formula with full conviction; only Stalin "taught" that before the "proletarian state" disappeared it would become strong as never before). Trubetzkoy came to the conclusion that the Soviet regime in Russia had nothing to do with the dictatorship of the proletariat: the essence of what has come to be known as partocracy (another wheel rediscovered after the Second World War) was absolutely clear to him. The Russian economy lay in ruins, yet Trubetzkoy observed that the main horror of the Soviet system was not so much starvation as the feeling of permanent suppression, the animal fear of death, and hopeless enslavement by a hated, despised master. What can be added to this statement?

All his life Trubetzkoy sought moral, religious factors that bound human communities. He knew that the Bolsheviks, for whom such factors did not exist, could rely only on the bugaboo of capitalist hostility. But the restoration of the bourgeoisie was a transitory danger, so, according to Trubetzkoy, the regime *needed* enemies: it was forced to create strawmen and whip up hatred to justify its existence. This policy was detrimental to Russia, but Trubetzkoy was again correct when he said that the Bolsheviks did not care about anything except staying in power. One should not be in a hurry to classify Trubetzkoy's pronouncements as truisms current in emigré circles. The Russian emigration of the early twenties presented a wide spectrum of convictions and beliefs, and one could run into attitudes from the royalist rejection of both revolutions to the Landmark Changers' servile acceptance of the Bolsheviks. Of course, Trubetzkoy was not alone in his assessment of the new rulers, but even against the background of the shrewdest professional journalism of that time his work is remarkable for its political acumen.

Predicting the future of great states is a fruitless occupation, and for decades discussions of how to govern Russia after the Bolsheviks seemed a waste of time. In the twenties nothing was known about police states and their longevity, but at present, when "rocks impregnable" are crumbling, people again live with the feeling that the Soviet Union is heading toward an unprecedented national catastrophe and they offer programs and plans for "the new epoch." Therefore, although couched in Eurasian terms, Trubetzkoy's words written in July 1921 still retain their poignancy:

> It is hard and terrible to think about Russia, especially if one does not want to hide one's head under one's wing and manufacture illusions. The rulers over there strike me as a rider who can hold onto a wild horse masterfully, so as not to fall, but who are absolutely unable to control this horse and have no idea where to go (the horse goes by itself). But owing to these characteristics of the rider, sooner or later he will have not to fall off, but to *dismount*. Any other rider will fail to keep his balance and fall off. And a horse without a rider will fall into the hands of horse thieves—the Romano-Germanic nations. Let it break loose; who cares if there is no real rider! And he is not yet to be seen (*LN*, 24-25).

With regard to many important issues Trubetzkoy turned out to be a good prophet. He said that the Bolsheviks' policy of promoting the national intelligentsia would produce unheard-of separatism and that the regime would scarcely be able to resist this trend. Along similar lines he predicted the speedy collapse of colonial empires, because the colonizers had taught their former slaves to fight other "masters" and had shown the privileged natives their true face. He was a more prescient realist than the Bolsheviks, who stopped repeating only after the debacle of 1941 that workers had no motherland, and replaced Marx's slogan with the most chauvinistic forms of nationalism (although here, as Agurskii

[1980] has shown, there were many interesting nuances in the Soviet Union itself).

In his article on the Ukrainian problem (1927a, no.10 above and 1928), Trubetzkoy provides a short sketch of what would happen in an independent Ukraine—how its separation from Russia would bring to power the most talentless elements of the Ukrainian nation, how these people, afraid of competition, abetted by the fanatics of nationalism, would leave on Ukrainian culture an imprint of petty provincial vanity, triumphant mediocrity, facelessness, and obscurantism, how the Ukrainians would be taught to hate Russia even at the expense of distorting their own past, and how culture would deteriorate into a tool of malicious, chauvinistic campaigns. Trubetzkoy could not know that very soon Ukrainian culture and the Ukraine would be trampled underfoot, subjected to genocide and merciless Russification, so that the options he discussed would become academic hypotheses devoid of any interest. But his Ukrainian opponents could not know that either. History played a nasty joke on Trubetzkoy and the Eurasians. Provincial vanity, triumphant mediocrity, obscurantism, and malicious, chauvinistic campaigns became the lot of *Russian* culture in its relation to the West when it closed the door to "Romano-Germanic civilization," and the Ukraine is more eager than ever to break loose from the "Union." But do we not think of the trials and tribulations of the Third World while reading Trubetzkoy's grim prophecy?

Trubetzkoy was not just a Eurasian, a literary historian, or a phonologist. He possessed a profound, searching mind, and, as it always happens when we come in contact with men of genius, we learn from them regardless of whether we agree or disagree with them. Herein is the justification for bringing together in English a number of little-known works published between two devastating wars by N. S. Trubetzkoy. Some of Trubetzkoy's answers may not satisfy us, but his quest for truth will surely stimulate readers—of Europe and mankind.

References

AN - "Autobiographische Notizen von N. S. Trubetzkoy" mitgeteilt von R. Jacobson [sic]. In: N. S. Trubetzkoy, *Grundzüge der Phonologie*. 4. Auflage. Göttingen: Vandenhoeck & Ruprecht 1967 [a reprint of the 1958 edition], 273-88.

Abeghian, Artasches. 1926. "Eurasien und die Eurasier." *Slavische Rundschau* 53, 86-90.

Agurskii, M. 1980. *Ideologiia natsional bol'shevizma* [The ideology of 'national Bolshevism']. Paris: YMCA.

Aleksandrovskii, B. N. 1969. *Iz perezhitogo v chuzhikh kraiakh. Vospominaniia i dumy byvshego èmigranta* [From my life in foreign lands. Recollections and thoughts of a former emigré]. Moscow: Mysl'.

Alekseev et al. 1929 = Alekseev, N. N., V. N. Il'in, P. N. Savitskii, *O gazete "Evraziia" (Gazeta "Evraziia" ne est' evraziiskii organ)* [On the newspaper *Eurasia* (The newspaper *Eurasia* is not a Eurasian organ)]. Paris.

Allen, Edwin. 1986. "The Genius and the Goddess." In: Jann Pasler (ed.), *Confronting Stravinsky: Man, Musician, and Modernist*. Berkeley: University of California Press, 327-31.

Amy, Gilbert. 1986. "Aspects of the Religious Music of Igor Stravinsky." In: Jann Pasler (ed.), *Confronting Stravinsky: Man, Musician, and Modernist*. Berkeley, etc.: University of California Press, 195-206.

Anonymous. 1928. *Russia in Resurrection. A summary of the views and the aims of a new Party in Russia.* By an English Europasian. London: George Routledge & Sons.

Anonymous. 1972. "Zum Geleit." *Wiener Slavistisches Jahrbuch* 17, 5-14.

Arsen'ev, N. S. 1959. *Iz russkoi kul'turnoi i tvorcheskoi traditsii* [On the Russian cultural and intellectual tradition]. Frankfurt am Main: Possev.

—. 1962. "O moskovskikh religiozno-filosofskikh i literaturnykh kruzhkakh i sobraniiakh nachala XX veka" [On some Moscow religious-philosophical and literary circles and gatherings at the beginning of the 20th century]. *Sovremennik* (Toronto) 6, 30-42.

Backus III, Oswald P., 1961. [Review of] Böss 1961. *Jahrbücher für Geschichte Osteuropas* 9, 595-99.

Berdiaev, N. 1925. "Evraziitsy" [The Eurasians]. *Put'* 1, 134-39.

—. 1927. "Utopicheskii ètatizm evraziitsev" [The utopian Eurasian theory of state]. *Put'* 8, 141-44.

Berg, B. G. 1941. "Kniaz'ia Trubetskiie. Kievskaia vetv'" [The Princes Trubetskoi. The Kiev branch]. *Novik* 3, 22-25.

Block, Heinrich. 1926. "Eurasien." *Zeitschrift für Geopolitik* 3/1, 8-16.

Bohachevsky-Chomiak, Martha. 1976. *Sergei N. Trubetskoi: An Intellectual among the Intelligentsia in Prerevolutionary Russia.* Belmont, Mass.: Nordland Publishing Company.

Böss, Otto. 1961. *Die Lehre der Eurasier. Ein Beitrag zur russischen Ideengeschichte des 20. Jahrhunderts.* Wiesbaden: Otto Harrassowitz.

—. 1973. "Zur wirtschaftskonzeption der 'Eurasier'". In: Werner Gumpel und Dietmar Keese (eds.), *Probleme des Industrialismus in Ost und West. Festschrift für Hans Raupach.* München, Wien: Günter Olzog Verlag, 481-92.

Chicherin, A. V. 1985. *Vospominaniia* [Memoirs]. In his *Sila poetichèskogo slova.* Moscow: Sovetskii pisatel', 230-318.

Chizhevsky. *See* Tschiževskij, Dmitrij.

Danilova, L. V. 1961. "Russkoie srednevekov'e v sovremennoi istoriografii SShA" [The Russian Middle Ages in modern American historiography]. *Voprosy istorii* 3, 63-91.

Dontchev, Nicolai. 1979. "Le Souvenir de N.S. Troubetzkoy." *A.I.O.N. Sezione slava* 20-21 (1977-78), 103-8.

Efron/Pasternak — *A. Efron B. Pasternaku, Pis'ma iz ssylki (1948-1957). Vkliuchaet 12 otvetnykh pisem Borisa Pasternaka* [A. Efron to B. Pasternak. Letters from Exile (1948-1957). Includes 12 letters to her from Boris Pasternak]. Paris: YMCA-Press, 1982.

Ferrand et al. 1984. *Recueil généalogique et photographique de la descendance du Prince Nicolas Petrovitch Troubetzkoy (1828-1900).* Paris.

Fleischman, L. et al. 1983. *Russkii Berlin 1921-1923...* [Russian Berlin 1921-1923...] Paris: YMCA-Press.

Florovskii, G. V. 1926. "Okameneloe beschuvstvie. (Po povodu polemiki protiv evraziistva.)" [A stony lack of sensitivity (apropos of the polemic against Eurasianism.)] *Put'* 2, 128-33.

Frank, S. L. 1926. *Osnovy marksizma* [Bases of Marxism]. Berlin: Evraziiskoe knigoizdatel'stvo.

Gapanovitch, J. J. 1946. *Introduction à l'histoire de la Russie. Historiographie russe hors de la Russie.* Tr. and with notes by Basile P. Nikitine. Paris: Payot.

Gasparov, Boris. 1987. "The Ideological Principles of Prague School Phonology." In K. Pomorska et al., 49-78.

Geller (Heller) Mikhail, Aleksandr Nekrich. 1986. *Utopiia u vlasti. Istoriia Sovetskogo Soiuza s 1917 goda do nashikh dne*i [Utopia in power. A history of the Soviet Union from 1917 to the present]. 2nd revised and expanded edition. London: Overseas Publications, Interchange Ltd.

Gessen [=Hessen], I. V. 1979. *Gody izgnaniia. Zhiznennyi otchet* [The years of exile. A report of my life]. Paris: YMCA-Press.

Gessen [=Hessen], S. I. 1925. "Evraziistvo" [Eurasianism]. *Sovremennye zapiski* 25, 494-508.

Gorlin, Michael. 1932-1933. "Die philosophisch-politischen Strömungen in der russischen Emigration." *Osteuropa* (Königsberg) 8, 279-94.

Gul', Roman. 1984. *"Ia unes Rossiiu"* ["I carried off Russia"]. Vol. 1. New York: Most.

Gumilev, L. N. 1989a. *Ètnogenez i biosfera Zemli* [Ethnogenesis and the biosphere of the Earth]. Leningrad: Leningradskii Universitet.

—. 1989b. *Drevniaia Rus' i Velikaia Step'* [Ancient Rus' and the great steppe]. Moscow: Mysl'.

Hafner, Stanislaus. 1977. "Die Phonologie und der literaturwissenschaftliche Strukturalismus." *Wiener Slavistisches Jahrbuch* 23, 58-69.

Hagège, Claude. 1967. "Extraits de la correspondence de N. S. Trubetzkoy." *La Linguistique,* 109-36.

Halperin, Charles J. 1983. "George Vernadsky, Eurasianism, the Mongols, and Russia." *Slavic Review* 41, 477-83.

—. 1985. "Russia and the Steppe: George Vernadsky and Eurasianism." *Forschungen zur osteuropäischen Geschichte* 36, 55-194.

Havránek, Bohuslav. 1939. "Nikolaj Sergejevič Trubeckoj (Trubetzkoy)." *Ročenka Slovanského ústavu* 11, 108-115.

Hjelmslev, Louis. 1939. "N. S. Trubetzkoy." *Archiv für Vergleichende Phonetik* 3, 55-60.

Il'in, V. N. 1980. *Arfa Davida. Religiozno-filosofskie motivy russkoi literatury.* 1. Proza [The harp of David. The religious-philosophical motifs of Russian literature, Vol.1. Prose]. San Francisco (n.p.).

Isačenko. *See* Issatschenko, A. V.

Ishboldin, Boris. 1946. "The Eurasian Movement." *The Russian Review* 5, 64-73.

Iskhod k Vostoku. Predchuvstviia i sversheniia. Utverzhdenie evraziitsev. Kniga I. [Exodus to the East. Forebodings and accomplishments. The self-assertion of the Eurasians. Book 1]. Sofia 1921.

Issatschenko, A.V. 1938. "N.S. Trubetzkoy als Lehrer." *Slavische Rundschau* 10, 323-28.

—. 1973. "Esli by v kontse XV veka Novgorod oderzhal pobedu nad Moskvoi. (Ob odnom nesostoiavshemsia variante istorii russkogo iazyka.) [If at the end of the 15th century Novgorod had won a victory over Moscow. (On a failed variant to the history of the Russian language)]. *Wiener Slavistisches Jahrbuch* 18, 48-55.

—. 1977. "Festrede." *Wiener Slavistiches Jahrbuch* 23, 9-18.

Ivanov-Razumnik, R. 1951. *Pisatel'skie sud'by* [Writers' fates]. New York: Literaturnyi fond.

Jagoditsch, Rudolf. 1950. "Die Lehrkanzel für slavische Philologie an der Universität Wien 1849-1949." *Wiener Slavistisches Jahrbuch* 1, 1-52.

—. 1964. "Nikolaj Sergeevič Trubetzkoy. Sein Bild als Mensch und Gelehrtenpersönlichkeit." *Wiener Slavistisches Jahrbuch* 11, 11-21.

—. 1965. "Die Slavistik an der Universität Wien 1849-1963." *Studien zur Geschichte der Universität Wien III.* Graz-Köln: Verlag Hermann Böhlaus Nachf., 28-54.

—. 1977. "Erinnerungen an N. S. Trubetzkoy." *Wiener Slavistisches Jahrbuch* 23, 19-24.

Jakobson, Roman. 1939. "Nikolaj Sergejevič Trubetzkoy." *Acta Linguistica* 1, 64-76. (Reprinted in Thomas A. Sebeok, ed., *Portraits of Linguists*...Bloomington and London: Indiana University Press,

1967, 526-42, and in his *Selected Writings,* vol. 2. The Hague, Paris: Mouton, 1971, 501-16).

—. 1971. "K kharakteristike evraziiskogo iazykovogo soiuza" [On the Eurasian language union]. In his *Selected Writings* 1. Second ed. The Hague, Paris: Mouton, 144-201 (written in 1930, first published in 1931).

Kizevetter, A. [A.]. 1928/29. "Evraziistvo i nauka" [Eurasianism and science]. *Slavia* 7, 426-30.

Kleiner, Iu. A. 1985. "Trubetzkoy: biografiia i nauchnye vzgliady" [Trubetzkoy: his biography and scholarly views]. *Kalbotyra* 35/3, 98-109.

Komin, V. V. 1977. *Politicheskii i ideinyi krakh russkoi melkoburzhuaznoi kontrrevolutsii za rubezhom* [The political and ideological collapse of the Russian petty bourgeois counterrevolution abroad]. Kalinin: Kalininskii universitet.

Kretschmer, P. 1939. "Nikolaus Fürst Trubetzkoy." *Almanach der Akademie der Wissenschaften in Wien für das Jahr 1938,* 88, 335-45.

LN - N. S. Trubetzkoy's Letters and Notes. Prepared for publication by Roman Jakobson with the assistance of H. Baran, O. Ronen, and Martha Taylor. The Hague: Mouton, 1975.

Lenin, V. I. 1960. "Po povodu smerti Trubetskogo" [On Trubetskoi's death]. *Polnoe sobranie sochinenii,* 5th ed., vol. 11, 333. Moscow: Gosudarstvennoe izdatel'stvo politicheskoi literatury.

Leppmann, Wolfgang. 1931. "Die russische Geschichtswissenschaft in der Emigration." *Zeitschrift für osteuropäische Geschichte* 5 (N.F. 1), 215-48.

Liberman, Anatoly. 1980. [Review of] *LN. Linguistics* 18, 543-56.

—. 1985. "N. S. Trubetzkoy as a Folklorist and Ethnographer." *American Folklore Society. 1985 Annual Meeting, Program and Abstracts.* Cincinnati/October 16-20, 1985, 49.

—. 1987. "Roman Jakobson and His Contemporaries on Change in Language and Literature. The Teleological Criterion." In K. Pomorska et al, 143-55.

Lubenskii, Stepan. 1931a. "Evraziiskaia bibliografiia 1921-1931. Putevoditel' po evraziiskoi literature. [The Eurasian bibliography

1921- 1931. A guide to Eurasian literature]. *Tridtsatye gody*. Izdanie evraziitsev, 285-317.

—. 1931b. "Bibliographie de l'Eurasisme." *Le Monde Slave*, 388-422.

Luks, Leonid. 1986. "Die Ideologie der Eurasier im zeitgeschichtlichen Zusammenhang." *Jahrbücher für Geschichte Osteuropas*. NF 34, 374-95.

—. 1990. "Evraziistvo" [Eurasianism]. *Novoe russkoe slovo*, June 8, pp. 20 and 28.

Malevsky-Malevitch, P. [N.]. 1928. *A New Party In Russia*. London: George Routledge & Sons.

Matejka, Ladislav. 1987. "Sociological Concerns in the Moscow Linguistic Circle." In K. Pomorska et al., 307-12.

Mayrhofer, Manfred. 1976. "N. S. Trubetzkoy und die Osterreichische Akademie der Wissenschaften." *Opuscula Slavica et Linguistica. Festschrift für Alexander Issatschenko*. (Schriftreihe Sprachwissenschaft. Universität für Bildungswissenschaften. Klagenfurt, Band 1). Klagenfurt: Verlag Johannes Heyn, 235-38.

Mazour, Anatole G. 1958. *Modern Russian Historiography*. 2nd ed., Princeton, N.J.: D. van Nostrand Co., Inc.

Meillet, A. 1928. [Discussion in:] *Bulletin de la Société de Linguistique de Paris* 29 (86.88-Séance du 18 Fevrier 1928), p. XVII.

Meisner, D. 1966. *Mirazhi i deistvitel'nost'. Zapiski èmigranta.* [Mirages and reality: An emigré's notes.] Moscow: Izdatel'stvo agentstva pechati "Novosti."

Meister, Richard. 1964. "Nikolaus S. Trubetzkoy." *Wiener Slavistisches Jahrbuch* 11, 7-10.

Meshcheriakov N. 1921. "O novykh nastroeniiakh russkoi intelligentsii" [On some new attitudes of the Russian intelligentsia]. *Pechat' i revolutsiia* 3, 33-43.

Miliukov, Paul. 1930. "Eurasianism and Europeanism in Russian History." In: *Festschrift Th. G. Masaryk zum 80. Geburtstage*. Erster Teil. Bonn: Verlag von Friedrich Cohen, 225-36.

Mirsky, D. S. 1927-1928. "The Eurasian Movement." *The Slavonic Review* 6, 311-19.

Mladenov, St. 1922. "Natsionalizŭm, kultura i choveshchina." *Sŭvremenik* (January-February 1922), 290-99.

Na putiakh. Utverzhdenie evraziitsev. Kniga II [On the Paths. The Self-Assertion of the Eurasians. Book 2]. Moscow-Berlin: Gelikon, 1922.

Nest'ev, I. 1987. "Chetyre druzhby. Petr Suvchinskii i russkie muzykanty" [Four friendships. Petr Suvchinskii and Russian musicians]. *Sovetskaia muzyka,* March, 83-93.

Nol'de, B. E. 1930. *Dalekoe i blizkoe. Istoricheskiie ocherki* [Things far and near. Historical essays]. Paris: Izdatel'stvo "Sovremennye zapiski."

Orchard, G. E. 1971. "The Last of the Westernizers." *Canadian Slavonic Papers/Revue Canadienne des Slavistes* 13, 91-95.

—. 1977. "The Eurasian School of Russian Historiography." *Laurentian University Review* 10, 97-106.

Pasternak, Boris. 1959. *I Remember. Sketch for an Autobiography.* Tr. by David Magarshak. New York: Pantheon.

—. 1982. *Vozdushnye puti...* Moscow: Sovetskii pisatel'.

See also Efron-Pasternak.

Pletnev, R. [V.]. 1972. "Russkoe literaturovedenie v èmigratsii" [Russian literary studies in emigration]. In: N.P. Poltoratskii (ed.), *Russkaia literatura v* èmigratsii [Russian literature in emigration]. Pittsburgh: University of Pittsburgh, Department of Slavic Languages and Literatures, 255-70.

Pomorska, Krystyna. 1977a. "Dramatika nauki (O Pis'makh Trubetskogo)" [The Dramatics of Science. On Trubetzkoy's *Letters*]. *Rossiia/Russia* (Torino) 3, 213-29.

—. 1977b. "N. S. Trubetzkoy o perevode ego knigi 'Evropa i chelovechestvo.'" [N. S. Trubetzkoy on the translation of his book *Europe and Mankind*]. *Rossiia/Russia* (Torino) 3, 230-37.

— et al. (eds.), *Language, Poetry and Poetics. The Generation of the 1890s: Jakobson, Trubetzkoy, Majakovskij. Proceedings of the First Roman Jakobson Colloquium, at the Massachusetts Institute of Technology, October 5-6, 1984,* Berlin: Mouton de Gruyter.

Pushkarev, S. G. 1983. "O russkoi èmigratsii v Prage (1921-1945)" [On the Russian emigration in Prague (1921-1945)]. *Novyi zhurnal* 151, 138-46.

Rasul-zade, M. E. 1930. *O Panturizme v sviazi s kavkazskoi problemoi.* S predisloviem N. Zhordaniia [On Panturanianism. In connection with the Caucasian problem. With a foreword by N. Zhordaniia] Paris: K[omitet] N[ezavisimosti] K[avkaza].

Riasanovskii, V. A. 1947. *Obzor russkoi kul'tury. Istoricheskii ocherk. Chast' pervaia* [A historical survey of Russian culture. Part 1]. New York: Copyright by the author.

Riasanovsky, Nicholas V. 1964. "Prince N. S. Trubetskoy's *Europe and Mankind.*" *Jahrbücher für Geschichte Osteuropas* 12, 207-20.

—. 1967. "The Emergence of Eurasianism." *California Slavic Studies* 4. Berkeley and Los Angeles, University of California Press, 39-72.

—. 1972. "Asia Through Russian Eyes." In: Wayne S. Vucinich (ed.). *Russia and Asia. Essays on the Influence of Russia on the Asian Peoples.* Stanford, California: Hoover Institution Press, Stanford University, 3-29.

—. 1984. *A History of Russia.* 4th ed. New York, Oxford: Oxford University Press.

Riha, T. 1958. "Russian Emigré Scholars in Prague after World War I." *The Slavic and East European Journal* 16, 22-26.

Rimscha, Hans von. 1927. *Russland jenseits der Grenzen 1921-1926. Ein Beitrag zur russischen Nachkriegsgeschichte.* Jena: Verlag der Fromannschen Buchhandlung (Walter Biedermann).

—. 1970. *Geschichte Russlands.* 2. überarbeitete und erweiterte Auflage. Darmstadt: Wissenschaftliche Buchgesellschaft.

Rossiia i latinstvo [Russia and Latinity]. Berlin, 1923.

Savickij. *See* Savitskii, P. N., *See also*: Lubenskii, Stepan

Savitskii, P. N. 1927. *Rossiia osobyi geograficheskii mir* [Russia as a unique geographical world]. Prague: Evraziiskoe knigoizdatel'stvo.

—. 1931a."L'Eurasie révélée par la linguistique." *Le Monde Slave,* 364-70.

—. 1931b. "Opoveshchenie ob otkrytii (Evraziia v lingvisticheskikh priznakakh) [Announcement of a discovery (Eurasia in its linguistic features). In: *Evraziia v svete iazykoznaniia* [Eurasia in light of linguistics]. Prague: Izdanie evraziitsev.

—. 1931c. "Les problèmes de la géographie linguistique du point de vue de la géographie." *Travaux du Cercle Linguistique de Prague* 1, 145-56.

—. 1931d. "V bor'be za evraziistvo. Polemika vokrug evraziistva v 1920-ykh godakh." [Struggle for Eurasianism. The polemic on Eurasianism in the twenties]. *Tridtsatye gody*. Utverzhdenie evraziitsev 7. Izdaniie evraziitsev [The Thirties], 1-52.

—. 1933. "Ist eine westlerische Auffassung der russischen Geschichte noch möglich?" *Slavische Rundschau* 5, 337-42.

—. [?] 1935. *Razrushaiushchie svoiu rodinu (snos pamiatnikov iskusstva i rasprodazha muzeev SSSR)* [The destroyers of their native land (demolition of art monuments and the auctioning off of museums in the U.S.S.R.).] Berlin: Izdanie evraziitsev.

Schultze, Bernhard. 1950. *Russische Denker. Ihre Stellung zu Christus, Kirche und Papstum*. Wien: Thomas-Morus-Presse im Verlag Herder.

Shevelev, I. 1990. "Rossiiskoe kraevedenie" [Russian *Landeskunde*]. *Novoe russkoe slovo*, May 30, p.5.

Shkarenkov, L.K. 1981. *Agoniia beloi èmigratsii* [The death throes of the white emigration]. Moscow: Mysl'.

Simeonov, Boris. 1976. "Nikolai Sergeevich Trubetskoi v Bolgarii." [N.S.T. in Bulgaria]. *Bolgarskaia rusistika* 3/2, 43-45.

—. 1977. "N. S. Trubetskoi v Bolgarii" [N.S.T. in Bulgaria]. *Balkansko ezikoznanie* 20/4, 5-12.

Spektorskii, E. 1927. "Zapadno-evropeiskie istochniki evraziistva" [The West European sources of Eurasianism]. *Vozrozhdenie* (Paris), May 26, No. 723, pp. 2 and 3.

Stählin, Karl. 1925. "Russland und Europa." *Historische Zeitschrift* 132, 197-246.

Stammler, Heinrich A. 1962. "Europa-Russland-Asien. Der "eurasische" Deutungsversuch der russischen Geschichte". *Osteuropa* (Stuttgart) 12, 521-28.

Stepun, F. 1924. [Review of] *Evraziiskii vremennik* 3 (1923). *Sovremennye zapiski* 21, 400-407.

Struve, Gleb. 1984. *Russkaia literatura v izgnanii. Opyt istoricheskogo obzora zarubezhnoi literatury* [Russian literature in exile. An attempt at a survey of <Russian> literature abroad]. 2nd ed. Paris: YMCA-Press. (1st ed. 1956 - New York: Izdatel'stvo imeni Chekhova).

Suvchinskii, P. P. et al. 1926. "Pis'mo v redaktsiiu 'Puti'" [A letter to the Editor of *Put'*]. *Put'* 2, 134.

Taruskin, Richard. 1987. "Stravinsky and the Traditions: Why the Memory Hole?" *Opus* 3/4 (June), 10-17.

Terapiano, Iu. 1953. *Vstrechi* [Encounters]. New York: Izdatel'stvo imeni Chekhova.

Timaschew, Nicholaus S. 1929. "Die politische Lehre der Eurasier." *Zeitschrift für Politik* 18, 598-612.

Timoféeff-Ressovsky, N. W. 1939. [N. S. Trubetzkoy]. *Archiv für vergleichende Phonetik* 3, 60-61.

Tiutchev, F. I. 1980. *Sochineniia v dvukh tomakh* [Works in two volumes], vol. 2. Moscow: Pravda.

Toman, Jindřich. 1987. "Trubetzkoy before Trubetzkoy." In: Hans Aarsleff et al. (eds.), *Papers in the History of Linguistics. Proceedings of the Third International Conference on the History of the Language Sciences. Princeton, 19-23 August 1984.* Amsterdam, Philadelphia: John Benjamins, 627-38.

Troubetzkoi, S. G. 1976. *Les Princes Troubetzkoi.* Labelle, Quebec.

Trubeckoj, Nikolaj. *See* Trubetzkoy, N. S.

Trubetskaia, Ol'ga. 1953. *Kniaz' S. N. Trubetskoi. Vospominaniia sestry* [Prince S. N. Trubetskoi. Recollections of a sister]. New York: Izdatel'stvo imeni Chekhova.

Trubetskoi, E. N. 1965. *Tri ocherka o russkoi ikone...* [Three essays on the Russian icon]. Paris: YMCA-Press.

—. 1973. *Icons: Theology in Color.* Tr. from the Russian by Gertrude Vakar...St. Vladimir's Seminary Press.

—. 1976. *Iz putevykh zametok bezhentsa* [From the journal of a refugee]. In his *Iz proshlago* etc. Newtonville, Mass.: Oriental Research Partners. [The latest reprint is E. N. Trubetskoi, *Minuvshee.* (Vserossiiskaia memuarnaia biblioteka. Seriia "Nashe minuvshee" 10). Paris: YMCA Press 1990].

Trubetskoi, S. N. 1906. *Uchenie o logose v ego istorii. Filosofsko-istoricheskoe issledovanie* [The doctrine of logos in its history. A philosophical and historical investigation]. Moscow: Tipografiia G. Lissnera i D. Sobko.

Trubetzkoy, G. N. 1913. *Russland als Grossmacht.* Tr. and with an intoduction by Josef Melnik. Stuttgart und Berlin: Deutsche Verlags-Anstalt (2nd ed.1917).

—. 1914. *Ryssland som stormakt*. Tr. by Walborg Hedberg. Stockholm: Bonnier.

—. 1915. *La Russia come Grande Potenza*. Tr. by Raffaele Guarglia. Milano: Fratelli Treves.

—. 1926. "Otvet na pis'mo evraziitsev" [A rejoinder to the Eurasians' letter]. *Put'* 2, 135-36.

Trubetzkoy, N. S. 1913. "Stefan Kirovich Kuznetsov. Lichnye vpechatleniia" [S. K. Kuznetsov. Personal Impressions]. *Ètnograficheskoe obozrenie* 25, 326-31. (Partly translated in Trubetzkoy 1990b, 107-9).

—. 1921. [Introduction to:] G. D. Uel's, *Rossiia vo mgle* [= Herbert D. Wells, *Russia in the Shadows*]. Sofia: Rossiisko-bolgarskoe knigoizdatel'stvo, iii-xvi.

—. 1922a. *Europa und die Menschheit* Tr. by S. O. Jacobsohn and F. Schlömer. With an introduction by Otto Hoetzsch. München: Drei Masken Verlag.

—. 1922b. "Religii Indii i khristianstvo" [The religions of India and Christianity]. *Na putiakh* 177-229.

—. 1923a. "U dverei. Reakciia? Revoliucia? "[At the door. Reaction? Revolution?]. *Evraziiskii vremennik* 3, 18-29.

—. 1923b. "Vavilonskaia bashnia i smeshenie iazykov" [The Tower of Babel and the confusion of tongues]. *Evraziiskii vremennik* 3, 107-24.

—. 1925. "My i drugie" [We and the others]. *Evraziiskii vremennik* 4, 66-81.

—. 1926. (Trubetsukoi-cho). 1926. *Seiobunmei to jinrui no shorai*. Tr. by Shimano, Saburo. Tokyo: Kochischa Suppanbu hakko.

—. 1927a. "K ukrainskoi probleme [On the Ukrainian Problem]. *Evraziiskii vremennik* 5, 165-84.

—. 1927b. [Vatroslav Jagić]. *Almanach der Akademie der Wissenschaften in Wien für das Jahr 1927*, 77, 239-46.

—. 1928. "Otvet D.I. Doroshenku" [Rejoinder to D. I. Doroshenko] *Evraziiskaia khronika* 10, 51-59.

—. 1930-31. "Viktor K. Porzhezinskii." *Slavia* 9, 199-203.

—. 1933. "Mysli ob avtarkii" [Thoughts on autarky] In: *Novaia epokha* (Narva), 25-26.

—. 1934. "Erinnerungen an einen Aufenthalt bei den Tscherkessen des Kreises Tuapse." *Caucasica* 11, 1-39.

—. 1935. "Ob idee-pravitel'nice ideokraticheskogo gosudarstva" [On the idea governing the ideocratic state]. *Evraziiskaia khronika* 11, 29-37.

—. 1937a. "Erich Berneker." *Almanach der Akademie der Wissenschaften in Wien für das Jahr 1937*, 87, 346-50.

—. 1937b. "Upadok tvorchestva" [The decline in creativity]. *Evraziiskaia khronika* 12, 10-16.

—. 1950. *The Common Slavic Element in Russian Culture* (ed. Leon Stilman). New York: Columbia University, Department of Slavic Languages.

—. 1963. "O vtorom periode tvorchestva Dostoevskogo" [On the second period of Dostoevsky's creative life]. *Novyi zhurnal* 71, 101-27.

—. 1973. *Vorlesungen über die altrussische Literatur*. Studia Historica et Philologica. Sectio Slavica 1. Firenze: Distr. Licosa-Commissionaria Sansoni.

—. 1982. *L'Europa e l'umanità. La prima critica all'eurocentrismo*. Ed. by Olga Strade. Introduction by Roman Jakobson. Torino: Einaudi. (Nova Politecnico 130).

—. 1987-88. *Evropa i chelovechestvo*. Veche 27, 89-113,28,127-49,29,99-111.

—. 1990a. "The Legacy of Genghis Khan." *Cross Currents* 9, 17-68.

—. 1990b. *Writings on Literature*. Edited, translated, and with an introduction by Anatoly Liberman. Minneapolis: University of Minnesota Press.

See also AN; *LN*.

Tschiżewskij, Dmitrij. 1938. "Kniaz' Nikolai Sergeevich Trubetzkoy" [Prince N. S. Trubetzkoy]. *Sovremennye zapiski* 68, 464-68.

—. 1966. "Antwort des Jubilars auf die Rede Prof. Dr. D. Gerhardts." In: Dietrich Gerhardt, Wiktor Weintraub, Hans-Jürgen zum Winkel (eds.), *Orbis Scriptus. Dmitrij Tschiżewskij zum 70. Geburtstag*. München: Wilhelm Fink Verlag, 21-22.

—. 1976. "Prager Erinnerungen. Herkunft des Prager Linguistischen Zirkels and seine Leistungen." In: Ladislav Matejka (ed.), *Sound,*

Sign and Meaning. Quinquagenary of the Prague Linguistic Circle. Michigan Slavic Contributions 6. Ann Arbor: Department of Slavic Languages and Literatures, The University of Michigan, 15-28.

Utechin, S. V. 1963 [1964]. *Russian Political Thought. A Concise History.* New York, London: Frederick A. Praeger.

Vachek, Josef. 1977a. "N. S. Trubetzkoy and the Prague Linguistic School." *Wiener Slavistisches Jahrbuch* 23, 103-109.

—. 1977b. [Review of] *LN. Language* 53, 424-28.

Vaillant, André. 1939. [N. S. Trubetzkoy]. *Revue des études slaves* 19, 200-202.

van Wijk, N. 1926. "Eurazisme." *De Gids* 91/4, 236-51.

—. 1939. "Levensbericht van N. S. Trubetskoj." *Jaarboek der Koninklijke Nederlandsche Akademie van Wetenschappen 1938-1939.* Amsterdam: N. V. Noord-Hollandsche uitgeversmaatschappij, 221-27.

Varshavskii, V. S. 1956. *Nezamechennoe pokolenie* [An unnoticed generation]. New York: Izdatel'stvo imeni Chekhova.

Veidle, Vladimir. *See* Weidlé, Wladimir.

Vernadsky, G. V. 1968. "P. N. Savitskii (1895-1968)". *Novyi zhurnal* 92, 273-77.

—. 1970. "Iz vospominanii" [From my recollections]. *Novyi zhurnal* 100, 196-221.

Vishniak, M. V. 1957. "*Sovremennye zapiski.*" *Vospominaniia redaktora* ["*Sovremennye zapiski.*" An editor's memoirs]. Indiana University Publications. Graduate School. Slavic and East European Series, vol. 7.

Weidlé, Wladimir. 1949. *La Russie absente et présente.* Gallimord. (In English - *Russia: Absent and Present.* New York: The John Day Company, 1952.)

—. 1956. *Zadacha Rossii* [Russia's task]. New York: Izdatel'stvo imeni Chekhova.

—. 1968. *Bezymiannaia strana* [The nameless country]. Paris: YMCA Press.

Williams, Robert C. 1972. *Culture in Exile. Russian Emigrés in Germany, 1881-1941.* Ithaca: Cornell University Press.

Wytrzens, Günther. 1964. "Fürst Trubetzkoy als Kulturphilosoph." *Wiener Slavistisches Jahrbuch* 11, 154-66.

Zen'kovskii, V. V. [1925]. *Russkiie mysliteli i Evropa. Kritika evropeiskoi kul'tury u russkikh myslitelei* [Russian thinkers and Europe. Criticism of European culture by Russian thinkers]. Paris: YMCA Press. (In English: V.V. Zenkovskii, *Russian Thinkers and Europe.* Tr. from the Russian by Galia S. Bodde. Ann Arbor: J.W. Edwards for American Council of Learned Societies, 1953.)

—. 1953. *A History of Russian Philosophy,* vol. 2, Authorized translation from the Russian by George L. Kline. London: Routledge & Kegan Paul Ltd.

Index

Index of proper, place, ethnic, and language names, occuring in Trubetzkoy's works and letters. *Europe, Eurasia,* and *Russia* occur passim and have been disregarded. Asterisks designate names mentioned only in the letters (pp. 295-375).

Index of Names

Subject Index